Sports and Christianity

Routledge Research in Sport, Culture and Society

Sports and Christianity

Historical and Contemporary Perspectives

Edited by

Nick J. Watson and Andrew Parker

NEW YORK   LONDON

First published 2013
by Routledge
711 Third Avenue, New York, NY 10017

Simultaneously published in the UK
by Routledge
2 Park Square, Milton Park, Abingdon, Oxfordshire OX14 4RN

First issued in paperback 2014

Routledge is an imprint of the Taylor and Francis Group, an informa business

Library of Congress Cataloging-in-Publication Data
Sports and Christianity : historical and contemporary perspectives /
edited by Nick J. Watson and Andrew Parker.
    p. cm. — (Routledge research in sport, culture and society v.19)
    Includes bibliographical references and index.
  1. Sports—Religious aspects—Christianity. 2. Sports and religion—
History. 3. Religion and culture—History. I. Watson, Nick J.
  II. Parker, Andrew.
  GV706.42.S67 2012
  796.01—dc23
  2012016010

ISBN 978-0-415-89922-2 (hbk)
ISBN 978-1-138-92057-6 (pbk)
ISBN 978-0-203-08462-5 (ebk)

Typeset in Sabon
by IBT Global.

From Nick: for him who shed blood for me and all humanity, Jesus of Nazareth

From Andrew: in memory of Dudley, who taught me to reach higher.

Contents

PART II
Contemporary Perspectives on Sport and Christianity

Foreword
Michael Novak

Sports requiring high skill and heroism have always generated electricity back and forth with religion, not only with Christianity. Not all who take part in sports are religious men or women, but religion and sport have always sprung out of the same deep waters of the human soul. More than that, they have nourished and been nourished by, inspired and been inspired by, each other.

One reason for this is that both belong to the kingdom of ends, not the kingdom of means. We do not worship God because God gets something out of it, or even because we do. Worship is not about means. It is about ends. To anyone who grasps the relative situation of Creator and creature, it is self-evident that the creature owes to her Creator everything she is and does and aspires to. We adore God, honor Him, give Him thanks because we recognize His immensity so far beyond us, and what He is and has done for us. He does not need our gratitude and honor and worship. But we would be disgracefully ungrateful, blind and self-centered not at least to voice what we owe Him. In doing so, we live up to the imperatives of our own nature; we reach toward fulfilling the high aspiration of our own destiny. We acquit all the duties and decencies expected of our own full nature.

We do something analogous in sports. We spend our whole selves, in the hope of achieving a moment of beauty in action, up to the tip-top best of our capacities. We stretch them to levels where they have never gone before. Our aim is upwards—in pursuit of the ends of our own nature. All this belongs to the kingdom of ends. It is beautiful in and of itself, and high achievement in sport, once it is reached, can never be taken away from us. It is part of our being. It has extended us.

The presently most famous athlete in the U.S. is Tim Tebow, the new first-year quarterback for the Denver Broncos in the National Football League (American football, that is). In his first year as a starter he led his team back from losing to winning in the last moments at least six times. He is a rather indomitable kid. What makes him so beloved to the public, however, is that he always goes down on one knee, his head in his hands, and communes with God. Win or lose, he thanks God.

Many Americans hate this, of course. Some religious people think it is too "showy" and that it be should kept in the secrecy of his own chamber. Many secular people hate it as just another aspect of their newly arisen passion to drive any and all sorts of public religious symbolic action out of public view.

My supposition is that Tebow is not asking God to bring about a miracle, or otherwise to intervene in the normal course of a football game. Rather, he is composing his own soul, in order to be on maximum alert for any "breaks" the ordinary course of a game may bring him. One man on the other team may end up out of place on the next play, and if Tim happens to catch that out of the corner of his eye, he will try to get the ball to that abandoned spot, in order to break open down the field.

Football is a game of "breaks." Even the ball is designed as an odd oval capable of taking unpredictable bounces. To have great mental clarity and acuity in the heat of battle is a way of honoring God, by living up to the full talent He has given one. Prayer that composes the mind and instincts to be on maximum alert for sudden chances, and whose very form is "Thy will be done," is never wasted. Win or lose, one plays to top capacity, and leaves the outcome in the Lord's hands. There is never cause for despair and simply giving up. Give your best even in the face of the seemingly impossible, and every so often the impossible happens. What an unrivaled joy that is! A joy for which one must give thanks. Both for the skills one has been given, for the alertness granted and for seeing "the break" in time to cut through the opening.

Such thoughts are reawakened in me by this treasure of careful and measured studies of aspects of this part of our lives—sports, play—that in earlier generations were not studied with so much attention and precision. Readers should not forget that research and study also belong to the kingdom of ends. Done right, they achieve something of beauty, worthy of the best the attentive human brain has to offer.

The many-colored threads with which the editors have beautifully woven this book together give it a symphonic quality. At first sight, the chapters seem to be on such disparate subjects. But it is extremely important to bring together a sampling of the themes considered herein. It is a part of our ongoing project of bringing sport—so large a part of human life, so delightful and intellectually rich—to the light of full self-consciousness and peaceful reflection.

In our earlier life as academics and intellectuals we may long have walked past the sports arenas all around us and not really noticed the sports sections of our newspapers (often the biggest and best-read of all sections). But the unrestricted *eros* of asking questions has now called us to inquire into one of the best-loved activities of our civilization. And to find it full of insight, puzzles and further questions. Sports are themselves a delightful field of inquiry.

Dip into this variegated collection and you will be enriched. And venture into a new field of intellectual delight.

Acknowledgments

Firstly, we would like to thank the editorial staff at the Routledge New York office for their patience, flexibility and professional approach to this project, in particular Max Novick and Jennifer Morrow. Secondly, we appreciate the time and effort of chapter contributors and their openness to our editorial requests. Finally, the editors would like to express their gratitude to scholars and sports practitioners who identified resources and/or read sections of our systematic review of literature (Chapter 1). These include: John White, Synthia Sydnor, Shirl Hoffman, Drew Gibson, Scott Kretchmar, Dominic Erdozain, Patrick Kelly, Stuart Weir, Joseph Price, Michael Grimshaw, Robert Higgs, Steve Overman, Kevin Lixey, Victor Pfitzner, Edward Hastings, Paul Heintzman, Mike McNamee, Tracy Trothen, Steven Waller and Sean Crosson. Last, but by no means least, we would like to thank our wives Kate and Beckie for their love, patience and support, and for taking care of all the things that we should have been doing while we were working on this project. Needless to say, the inadequacies and inconsistencies found herein are entirely our own.

Introduction

Andrew Parker and Nick J. Watson

Over the past thirty to forty years there has been a steady growth in the academic literature concerning sport and religion. Within this genre authors have explored a variety of topics and issues. There are books about sport and faith, sport and spirituality, sport and religious ethics; this is a book about sport and Christianity and, specifically, the connections between the two. One of the things that stands out in the more recent sport–Christianity literature is the way in which this relationship has developed over time, not simply because scholars have had the compulsion to delve deeper into the similarities between these two cultural stalwarts, but also because of the fact that the Church was one social institution among many that got caught up in the momentum surrounding the wider popularization of sport. Since then the relationship has ebbed and flowed, characterized on the one hand by a more general (and growing) Christian acceptance of sport as a 'useful' physical, moral and emotional practice, and on the other by an increasingly commercialized sporting world the values of which, as time goes on, appear to sit less and less easily with formal religion of any kind.

Of course, what all of this illustrates is that sport does not exist in a social vacuum. On the contrary, it evolves and develops in accordance with a variety of broader factors and forces while at the same time embedding itself further into the very fabric of everyday life. Modern-day sport looks like it does because it has been (and continues to be) shaped and formed in line with the turbulence of social existence (economics, politics, etc.), which, in turn, makes it what it is. The sport–Christianity relationship is no different. This too is a reflection of the way in which sport has increasingly impacted wider society and has progressed from being a marginal social pastime to an established feature of daily living. It is neither the intention nor the remit of this book to debate the pros and cons of such matters, but what the following chapters do illustrate is the way in which this relationship has developed in specific social and cultural contexts and how we might think further about the intimate connections (and disconnections) between sport and the Christian faith.

So, why this particular book and why now? Amid the growth of publications on the relationship between sport and all major world religions, this volume comes out of a sense of urgency; an urgency to publish a collection of chapters by some of the most established academics in the sport and Christianity field; this, so that students, scholars and lay readers alike may have access to a resource that provides both a flavor and an overview of the variety and quality of previous and ongoing work in the area. What transpires is a series of chapters produced by a selection of writers who have had much to say on their respective subjects and who, as a consequence, present us with a sense of their drive, focus and enthusiasm on the key facets of scholarship that have engaged them most. To this end, the book explores two main themes that encapsulate the chosen topics of the featured authors and the mainstay of their academic interests. These comprise: (i) the history/genealogy of debates surrounding the sport–religion relationship (Watson and Parker, Pfitzner, McLeod, Hoffman, Higgs), and (ii) contemporary philosophical debates surrounding sport and Christianity (Watson, Trothen, Goodson, Lixey, Kretchmar).

And so to the contents. On the face of it the book starts out somewhat indulgently; it is far too easy for authors to abuse editorial license but, rest assured, this is not the case here. The reason why Watson and Parker open proceedings in Chapter 1 is simply because their substantive offerings serve to set the scene for the remaining contributors. Accordingly, what their chapter provides is a mapping of the academic landscape on sport and Christianity. Addressing topics as broad and diverse in content as they are in chronology, the main objective for Watson and Parker (in their position as relative newcomers to the field) is to chart the historical terrain of this discursive canvas while at the same time highlighting possible avenues for future research.

Tracking the historical trajectory of the sport–Christianity relationship has been a central preoccupation for a number of scholars over the years. Much has been written, for example, on St Paul's use of athletic/sporting metaphor in Scripture and Chapter 2 features the work of a key contributor to these debates, Victor Pfitzner. Reflecting on his extensive investment in this area, Pfitzner suggests that Paul's use of metaphor tells us much about the cultural context in which he lived, especially the way in which such linguistic habits may have been recognizable to his audience as a consequence of their commonsense meanings in everyday life. Pfitzner goes on to suggest that ultimately the simplest way to view Paul's use of agonistic imagery is to do so both in terms of 'social reality'—that is, a knowledge of contemporary athletics—and as part of a 'tradition' of appropriating athletic metaphors. The chapter also presents an overview of recent research in the field and how the adoption of new methodologies has served to uncover more about the apostle's metaphorical pursuits.

Another central tenet of the literature in this field is that of muscular Christianity. That said, relatively few accounts have explored either the broader social significance or the denominational complexities of this popular tale. Even fewer have been written by eminent historians. In achieving all of these objectives Hugh McLeod's work in Chapter 3 seeks to uncover details of the way in which those from various church traditions differed in their perceptions of, and approaches to, sporting involvement in Victorian Britain. Moreover, McLeod analyzes how a series of wider issues impacted the sport–religion relationship during that period, the emergence of modern sporting forms, the impact of 'professionalism' and the 'problem' of sporting obsession. This is a story of ideologies and institutions but also of the individuals who mobilized the muscular Christian movement: those who had the wherewithal to step out in faith, often against the tide of social and spiritual momentum, in order to change and challenge the way in which sport was viewed by those within the Church.

It was not long, of course, before Christian leaders realized the benefits of sport. Certainly by the end of the nineteenth century there was widespread acceptance among a number of denominations that the broader popularization of sport was becoming part and parcel of religious life. The challenge then became one of how the Church might maintain the attentions of its members (and others) amid the emergence of this rapidly expanding cultural phenomenon. It has been well documented that the UK and the U.S. were trailblazers in recognizing the benefits of the Church's engagement with sport, and details of how this took shape in the North American context is the focus of Shirl Hoffman's discussion in Chapter 4. With a wealth of expertise and experience in hand, what Hoffman provides is a sense of the way in which the rationale for the acceptance and integration of sport into church life changed from the mid-nineteenth century onwards; at first being seen as a form of physical, moral and emotional refreshment, later being recognized as a strategic tool for evangelism. What Hoffman also charts is the way in which the relational bonds between sport and the Christian faith then became inextricably linked and how, over time, a general acceptance of the values and practices of 'big-time' sport has inevitably led to a series of emergent ethical dilemmas for Christian sports practitioners and advocates alike. The ultimate question for Hoffman is not are sport and Christianity compatible bedfellows, rather, to what extent can and should the Christian church impact the moral crisis evident in modern-day commercialized sport and, moreover, how might such an undertaking be carried out.

What Hoffman's work also eloquently articulates is the way in which the popularization of sport at a social level has led to a popularization of sporting Christianity. Just as in the post-1945 era sport has been celebritized, so too has the cultural significance of the sport–Christianity relationship been proselytized by any number of organizational advertisements, websites, autobiographies, self-help manuals, pamphlets and devotionals. The commercialization of modern-day sport is often derided for the media hyperbole that surrounds it, but, like it or not, the sport–religion nexus is both a contributor to and a beneficiary of this. At the center of the vortex of 'big-time' sports are the athletes themselves for whom demigod status, celebrity lifestyles and transcendent fame are part of the everyday. Amid all of this it is easy to lose sight of the fact that contemporary sports performers are, like you and I, real people. Indeed, in Chapter 5 Robert Higgs suggests that one way to analyze how sport has evolved over time is to think about who sports performers are, what they represent and how their identities both create and reflect particular cultural values. In a novel and challenging contribution, Higgs draws upon his in-depth knowledge of the work of various historical and literary scholars in order to investigate more closely the intertwining complexity of the sport–Christianity dyad and, specifically, how stereotypical and archetypal patterns of sporting representation intersect and react to make our games and religions what they are—and what they are not.

And so to Part II, where we take a slightly different tack, one that is grounded in philosophical reflection. Countering the dearth of academic literature addressing the Christian theological dimensions of disability sport, in Chapter 6, Nick Watson builds upon some of the issues raised in the opening part of the book by exploring the extent to which commercialized sport has embedded itself into the very fabric of social life and, by way of its normative and often questionable values, has come to represent a form of cultural idolatry. Drawing on the work of Jean Vanier, Stanley Hauerwas, Amos Yong and Wolf Wolfsenberger, Watson examines how sportspersons with disabilities, especially intellectual disabilities (and the 'movement' that represents them, the Special Olympics), may thus be seen as a 'prophetic sign' to the multibillion-dollar business of contemporary sport that he (along with others) suggests is a major edifice in the modern 'Tower of Babel.' In conclusion, Watson identifies themes and issues within disability sport that may benefit from further theological reflection and highlights current Church and para-Church initiatives that seek to raise awareness and affect change in this area.

Discussions of normative values necessarily bring with them notions of 'difference,' which are also central to Tracy Trothen's contribution in Chapter 7. Here Trothen builds upon her well-established reputation in the area of sport, religion and technoscience by examining notions of 'normativity,' 'transcendence' and 'difference' within the context of elite sport. In an exploration of the values that underpin the assessment of what constitutes acceptable sporting enhancement, Trothen argues that while normative embodiment discourse (and its assumptive underpinnings) are operative in modern-day sport they are not always visible. Utilizing case study examples of the ways in which sporting technology has, of late, undergone increased exposure and scrutiny, Trothen goes on to argue that this new level of visibility provides opportunities for an increased recognition of (and favorable disposition to) a sense of diversity, while at the same time facilitating a retrenchment of dominant categories and further marginalization of those who depict and display 'different-ness.' The chapter concludes by suggesting that the intersection of technology, sport and religion has the potential to intensify normative constructions of embodiment while being able to promote a greater interrogation of such norms and values. In turn, the intersection between sport (as a religion) and technoscience (which fosters visible difference) has the potential to evoke a relational transcendence in which hospitable relationships with the diverse Other become more pervasively desired and valued.

With the benefit of equally well-grounded expertise (and the hindsight that comes with it), in Chapter 8 Jacob Goodson advances the theme of sporting enhancement by exploring the philosophical arguments surrounding the use of anabolic steroids in U.S. Major League baseball. Constructing a critique of the way in which sport media has framed baseball as 'steroid' fueled, Goodson proposes a virtue-centered approach for making judgments on the use of steroids within the game particularly in relation to the 'quest for excellence and perfection.' Baseball, Goodson argues, has become overdetermined by and reliant upon performance-enhancing drugs to the extent that excellence and perfection are measured in relation to the use of steroids, rather than the skills and virtues that the game naturally nurtures and requires. Goodson goes on to challenge the 'now common assumption that baseball ought to be narrated by steroids.' In so doing he demonstrates how a virtue-centered account of the professional game offers a different way of understanding its nature and purpose and, as a consequence, a useful means by which to make moral judgments about those players who have used steroids in their quest for excellence and perfection. Goodson concludes that while we might be sympathetic to the plight of injured or older players who use performance-enhancing drugs in order to continue their careers, morally we have to say that the practice in the round is unjustifiable.

One of the things that often comes into question when performance-enhancement arguments surface in sporting contexts are notions of integrity and character. If, amid a climate of moral decomposition, modern-day sport is to be seen as a social setting that promotes positive values and qualities where, we might ask, should we look to stimulate a regeneration of such values and, moreover, what steps can be taken to set this process in motion? Of course, the Catholic Church has long since engendered an affinity for sport and, in particular, its character-building qualities. Hence, it is highly appropriate that in Chapter 9 Kevin Lixey draws on his unique experience as Head of the Church and Sport section of the Pontifical Council for the Laity to make a renewed call for the recognition of the role of sport in character development. Outlining the vagaries of contemporary social life and its ability to breed a sense of 'apathy and indifference' in young people, Lixey cites sport as liberatory force with the potential to promote the 'fulfillment of spiritual and human development' by way of a 'recuperation and strengthening' of its 'recreational, educational, and pastoral dimensions.'

Drawing on the words of Pope Benedict XVI and John Paul II, Lixey argues for the ability of sport to reinvigorate a sense of enthusiasm in young people not simply toward sporting pursuit per se, but towards life in general. In this view, Lixey goes on, the promotion of excellence in sport can inspire young people to seek a life of 'moral virtue,' lived with 'compassion, interest and goodness' while at the same time representing a stimulus for the pro-active construction of individual futures. The key factor for Lixey within all of this is the role of the sports educator, i.e., coach, parent, teacher or volunteer, and how such positions of responsibility should be more readily viewed as 'pastoral,' rather than simply instructive or 'neutral.'

One of the personal characteristics and qualities that sport (competitive sport in particular) is often said to engender is that of humility, and it is to this topic that Scott Kretchmar turns in Chapter 10. For Kretchmar humility is connected to finding a realistic sense of self, finding out who we are in comparison to others, finding what we can and cannot do, finding our weaknesses and vulnerabilities. Sporting endeavor is a world where our vulnerabilities are there for all to see. With these things in mind Kretchmar carries out an investigation into the philosophical underpinnings of humility and discusses its role in three world religions, Christianity, Islam and Buddhism. Utilizing the concepts of 'practice' and 'tradition' as set out in the work of MacIntyre, Kretchmar then draws upon the similarities between these religious traditions to make a case for sport and spirituality as potential sites of both humility and pride; that is, they have the potential and ability to 'force us to confront and reconcile opposites'; to manifest confidence, security and status while at the same time exhibiting dependency, vulnerability and weakness. In conclusion, Kretchmar addresses the question of whether sport (as we know it today) is a useful venue for the cultivation of spiritual humility and whether or not it represents a 'pedagogy' for a healthy version of pride.

In sum, *Sports and Christianity* aims not only to reflect on the ways in which the underpinning principles of the Christian faith might allow us to consider and challenge the values and practices of modern-day sport, but also how they might enhance the way in which we see the future of sport both in terms of its participatory and structural formation. We believe that it is by way of such reflection that our understandings of the relationship between sport and Christianity can continue to thrive and that the desire for ongoing empirical scholarship will be stimulated and encouraged. Needless to say, we trust that this book will be both a stimulus and an encouragement to our readership.

Part I

Historical Perspectives on Sport and Christianity

1 Sports and Christianity
Mapping the Field

Nick J. Watson and Andrew Parker

> *Sport seduces the teeming 'global village'; it is the new opiate of the masses; it is one of the great modern experiences . . . sport is a mirror . . . that reflection is sometimes bright, sometimes dark, sometimes distorted, sometimes magnified. This metaphorical mirror is a source of mass exhilaration and depression, security and insecurity, pride and humiliation, bonding and alienation. Sport, for many, has replaced religion as a source of emotional catharsis and spiritual passion . . . the story of modern sport is the story of the modern world . . . sport demands the attention of the academic.*
>
> (Mangan, Majumdar and Dyreson, 2009: xii–xiii)

INTRODUCTION

Scholars who have written on the relationship between sport and Christianity are in general agreement that academics outside the traditional social-science sports studies disciplines,[1] such as theologians and philosophers of religion, have been slow to recognize the cultural significance of modern sports (e.g., Watson, 2011b; Hoffman, 2010a; Twietmeyer, 2009, 2008). As this review demonstrates, this trend is slowly changing. In addition to the birth of research centers, academic journals and Church-based sport–faith initiatives, the contributors to recent monographs and anthologies that analyze the various aspects of the relationship between the Christian religion and sport now include scholars from across a plethora of disciplines and denominations (see Table 1.1).[2]

Historians and anthropologists have mapped a relationship between religion and sport that spans approximately three thousand years, and many of the more recent scholarly examinations of the dialectical relation between sports and Christianity are indebted to this work. Links between the sacred and sport have been identified in a number of historical epochs. These include primitive times when ritual-cultic ball games were played to appease the gods (for fertility); the athletic spectacles of ancient Greece and the Olympic games that were held in honor of mythological deities; the gladiatorial contests of Rome; the festivals and folk-games of the Middle Ages; the general Puritan suspicion and prohibitions against sports; and, lastly, Victorian muscular Christianity (1850–1910), a socio-theological movement, and some would argue ideology, that significantly shaped the character of modern sports (see McLeod, this volume; Koch, 2012; Baker, 2010, 2007b, 1988; Lipoński, 2009; Mathisen, 2005; Guttman, 1978/2004; Coleman, 1989; Carter, 1984a, 1984b; Eisen, 1975; Ballou, 1973; Brasch, 1970).[3] Additionally, there is a small corpus of work that has explored how sport interacts with other monotheistic and eastern (pantheistic) world religions, such as Islam, Judaism, Buddhism and Shintoism, which provides useful comparative insights for scholars examining the Christian faith and sport relation (e.g., Benn, Dagkas and Jawad, 2011; Benn, Pfister and Jawad, 2010; Meyer, 2009; Hargreaves, 2007; Magdalinski and Chandler, 2002; Prebish, 1993; Hyland, 1990).

Considering Christianity's Hebraic roots in the old testament and its inseparable ties to Jewish history, faith and tradition, the discourse that is fast developing around Judaism and sporting pursuits will undoubtedly assist scholars when examining the relationship between sports and Christianity, especially in relation to historical, theological and sociological research on gender, embodiment and identity (e.g., Borish, 2009, 2002; Kaufman and Galily, 2009; Mendelsohn, 2009; Meyer, 2009; Kugelmass, 2007; Gurock, 2005; Eisen, 1998). From this point forward, however, we focus on systematically (and thematically) reviewing the empirical research and scholarship on sport and Christianity.[4] While unavoidably touching on aspects of the sport–faith relationship throughout the last two millennia to ensure that we historically and culturally situate our analysis,[5] the overriding focus is the modern forms of sport that were birthed in Victorian Britain in the middle to late part of the nineteenth century (1850–1910). The review comprises four themed sections:[6] (i) theologies of play in sport, (ii) muscular Christianity and sports ministry, (iii) theological ethics in sport (with psychological considerations) and (iv) emerging research topics. In turn, the review is prefaced by a brief overview of pioneering scholars and initiatives in the field and an outline of the aims and the methodological approach.

AIMS AND METHOD

The aim of this systematic literature review is to: (i) comprehensively identify, critically appraise and synthesize scholarship (in English),[7] primary empirical research and initiatives (e.g., research centers and organizations) concerning the relationship between sport and Christianity, and (ii) to identify areas for future research and to provide related resources. While not exhaustive the review identifies key debates, seminal articles and scholarly texts and initiatives, allowing the reader to further explore specific themes of interest.[8] This review adopts a 'systematic approach,' although as the topic sits within the social sciences, it does not adhere to the stringent requirements of the *Cocharne Collaboration* format of a systematic review (Aveyard, 2008).

PIONEERING SCHOLARS AND INITIATIVES IN THE FIELD[9]

Until relatively recently, the majority of academic reflection on the relationship between sport and Christianity, has come from American scholars. During the postwar years of the 1960s, amid a swathe of civil and human rights movements the U.S. was reassessing and critiquing all its major institutions in one form or another, which included sports. In this era sports became increasingly professionalized and driven by free-market capitalist forces and political agendas, and thus, were ripe for social-scientific and theological analysis. While the pioneers in this particular field had only a small number of isolated writings published in Church periodicals (McNeill, 1948; Brasch, 1970; Anderson, 1925)[10] and popular sports magazines (Deford, 1976a, 1976b, 1976c, 1976d, 1986), as academic journal papers, chapters and books and popular Christian literature (Peale, 1957),[11] which included an edited collection (Simonson, 1962) of testimonies from athletes that were associated with the Fellowship of Christian Athletes (FCA, 1952/54–), it was Michael Novak's seminal book, *The Joy of Sports* (1967/1994), that provided the foundation for what was to follow.

Novak's book was the first systematic study of the sport–faith interface.[12] Since then, Novak has made numerous conference presentations on the topic, published a small number of articles in periodicals and has recently written the foreword to an edited anthology on sports and Christianity (this volume). Due to his wider professional interests and responsibilities,[13] however, he has not produced any further in-depth scholarly analyses. One of the chapters from his groundbreaking book was republished in Shirl Hoffman's edited anthology on sport and religion, the first of its kind.

Shirl J. Hoffman, a retired professor of kinesiology at the University of North Carolina (Greensboro, North Carolina) and former college basketball coach and official, started his work on sport and the Christian faith with a handful of academic papers (Hoffman, 1991, 1986, 1985, 1976), then published the first edited anthology on the topic in 1992, which includes contributions from other pioneers in the field (i.e., Novak, Higgs, Price and Mathisen).[14] Following nearly four decades of engagement in the field he recently published a single-authored text, *Good Game: Christianity and the Culture of Sports* (2010a),[15] which is essentially a representation of his life's work.[16] Hoffman has been successful in disseminating his ideas in the media, regularly contributing to documentaries televised on networks such as CBS, ESPN and Channel 4 in Britain, and to radio broadcasts for the BBC, CBS and NPR. Robert (Jack) Higgs, a chapter contributor to Hoffman's anthology, has also been a leading authority on the topic over the last three decades.

The first scholarly contribution of Higgs, a retired English literature professor at East Tennessee State University was a book that examined sport and religion (Christianity) in classic American literature (Higgs, 1981). This was followed by a review of 'Philosophy and Religion' in sports that includes an extensive bibliography (Higgs, 1982), which has subsequently been updated and revised (Deardorff, 2000). After publishing further related chapters and articles (e.g., Higgs, 1990, 1985, 1983), he produced a monograph, *God in the Stadium: Sports and Religion in America* (1995), which was highly critical of the American sports institution while championing the good of sport *per se*. This text has been widely cited in the related literature and was formed the basis of over eighty-five conference and invited presentations by Higgs. A coauthored book followed (Higgs and Braswell, 2004) that covered a wide range of literary, theological, sociological and philosophical themes. Most recently, Higgs has written on archetypes and stereotypes in religion and American sports (Higgs, this volume). Another prolific scholar in the field is Joseph L. Price.

Price, a professor of Religious Studies at Whittier College (U.S.), is the editor of the 'Sports and Religion' book series for Mercer University Press and a text (Price, 2001a) on the religious aspects of American sports and their manifestation as a 'civil or surrogate religion.' He has also produced a monograph entitled *Rounding the Bases: Baseball and American Religion* (2006). While Price has published on a range of topics in the area (e.g., 2009, 2007, 2002, 2001a, 1996, 1984, 1991, 1994), his corpus of work is more focused and specific than the broad-ranging analysis of the sports and Christianity relationship provided by Hoffman and Higgs, in that his primary research interests are American baseball and football adopting mainstream sociological theories and the tools of religious studies to analyze his subject matter. In addition to Novak, Hoffman, Higgs and Price, two other scholars, William J. Baker and James Mathisen, have also made significant inroads into the scholarly investigation of the sport–faith relationship.

The major contribution of Baker, an emeritus historian at the University of Maine, is his scholarly and yet accessible sociohistorical analysis of the American modern sports institution, *Playing with God* (Baker, 2007b). This was preceded by his book provocatively entitled, *If Christ Came to the Olympics* (Baker, 2000a) that is particularly useful for those wanting to critically analyze modern Olympia. He has also published on the sociocultural movement of Victorian muscular Christianity (Baker, 2000b) and the historical relationship between Western sports and religion (Baker, 2010, 1988). In this vein, the key area of expertise of Mathisen, a retired sociologist of religion at Wheaton College (U.S.), is muscular Christianity in American culture, while he has also published on sport and religion, Pauline athletic metaphors and the evolution and development of sports ministry organizations (Mathisen, 2005, 2002, 2001, 1998, 1994/2006, 1990). His coauthored book with Tony Ladd, *Muscular Christianity: Evangelical Protestants and the Development of American Sport* (1999), is his most well-known and, for some practitioners of 'sports ministry,' a controversial work. One of Mathisen's (1994/2006) earlier contributions on muscular Christianity was published in a book that comprised papers from the annual American conference (1989–) of the Christian Society for Kinesiology and Leisure Studies (CSKLS), which until recently was the only professional scholarly organization to focus on sport and the Christian faith (see Table 1.1).

CSKLS was officially launched in 2002, but its roots go back to 1989 when Glen Van Andel, a professor of recreation (now retired) at Calvin College (U.S.), founded the annual Symposium on Christianity and Leisure Studies. Tom Visker, a professor of sport and physical education (Bethel College, U.S.) and Paul Heintzman, a professor of leisure studies (University of Ottawa, Canada) both attended the 1989 conference and, along with Van Andel, played key roles in the early development of this organization. In the early years of the annual symposium there was a focus on leisure and recreation studies, and the first book of papers from the conferences, titled *Christianity and Leisure: Issues in a Pluralistic Society* (Heintzman, Van Andel and Visker, 1994/2006), reflects this. During the mid-1990s the overall scope of the organization extended to kinesiology. A second book of conference papers reflects this sports emphasis, entitled *Physical Education, Sports, and Wellness: Looking to God as We Look at Ourselves* (Byl and Visker, 1999).[17] The significance of CSKLS as a 'pioneering organization' is further supported by the fact that both Hoffman (1994/2006) and Mathisen (1994/2006) have contributed chapters to these edited collections. Hoffman delivered invited keynote presentations at the 1991 and 2010 CSKLS conferences, while Mathisen has presented papers at the event on more than one occasion. With the recent launch of a professional journal, the *Journal of the Christian Society for Kinesiology and Leisure Studies* (2010–), CSKLS continues to be an important vehicle for research and scholarship in the field. The pioneering work of CSKLS and the scholars noted in the preceding narrative, excluding Novak as a Catholic, have a strong Protestant theological focus. This, however, does not mean that the Catholic Church and community of scholars have not passionately engaged in reflecting upon sport and religion.

Until recently, Novak's (1967/1994) influential book has stood alone as the only systematic analysis of sport and the Catholic faith in the English language. That said, scholars from Germany, Italy and Poland have contributed to such debates in their own languages, often in the form of documents written at the national level by the country's Catholic bishops. Recently, however, and especially during the last decade, there have been a growing number of academic texts (e.g., Lixey et al., 2012; Lixey, 2012, this volume; Kelly, 2012; O'Gorman, 2010b; Sing, 2004; Feeney, 2006, 1995; Baum and Coleman, 1989; Ryan, 1986); empirical studies (Hastings and DelleMonache, 2007; Hastings et al., 2006); scholarly essays;[18] sports coaching books (Hess, 2012; Costantini and Lixey, 2011; Penrice, 2009;

Yerkovich and Kelly, 2003; Brown et al., 2006); and a special edition of the periodical *New Catholic World* (1986, July–August). These have undoubtedly been driven by the Pontificate of John Paul II, which we would argue has been as significant for the Catholic community as the body of work developed by the Protestant thinkers described in the preceding.

Building on the work of his predecessor, Pope Pius XII, who addressed numerous Catholic sport associations, John Paul II, who in his earlier life was a passionate sportsman (i.e., football goalkeeper, skier and mountain climber; see Feeney, 2006, 1995), held two international sport gatherings in Rome's Olympic stadium speaking no less than 120 times on the subject, addressing Olympic committees and able-bodied and disabled athletes (Müller and Schäfer, 2010). The launch of the 'Church Sport' office within the Pontifical Council for the Laity in 2004, led by Father Kevin Lixey, is arguably the most significant outcome of the long-held enthusiasm of the Holy See for sport, culminating in the pontificate of John Paul II. To date, this new office has held three international seminars at the Vatican, each of which has had a specific focus: (i) chaplaincy, (ii) evangelism and (iii) mission and education in sport. These events have resulted in the publication of three books (Liberia Editrice Vaticana, 2011, 2008, 2006). Most recently, Pope Benedict XVI, while on a state visit to Great Britain (and in addition to his own reflections on the sports world; see Clemens, 2009), launched The John Paul II Foundation for Sport (2008–), safeguarding the enduring legacy of his predecessor. A central historical motif of Catholic discourse on sports and faith is the need to emphasize the joyful, festive and intrinsically playful nature of sport, a topic that is at the heart of the field and to which we now turn.

THEOLOGIES OF PLAY IN SPORT

> I wonder whether it is possible (it almost seems so today) to regain the idea of the Church as providing an understanding of the area of freedom (art, education, friendship, play), so that Kierkegaard's "aesthetic existence" would not be banished from the Church's sphere, but would be re-established within it? (Dietrish Bonhoeffer 1944)[19]

Over the past eighty years the study of the human impulse to play has entertained scholars from a wide range of academic disciplines and was a topic that the ancient Greek philosophers, Plato (424–348 BC) and Aristotle (384–322 BC), acknowledged as integral to human (and animal) experience (Ardley, 1967). Most of the academic work published on sport and the Christian religion that are cited in this review discusses to varying degrees the role of play in modern sport and, in particular, the lack of playfulness, a historical process that Guttman (1978/2004) describes as the 'ludic diffusion.' These reflections are, however, rooted in literature that emanates from a number of social science disciplines.

Empirical research and scholarly essays that analyze play, often with a link to games and organized sports, have come from the disciplines of psychology (e.g., Csikszentmihalyi, 1975a, 1975b), education (e.g., Piaget, 1951), cultural anthropology (Geertz, 1973),[20] sociology (e.g., Gruneau, 1980; Berger, 1970, 1967; Mead, 1934), the philosophical and social study of sport (e.g., Schmid, 2011; Giamatti, 1989/2011; Morgan and Meier, 1995, section1: 1–66; Hoffman, 1994/2006; Oriard, 1991; Higgs, 1990; McIntosh, 1979b), history (e.g., Eisen, 1991; Huizinga, 1950); biological and physical anthropology (Sands and Sands, 2010; Burghardt, 2005; Bekoff and Byers, 1998), leisure studies (e.g., Heintzman, 2006, 2003a; Heintzman, Van Andel and Visker, 1994/2006; Hoffman, 1994/2006; Ryken, 1987; Holmes, 1981; Pieper, 1948/1998),[21] evolutionary theory (Caroll, 2000), and, most importantly here, theology. The foundational study of play by Dutch cultural historian Huizinga (1950) has provided a starting point for a number of scholars wishing to explore the relationship among play (the ludic element), sports (the agnostic element that involves a contest/test) and games, a well-documented and complex triad.[22] The following quote represents the basic tenets of his work:

> We may well call play a "totality" in the modern sense of the word . . . In all its higher forms [play] at any rate belongs to the sphere of festival and ritual—the sacred sphere . . . The Platonic identification of play and holiness does not defile the latter by calling it play, rather it exalts the concept of play to the highest regions of the spirit . . . In play we move below the level of the serious, as the child does; but we can also move above it—in the realm of the beautiful and sacred.[23]

Clearly, for Huizinga (1950), play is imbued with a sacred or spiritual dimension. While his theory of play courts some theological themes, it was Rahner (1972), a Jesuit Catholic theologian, who added a strong theological foundation to the concept of play, by locating God the Creator as the 'ultimate player.' A series of philosophical and theological studies of play followed, all of which in some way are indebted to the Protestant liberal theologian Tillich (1886–1965), who pioneered theological analysis of culture in the twentieth century (Johnston, 1983; Grimshaw, 2012). These scholars variously commented on the role of play and festivity (Cox, 1969; Pieper, 1965; see also Eichberg, 2009b) in understanding God's creation and mission; the evolution of civilization; human interactions; and the relationship between, and significance of, play, games and sports (e.g., Johnston, 1983: Moltmann, 1972; Söll,1972;[24] Miller, 1971, 1969; Callois, 1958) and how Christian athletes may view playful sport as a form of worship, an expression of devotion and love toward God (Neale, 1969). Collectively, these authors, alongside more recent chapters and articles (e.g., Erdozain, 2012b; Harvey, 2012; Sing, 2011; Kelly, 2011; Kretchmar, 2011; Hoffman,

2010a: 273–80; Twietmeyer, 2009; Preece, 2009; Hamilton, 2008b; Thoennes, 2008; Feeney, 2006, 1995; Koch, 2003; Kliever, 2001; Heintzman, Van Andel and Visker, 1994/2006[25]), are in general agreement that play can be characterized by a sense of freedom and autonomy, a nonutilitarian ethic, a celebratory and spontaneous spirit, creativity, joy, intrinsic enjoyment (the autotelic), a transcendence of ego-boundaries and a feeling of psychic (and spiritual) holistic integration.[26] Arguably, it is Johnston's book *The Christian at Play* (1983) that provides one of the most comprehensive overviews of 'Christians at play.'[27]

Charting the theological reflection of play from Augustine (c. 354–430) and other Church fathers through to the modern era, Johnston (1983) provides a biblical model of play (i.e., Hebraic, Greek and Protestant),[28] an exploration of leisure, work, play and sport and the differing theological options that have emerged (e.g., Moltmann, Berger and C. S. Lewis[29]). Following others, he warns against the risk of framing a 'theology of play' as another 'pop theology' (e.g., the death of God and human potential movements), by humanizing or deifying play and thus mistakenly adopting current opinion and identifying it with the Christian religion *per se*. On the whole, Johnston is optimistic about 'Christians at play' but acknowledges the Church's suspicious (e.g., Augustine and Puritans) and ambivalent attitude toward play, pleasure and sport.[30] He also suggests that Protestant 'evangelical Christians are so prone to instrumentalize everything' (ix), including play, that modern commercialized sport has lost its playfulness, and thus its sacred roots.

This claim has been at the center of scholarly debate on this topic since the late 1960s, especially in America, and leading Catholic voices, such as Novak (1967/1994), point to the Protestant work ethic (rooted in individualistic Calvinistic doctrine) and Marxist ideology as the major forces that have transformed sport into a soulless utilitarian endeavor. Huizinga (1950: 199) concurs, stating that 'we have an activity nominally known as play but raised to such a pitch of technical organisation and scientific thoroughness that the real play-spirit is threatened with extinction.' Following a number of devastating Marxist critiques of the modern sporting institution (Rigauer, 1981; Brohm, 1978), which have suggested that 'sacred play moments' in sports have been lost through the pervasive forces of industrial capitalism (Gruneau, 1980),[31] a number of scholars in support of Huizinga (Overman, 2011, 1997; Lasch, 1980; Guttman, 1978/2004) have argued that 'sport has become work' (an individual calling in Calvinist doctrine) for many, characterized by rationality, quantification, bureaucracy, commercialism, greed and a quest for personal glory. The ethical sporting quandaries that arise from this institutional and instrumental approach to sport are many and varied and represent a topic to which we will turn in due course. Another reason why sport may be perceived to have lost its playfulness, remembering that a key characteristic of play is anthropological holism (i.e., mind, body and spirit), is the historical baggage of

Platonic–Cartesian dualism in Western theology and the theory and practice of physical education (i.e., the mind–body split).

Addressing themes of embodiment and theological dichotomies (an insufficient epistemology that underplays the complexity of things) in the modern discourse on sports, a number of scholars have presented frameworks for thinking about sport rooted in holistic Judea-Christian and Pauline theology (Barrajón, 2012; White, 2012a; Kretchmar, 2011; Scarpa and Carraro, 2011; Hochstetler, Hopsicker and Kretchmar, 2008; Twietmeyer, 2009, 2008; Watson, 2007a; also see Thaden, 2003). The Thomist scholar Pieper (1965, 1948/1998) has been arguably the most important thinker from the Catholic community with regards to orthodox theological understandings of leisure, play, work and recreation. Drawing mainly on Aquinas (c. 1225–1274) and thus Aristotle, Pieper extols the worth and necessity of leisure and play and attacks the 'cult of work' that has embroiled industrialized Western civilization, by presenting a holistic theological anthropology that views the body as inherently good and spiritual. Pieper's thesis has significantly influenced Protestant accounts of sport and play, as well as recent analyses of play (and related psychological concepts, such as 'flow'[32]) by Catholic sports scholars (Kelly, 2011; Sing, 2011, 2004) that have helped to counter the epistemological and theological error of dualism in Western theology and the study and understanding of sport. The Greek dualistic philosophy of Plato, as used especially in the writings of church father Origen (c. 182–251), have been extremely influential in denigrating the worth/sacredness of the body and thus sport and physical education (in comparison to academics and other cultural forms) in the last two millennia (Wilson, 1989). This trend has also permeated the predominantly secular based sports studies disciplines, such as sport psychology, which we also discuss after providing a historical backdrop.

Beginning with the Church fathers and practices of desert monasticism in the early centuries of Christendom, spiritual writers from across the traditions have advocated the sacrament of the 'present movement,' in which a person can experience God bodily, a sense of wholeness, centeredness and peace (Williams, 2003; Quoist, 1965; Merton, 1948).[33] This 'present' disposition (based on the presence of the Holy Spirit) allows for negative experience and feelings from the past, and fears of the future, to be largely surrendered to God. Interestingly then, four decades of sport psychology research has consistently demonstrated that heightened levels of competitive anxiety, largely due to personality traits, external influences (e.g., presence of significant others), past poor performance and fear of failure (the opposite disposition to flow; see Sager, Lavallee and Spray, 2009), most often results in maladaptive stress, a reduced sense of overall well-being and a resultant decrements in performance (Weinberg and Gould, 2011a). Indeed, longitudinal empirical studies have shown that when athletes attain 'flow states,' being able to stay in the present (as with play) is a key aspect of this experience (Jackson and Csikszentmihalyi, 1999). For example, the golfer Tiger Woods comments that 'I get so entrenched in the moment . . . that . . . there are many shots or many putts I don't remember hitting. The more intense the situation gets that calmer I feel and the more things slow down. It's a weird sensation' (Shedloski, 2011: 62). This raises two key questions: (i) are there any ontological and epistemological similarities in the experiences of religious devotees and sports performers? and (ii) Is there a possibility that Christians may observe improvements in sports performance due to the peace and centeredness they may experience?

The tendency to dichotomize subjective, playful sporting experience and sport psychology consultancy work has been critiqued by humanistic sport psychologists (e.g., Ravizza, 2002, 1984) and popular sports theorists (e.g., Cooper, 1998; Murphy and White, 1995). Cooper and Murphy and White, have subsequently gone on to make a series of claims that athletes' reports of 'being in the zone,' 'in the present moment' and/or 'in flow,' are in some way spiritual, religious, sublime (Kant and Burke), mystical or numinous (Otto) ecstatic experiences that parallel those of Moses, St. Paul or the medieval mystics, such as St. John of the Cross and St. Theresa of Avila. Philosophically eclectic work surrounding the so-called 'runner's high' (i.e., euphoric sensations experienced while long-distance running) has been central to this genre of scholarship (e.g., Sands, 2010; Sands and Sands, 2009; Battista, 2004; Jones, 2004; Joslin, 2003) and arguably stems from Sheehan's seminal text, *Running and Being* (1978), which is often cited in sport–religion studies that explore religious experience and flow states.

Although some psychologists (Csikszentmihalyi, 1988) and Catholic scholars (Hastings, 2004; Kelly, 2011) have noted conceptual, if not ontological and epistemological, parallels between 'flow' experiences and the meditative and contemplative practices of Catholic communities (e.g., Jesuit and Ignation), Christian scholars have critiqued this eclectic body of work for its etymological and philosophical naivety, while championing the good of these sporting experiences in themselves (Watson, 2007b; Higgs and Braswell, 2004; Hoffman, 1992a, 1992b, 1992c; Higgs, 1983). In particular, these writers ask whether so-called spiritual experiences and the use and interpretation of sporting metaphors,[34] such as 'sporting spirit,' in traditional and alternative/extreme sports (see O'Gorman, 2010b; Watson, 2007b), lead the athlete to a deeper commitment to God, purification from vices and the development of humility, the benchmark of Christian mysticism down the centuries?[35] In this vein, is it then theologically plausible to consider that the Christian belief of an athlete may lead to enhanced performance and/or winning?

Based on data from interviews with professional athletes who have made a commitment to the Christian faith during their career (Hubbard, 1998),[36] it could be argued that the process of Christian salvation and the lifelong surrendering of the heart to God (alongside technical physical practice and fitness conditioning), which according to Christian teaching leads to inner peace and a sense of identity rooted in God the father (Romans 8: 1–18), may inadvertently lead an athlete to improved performance in competition. This said, it is vital to point out that while the quest for excellence in any human endeavor is a very positive goal, success, enhanced performance and winning in sport is certainly not the central message of the Christian gospel (Brock, 2012; Watson, this volume, 2012, 2011a).

Considering the wealth of research on play and related concepts and the fact that it has been argued that moderns in a rationalized scientific age have lost their playful 'sense of wonder' (Dubay, 1999) and the ability to 'see contemplatively' beyond the material world (Rolheiser, 2001), further research on play in organized sport is vital. In fact, Hoffman (2010a) has argued, in support of many others, that the recovery of the play ethic in modern sport is essential for its long-term health and re-creation. Questions for future research include: in light of the historical suspicion and ambivalence of the Church with regard to play, how can playful activities such as sport, dance, music and the arts (see Begbie, 2000) be further integrated into ecclesiological praxis?[37] Building on theological works of joy in sports (Altrogge, 2008; Null, 2004) and interdisciplinary analyses of humor in sporting contexts (Eichberg, 2009a, 2009b; Walford, 2009; Levine, 1967), what are the links between humor, laughter and play in sporting locales (see Eldredge, 2011; Martin, 2011; Capps, 2006; Berger, 1997; Heddendorf, 1994/2006; Kuschel, 1994)? As the majority of previous research has largely assumed that play is a uniform concept, how does the experience of different depths of play ('deep/profound' and 'shallow/diversionary'; see Ackerman, 1997) impact the sportsperson? How can theologies and philosophies of play help to counteract the commercialized and scientized world of sport? Does the theological basis of religious disability communities, such as *L'Arche* (i.e., cooperation, celebration, festivity, humor, forgiveness, humility and vulnerability), whose activities including sports and leisure (see O'Keefe, 1994/2006), hold a prophetic and corrective message for the commercialized sports institution (see Watson, this volume, 2012; Watson and Parker, 2012a)?[38] What is the role of neuro-theological research in holistically understanding playful moments of transcendence during sports participation (see Ward, 2012; Dietrich, 2003)?

Play experiences permeate our culture, with Berger (1970) famously calling these moments 'signals of transcendence' in the human condition. Examining how such moments have contributed to the development of muscular Christianity over the last 150 years is our next task.

MUSCULAR CHRISTIANITY AND SPORTS MINISTRY

> First, convert the athletes, who are among the most visible individuals in our society, then, use these stars for what is generally known in the business as 'outreach,' an up-to date rendering of the old-fashioned phrase 'missionary work.' (Deford 1976d: 66)

Due to the historical significance of the Anglo-American (and largely Protestant)[39] movement of Victorian muscular Christianity (1850–) on modern sport, physical education and the evolution of modern 'sport ministry' (i.e., neo-muscular Christian groups), there are numerous books and scholarly articles on this subject.[40] In short, the ideology of Victorian muscular Christianity proffers the notion that sport and physical education has the potential to build manly and virtuous character, which is characterized by 'fair play, respect (both for oneself and others), strength (physical and emotional), perseverance, deference, subordination, obedience, discipline, loyalty, cooperation, self-control, self-sacrifice [and], endurance' (Collins and Parker, 2009: 194). This philosophy materialized during an age when the colonial, military and industrial aspirations of the British Empire were high on the agenda of the ruling classes, and thus sports in Victorian public schools were a vehicle to create leaders, that is, 'good Christian gentlemen' (Watson, Weir and Friend, 2005; Mangan, 1981/2000). Heavily influenced by the incarnational theology of F. D. Maurice and champions of the Christian Socialist movement (one aspect of the 'social gospel' rhetoric), such as J. M. Ludlow (1821–1911), it was Charles Kingsley (1819–1875) and Thomas Hughes (1822–1896) who developed and applied the doctrine of muscular Christianity, which also quickly gained acceptance in America, in particular though the Young Men's Christian Association (YMCA) and the ministry of D. L. Moody (Bloomfield, 1994; Norman, 1987). Over the last 150 years but especially since Protestant evangelicals began to recognize sport as a cultural vehicle to proselytize in the 1950s (Watson, 2007a), muscular Christianity (or more accurately, aspects of this movement) has morphed into a largely evangelical endeavor, under the banner of 'sports ministry.'

For scholars wishing to study this influential movement, the key scholarly texts that focus mainly on the British context, which we would argue are indebted to Mangan's (1981/2000) seminal work, are Erdozain (2010), Hall (1994), Vance (1985), Haley (1978) and McLeod (forthcoming) with sociohistorical treatments of Victorian sport being important complementary resources (Huggins, 2004; Birley, 1993; Dunning and Sheard, 1979/2005). The notable academic analyses of muscular Christianity in an American context are Putney (2001a, largely a history) and Ladd and Mathisen (1999), the latter being especially insightful with regards to modern-day sports ministry organizations and the use/misuse of Pauline athletic metaphors by modern 'muscular Christians.' Along similar lines, Hoffman's (2010a) and Krattenmaker's (2010) texts, while noting the historical development of muscular Christianity, document and critique the approach of modern American neo-muscular Christian sports ministry organizations, such as the FCA, and the practice of 'sports chaplaincy' (see Table 1.1).[41] There are also a handful of scholars from other Christian traditions and world religions who have examined 'muscular Catholicism' (Chandler, 2002; McDevitt, 1997), 'muscular Judaism' (Meyer, 2009;

Mendelsohn, 2009; Pressner, 2007; Gurock, 2005; Eisen, 1998; Hughes, 1996); 'muscular Islam' (Baker, 2007a; Smith, 2002); 'muscular Hinduism' (Alter, 2004); 'muscular Mormonism' (Kimball, 2008); and 'muscular Quakerism' (Freeman, 2010). These resources are helpful when seeking to more fully understand the evolution of muscular Christianity in a culturally and religiously pluralistic world.

Conceptually, Ladd and Mathisen's (1999) 'four models' of muscular Christianity are helpful in reviewing how this movement has evolved in Britain and America in the last 150 years.[42] These are: (i) the classical model, based primarily on the ideology and social praxis of Kingsley and Hughes that had significant impact on the development of the English public school system in the late nineteenth century (e.g., Eton, Uppingham, Marlborough, Harrow and Rugby schools); (ii) the evangelical model, which was championed by C. T. Studd (1860–1931) and D. L. Moody (1837–1899) in the early years and then athletes, such as Eric Liddell (1902–1945), whose athletic and religious accomplishments were depicted in the 1981 film *Chariots of Fire* (see Cashmore, 2008; Preece, 2009); (iii) the YMCA model that was birthed in 1844 in London, England, and 1851 in Boston, Massachusetts, and whose ideas were supported by all those who saw the importance of care for the poor and advancement of the gospel through masculine and moral young men (e.g., Fretheim, 2008; Garnham, 2001; Binfield, 1973);[43] and (iv) the Olympic model, whose principle advocate was the founder of the modern Olympic Games (1896–), the French aristocrat and philanthropist Baron Pierre de Coubertin (1863–1937), who read *the* muscular Christian novel, *Tom Brown's Schooldays* (Hughes, 1857) and visited Rugby School in 1883. Both these events having a significant role in forming his ideology that birthed the modern Olympic games.[44]

There are, of course, scores of book chapters and articles that address many of the subtopics within Ladd and Mathisen's (1999) four-point model. Some include the historical roots of muscular Christianity in the Old Testament and medieval Europe, which explored, for example, notions of chivalry and knighthood in the Middle Ages and war and dance in the Jewish faith (Higgs and Braswell, 2004; Carter, 1984a, 1984b; Thomas, 1976; Eisen, 1975; Ballou, 1973); the connections between war, modern sports and American Christianity/muscular Christianity (Dowland, 2011);; the relationships between the Puritan view of sport and muscular Christianity (e.g., Overman, 2011; Ryken, 2006, 1987, 1986; Swanson, 1978); the development of the muscular Christian idiom in British literature (Stakweather, 2011); how the secularization of Western society impacted sports and leisure in Victorian England and, conversely, how the modern-day obsession with sport may contribute to the secularization of churches by diverting their mission focus (Erdozain, 2010; Collins and Parker, 2009); the social and ethical issues that are implicit within the muscular Christian movement (Hoffman, 2010a, 1986; Bradley, 2007; Watson, 2007a; Grace, 2000; Spencer, 2000; Higgs, 1983; McIntosh, 1979a); the role of muscular

Christianity in the evolution of the modern Olympic games (Krüger, 1993; Lucas, 1976, 1975); muscular Christian motifs in *Tom Brown's Schooldays* and classic children's literature that predate the birth of the movement in the 1850s (Redmond, 1978; Winn, 1960); and how British colonialism has spread the muscular Christian message and thus traditional British sports (e.g., Macaloon, 2009; Alter, 2004). Likewise, scholarship surrounding 'Sunday sport' (i.e., sport on the Sabbath) has been quite extensive.

Over the last century Church attendance has sharply declined in the Western world, especially in the UK (see Brierley, 2006; Gill, 2003). This has led Deford (1976c: 92) to observe that 'the churches have ceded Sunday to sports . . . Sport owns Sunday now, and religion is content to lease a few minutes before big games.' This scenario has been briefly examined by sports historians (e.g., Brailsford, 1991; Holt, 1990) and others who address a range of issues surrounding the doctrine of Sabbatarianism (e.g., Waller, 2009; Helman, 2008; Heintzman, 2006; Price, 2001a). To varying degrees, most of these authors frame their analyses around the well-known story of Scottish athlete Eric Liddell, whose decision not to compete on a Sunday (Exodus 20:8) in a qualifying heat of the 100 meters at the 1924 Paris Olympics was depicted in the film *Chariots of Fire* (see Cashmore, 2008; Preece, 2009; Keddie, 2007; Watson, 2007a). The former triple-jump Olympic champion and world record holder Jonathan Edwards was until recently (when he renounced his Christian faith),[45] often viewed as a modern-day 'muscular Christian' comparable to Liddell (Folley, 2001). Such comparisons were principally based on Edward's decision not to compete in the British athletic trials for the 1988 Seoul Olympics, as they also took place on a Sunday. In time, however, Edwards had a change of heart and started to compete on Sundays, after becoming aware of a new covenant bible verse (Romans 14:15) that states that 'one man considers one day more sacred than the other; another man considers everyday alike' (Folley, 2001). In more recent times, both Euan Murray (a Scottish rugby international) and Dan Walker (a BBC sports presenter) have followed in the footsteps of Liddell. Murray refuses to play rugby on a Sunday and when signing autographs includes a bible verse (Kessel, 2010). Likewise, in order not to compromise his Sabbatarian beliefs, Walker (2009) refuses to work for the BBC on the Sabbath.

Other niche areas of research on muscular Christianity include: Catholic reflections on the movement (Costantini and Lixey, 2011; Vost, 2011;[46] McGrath, 2008; Chandler, 2002; McDevitt, 1997),[47] which include empirical research from *The Mirenda Centre for Sport, Spirituality and Character Development* (Hastings et al., 2006; Hastings and DelleMonache, 2007); the links between revivalism and rugby in Edwardian Wales (Morgan, 2005); critiques identifying an emphasis of the physical over the moral in the ideology and practice of muscular Christianity (Mangan and Walvin, 1987); examination of gender construction in Victorian educational ideology (Neddam, 2004); the neglect and celebration of 'muscular women'

(Deardorff and Deardorff, 2008; Millikan, 2006; Stebner and Trothen, 2002; Putney, 2001b; Borish, 1987; Bederman, 1989; Vertinsky, 1987; Chen and Zhao, 2001); the role of muscular Christianity in the emergence of 'men's movements' such as the Promise Keepers (1990–) in America in the 1990s (Harper, 2012; Gelfer, 2010; Bartowski, 2004; Armato and Marsiglio, 2002; Allen, 2002; Randels and Beal, 2002; Balmer, 2000; Hawkins, 2000; Beal, 1997; Web-Mitchell, 1997); the enmeshed imperialistic and political agendas of militarism, social Darwinism and muscular Christianity (Mangan, 2011; Pope, 2010); the historical and social process that at least partially wed soccer to Christian masculine ideals (Mangan and Hickey, 2008; Kwauk, 2007; Lupson, 2006); and the influence of the 'social gospel' movement and leisure revolution that led to the notion of 'rational recreation' (Cavallo, 1981; Cunningham, 1980), a class-based and political 'movement designed to counter moral slippage, mass delinquency and mob culture' (Collins and Parker, 2009: 196). The 'games playing' ethos inculcated by the muscular Christian message in English public schools and implicit in 'rational recreation' was not, Mangan (1982: 33) observes, the 'exclusive prerogative of didactic muscular Christians . . . Hedonists, opportunists, pragmatists and moralists . . . embraced the cult of games . . . in late Victorian England.'

For sure, political leaders through the twentieth century have continued to advance the long-held (and controversial) muscular Christian idea that 'sport builds character' (Coakley, 2011). A wide range of social and religious movements have also emerged during the last 150 years, which have advocated physical endeavors, such as sport and physical training (later to be called physical education) as a vehicle to contribute to the positive development of civil and moral character (sometimes with militaristic undertones). Social historian Freeman (2010), suggests that these include the utilization of sports in the *Sunday School* movement in the 1880s (see McLeod, 2007);[48] the *Scouts*, founded by Sir Baden-Powell (1857–1941) in 1907 (see Turner and Posner, 2010); the *Boys Brigade* (1883–); and the *Outward Bound* movement (1941–), the latter of which was instigated by the German educationalist, Kurt Hahn (1886–1974). Freeman goes on to note that during the 1960s there was a shift away from a focus on 'character training' and education for leadership (a corporate vision) to an individual quest for 'personal growth' and 'self-discovery.'

Arguably, this reflects the secularization of Western culture and the individualism and promulgation of theories of 'self-actualization' from humanistic psychology and sport psychology (e.g., Bellah, 2007; Maslow, 1968; Ravizza, 1984). Indeed, Aitken (1989: 401), in support of sport sociologists who have evaluated the prevalence and validity of the use of prayer, superstitions and rituals in sports (e.g., Coakley, 2007), argues that '"Born-Again Sport," like fundamentalist Christianity, holds to a very traditionalist view of American life where winning is a virtue . . . [which] . . . has contributed to the ongoing process of secularization by reducing religion to magic.' Possibly the most controversial and widely documented example of this kind of scenario is when athletes are seen (or heard) to pray for 'God to be on their team' in an attempt to influence the outcome of the game and in the ultimate interests of winning (see Hoffman, 2011; Price, 2009; Kreider, 2003). Over the last four decades, Hoffman (1986: 18) has been the most vociferous critic of this kind of utilitarian approach to sport:

> Christian athletes confront an inevitable contradiction. Sport which celebrates the myth of success is harnessed to a theology that often stresses the importance of losing. Sport which symbolizes a morality of self-reliance and teaches the just rewards of hard-work is used to propagate a theology dominated by the radicalism of grace (the first shall be last and the last shall be first). Sport, a microcosm of meritocracy, is used to celebrate religion that says that all are unworthy and undeserving.

While championing the many positives of sports, this ethic, Watson (2011a, 2007b) argues, is diametrically opposed to the Christian injunction to 'die to oneself' and thus is more analogous to the atheistic existentialism of philosophers such as Sartre, Camus or Nietzsche. Echoing such thoughts, Erdozain (2010: 105) proposes that the foundational muscular Christian doctrine of manliness (and competitiveness) that frequently seems to indoctrinate humanistic virtues, is 'the opposite to the Pauline concept of divine strength being made "perfect in weakness': the [competitive sport] model is divine approval for human strength, albeit strength of will rather than mere physicality.'[49] Historically, this stems from what Overman (2011: 61) calls the 'great Protestant delusion,' that is, that human existence is principally directed and shaped by the force of human will, a point of critique for most Catholic scholars reflecting on Protestant models of sport (e.g., Novak, 1967/1994). Observations such as this have sparked a growing genre of scholarship that has vigorously questioned the 'theologies of competition' that have emerged within modern sports ministries.

At the heart of this literature is the proposal that modern-day advocates of muscular Christian ideals often uncritically adopt tenets of contemporary sporting culture that have little, if any, affinity with the gospel of Christ (e.g., Brock, 2012; Hoffman, 2010a; Krattenmaker, 2010; Erdozain, 2010; Ladd and Mathisen, 1999; Mathisen, 1994/2006, 1998, 1990; Aitken, 1989). Sociologists of religion Ladd and Mathisen (1999) have conceptualized the broader ideology that has developed within the short history of modern sports ministry (1950s–) as a 'folk theology' comprising five facets: (i) pragmatic utility, (ii) meritocratic democracy, (iii) competitive virtue, (iv) heroic models and (v) therapeutic self-control. Perhaps the most oft-cited aspect of this 'folk theology' is 'pragmatic utility,' that is, sports usefulness as a means to attract and convert people.[50] Notwithstanding the criticisms surrounding modern sports ministry, there are a number of scholars (and notably the majority of Catholic Popes of the twentieth century; see Koch,

2012) who also believe in the goodness and worth of the endeavors of sports ministries (e.g., Pfitzner, this volume; White, 2012b; Watson, 2007a; Liberia Editrice Vaticana, 2006).

Reflecting on this, we provoke scholars to consider that sports ministry organizations, particularly in America, might just be an intimation, albeit an imperfect one, of the 'local tradition' or 'light' in the microcosm of modern sport. This thesis stems from our reading of the Old Testament theologian Brueggeman (2010: 18), who, in resonating with other prophetic voices such as Jim Wallis, William Stringfellow (1973/2004) and Jacques Ellul, argues that the hegemonic 'American Empire' is a modern-day Babylon that is 'living in a cocoon of self-justification' and unconscious denial, as was the case for previous empires, for example, Roman, Persian and British. The American Church, the faithful body of believers, is the 'local tradition' for Brueggeman, as were the exiled Jews in Babylon before the intervention of Cyrus, and thus should actively resist the imperialistic self-indulgent greed, pride, power and arrogance of the empire (as did the prophets). Do sports ministry organizations, in some small way, fulfill this role of the 'local tradition' in what Watson and White (2007) have called the modern sporting Babel? If it is true, as Hoffman (2010a) has consistently claimed, that modern sports ministry groups uncritically embrace the cultural norms of this sporting Babel, then Brueggeman has a stark warning, but one which also provides a glimmer of hope for our thesis:

> The local tradition, which stands in deep tension with the empire, knows the denial cannot finally cover over the reality . . . [of] anxiety . . . The congregation of the local tradition, having inhaled so much imperial air, is itself slow and reluctant to realise what has been entrusted to it . . . Such a congregation is tempted to collude with and accommodate itself to the loud, insistent practices of the empire. At best, however, the congregation, funded by the local tradition, knows better . . . it tells an alternative and opposing story to that of the empire centred on the covenant with YHWH.[51]

So it seems that, as Brueggeman (2010) goes on to explain, scholars wanting to pursue this line of reasoning must do so with care so as not to dichotomize (or demonize) a complex and dynamic relationship between empire and local tradition, as any organization or institution can occupy, to varying degrees, both roles simultaneously. Future scholarship, could, however, examine how this dynamic operates within sport ministry locales and how models of 'overt' (e.g., proselytizing)[52] and 'covert' (incarnational modeling through service to others) ministry could both be affectively embraced (see Johnson, 2006). Beyond institutional analyses of the sport–faith dyad, there are a whole range of more specific research questions and topics that Watson (2007a) has urged scholars and practitioners from across the traditions of Christendom to collaborate on.

Perhaps initially, one of the most important tasks is to undertake a comprehensive mapping of sports ministry publications, provision and practice across different countries and Christian traditions (e.g., UK and America/ Catholic and Protestant). In addition to the largely critical works on muscular Christianity and the resources[53] of sports ministry organizations (e.g., White et al., 2008; Neal, 1981, 1972[54]), to date the key sources from a Protestant perspective are Mason (2011, 2003), Null (2008b, 2004), White and White (2006), Garner (2003), Connor (2003), McCown and Gin (2003), Shields (2002), Voss (1997) and Yessick (1996)[55]. From a Catholic standpoint they are White (2012b), Liberia Editrice Vaticana (2006) and Hastings et al. (2006). Beyond use in sports ministry praxis, some of these resources are used on a range of postgraduate courses in America and more recently in the UK at the University of Gloucestershire (Collins and Parker, 2009), which have a specific focus on sports ministry and/or chaplaincy. The systematic mapping of such educational courses and publications would provide an objective sociological and theological foundation, and rationale, for further research and course development in all levels of tertiary education. The results of such a project would also pave the way for greater ecumenical and intercultural dialogue through sport–faith organizations that Catholic scholars have recently identified as an important initiative (Müller, 2011; Kammogne, 2011) and that, we argue, could provide a forum via which to broach more divisive ecclesiological matters.

Considering that *Sport Alpha* (2012–)[56] has recently been launched at Holy Trinity Brompton Church, London, UK, scholars should also investigate how the medium of sport can be used as a means of outreach and evangelism within Church structures, as the majority of sports ministries are currently para-church organizations (see Cornick, 2012; Oakley, 2012; Daniels and Weir, 2008; Carpenter, 2001). In addition to 'sports ministry groups,' a number of 'individual sport evangelists,' such as the extradited Zimbabwean international cricketer Henry Olonga, have recently emerged and have used their sporting success/fame as a means by which to combat human rights abuses and to share their faith (see Batts, 2010; Olonga, 2010).[57] Research investigating the experiences and effectiveness of lone 'modern-day muscular Christians,' such as Olonga and others (Bolt, 2012; Gibbons, Dixon and Braye, 2008),[58] would be valuable, in terms of comparing and contrasting these biographies with previous Christian sports figures, such as Eric Liddell.

Conceptualizations of Christian masculinity within sporting contexts is also a niche area that has received little attention to date. While not neglecting the wealth of research on masculine identities in modern sport (e.g., Wellard, 2009; Messner, Mckay and Sabo, 2000), scholars looking for a holistic understanding of this topic should access both Protestant and Catholic writings (e.g., Aune, 2010; Gelfer, 2010; Rohr, 2005, 2004a, 2004b; Eldredge, 2001; Putney, 2001a; Claussen, 2000; Ward, 1999) and the work of Deardorff and Deardorff (2008), who have drawn on some of this literature in their theological analysis of both masculine and feminine templates in sports settings.[59] Similarly, the challenges that Christian sportswomen face in negotiating their femininity in male-dominated sports is a topic with very little reflection, except that of Deardorff and Deardorff and a small handful of scholarly essays from Catholic (Sydnor, 2012, 2009, 2006a, 2006b, 2005) and Protestant thinkers (Millikan, 2006; Stebner and Trothen, 2002; Chen and Zhao, 2001; Putney, 2001b; Bederman, 1989; Borish, 1987; Vertinsky, 1987; Carmody, 1986). The scope for further research is, therefore, significant and we would argue crucial if the Church and sports ministry organizations are to more fully engage with and provide instruction and guidance for Christian women who are passionate about sport.

Another closely related topic is that of the exegesis and use of Pauline athletic metaphors (e.g., 1 Corinthians 9:24–27) and in particular, the *agon* motif, in the literature and praxis of sports ministry organizations; what Mangan (1982) terms 'agnostic muscularity.' In addition to Catholic analyses on this topic (e.g., Arnold, 2012; White, 2012b; Costantini and Lixey, 2011; Feeney, 2006, 1995; Koch, 2005b, 2003), it is the work of Lutheran theologian Pfitzner (this volume, 2009, 1981, 1967) that encompasses historical, cultural, philosophical and theological dimensions of the study of such metaphors, which scholars argue is the most authoritative resource (Ladd and Mathisen, 1999; Hoffman, 2010a; Watson, 2007a). This area of research comprises three broad themes: (i) exegetical and hermeneutical issues surrounding the praxis of Pauline athletic metaphors in preaching and sports ministry contexts; (ii) historical, cultural and archaeological evidence that situates and contextualizes the use of Paul's athletic metaphors and related concepts, such as asceticism, endurance, suffering, self-sacrifice, martyrdom and death, victory, heroism, contest and struggle towards the fulfillment of a spiritual (eschatological) or earthly goal (victory in sport), all aspects of modern sports; and (iii) the use of athletic metaphors to construct a 'theology of sport' and/or a 'theology of sports competition' based on the controversial premise that 'sport builds character' and is a vehicle for evangelistic endeavors.[60]

Following this theme, Kidd (2010: 163) has recently suggested that the myriad of 'sport-peace' enterprises that have emerged over the last decade, whose aim it is to combat ethical and social issues through the vehicle of sport are a 'striking reassertion of Thomas Hughes' nineteenth-century ideals of sport as a pedagogy of beneficial change.' Our next task then, is to review the literature that has documented and analyzed the ethical issues surrounding modern-day sports.

THEOLOGICAL ETHICS IN SPORT (WITH PSYCHOLOGICAL CONSIDERATIONS)

Reducing sporting performances to matters of science, money, power or fame ultimately destroys their internal significance, and becomes a kind of moral defeatism. (Grace, 2000: 12)

Professional athletes have become the naughty vicars of the 21st century, required to set a moral example for which they have no inclination and little aptitude . . . A moral burden . . . is placed on the back of every professional athlete. (Barnes, 2011: 93)

In 1986 Hoffman published an article in the periodical *Christianity Today* entitled 'The Sanctification of Sport: Can the Mind of Christ Coexist with the Killer Instinct?' In many ways this question provides a basic starting point for theological ethicists examining the sports world that has, since Victorian times been upheld up as a 'moral laboratory' (see McFee, 2004).' Not forgetting the many positive values that can be experienced in sport, such as teamwork, altruism, strength, self-control, justice, loyalty, wisdom, self-sacrifice, equality, courage, generosity, joy, honesty, tenacity, hard work, solidarity, peace, love (*Philia*, friendship love) and community spirit (McNamee, 2011, 2008; White, 2012b, 2008; Scarpa and Carraro, 2011; Corlett, 1996), which Pope John Paul II recognized as the 'the most authentic dimension of sport,'[61] the multibillion-dollar global institute of professional and American College sport (see Overman, 2011) has been fraught with ethical and moral issues for over a century. This led historian and social commentator Lasch (1980) to title his oft-cited chapter 'The Degradation of Sport,'[62] which he argues partially stems from the loss of the sacred dimension in the modern sporting milieu.

Beside the secularization of Western culture (Taylor, 2007; Ratzinger, 2005) and consequently the microcosm of sport (Yamane, Mellies and Blake, 2010; Guttman, 1978/2004), the scientization, commodification and professionalization of sport since the 1960s has largely been driven by the allied growth of televised sport and mass sponsorship (Whannel, 1986). This shift has been a major determinant in the decline of ethical values in the sporting realm (Cashmore, 2012; Beamish and Ritchie, 2006; Hoberman, 1992). Recognizing that the application of science to sport (i.e., biomechanics, physiology and psychology) is not a negative development in itself, Twietmeyer (2008: 461) highlights that these historical changes may have inadvertently led to a more utilitarian approach to sport: 'science (a necessary, although not sufficient, good in Kinesiology) ends up overwhelming the field. Consequently the study of human movement is unalterably crippled.' Any quest for deeper spiritual meaning, or simply a spirit of freedom and playfulness in sporting contexts, is then often lost in a quest for external gains, such as winning for personal glory and status and/or financial greed.

The moral and ethical issues that have materialized from this instrumental approach to sport are innumerable and have been at least partially driven by what Walsh and Giulianotti (2007) call the 'Sporting Mammon' that rapidly emerged as sport was professionalized and became big business. Key areas of research include: physical and verbal abuse of opponents (and even teammates); fan violence, including sectarianism (e.g., Lawrence, 2011; Sugden and Bairner, 1993); intimidation; blatant disregard for the spirit of the rules; mistaking legality for ethicality; sexual abuse of athletes by coaches; praying to win (Kreider, 2003); trash talk; cheating; playing with pain and injuries (Sinden, 2012; Howe, 2004; Nixon, 1992); financial greed and corruption; alienation in individual and international relations (e.g., political boycotting of the Olympics and the threat of global terrorism);[63] invasive noncorrective surgery for athletic performance enhancement (Hamilton, 2006); drug-doping; abuse of officials; genetic-enhancement technologies; abusive child and youth elite development academies (e.g., in former Eastern Bloc countries and China; see Hong, 2006); overtraining and abuse of one's body; and the potential deleterious effects of excessive expectations and pressure from parents, coaches and even nations (see McNamee, 2010; Miah, 2010, 2004; Morgan, 2007; Simon, 2004; Lumpkin, Stoll and Beller, 2002; McNamee and Parry, 1998; McIntosh, 1979c).[64] This burgeoning sports ethics literature identifies many moral problems within professional sport and in turn has spawned a number of practical initiatives, both in America and across continental Europe. Examples include the American Sport Education Program (1981–); the Centre for ETHICS (1993–);[65] the Character Counts project (Josephson Institute, Centre for Youth Ethics, 1987–); the Positive Coaching Alliance (1998–); and the Vatican Church Sport office (2004–), all of which promote ethical practice (and scholarship) in sport through educational programs and workshops.

Within the discipline of sport philosophy, this corpus of ethical studies and concomitant initiatives far outweigh contributions from other philosophical subdisciplines, such as epistemology, aesthetics and metaphysics (e.g., McNamee, 2010; Morgan, 2007; Simon, 2004). For the Christian theologian, it is the divorce of ethics from metaphysics that presents a serious epistemological error (see Kretchmar, 1983), which is rooted in the fact that for the first 20 years of the discipline the bulk of ethical reflection in sport was underpinned by secular analytical philosophy (McNamee, 2010, 2007a). Schools of thought, such as pragmatism (especially Jamesian) and phenomenology that appear more compatible with spiritual concepts have slowly begun to emerge in the discipline of the philosophy of sport, which is a promising sign. Notwithstanding all of this, Watson (2011b: 10), recently asked, 'Has the world of sport, especially big-business professional sport, actually changed significantly' following forty years of philosophical reflection and programming?

Critiquing the values of modern sport, utilizing Augustinian ethics, philosopher Hamilton (2011) suggests not and argues that we need to explore the metaphysical roots of the problems in sport, rather than seeking piecemeal solutions. Kretchmar (1998), in agreement, has argued that when studying sport, 'to do ethics *in vacuo*, without some sort of metaphysical basis, is a questionable endeavour.'[66] It is encouraging then that the two leading journals in the field, *Sport, Ethics and Philosophy* and the *Journal of the Philosophy of Sport*, have published papers and book reviews with a spiritual and/or Christian theme (e.g., Thompson, 2011; Scarpa and Carraro, 2011; Hopsicker, 2009; Kreider, 2003; Abe, 1986; Wertz, 1977; Hoffman, 1976). Theological ethicists interested in sport who wish to build on these foundations have a range of theoretical options.

Sports ethicist Parry (2011) suggests that these options include 'Divine Command Theory,' which has historically dominated Christian ethics, but also a number of well-used ethical frameworks that have a theological basis. Examples are the virtue ethics of Aristotle and MacIntyre (e.g., Goodson, this volume; McNamee, 2011, 2008); Paley's Utilitarianism; and Aquinas's Natural Law theory. Other theological investigations of morality in sport that have concentrated on the sin of pride and the virtue of humility (Watson, this volume; Watson and White, 2007), have in part utilized the Catholic model of the 'Seven Deadly Sins' (i.e., wrath, greed, sloth, pride, lust, envy and gluttony) to examine sports experience, drawing specifically on interpretations of this concept from pastoral theology (Capps, 1987) and psychiatry (Menninger, 1973). Helpfully, Parry (2011: 21) outlines a range of topics that could be addressed using the ethical theories suggested in the preceding:

- The application of the insights of theological thinkers to ethical issues in sport (e.g., Augustine)
- The understanding of religious practices in relation to sport (e.g., prayer)
- The clarification and exploration of theological concepts, and their relevance in sporting environments (e.g., evil, sin and redemption)
- The significance of religious beliefs in terms of social and lifestyle issues (e.g., Christian beliefs and sporting identity)
- The application of religious morality to sporting practices
- The interpretation of sporting events, institutions and relationships in religious terms
- The critique of sport from a theological point of view

Drawing on the sport ethics literature and applying some of the Christian ethical theories outlined in the preceding, anthologies and monographs by Kelly (2012); Lixey et al. (2012), Watson and Parker (2012), Parry, Nesti and Watson (2011: part I), Deardorff and White (2008), Parry et al. (2007), Hoffman (2010a, 1992b), Feeney (2006, 1995), Higgs and Braswell (2004), Higgs (1995), Heintzman, Van Andel and Visker (1994/2006), Baum and Coleman (1989), and Novak (1967/1994) contain numerous chapters discussing ethical sporting dilemmas and proffer ways to bring redemption to the sporting institution. Along these lines, there is also an emerging body of empirical research and essays that seek to shed further light on this subject matter.

Empirical qualitative research in this field is relatively scarce, but what does exist features examinations of how Christian athletes negotiate the paradoxical cultures and norms of elite-competitive sport and Christianity

(Stevenson, 1997, 1991; also see Sinden, 2012; Stevenson, 2008; Schroeder and Scribner, 2006; Curry, 1988); the experience of athletes in Christian sports leagues (Dunn and Stevenson, 1998); and a case study exploring how a Christian intercollegiate coach at an evangelical American college responds to the dominant values of competitive sport (Bennett et al., 2005; also see Hunt, 1999). Scholars have also explored embodiment in relation to identity construction in Christian physical education teachers (Macdonald and Kirk, 1999; Macdonald, 1998; also see Riesen, 2007) and the notion of 'athletic identity' through a theological and psychological lens (Watson, 2011a). Closely related to this work are educational studies in sporting locales (in particular physical education) that have a strong moral and spiritual underpinning. These studies have drawn variously on Kohlberg's (1984) theory of the 'stages of moral development' (building on Jean Piaget's theory of cognitive development), Aristotelian and Platonic ethics, theological virtue ethics and the educational doctrine within the philosophy of Olympism (e.g., Lixey, this volume; Costantini, 2011; McNamee, 2011, 2010;[67] Robinson, 2007; Parry, 2007b; Feeney, 1995; Arnold, 2001, 1999, 1997, 1994, 1989; Shields, 1996; McIntosh, 1979c). This corpus of work is intimately related to the literature on 'moral reasoning' and 'character development' in sport (e.g., Stoll and Beller, 2008) and how competition in sport is understood.

The theme of competition in sport, the 'win-at-all-costs' culture and the possible moral issues that this may engender are the central themes of a number of scholarly works with a Christian emphasis that are helpful to contextualize this empirical work and that reflect the importance of psychological insight in this area of study (e.g., Shields and Bredemeier, 2011a, 2009; Watson, 2011a; Clifford and Feezell, 2009; Weir, 2008; Watson and White, 2007; Henkel, 2007; Grace, 2000; Spencer, 2000; Koch, 2005a, 1994; Robinson, 1997; Aitken, 1989; Arnold, 1989; Hoffman, 1986; Higgs, 1983; also see Walker, 1980). Intense, and often unhealthy, competition between nations to top the Olympic and Paralympic medal table has also been evidenced and is closely tied to a quest for geopolitical power on the world stage (De Bosscher et al., 2008; Close, Askew and Xin, 2007), which Higgs (1982) suggests is frequently rooted in pride of heart.

Ethicists, psychologists, philosophers, theologians and those involved in sports ministry that have examined the nature of 'sport competition,' have wrestled with a number of challenging questions.[68] These include: how might one define sport and competition? Is competitive sport ethically defensible, considering it always produces a zero-sum outcome—a winner and loser? Can Christianity transform the potentially negative elements of zero-sum outcomes into mutual benefits? How do sporting opponents 'compete' and/or 'cooperate' with one another in the quest for excellence? Does sport build positive Christian character and can it be measured? If so, how might one define it? Does participation in competitive sport augment or lessen 'moral reasoning' in the athlete? Do athletes with Christian beliefs demonstrate higher levels of moral reasoning than nonbelievers, and thus behavior in line with the biblical code? And if not, why not?

Etymologically, sport competition can be understood as a 'mutual striving together for excellence' (Greek, *arête*)[69] in which opponents honor their opponents and cooperate to bring out the best in one another (see Weinberg and Gould, 2011c; Kretchmar, 1995; Hyland, 1988, 1978; also see Newman, 1989; Mead, 1937).[70] There are important links here to Pauline athletic metaphors and the meaning of 'challenge' or 'contest' in sporting competition, in the original Greek, the *agon*, a term that the 'apostolic athlete,' Paul, regularly used to help describe the ethics of the Christian life in his broader eschatological vision (see Brock, 2012; White, 2012b; Pfitzner, this volume, 1967). Of course, in the emotionally charged world of sport, this ideal sometimes dissolves into 'alienation and violence' and a host of other moral issues (Hyland, 1988: 177; see also Young, 2011; Trothen, 2009; Messner, 1990; Bredemeier et al., 1987; Bredemeier and Shields, 1986, 1985). This has led some social scientists and psychologists to question whether sporting competition is ethically defensible at all, or whether it can assist in building positive character (e.g., Kohn, 1992;[71] Olgilvie and Tutko, 1971). Nevertheless, the general consensus among scholars from across the disciplines, according to Lixey (this volume), McNamee (2011) and Watson and White (2007), is that sporting competition is essentially 'good' and has the potential to lead to positive outcomes such as mutual excellence and friendship and the development of positive (Christian) character attributes. There is, however, limited empirical evidence to support this complex thesis (Coakley, 2011), in part because of the many variables that White (2012b: 14n54) acknowledges are 'difficult to isolate when analysing empirical and anecdotal evidence for and against' the theory that sport builds character.[72]

Stoll and Beller's (2008) longitudinal (over twenty years) sports ethics research demonstrates that athletes in American Christian and secular schools show little, if any, difference, in moral reasoning and that Christian athletes have a tendency to compartmentalize their faith and exclude it from competitive sport (see also Erdozain, 2012a; Bell, Johnson and Peterson, 2011; Shields and Bredemeier, 2011b, 2010, 2005, 1995; Weinberg and Gould, 2011b; Storch et al., 2004; Storch and Storch, 2002a; Storch et al., 2001; Bredemeier and Shields, 2005; Shields et al., 2005; Mara and Barber, 2000; Beller et al., 1996; Kelly, Hoffman and Gill, 1990). Such an approach that accepts unethical and violent behavior on the field of play but not off it is what Walsh and Guilianotti (2007: 1) aptly term 'white line fever' (also see Upton, 2011), whereby 'sporting arenas are special spheres where the rules of life do not apply.' An example of this is illustrated in the normativity of explicit violence in Canadian ice hockey participation and fandom (Klein and Austen, 2011; Trothen, 2009).

Commenting on this theme and on Stoll and Beller's findings, Watson (2011a) advocates the need to balance the spiritual development of the 'heart' of the athlete, or fan (Proverbs 4:23; Matthew 12:34), with sound ethical/biblical instruction and habitual practice of virtuous behavior. This is largely based on the theological proposition that it is not 'self-control' that is the master Christian virtue but rather 'surrender of self' to Christ, in which both the motivations of the heart and the ethical knowledge accrued through instruction (Watson, 2011a) play a determining role in sporting attitudes and behaviors (Worthington and Berry, 2005).[73] This thesis is in some way supported by McNamee (2011: 41), who, by drawing on Aristotelian ethics, observes that moral behavior in sport is a combination of virtuous action and 'emotional sensibility' (of the heart?),[74] which makes up a 'fuller model of virtue development.'

Of course, the notion of 'self-control' in moral reasoning is deeply embedded in the psyche of nations (e.g., America) founded on the Protestant work ethic and the moral imperatives of Calvinism and Puritanism (e.g., emphasizing individual calling and moral perfection). Sociologist Overman (2011: 61) has argued that the 'great Protestant delusion was (and is) that human existence is shaped by human will.' He defines 'seven Protestant virtues' (with apologies to Thomas Aquinas) that characterize American (and other largely Protestant nations') culture and sport: (i) worldly asceticism, (ii) rationalization, (iii) goal-directed behavior, (iv) achieved status, (v) individualism, (vi) work ethic and (vii) time ethic. This said, 'self-control' is a biblical virtue that is essential to the Christian life and sport. But as Taylor (2007: 497–98) has observed, 'moralism' (i.e., the autocratic application of codes of behavior) and, in turn, a repression of bodily pleasures in the modern secular project (Erdozain, 2010), has largely failed to inculcate Christian moral and ethical behavior and character:

> This [moralism] is perhaps not an outlook which is easy to square with a reading of the New Testament, but it nevertheless achieved a kind of hegemony across the broad reaches of the Christian Church in the modern era. The outlook ends up putting all the emphasis on what we should do, and/or what we should believe, to the detriment of spiritual growth.

The result of a legalistic and mechanized approach to sport (versus the play ethic), what Brock (2012: 19) calls a *culture of individualized economic competition* and *introspection* entrenched in capitalist ideology (also see Bellah, 2007; Vitz, 1977/1994; Lasch, 1980), is clearly demonstrated in a large body of sport and exercise psychology research. Of particular interest here is the significant literature that indicates the prevalence of physical and psychological 'burnout and overtraining' in elite adult and youth sport (Smith, Lemyre and Raedeke, 2007). The prevalence of such a condition, we argue, is a direct consequence of the obsessive, driven and results-oriented Protestant 'work ethic' (and Marxist ideologies) that has shaped modern life and professional sport in many Western nations (Erdozain, 2012c; Overman, 2011; Guttman, 1978/2004; Weber, 1958). Catholic sports scholars, for example, Novak (1967/1994), have warned against this ethos and called for a renaissance of the 'play ethic' in sport, yet such calls have largely fallen on deaf ears.

Relatedly, other psychiatric, philosophical and theological writings (see Watson, 2011a)[75] and quantitative studies from the fields of 'clinical sport psychology' and 'religion and health' on sports performers (especially American university student athletes) have recorded a wide range of maladaptive responses from participating in sports that are permeated with questionable ethical practices (Sinden, 2012; Zenic, Stipic and Sekulic, 2011; Cavar, Sekulic and Culjak, 2010; Rodek, Sekulic and Pasalic, 2009; Storch and Farber, 2002; Storch et al., 2003, 2002; Storch and Storch, 2002b; Storch, Storch and Adams, 2002; Storch et al., 2001; Begel and Burton, 2000). These include clinical levels of social and competitive anxiety, substance abuse, eating disorders, narcissistic tendencies and moral emotions, such as guilt, shame, depression, suicide and suicidal ideation, which research has also demonstrated in athletes that have suffered career-ending injuries, retirement and de-selection (especially in professional sports, see Watson, 2011a; Null, 2008a). An important caveat in this research is that religiousness in American university sport students (male and female) has been found to have a significant buffering affect against binge (alcohol) drinking and drug taking (e.g., Zenic, Stipic and Sekulic, 2011; Cavar, Sekulic and Culjak, 2010). Bearing in mind the moral malaise surrounding 'Jock Culture' in modern sports settings, in particular university sport settings (Waldron, Lynn and Krane, 2011; Sparkes, Partington and Brown, 2007; Martens, 1979), these results elucidate the importance of further psychological research from a Christian viewpoint that is to date limited (see Nesti, 2011, 2007a, 2007b, 2007c; Watson, 2011a; Lynn, Pargament and Krane, 2010; Smith, 2010; Watson and Nesti, 2005; Peña, 2004; Cook, 1985). Additional ethical inquiry to complement and underpin this body of work will be crucial if we are to begin to counter the wave of systemic moral problems in global sports, not least from trained theologians and Christian psychologists and ethicists.

In concluding their recent essay on sports ethics, Scarpa and Carraro (2011: 120) identified 'a commonality and reciprocity of values between sports and Christian ethics' that should encourage scholars to explore a gamut of ethical questions in the sporting domain (also see Kretschmann and Benz, 2012). Of course, resources from the sports philosophy field and those from the embryonic literature on theology and sport, discussed here are a solid foundation from which to begin this task. Importantly, however, academics might also more fully engage with the foundational writings of the early Church fathers, Christian philosophers and medieval theologians. For example, Tertullian, Philo, Augustine, John Chrysostom, John Cassian and Thomas Aquinas, who provided exegesis on Pauline athletic metaphors (e.g., Cor. 9:24–27) and ideas surrounding embodiment in response to different gnostic heresies (typically dualisms) and pagan and gladiatorial sports that have emerged down the ages (see Koch, 2012; Pfitzner, this volume; Scarpa and Carraro, 2011; Hoffman, 2010a, chap. 1; Carter, 1984a). Major theologians, from both Catholic and Protestant traditions during the twentieth century, have made passing reference to sport in their ethical musings (e.g., Bonhoeffer, 1955; Barth, 1981),[76] with Moltmann (1989,

1972) being an exception, having written specific papers on the ethics of modern Olympic games and a book on the theology of play. This said, during the last eighty years a succession of popes, drawing chiefly on Catholic moral theology (e.g., Curran, 2005)[77] and reflections on culture (e.g., Rowland, 2003), have used what Pope Pius XII called the 'Sport Epistle'—Paul's Corinthian correspondence, in particular his athletic metaphors (Koch, 2012)—as a framework for cultural reflection when delivering homilies and speeches in sporting locales (see Lixey et al., 2012; Mazza, 2012; White, 2012b; O'Gorman, 2010b, chap. 6; Müller and Schäfer, 2010; Liberia Editrice Vaticana, 2006; Feeney, 2006, 1995). This is encouraging, although further Catholic and Protestant biblical and systematic theological study is paramount if the discourse on sport is to advance in credibility and depth.

A recent conference on 'Christian Ethics and Sport' (2011), hosted by the well-respected Society for the Study of Christian Ethics, and three international seminars, hosted by the Vatican's 'Church Sport' office (2009, 2008, 2005) that addressed (among other things) the ethical dimension of sport, are promising signs that the discipline of theology and the Church is beginning to take sport more seriously.[78] This work is complemented by the vital contributions of Christian ethicists who have helped counter the insightful but largely trans-humanist and post-humanist literature (e.g., McNamee, 2010;[79] Miah, 2010, 2004; Butryn and Masucci, 2009; Tamburrini and Tannsjo, 2005), addressing genetic enhancement technology in sport (Trothen, this volume, 2011, 2008a, 2008b; President's Council on Bioethics, 2003). Applying MacIntyre's (2007) virtue ethics, Goodson (this volume) analyzes both genetic sport technologies and performance-enhancing drugs, which have plagued professional sports for decades. This genre of work will continue to be important, given that 'creating a super-athlete' (Green, 2007: 171) amid futurological movements (i.e., trans-humanism and post-humanism) that have been recognized as 'new religions' (Hefner, 2009; Amarasingam, 2008) will undoubtedly be on the agenda for those wedded to the 'victory-cult.' Related technological innovations from the fields of robotics, artificial intelligence, nanotechnology and cognitive science may also begin to infiltrate the sports world and thus will need careful attention from theologians. In order to provide sound ethical and theological reflection on the interface between humans and technology in sport, Watson (2011a) has urged scholars to embed their reflections in a sound biblical anthropology and psychology—Christian personhood (e.g., Miller and Delaney, 2005, section II;[80] John Paul II, 1997; Schwobel and Gunton, 1991; McFadyen, 1990; Chambers, 1936/1962).

Further research questions and topics that require Christian ethical attention include: how can classic devotional literature, such as the writings of Thomas á Kempis, Oswald Chambers, Francois Fenelon, Andrew Murray and C. S. Lewis, be used to reflect on ethical issues in sport and the need for humility, love and 'spiritual growth' of the heart (Gal. 5:22–25), so to produce accessible literature (e.g., White and White, 2006; Fellowship of Christian Athletes, 2008) for athletes, coaches and parents (see Goodson, this volume; Kretchmar, this volume; Simmons, 2011; Kluck, 2009b; Holowchak, 2008; Hastings and DelleMonache, 2007; Watson and White, 2007)?[81] Closely linked to this, scholars could further examine what constitutes Christian character in sports competition, and how 'moral codes' of behavior and typologies of good character fit, if at all, with the many biblical biographies, such as that of King David, where multiple moral failures are evident?[82] How, or to what extent, can Christians endorse or participate in violent sports,[83] such as boxing and Mixed Martial Arts[84] that has experienced an exponential increase in popularity and participation in the last decade (Garcia and Malcolm, 2010), and which partially mirrors the gladiatorial contests of ancient Rome and the Pankration of Ancient Greece (see Carter, Kluck and Morin, 2012; Borer and Schafer, 2011; Spencer, 2011, 2009; Gore, 2011; Schneiderman, 2010; Dixon, 2007; Marty, 2007; Simon, 2007; Seesengood, 2006a, 2006b; Van Bottenburg and Heilbron, 2006; Goldstein, 1998; Leone and Leone, 1992; Nixon, 1992; Messner, 1990; Poliakoff, 1987, 1984; Watson and Brock, forthcoming)? Can Christians morally justify partaking in animal hunting as a competitive sport (see Peiser, 1997; Morgan and Meier, 1995;[85] Campolo, 1988; White and Hill, forthcoming, 2014)? What are the Christian ethical questions that surround participation in alternative/extreme sport forms, for example, in relation to the tension between risk-taking, autonomy and paternalism (see Watson, 2007b; McNamee, 2010,[86] 2007b)?

How do models of 'servant leadership' in sport, rather than 'top-down' leadership styles, inform the ethical practice and effectiveness of sports leaders, for example, coaches, managers, officials and team captains (see Dungy, 2010, 2008; Rieke, Hammermeister and Chase, 2008; DeSensi and Rosenberg, 2003; Greenleaf, 1977/2002; Degraaf, Jordan and Degraaf, 1999)? What are the tensions surrounding notions of the modern sporting celebrity and idolatry and is there theological justification for sporting celebrities to 'sell the gospel' (i.e., 'platform ministry') based on their fame and human abilities? This is what Macarthur (2003: 40), in support of others (Brock, 2012; Watson, this volume, 2012), calls 'posturing from positions of prestige,' which he argues is the antithesis of the gospel (1 Cor. 1:27–29; Phil. 2:5–11). Any scholar pursuing this avenue of research should, Ward (2011) suggests, guard against the danger of being sucked into judgmentalism when theologizing about specific celebrities, as we may so easily become gods ourselves.[87] There are also a number of broader research topics that are emerging at the present time that raise a whole host of ethical questions.

According to many social scientists and theologians, we live in a 'fatherless generation' that is characterized by family breakdown and dysfunction and is leading to social and moral fragmentation (e.g., Kay, 2009; Sowers, 2010; Marx, 2003; Blankenhorn, 1995). Recognizing this as the sociocultural context in which sport is experienced raises a number of related ethical questions. What are the historical spiritual roots of fatherlessness in our age, and what does the biblical narrative suggest as a remedy for this problem (see Harper, 2012; Gelfer, 2010; Aune, 2010; Sowers, 2010; Stibbe, 2010)? How can sport be used as a vehicle to 'father' (bonding) and 'mentor' children and youths and thus inculcate desirable character attributes and practices for healthy civil engagement (see Kay, 2009; Watson, forthcoming)? In turn, how can sport be used as a means of developing strong family bonds and relations? What is the role and impact of 'fatherlessness' on the prevalence of moral and ethical concerns in professional and amateur sport? How can coaches, physical educators and support staff, such as sport psychologists and club chaplains, through sensitive pastoral care and leadership, help to counter the deleterious effects of fatherlessness (see Brown, 2012; McCuaig, Öhmans and Wright, 2011; Dzikus, Waller and Hardin, 2010; Liberia Editrice Vaticana, 2008; McGuire, Cooper and Park, 2006; Waller, Dzikus and Hardin, in press)? Disability sport is another broad area of research that warrants attention from a Christian standpoint.

Building on recent research in sports ethics (Jesperson and McNamee, 2009); theology (e.g., Brock and Swinton, 2012; Swinton, 2011); and embryonic work on the theology of disability sport (e.g., Watson, this volume, 2012; Watson and Parker, 2012a; Watts, 2007; O'Keefe, 1994/2006; Watson and Parker, forthcoming),[88] there are a plethora of questions that need to be addressed in relation to a Christian understanding of physical and intellectual disability in sport. For example, what are the societal values and norms that dictate that there are markedly different funding models and levels of media and cinematic representation in physical and intellectual disability sports (e.g., Paralympics and Special Olympics) in comparison to able-bodied sports (e.g., Olympics), and, relatedly, why have no celebrities emerged from the Special Olympics? A further area of investigation is the moral attitudes and emotions that permeate competitive sport, such as shame and guilt (McNamee, 2008; Hamilton, 2002); joy (Null, 2004); narcissism (Begel and Burton, 2000); pain and suffering (Nesti, 2007c; Howe, 2004); relational difficulties and experience of failure and success.

The content of the preceding sections reflect the key themes of scholarship that have developed in the past four decades in the sport–religion literature. The questions and topics identified at the end of each of these sections provide a starting point for further research within these subject areas. However, it is worthwhile to briefly identify a series of additional emerging research areas and related resources to stimulate further Christian reflection on modern sports.

EMERGING AND NEEDED RESEARCH

- *Theological analysis of disability sport, including reflection on institutions, such as the Paralympics and Special Olympics.* Past work in this area is sparse with a small handful of exceptions (Watts, 2007; Yong, 2007: 114; O'Keefe, 1994/2006), although recent publications (Watson, this volume, 2012; Watson and Parker, 2012) and a forthcoming special edition of the *Journal of Religion, Disability and*

Health titled 'Sport, Religion and Disability,' which will comprise seventeen papers, consisting of a mix of scholarly essays and empirical research studies, is a promising sign (Watson and Parker, forthcoming). Resources from the theology of disability that will assist scholars in addressing this topic in the sports domain include Swinton's (2011) recent 'research report' and a 'reader' on Christian theology and disability (Brock and Swinton, 2012).

- *The various uses of prayer in sport.* While prayer in sport has been a topic of discussion in many publications on sport and religion, specific research has been limited. As a starting point, I would argue the recent work of Hoffman (2011) and Price (2009) are the most comprehensive examinations of this topic; for a clear and simple overview of the key themes, see Coakley's (2007) chapter. Other studies have addressed the legality of prayer in American physical education settings (Lee, 2005; Sawyer, 1997), praying to win (Kreider, 2003), providence; prayer and sport (Hamilton, 2009), and a range of empirical studies and essays that explore existential themes often with reference to psychological variables identified in the sport psychology literature (Hochstetler, 2009; Czech and Bullet, 2007; Murray et al., 2005; Watson and Czech, 2005; Watson and Nesti, 2005; Czech et al., 2004; Lee, 2003; Park, 2000).

- *The theory and practice of sport chaplaincy.* Until recently, the majority of reflection on this topic has stemmed from the work of practicing sport chaplains (Boyers, 2011, 2000; Wood, 2011; Heskins and Baker, 2006). Nonetheless, the Vatican 'Church Sport' office (Liberia Editrice Vaticana, 2008) and academic practitioners contend that the professional training and accreditation of chaplains in sporting locales is long overdue and thus there are numerous avenues of research to investigate (see Dzikus, Waller and Hardin, 2010; Waller, Dzikus and Hardin, 2010; Waller, Dzikus and Hardin, in press).

- *Theological reflection on exercise and health, two concepts that are closely linked to sports.* Some scholars have argued that health clubs and gyms have become the new Church for many, sometimes characterized by a narcissistic quest for bodily perfection (e.g., Brock, 2012; Hoverd and Sibley, 2007; Hoverd, 2005; Lelwica, 2000). Hoffman (1992b: 157) has termed this phenomena as *culticus aerobicus*, in that he states: 'the horde of Sunday morning joggers . . . who claim to have found on the roads passing the Church what they could never find within its walls.' Similarly, the *Lord's Gym* (a wordplay on *Gold's Gym*) and *Faith and Fitness* magazine in America are interesting dimensions of Western exercise culture and the comingling of sports, exercise, health (and diet) and religion that deserve closer academic attention (see Sinden, 2012; Griffith, 2004). There is also a small body of work from both Catholic and Protestant thinkers that recognizing the body as the 'temple of the Holy Spirit' provides a more positive analysis on exercise and the pursuit of health and wellness (e.g., Thomas, 2011; Vost, 2011, 2008; Walters and Byl, 2008; Hill, 2005; Byl and Visker, 1999; Feeney, 1995; Ryan, 1986). To date, scholars exploring this area have arguably neglected a significant body of research that has examined the relationship between religion and health (e.g., Koeing, 2008, 2001). A focal source of this research has been the Centre for Spirituality, Theology and Health at Duke University Medical Centre, U.S. With reference to the global obesity epidemic that has multifarious causes, future studies could also apply the doctrine of gluttony and sloth (see Thomas, 2011; Hoverd and Sibley, 2007; Hoverd, 2005; Griffith, 2004; Prentice and Jebb, 1995), in relation to people's eating and exercise/physical activity patterns.

- *Women, sport and the Christian religion.* There has been a paucity of theological reflection on women in sport, with the majority of academic books and papers cited in this review, at most making only passing reference to this important topic.[89] Building on a handful of papers and chapters that have explored the role of women in the muscular Christianity movement (Millikan, 2006; Stebner and Trothen, 2002; Putney, 2001b; Chen and Zhao, 2001; Bederman, 1989; Borish, 1987; Vertinsky, 1987) and issues of embodiment/anthropology with regard to how women negotiate their femininity in male-dominated sports settings (Sydnor, 2012, 2009, 2006a, 2006b, 2005; Deardorff and Deardorff, 2008; Carmody, 1986), scholars have a wide array of questions to examine. Importantly, any subsequent work in this area should consult the burgeoning literature on women's sports that has emerged from the social sciences since the 1960s (e.g., Bandy, 2010; Hargreaves, 2001; Scraton and Flintoff, 2002). However, as 'Christianity itself is usually depicted as naïve and repressive, a religion at odds with sophisticated critical [feminist] studies in sport' (Sydnor, 2009: 83), this will be a challenging task, but one that is worth embracing to shed further light on women's engagement in the world's most popular pastime. Finally, there has been virtually no Christian scholarship to date that has examined the links between sports participation and 'eating disorders' in women,[90] something that has become a major issue in certain sports, for example, gymnastics, cheerleading, dance and long-distance running (see Lelwica, 2000, 1999; Quinn and Crocker, 1999).
- *Sport, religion and popular culture.* Scholars wishing to examine the social and cultural dynamics and interplay of Christianity and sports could access Niebuhr's (1951) classic work *Christ and Culture* and emerging scholarship in sport adopting the theology of 'radical orthodoxy' (Meyer, 2012; Meyer and Watson, forthcoming; Sydnor, 2006b, 2003).[91] Niebuhr's five-point typology, which has been adapted by Wittmer (2008) to examine modern sport, would be an invaluable tool for examining a plethora of sociocultural movements, such as Victorian muscular Christianity and modern sports ministry, sport, religion and film (see Poulton and Roderick, 2009; Cashmore, 2008; Roubach, 2007; Johnston, 2006; Crosson, 2012) and sport–faith

initiatives, such as the 'Maradonian Church' (Archetti, 2002), which could be classed as a 'surrogate religion' organization.

- *Beauty and aesthetics in traditional and alternative/extreme sports.* Drawing on recent philosophical and theological treatments of beauty and the sublime in various sporting locales (e.g., Hübenthal, 2012; Ilundian-Agurraza, 2007; Dougherty, 2007; Watson, 2007b; Stranger, 2007; Gumbrecht, 2006; Higgs, 1983), future studies could investigate this positive dimension of sports participation and spectating. Some key theological works that may assist scholars in this project are Kant's (1790/1952) and Burke's (1757/1990) seminal works on the sublime and more recent treatments of beauty and aesthetics in academic theology (e.g., Dubay, 1999).

- *Relationships in sporting contexts.* Jowett and Wylleman (2006) recently noted that the study of interpersonal relationships in sport psychology is 'unexplored territory.' In support of this, Watson (this volume) has argued that while there is some reflection on relationships in the physical education and coaching literature (e.g., Martens, 2004), valuable insights provided in sports ministry and sport chaplaincy texts (e.g., Heskins and Baker, 2006; Fellowship of Christian Athletes, 2008) and popular books on coaching from a Christian perspective (Costantini and Lixey, 2011; Riesen, 2007; Brown et al., 2006; Wooden, 2005; Yerkovich and Kelly, 2003), there are, at present, no academic publications that specifically address relationships from a Christian worldview. This, it would seem, represents a major oversight, in that the notion of relationship is at the heart of the Christian religion. Scholars could explore issues such as listening in the 'relational encounter' utilizing Buber's (1923/1958) dialogical concept of *I-Thou* (Nesti, 2007a; Watson and Nesti, 2005; Progen and DeSensi, 1984) and friendship in sport (Gallagher, 2008). Leadership is another key aspect of relations in sport, and future studies may wish to explore the merits of the Christian based 'servant leadership' model (Greenleaf, 1977/2002) that has recently been applied to sport and recreation contexts (Rieke, Hammermeister and Chase, 2008; Degraaf, Jordan and Degraaf, 1999).

CONCLUSION

The aim of this systematic review of literature has been twofold: (i) to comprehensively identify, critically appraise and synthesize scholarship, primary empirical research and initiatives on the relationship between sport and Christianity from 1850 to the present day, and (ii) to identify areas for future research and scholarship and provide related resources. The themed sections and emergent research topics outlined above (see also Table 1.1) provide conceptual and theoretical direction for future empirical research and scholarship.

In conclusion, whether it is in the domain of research, teaching or practice, individuals engaged in the sport-Christianity field will need to adopt a critical and careful hermeneutic in their endeavours. As a starting-point, teachers from all levels of tertiary education looking to design courses on sport and religion (Christianity) could adopt accessible summary chapters on the topic, which will serve as introductory reading for pre-university students and undergraduates (e.g., Jarvie, 2012; Delaney and Madigan, 2009; Stevenson, 2008; Coakley, 2007; Woods, 2007). However, one of the key findings of this review is that while there is a significant amount of scholarship on sports and Christianity (i.e., essays), there is a distinct lack of quality empirical research. Therefore, further quantitative and qualitative research studies are needed to develop evidence-based resources for educators. For example, survey studies that examine the provision and quality of sport-religion courses across the educational spectrum would provide benchmarks for scholars, publishers, grant awarding bodies and Churches. Interview based research that explores how modern-day Christian athletes, coaches and officials, reconcile their religious beliefs with those of modern sporting culture, is an example of a study adopting a qualitative approach. In short, a widening of the research agenda would benefit the field in numerous ways and would encourage theologians and religious studies scholars to more fully engage in this endeavour.

Reflecting upon this proposal, if the community of scholars and practitioners invested in this area of study fail to move the discussion forward through collaborative high-quality research, and thus fail to effect positive change in sports, President Barack Obama's (2008: 9) prophetic warning about American societal structures may be true for the institution of sport: ' . . . if we don't change course soon, we may be the first generation in a very long time that leaves behind a weaker and more fractured America than the one we inherited'.

On a more positive tack, if we are to leave behind a stronger and more virtuous model of sport the 'course' we must take, according to Queen Elizabeth II, must be guided by Christian philosophy. Indeed, in her Christmas Speech of 2010 that focused on the four hundredth year celebration of the *King James Bible* and the central unifying role of sport in society, Her Majesty observes:

> King James may not have anticipated quite how important sport and games were to become in promoting harmony and common interests. But from the scriptures in the bible which bears his name, we know that nothing is more satisfying than the feeling of belonging to a group who are dedicated to helping each other: Therefore all things whatsoever ye would that men should do to you, do ye even so to them.[92]

Let us then hope that there is a similar common vision and dedication to assist one another within the diverse group of scholars, sport–faith practitioners, participants and teachers of sport, as they seek to combat the 'ludic diffusion' that Guttman (1978/2004) identified over three decades ago.

Table 1.1

Academic Research Centers and Study Groups	Key Academic Books on Sport and Christianity[93]
Religion, Sport and Play, specialist group/section of the American Academy of Religion, 2012–(Co-chairs of Steering Committee, Professors Rebecca Alpert and Eric Bain-Selbo).	Bain-Selbo, E. (2008) *Game Day and God: Football, Faith and Politics in the American South.*
Centre of Sport, Spirituality and Religion, 2009–(University of Glouscestershire, UK, Founding Director, Professor Andrew Parker).	Baker, W. J. (2007) *Playing with God: Religion and Modern Sport.*
The Mirenda Centre for Sport, Spirituality and Character Development, which is home to the *Institute for Sport, Spirituality and Character Development*, 1999–(Neumann University, U.S., Founding Director, Dr. Edward Hastings).	Baker, W. J. (2000) *If Christ Came to the Olympics.*
Centre for the Study of Sport and Spirituality, 2003–2009 (York St. John University, UK, Founding Co-directors, Nick Watson and Dr. Mark Nesti).	Baum, G. and Coleman, J. (eds.) (1989) *Sport.*
Centre for Sport and Peace, 2012–(University of Tennessee, U.S., Founding Director, Dr. Ashleigh Huffman).	Byl, J. and Visker, T. (eds.) (1999) *Physical Education, Sports, and Wellness: Looking to God as We Look at Ourselves.*
	Costantini, E. and Lixey, K. (2011) *Sport and Paul: A Course for Champions.*
	Deardorff II, D. and White, J. (eds.) (2008) *The Image of God in the Human Body: Essays on Christianity and Sports.*
	Ellis, R. (forthcoming) *The Games People Play: Theology, Religion and Sport.*
	Evans, C. H. and Herzog, W. R. (eds.) (2002) *The Faith of 50 Million: Baseball, Religion and American Culture* (foreword by Stanley Hauerwas).
	Feeney, F. (2006) *The Catholic Ideal: Exercise and Sport* (Catholic).
	Feeney, F. (1995) (Ed.) *A Catholic Perspective: Physical Exercise and Sport* (Catholic).
	Forney, C.A. (2010) *The Holy Trinity of American Sports: Civil Religion in Football, Baseball and Basketball.*
	Heintzman, P., Van Andel, G. and Visker, T. (eds.) (1994/2006) *Christianity and Leisure: Issues in a Pluralistic Society.*
	Higgs, R. J. (1995) *God in the Stadium: Sports and Religion in America.*
	Higgs, R. J. and Braswell, M.C. (2004) *An Unholy Alliance: The Sacred and Modern Sports.*
	Hoffman, S. J. (2010) *Good Game: Christians and the Culture of Sport.*
	Hoffman, S. J. (ed.) (1992) *Sport and Religion.*
	Kelly, P. (2012) *Catholic Perspectives on Sports: From Medieval to Modern Times* (Catholic).
	Kluck, T. (2009) *The Reason for Sports: A Christian Manifesto.*
	Krattenmaker, T. (2010) *Onward Christian Athletes: Turning Ballparks into Pulpits and Players into Preachers.*
	Ladd, T. and Mathisen, J. A. (1999) *Muscular Christianity: Evangelical Protestants and the Development American Sport.*
	Liberia Editrice Vaticana (2011) *Sport, Education and Faith: Toward a New Season for Catholic Sports Associations* (Catholic).

Liberia Editrice Vaticana (2008) *The World of Sport Today: A Field of Christian Mission* (Catholic).

Liberia Editrice Vaticana (2006) *Sport: An Educational and Pastoral Challenge* (Catholic).

Lixey, K., Hübenthal, C., Mieth, D. and Müller, N. (eds.) (2012) *Sport and Christianity: A Sign of the Times in the Light of Faith* (Catholic).

Magdalinski, T. and Chandler, T. J. L. (eds.) (2002) *With God on their Side: Sport in the Service of Religion*.

Novak, M. (1967/1994) *The Joy of Sports: End Zones, Bases, Baskets, Balls and Consecration of the American Spirit*.

O'Gorman, K. (2010) *Saving Sport: Sport, Society and Spirituality* (Catholic).

Overman, S. J. (2011) *The Protestant Work Ethic and the Spirit of Sport: How Calvinism and Capitalism Shaped American Games*.

Overman, S. J. (1997) *The Influence of the Protestant Ethic on Sport and Recreation*.

Parry, J., Watson, N. J. and Nesti, M. S. (eds.) (2011) *Theology, Ethics and Transcendence in Sports* (foreword by Robert Higgs).

Parry, J., Robinson, S., Watson, N. J. and Nesti, M. S. (2007) *Sport and Spirituality: An Introduction* (foreword by Shirl Hoffman).

Preece, G. and Hess, R. (eds.) (2009) *Sport and Spirituality: An Exercise in Everyday Theology*.

Prebish, C. S. (1993) *Religion and Sport: The Meeting of Sacred and Profane*.

Price, J. L. (2006) *Rounding the Bases: Baseball and American Religion*.

Price, J. L. (ed.) (2001) *From Season to Season: Sports as American Religion*.

Sing, S. (2004) *Spirituality of Sport: Balancing Body and Soul* (Catholic).

Watson, N. J. and Parker, A. (eds.) (2012) *Sports and Christianity: Historical and Contemporary Perspectives* (foreword by Michael Novak).

Major Sports Ministry and Chaplaincy Organizations[94]

Sports Ministry Organizations

Athletes in Action (U.S., 1966–, President, Mark Householder).

Ambassadors in Sport (UK, 1990–, Executive Director, David Oakley).

Baseball Chapel (U.S., 1974–, President Vince Nauss).

Christians in Sport (UK, 1980–, Directors, Graham Daniels and Keith Proctor).

Church Sport and Recreation Ministries (U.S., 1994, Executive Director, Dr. Greg Linville).

European Christian Sports Union (Europe, 1989–, Director Hannes Schmidts).

Fellowship of Christian Athletes (U.S., 1952/1954–, President, Lee Steckel).

Academic International Conferences, Seminars and Lecture Series

Sports, Leisure, Religion and Spirituality in Africa and the African Diaspora, the 5th Annual Conference of the African Association for the Study of Religions, Egerton University, Njoro, Kenya, 18–23 July 2012. Organized and chaired by Dr. Afe Adomgame.

Everybody Has a Place: Catholic International Conference (theology of disability/paralympic sport), The Methodist, Westminster Central Hall, London, UK, 2 July, 2012. Co-organized by the Catholic Paralympic 2012 Committee and The Kairos Forum for Cognitive Disabilities (University of Aberdeen).

(*continued*)

Table 1.1 (continued)

The Soul of Youth Sport Symposium, University of Notre Dame, U.S., 24–26 June 2012. Organized by Father Patrick Kelly, S. J. This is an annual joint-event and partnership organized by Seattle University, University of Notre Dame, Neumann University and the National Catholic Education Association.

Spirituality and Physicality: Crossing the Boundaries, The 12th International Conference of Children's Spirituality, University of East Anglia, UK, 1–5 July 2012. Organized and chaired by Drs. Linda Rudge and Jacqueline Watson. A special edition of the journal *International Journal of Children's Spirituality* (forthcoming, 2013) comprising papers from this conference will be published and is edited by Dr. Jacqueline Watson.

Christian Ethics and Sport, Annual Conference of the Society for the Study of Christian Ethics, University of Cambridge, UK, 2–4 September 2011. Organized by Dr. Robert Heimburger. A special edition of the journal of the SSCE, *Studies in Christian Ethics* (2012: 25, 1), comprising plenary papers from the conference has been published.

Sport and Religion Seminars, Annual Conference of the American Academy of Religion in 2008 (Chicago), 2009 (Montreal), 2010 (Atlanta) and 2011 (San Francisco). The papers presented at these seminars have focused on a range of sport–religion themes, for example, sport chaplaincy, sport and film, sport as a surrogate religion and religion and baseball.

Towards a Theology of Sport, Sports Ministries Think Tank Annual Day Conference, Hosted by the Centre for Sport, Spirituality and Religion, University of Gloucestershire, UK, 4 May 2011. Organized and chaired by Professor Andrew Parker.

Christianity and Sport, Public Lecture Series, Regent's Park College, University of Oxford, UK, Oxford Centre for Christianity and Culture, Six Weekly Lectures, 18 January–1 March 2011. Organized and chaired by Dr. Andrew Moore. A special edition (on sport) of the journal *Anvil: An Evangelical Journal for Theology and Mission* (2012: 28, 1) comprising papers from the Lecture Series has been published and edited by Dr. Andrew Moore.

Story, Sport and Spirit: A Conference to Explore the Theory and Practice of Storytelling in Athletics, 19–21 May 2010, hosted by the *Institute for Sport, Spirituality and Character Development*, Neumann University, U.S. Organized and chaired by Dr. Edward Hastings.

International Sports Coalition (Worldwide, 1985–, Director and Global Coordinator, Paul Moses).

Professional Athletes Outreach (U.S., 1974–, Director Jim Horsley).

Sports Ministry UK (UK, 2004–, Administrator, Mark Blythe).

For web links to all the preceding organizations and multiple ministry organizations for 'specific sports,' see: UK Sports Ministries, http://uksportsministries.org/category/organisations-list; and 'Links' page of the *Centre of Sport, Spirituality and Religion*, http://www.glos.ac.uk/research/dse/cssr/Pages/links.aspx.

Sports Chaplaincy Organizations

Baseball Chapel (U.S., 1974–, President Vince Nauss).

Sport Chaplaincy UK (formerly, SCORE) (UK, 1991–, Founding Director, Reverend John Boyers)

Sports Chaplaincy Australia (Australia, 1980–, National Director, Cameron Butler).

Inaugural International Conference on Sport and Spirituality, 28–31 August 2007, hosted by the Centre for the Study of Sport and Spirituality, York St. John University (2003–2009), UK. Organized and chaired by Nick Watson. An edited book has been published by Routledge, comprising a selection of papers from the conference (Parry, Nesti and Watson, 2011).

Think Tank, Lord of Sport: A Quest to Discover God's Wisdom for Sport, hosted by Athletes in Action and organized and chaired by Dr. John White, Dayton, Ohio, U.S., 13–16 May 2005. An edited book was published by Edwin Mellen Press, comprising a selection of papers authored by selected delegates from the conference (Deardorff and White, 2008).

First International Conference, Sport and Religion: An Inquiry into Cultural Values, St. Olaf's College, Minnesota, U.S., 24–26 June 2004. Organized and chaired by Dr. Gary Wicks.

Second International Conference, Sport and Religion: An Inquiry into Cultural Values, St. Olaf's College, Minnesota, U.S., 28–29 October 2005. Organized and chaired by Dr. Gary Wicks.

The 'Church and Sport Office,' within the Pontifical Council for the Laity in the Vatican, Italy, has hosted three international seminars on various aspects of the relationship between Catholicism and sports in 2005, 2007 and 2009 (see Liberia Editrice Vaticana, 2011, 2008, 2006). Organized and chaired by Father Kevin Lixey.

The *Christian Society for Kinesiology and Leisure Studies* has held an annual conference at various Christian colleges in the U.S. since 1989. This organization was founded by Professors Glen Van Andel, Tom Visker and Paul Heintzman. Two books have been published that comprise papers from annual conferences (Van Andel, Heintzman, and Visker, 1994/2006; Byl, and Visker, 1999).

Journals, Special Editions and Book Series on Sport and Christianity

Journals

International Journal of Religion and Sport (Founding Editors, 2009–, Dr. Chris Anderson and Professor Gordon Marino. Current editors, 2010–, Professors Andrew Parker and Eric Bain-Selbo. This journal is hard copy only and published by Mercer University Press, U.S.).

Journal of the Christian Society for Kinesiology and Leisure Studies (Founding Editors, 2010–, Dr. Valerie Gin and Professor Dale Connally. This journal is 'online' only).

Church-Based Sport Organizations and Related Initiatives

More than Gold is a temporary organization that has representatives from all the major Christian denominations for the London 2012 Olympic and Paralympic Games, CEO, David Willson.

The John Paul II Foundation for Sport (2008–), commissioned by Pope Benedict XVI.

The *Church and Sport Office*, within the Pontifical Council for the Laity in the Vatican, Italy (2004—), commissioned by Pope JPII. Founding Director, Father Kevin Lixey.

Catholic Athletes for Christ (2006–), Founder, Ray McKenna.

(continued)

Table 1.1 (continued)

Journal Special Editions

Duyvenbode M. van. (ed.) (2012, Spring) Special Edition, Sporting Life: Reflections on Sport, Culture and the Church, *The Bible in Transmission* (the journal of the Bible Society). Full text available online: http://www.biblesociety.org.uk/resources22/ (accessed 6 June 2012)

Parsons, S. (2012: 25, 1, February) Special Edition, Christian Ethics and Sport: *Studies in Christian Ethics*. Plenary Papers from the Annual Conference of the Society for the Study of Christian Ethics, University of Cambridge, UK, 2–4 September 2011.

Plant, S. J. (ed.) (2012: 114, 4, July/August) Special Edition, Sport and Theology: *Theology* (SPCK/Sage).

Moore, A. (ed.) (2012: 28, 1) Special Edition, Christianity and Sport, *Anvil: An Evangelical Journal for Theology and Mission.*

Stoddart, E. (ed.) (2012: 5, 2) Special Edition, Sport: *Practical Theology.*

Lämmer, M., Smith, M., and Terret, T. (2009: 35) Special Edition, Sport and Religion: *Stadion: International Journal of the History of Sport.* (Not all papers are on sport and the Christian religion.)

Preece, G. and Hess, R. (eds.) (2009: 11, 1) Special Edition: *Sport and Spirituality: An Exercise in Everyday Theology, Interface: A Forum for Theology in the World* (also published as a book: Preece and Hess, 2009).

Baum, G. and Coleman, J. (eds.) (1985: 5, 205) Special Edition, Sport: *International Journal of Theology* (also published as a book: Baum and Coleman, 1989).

Watson, N. J. and Parker, A. (guest eds.) (forthcoming, 2014/2015) Special Edition, Sports, Religion and Disability, *Journal of Religion, Disability and Health.*

Watson, J. (forthcoming, 2013) Special Edition: Spirituality and Physicality: Crossing the Boundaries, *International Journal of Children's Spirituality.* Papers from the 12th International Conference of Children's Spirituality, *Spirituality and Physicality: Crossing the Boundaries,* University of East Anglia, UK, 1–5 July 2012.

Book Series/Themes on Sport and Religion (Christianity)

Nine books with a general focus on sport and Christianity have been published in the 'Sports and Religion' Series, by Mercer University Press, U.S. Series Editor, Professor Joseph Price.

Sports Faith International (2008–), Chairperson, Patrick McCaskey.
Sport Alpha (2012–), Holy Trinity Brompton Church, Knightsbridge, London, UK.
Faith and Football (2002–), Founders, Linvoy Primus and Darren Moore.
Young Men's Christian Association, YMCA (1844–), Founder, Sir George Williams.
Young Women's Christian Association, YWCA, (1855–), Founders, Lady Mary Jane Kinnaird and Emma Roberts.

Routledge has published four books on sport and religion, with a main focus on sport and Christianity (Watson and Parker, 2012; Parry, Nesti and Watson, 2011; Parry, Robinson, Watson and Nesti, 2007; Magdalinski and Chandler, 2002). The University Press of Kentucky has published a number of books in the *Philosophy of Popular Culture* book series (Going Deep) that have some chapters with themes on Christian faith and sports (e.g., Hamilton, 2008a, 2007, 2004).

Sport and Religion Courses in Higher Education[95]

Examples of Undergraduate Modules

Grace and Play: Christianity and Meaning of Sport (summer school), Regent College (2011–), Vancouver, Canada, Module Leader, Dr. Dominic Erdozain, King's College, London.

Sport and Spirituality (2007–), York St. John University, UK, Module Leader, Nick Watson.

Sport and Spirituality (2000–), *Spiritual Themes in Sports Movies* (2011–) and a *Spirituality of Coaching* (2012–), Neumann University, U.S. (2000–), Module Leader, Dr. Edward Hastings.

Sport and Spirituality (2007–), University of Western Australia, Perth, Australia, Module Leader, Reverend Canon Richard Pengelley. From 2012 this module will be renamed as *The Spirit of Sport.*

Postgraduate Courses and Modules

Postgraduate Certificate/Postgraduate Diploma/MA *Sports and Christian Outreach* (Sports Ministry), University of Glouscestershire, UK, Course Leader, Professor Andrew Parker.

Postgraduate Certificate/Postgraduate Diploma/MA *Sports and Christian Outreach* (Sports Chaplaincy), University of Glouscestershire, UK, Course Leader, Professor Andrew Parker.

Sport, Psychology and Spirituality (2008 and 2009, module on MSc Sport Psychology), York St. John University, UK, Nick Watson.

The Soul of Athletics, Neumann University, U.S. (2002–, module on MA Education), Module Leader, Dr. Edward Hastings.

Sports Ministry Concentration (2012–module on Master of Divinity), Baylor University, U.S., Course Leader, Dr. John White.

Movies with a Sports–Christian Theme and Related Publications
(see Crosson, 2012; Poulton and Roderick, 2009)

Sport Movies with a Central Christian/Religious Theme
Blind Side (2009). See Montez de Oca's (2012) sociological analysis.
Invictus (2009).
Hansie (2008).
Facing the Giants (2006).
Million Dollar Baby (2004). See Roubach's (2007) theological analysis.
Field of Dreams (1989).
Chariots of Fire (1981). See Cashmore's (2008) sociohistorical analysis.
Sport Movies with a Christian/Religious Subtext
Hoosiers (1986).
Rocky (1976).
The Babe Ruth Story (1948).
The Pride of the Yankees (1942).
Trouble along the Way (1953).
The Leather Saint (1955).
Angels in the Outfield (1951, remade under the same title in 1994).

NOTES

1. These include sociology, history, anthropology, philosophy and psychology.
2. See the 'overview' in Table 1.1, which provides a concise summary of academic and practical developments in the area. This is a helpful resource and reference point for readers wishing to grasp an historical snapshot of developments and resources in the field as they read individual sections of this review.
3. For a brief overview of the sport-religion relationship, see Baker (2010) and Mathisen (2005).
4. To our knowledge, the only 'literature reviews' on 'sport and religion' (not specifically Christianity) are those of Higgs (1982) and Deardorff (2000), the latter being an updated and revised edition of Higgs's earlier work.
5. For example, the exegesis and use of Pauline athletic metaphors, the principles of medieval sport and the perspectives of the Church Fathers (Patristic writings) on physical education and culture.
6. While there are other thematic sections that could be included in this review, for example, 'sport, religion and popular culture' (see Blazer, 2012; Bauer, 2011; Cusack, 2010; Borer, 2008; Price, 2001b; Coakley, 2007; Edwards, 1973) and 'institutions (e.g., the Olympic Games) and governance of sport' (see Overman, 2011, 1997; Baker, 2000a; Guttman, 1978/2004; Watson and White, 2012; Watson and White, 2007; Watson and Parker, under review), these are beyond the scope of this work.
7. There have been a number of academic books on sport and Christianity published in the German and Italian languages, most notably by Alois Koch, who has had some of his academic papers and book chapters translated into English, which are available online: http://www.con-spiration.de/koch/#english (accessed 6 June 2012). In addition, the *Religioni e Società* (trans. *Italian Review of the Sociology of Religion*, 2011: vol. 71) has recently published a special edition on 'sport and spirituality' (only available in Italian) and *Stadion: International Journal of History* (2009: vol. 35) published a special edition on 'sport and religion' that is composed of essays in English, German and French.
8. For example, while the numerous biographies of Christian sportspersons (e.g., Tebow, 2011; Dungy, 2008; Keddie, 2007); devotional literature (e.g., Lipe, 2005; O'Toole, 2001); and postgraduate theses provide invaluable insights for academic researchers, they are beyond the scope of this review. For a comprehensive list of sport–faith biographies, PhD and master's theses on sport and Christianity, see Stuart Weir's 'Sport and Christianity Booklist' online bibliography (http://www.veritesport.org/downloads/Sports_bibliography_shorter.pdf, accessed 23 August 2011).
9. Details concerning the individuals discussed in this section have been verified through email correspondence and personal communication with the individuals concerned.
10. Two decades later the American periodical *Christianity Today* (1986, 4 April) published a special edition on sports.
11. Some key books included: Edwards (1973), Brasch (1970), Miller (1969), Neale (1969), Weiss, (1969), Slusher (1967) and Callois (1958). Oft-cited chapters and journal articles included: Deford (1979), Dirksen (1975), Miller (1971), Hogan (1967) and Wenkert (1963).
12. Novak's book is widely cited across the academic disciplines and is acknowledged by *Sports Illustrated* as one of the 'Top 100 Sports Books of All Time' (Cited in 16 December 2002 issue of *Sports Illustrated*; see http://

www.michaelnovak.net/index.cfm?fuseaction=bookshelf.welcome&id=18, accessed 23 October 2011).

13. Michael Novak, a philosopher, theologian and author, is the 1994 recipient of the Templeton Prize for Progress in Religion. He has been an emissary to the United Nations Human Rights Commission and to the Conference on Security and Cooperation in Europe. He has written twenty-seven books on the philosophy and theology of culture, especially the essential elements of a free society (see http://www.aei.org/scholar/44). For further details, see Novak's personal webpage (http://www.michaelnovak.net/).

14. Following Hoffman's (1992b) anthology he published a number of other papers (e.g., 2003, 1999).

15. White (2012a) has written a 'review article' of Hoffman's (2010a) recent book, exploring, in particular, theological dualism in this work.

16. An article based on a chapter of Hoffman's (2010a) book has been published in the periodical *Christianity Today* (Hoffman, 2010b), whose current managing editor Mark Galli (2010, 2005) also has an interest in the topic. Also, Hoffman (2012) has republished a chapter from his book (Hoffman, 2010a).

17. Kinesiology is an American term and is broadly speaking synonymous in its usage with the disciplinary descriptors, 'sports studies' and 'sports sciences.'

18. These scholarly essays include: Maranise, 2009; Sydnor, 2009, 2006b, 2005; Munoz, 2009; Nesti, 2007a; Hastings, 2004; Miroslaw, 2003; Savant, 2003; Cronin, 2000; McDevitt, 1997; Gems, 1993; Kerrigan, 1986; Ryan, 1985; Söll, 1972.

19. Cited in Johnston (1983: unnumbered page prior to the introduction).

20. Geertz's (1973: 412–54) classic essay 'Deep Play: Notes on the Balinese Cockfight' explores rituals and social interactions between those involved in illegal cockfighting in Indonesia in the 1950s. He examines how the experience of the risk of arrest (mainly due to betting large amounts of money) and potential loss, or gain, of social status that characterizes illegal cock fighting lead to moments of 'deep play' in which individuals transcend the rational (a key aspect of play) for short periods of time.

21. See 'Selected Bibliography on Play (and Work),' prepared by Herbert F. Lowe for *Religion Online* that was originally published in Johnston (1983: 163–66) and is available online (http://www.religion-online.org/showchapter. asp?title=3366&C=2763, accessed 26 October 2011).

22. The relationship between play, games and competitive sports has been an important topic in the history of the philosophy of sport literature. Part 1 of Morgan and Meier's (1995: 1–66) book, which focuses on 'Ontological Frameworks' and is titled 'The Nature of Play, Sport and Games,' while dated, is arguably the most diverse and academically rigorous collection of essays. Articles by pioneering modern sport philosophers, such as Bernard Suits, Klaus Meier and Scott Kretchmar, alongside classic essays by pioneering play scholars, such as Huizinga, make this edited collection invaluable for those wishing to understand the complexities of this topic. The part on metaphysics in Weiss's (1969) seminal book and Part 1 of McNamee's (2010: 9–92) recent 'reader' on sports ethics, titled 'The Roots of Sports Ethics: Games, Play, Sports,' are also helpful for examining play.

23. This quote was cited in Mathisen (2005: 281), whose chapter we would like to acknowledge was very helpful in charting the historical developments of the study of play for this section.

24. While Söll's (1972) chapter on a Catholic of sport theology (mainly based on the work of German Catholic theologians) does not specifically address play,

there is some reflection on this point, as in later Catholic writings (Feeney, 2006, 1995).

25. Part 4 of this text, titled, 'Play, Sport and Athletics,' has seven essays that to varying degrees discuss the role of play in modern sport.

26. It is then interesting to note that Burstyn (2005) has called modern sports a 'secular sacrament'.

27. These are: 'the discharge of surplus energy (Herbert Spencer, J. C. Friedrich von Schiller) . . . relaxation, as recuperation from exhaustion (G. T. W. Patrick and Moritz Lazarus) . . . an internal educator (Karl Groos); as a means of catharsis, a safety valve to vent emotions (Aristotle); as a creative modelling of situations that enables the player to better handle experience (Erik Erikson); as a means of resolving psychic conflict (Sigmund Freud), or, on the contrary, as activity *not* motivated by the need to resolve inner conflict (Robert Neale)' (Johnston, 1983: 32).

28. While Johnston (1983) writes from a Protestant perspective, his considerable positive engagement with key Catholic scholars, such as Novak, Pieper and Rahner, in many ways makes this text transcend theological and ecclesiological boundaries.

29. Johnston's (1983) discussion of C. S. Lewis's (1955) autobiography, in which Lewis describes his joyful play experiences in childhood that had a transcendent dimension, has clear links to more recent theological treatments of joy in sports (Null, 2004).

30. Waller's (2010) resent research on play, leisure and sport in the 'black church' is a positive sign that churches are beginning to recognize the value of play and sport.

31. Cultural Marxist Gruneau (1980) provides a thorough and balanced analysis of classical Marxist critiques of sport (Rigauer, 1981; Brohm, 1971), while also considering Novak's (1967/1994) theological position on play and Guttman's (1978/2004) Weberian analysis of modern sport and play.

32. The *flow* construct comprises nine dimensions (Jackson and Csikszentmihalyi, 1999): a balance between perceived challenges and skills; having clear goals; having a sense of control over one's actions; merging of action and awareness; receiving unambiguous feedback; being fully concentrated on the task; not being self-conscious; loss of time awareness; and, the end result, an *autotelic* experience (a high level of intrinsic satisfaction).

33. Research from the religion–health field has also identified clear links between 'sacred [playful] moments' in a range of human endeavors, including sports, as a means to enhancing physical and emotional health and well-being (King, 1986).

34. Spiritual experience based on the premise that spiritual revelation is received during the experience.

35. Work by Moore (2012), Heintzman (2003a, 2003b), Watson (2007b) and Price (1996) explores spiritual, mystical, numinous experiences in alternative sports (sometimes called extreme sports) and activities that are often undertaken in wilderness/nature-based environments and may involve opportunity for contemplation in nature, risk-taking and experiences of the sublime, etc.

36. In Hubbard's (1998: 156) popular book that documents the lives and sports careers of Christian (and Muslim) athletes, there are a number of allusions to this idea. For example, in summarizing the testimony of Loren Roberts, an American professional golfer, he reported, 'When golf was his God, he realized, he was putting incredible pressure on himself. When he placed God first, family second, and golf third, he began to relax—essential for a sport that is as much mental as physical.'

37. Bart's theological musings regarding Wolfgang Amadeus Mozart's playful creativity and imaginative expression of his gift (Metzger, 2003) have been used in previous analyses of play in sport (Watson, 2011a).
38. *L'Arche* (French for Ark) is a Catholic, yet wholly ecumenical, international federation of 137 communities in forty countries where people with and without learning difficulties live in community. Its founder is Jean Vanier, a pioneer, celebrated writer and practitioner in this area.
39. As McGrath (2008) suggests, the muscular Christian movement was largely Protestant in origin but not exclusively, with a range of Catholic related initiatives and educational institutions that adopted its principles.
40. The majority of books cited in this review and Table 1.1 have chapters or sections that reflect on muscular Christianity.
41. While discussion in this section focuses on neo-muscular Christian sports ministry organizations, it is important to recognize that, in general, sports chaplaincy practice in America is sometimes more closely tied to the evangelical concerns of sports ministry organizations. However, in the United Kingdom, the practice of sports chaplaincy is more traditional in that it focuses on pastoral concerns of athletes and club support staff. Of course the degree to which this statement is true varies greatly in regard to context, denominational differences in chaplaincy practice and the policy of the sports club at which the chaplain works.
42. For scholars wishing to examine the historical development of muscular Christianity in Anglican and Non-Conformist churches in the UK, McLeod (2003) has provided a chronological map with five broad phases (also see Parker and Weir, 2012).
43. A caveat in regard to the strength and significance of the historical and philosophical relationship between muscular Christianity and the YMCA is that some administrators and evangelists within the YMCA disavowed the phrase *muscular Christianity* (Erdozain, 2010).
44. See Parry (2007a), Lucas (1976, 1975) and Koch (2005c) for further information with regard to the links between 'muscular Christianity' (and religion) and the modern Olympic Games.
45. The authors of a recent book that explores the win-at-all-costs culture of modern professional sport adopting a neo-Freudian framework publish a verbatim transcribed interview with Jonathon Edwards that focused on his retirement from athletics and subsequent loss of his Christian faith (Gogarty and Williamson, 2009: 214–24). The interview transcript is titled 'An Interview with Jonathon Edwards: Judgment Day—Resolving Pathology,' which clearly reflects the Freudian perspective. While there has been speculation in the media regarding the degree to which Edwards has lost his faith, there is clear evidence within this transcript of this, for example: 'I didn't find losing my faith devastating. I analysed what I had always believed and it didn't seem to make sense in the way that it had done before and I just accepted it and moved on' (219).
46. Kevin Vost, a former Olympic weightlifter and well-known academic Catholic apologist, has written two books (Vost, 2011, 2008) that focus on exercise, weightlifting and healthy eating that have clear links to muscular Christian ideals (see West, 2011).
47. Aitken (1989) notes that the ethos of muscular Christianity became very popular in American Catholic universities from around the 1950s, for example, Georgetown, Notre Dame, Boston College and St. John's.
48. An interesting caveat regarding the relationship between Sunday schools and sport is the fact that when most UK youth soccer leagues moved to Sunday

mornings in the 1990s, this had a significant negative impact upon attendance and participation in Church Sunday schools (Collins and Parker, 2009).

49. On this point also see Brock (2012), Erdozain (2012a) and Watson (this volume).

50. For example, during Billy Graham's evangelistic crusades in the 1950s, Christian sporting celebrities (e.g., Jill Dodds; see Mathisen, 1990) were invited to share their testimonies, which some argue is not the typical way that authentic Christian conversion is initiated (e.g., Macarthur, 2003: 40).

51. Cited in Brueggeman (2010: 18–19, 45).

52. Some scholars have been very critical (perhaps overly) of athletes' who openly testify to their faith in Jesus Christ on winning a match or championship (e.g., American footballer Tim Tebow and PGA golfers Zach Johnson and Bubba Watson, see Bolt, 2012). However, we would argue that the Bible teaches that it is the 'motivation of the heart' behind the testimony of the individual that determines whether or not a testimony is authentic or not. In addition, unless the athlete explicitly states otherwise, it is often very difficult to know whether these testimonies are to thank God for winning (which could be problematic) or to thank God for who He is in their lives. Thus, we would urge scholars to be careful not to fall into judgmentalism when analyzing the testimonies of professional athletes. See the Foreword of this book for Michael Novak's reflections on this topic (e.g., Tom Tebow).

53. In addition to sports ministry 'instruction' handbooks there are a number of sport-themed Bible editions, for example, Branon's (2002) *NIV Sports Devotional Bible: Daily Inspirations for Sports Enthusiasts*, which include testimonies of famous athletes.

54. Aitken (1989: 396) argues that Wesley Neal's (1981, 1972) books provided the foundational theology for the FCA and Neal 'became the principal theologian in the movement [FCA].'

55. Also, see the recent empirical study of Tucker and Woodbridge (2012).

56. For Sport Alpha website, see http://uk-england.alpha.org/alpha/sports-alpha.

57. Olonga's ministry mainly involves after-dinner speaking and Church visits. In regard to Church visits (the first author has attended one), he typically sings gospel music (he is a well-respected soloist), is interviewed regarding his life as a Christian sportsperson and his experience of being extradited from Zimbabwe due to his protest against the human rights abuses of President Mugabe. Toward the end of the evening he shares the gospel message and signs copies of his biography that are on sale (Olonga, 2010). For further information, see his personal website: http://www.henryolonga.net/container/ (accessed 6 June 2012.

58. Gibbons, Dixon and Braye's (2008) paper explores the dramatic conversion experience of an English football hooligan, who then became a well-known Christian minister in the north of England and who used his life story within sporting locales to assist in sharing the gospel message.

59. The following three journals are good sources of information on this topic, *Men and Masculinities*, the *Journal of Men's Studies* and *THYMOS: Journal of Boyhood Studies*.

60. Helpful resources for these three topics are: (i) *Exegesis and hermeneutics* (Brock, 2012; White, 2012b; Pfitzner, this volume, 2009, 1981, 1967; Yinger, 2008; Seesengood, 2006a, 2006b, 2005; Esler, 2005; Garrison, 1993; Thaden, 2003; Williams, 1999; Garrison, 1997; Gudorf, 1998; Henderson, 1997; Duff, 1991; De Vries, 1975; Ringwald, 1971; Howson, 1868; Yong, forthcoming). For specific application of Pauline athletic metaphors in modern sports ministry, see Costantini and Lixey (2011), Hoffman (2010a),

Krattenmaker (2010), Ladd and Mathisen (1999), Mathisen (2002) and Watson (2007a). (ii) *Historical, cultural and archaeological* (see Pfitzner, this volume, 1967; Hoffman, 2010a: 41–45; O'Gorman, 2010a; Harrison, 2008; Combes, 1997; Seesengood, 2006b, 2005; Hullinger, 2004; Savage, 2004; Krentz, 2003; Fredriksen, 2002; Murphy-O'Conner, 2002; Kajava, 2002; van Nijf, 2001; Williams, 1999; Raschke, 1986; Freyne, 1989; Poliakiff, 1987, 1984; Broneer, 1971, 1962a, 1962b). (iii) *The use of athletic metaphors to construct a 'theology of sport' and/or a 'theology of sport competition* (see Pfitzner, this volume, 2009; Brock, 2012; White, 2012b; Hoffman, 2010a; Krattenmaker, 2010; Watson, 2007a; Seesengood, 2006b; Koch, 1999; Novak, 1967/1994, chap. 9; Freyne, 1989; Yong, forthcoming).

61. Cited in Feeney (1995: 69).
62. Lasch's chapter has recently been republished in a 'reader' on sports ethics (McNamee, 2010: 369–81).
63. The ever-present threat of terrorism at sporting mega-events cannot be illustrated more clearly by the potential mooring of a Royal Naval Warship (type-45 destroyer) with air defense capability in the Docklands of east London during the 2012 Olympic and Paralympic games (Coghlan, Schlesinger and Savage, 2011).
64. For those wishing to critique the ethics of the modern sporting institution, Part 6 of McNamee's (2010: 363–434) 'reader' text, titled 'Commercialism, Corruption and Exploitation in Sport,' which has six essays from leading thinkers addressing the ethics of adult and child sports, is very helpful.
65. Stoll and Beller's (2008) longitudinal research on moral reasoning in sporting contexts and related examination of whether sport builds character stems from the Centre for ETHICS, University of Idaho, U.S.
66. It is interesting that the seminal academic book written by a Catholic philosopher (Weiss, 1969) for the discipline of the philosophy of sport had a section on metaphysics and yet this school of thought has not, until recently, received any sustained attention and has largely been divorced from ethical reflection.
67. Part 5, titled 'Ethical Development in and through Sports: Rules, Virtues and Vices,' in McNamee (2010: 301–62), has five essays from leading thinkers in this area of study.
68. Greg Linville, of the Association of Church Sports and Recreation Ministries, has published a series of articles on the 'theology of competition' that are available online: http://www.csrm.org/index.html (accessed 6 June 2012).
69. As McNamee (2011: 36–44) has noted, the concept of arête (i.e., excellence) in Greek culture was closely tied to virtue ethics, as it is in modern sport.
70. The word 'competition' is derived from the Latin *com-petito*, which translates 'questioning or striving together.'
71. For a recent evaluation of the validity of Kohn's (1992) oft-cited work, see Shields and Bredemeier (2010).
72. Also see Clifford and Feezell (2009), who provide an extensive study of this topic.
73. The balance between the development of the heart and ethical knowledge in determining attitudes and behavior in sport is indicative of a much wider and vigorous historical Church debate that has continued down the centuries (especially around the Reformation period), in regard to the balance of emphasis between 'faith (leading of the heart) and reason (the Bible)' or 'word (the Bible) and spirit (leading of the heart)' in ecclesiological praxis in different denominations.
74. Orthodox Christian anthropology holds that humans consist of soul, body and spirit (see 1 Thessalonians 5:23) and the soul (or *psyche*) of the person

consists of the 'will, intellect and emotions.' But fundamentally, it is our spirit that relates to God's spirit (Romans 8:16), not our emotions/emotional sensibility. This said, McNamee's proposal of 'emotional sensibility' is interesting due to the *holistic* and inseparable nature of all aspects of human personhood that are often referred to collectively as the 'heart' (see Chambers, 1936/1962). Thus, God relates to the person via the spirit but also through the soul of the individual, the *emotions*, will and intellect (see Watson, 2011a; Miller and Delaney, 2005; John Paul II, 1997).

75. Watson's (2011a) chapter contains reference to a wide range of research from across the disciplines.

76. In discussing the theology of play, Bonhoeffer (1955) touches on a range of ethical issues related to sport, as does Barth, in the *Church Dogmatics*, where he talks about the institution of sport becoming the 'playground of a particular-earth-spirit' (1981: 229), that is, a form of idolatrous spirit that *partially* characterizes institutions.

77. There are subtle differences between Catholic moral theology (closely allied to the Church magisterium) and Christian ethics, for example, as Kirk (1949: 223–24) notes, 'moral theology is concerned not so much with the highest standards of Christian conduct (that is perhaps the special province of Christian ethics) as with the *minimum* standard to which conduct must attain if it is to be adjudged Christian at all.'

78. Plenary papers from this meeting at the University of Cambridge are to be published in a special edition of the society's journal, *Studies in Christian Ethics: Christian Ethics and Sport* (2012: Vol. 25, 1, February). In response to London hosting the 2012 Olympic and Paralympic games, a number of other theological and religious studies journals are publishing special editions on sport (see Table 1.1) that have a focus on theological ethics.

79. See Part 3, titled 'Doping, Genetic Modification and the Ethics of Enhancement,' in McNamee (2010: 153–224), which includes six essays from key thinkers in this topic area.

80. Part II of Miller and Delaney's (2005) book, titled 'The Nature of the Human Person,' is especially helpful. Also, see the *Journal of Psychology and Theology*, the *Journal of Psychology and Christianity* (studies of prayer in sport have been published in this journal) and the *Journal of Psychology and Judaism* for psychological insights of human nature from a Judea-Christian standpoint. A Special Edition (2005: Vol. 59, 4) of the journal *Interpretation: A Journal of Bible and Theology* that focuses on biblical anthropology and biblical portraits of personhood is also a rich source of theological insights.

81. Catholic theologians, such as Richard Rohr, and the philosopher of sport Kretchmar (this volume) have challenged Christian scholars to learn about things such as humility in sport from the writings of others faiths traditions, suggesting that we can learn from supposed 'outsiders.'

82. This is an interesting line of inquiry due to the fact that 'moralism' has failed in the modern world (see Taylor, 2007) and while personal character attributes such as consistency, trustworthiness, faithfulness, loyalty, self-control and being principled are desirable traits in a Christian, if an individual builds a reputation on these principles and glories in them, the danger of self-righteousness and religious pride always lurks at the door (i.e., moralizing about others). As C. S. Lewis (1952/1997) noted, a prostitute that knows her desperate need of God may be far closer to Him than a churchgoer of many years that is 'highly principled' and seen as a pillar of the community. This is the offense of grace. Jesus had a total disinterest in building a reputation for himself (see Phil. 2:1–11) and King David, after committing murder and adultery, was famously described as 'a man after God's own heart,' *because*

he had a broken and contrite spirit (Ps. 51), not because he always acted in a principled and ethical manner. Based on this, perhaps, Christian character could be better understood as a *combination* of moral principles evident in an individual's life but also the existence of a 'tender (broken) heart that is always willing to repent quickly' and that extends mercy and grace to those that persecute them (i.e., a state of heart that wants the offender to get off free and not to suffer consequences/punishment).

83. As theorists have noted (Dixon, 2007), violence and physical harm (injury) are also clearly evident in more broadly conceived 'combative sports' such as, rugby, American football, etc., and thus these activities could also be a focus of research from a Christian perspective.

84. Mixed Martial Arts (MMA) is also known as Cage Fighting and gained in popularity as a sport mainly through the televised *Ultimate Fighting Championship* (1993-). Borer and Schafer (2011: 167) note that roughly 700 American churches 'have begun incorporating MMA into their ministry in some capacity', a development that has been controversial for many Christian ministers (see Schneiderman, 2010). Additionally, in a recent blog on the *Sydney Anglican Network* titled 'The Christian and the Cage Fighter,' Craig Schwarze (2010), notes that there is no literature on this topic to date and as the controversial American pastor, Mark Driscoll, has endorsed the *Ultimate Fighting Championship* as a vehicle to develop 'muscular Christians' in a feminized world church, academic analysis is urgently needed. See: http://sydneyanglicans.net/life/daytoday/the_christian_and_the_cage_fighter/ (accessed 6 June 2012).

85. Part XVII of Morgan and Meier's (1995) book, titled 'The Morality of Hunting and Animal Liberation,' which has five essays on the topic, provides a secular ethical perspective.

86. See Part 7 of McNamee (2010: 435–500), titled 'Ethics and Adventurous Activity,' for five essays that address this topic.

87. It is then interesting that the All American Speakers Bureau and Celebrity Network that includes the details of a number of high-profile Christian athletes (some charging up to $50,000 for one speaking engagement) advertise that 'we know the power of celebrity endorsements, stated or implied, and there are few bigger celebrities than famous athletes from the world of sports. When a top athlete makes an appearance at your corporate event, you get the benefits of his or her star power . . . they help give you . . . media and public attention', see: http://www.allamericanspeakers.com/ (accessed 6 June 2012). Also, see the related sport story in Manning (2002: 39–40) that challenges the notion of 'sport platform ministry' in some ways but avoids judgmentalism.

88. A Special Edition (and double edition) of the *Journal of Religion, Disability and Health* titled 'Sport, Religion and Disability,' which focuses on sport and leisure, will include seventeen papers, consisting of a mix of scholarly essays and empirical research studies, and will provide a starting point for this research area. It is projected that this will be published in 2014 and will also be republished as a book.

89. However, there is a significant body of scholarly publications on Christian theology, women and embodiment more generally, for example, the writings of Rosemary Radford Ruether, Sallie McFague, Marcella Athaus Reid and Ivone Gebara.

90. While the eating disorders are far more prevalent in women's sports, this has become more and more of a problem for sportsmen, in sports such as boxing, wrestling and horseback riding (i.e., jockeys), which require the participant to reach/maintain a specific bodyweight.

91. Radical orthodoxy is a relatively recent school of theology-philosophy that has evolved from the writings of John Milbank, Graham Ward and Catherine Pickstock in the early 1990s (see Milbank and Oliver, 2009). Its principal thesis, which now stems from thinkers across the Christian traditions, is that the theologian's task is to view all contemporary phenomena (i.e., explored in the social sciences) through the lens of orthodox Christian doctrine (theological ontology and epistemology) laid down in the early Church creeds and writings of the Church fathers and rearticulated and interpreted by modern theological reflection, for example, in the works of Protestant Karl Bart and Catholic Hans Urs Balthasar. This precludes that radical orthodoxy provides a strong attack on the paradigms of secularization in modern Western culture.
92. For a full transcript of the Queen's speech (Christmas, 2010), see: http://www.bbc.co.uk/news/uk-12079065 (accessed 6 June 2012)
93. This is not an exhaustive list, but to our knowledge, includes all the major protestant and Catholic 'academic' texts (or books written by journalists and freelance authors that have academic credibility) that focus *broadly* on the sport–Christianity interface discussing a range of themes. Some of the book listed (e.g., Magdalinski and Chandler, 2002; Prebish, 1993) do not focus exclusively on Christianity and sport, although the majority of the chapters are on this theme. Books specifically on muscular Christianity and some other specific topics are not cited, with the exception of Ladd and Mathisen's (1999) book, as this oft-cited work analyzes Christianity and American sport in a broader context, including a socio-ethical analysis. Many of these texts have chapters from both Catholic and Protestant scholars (e.g., Parry, Nesti and Watson, 2011); however, for clarity we have noted which texts are written purely from a Catholic perspective: (Catholic).
94. The dates provided for the founding/launch of each these organizations is the date that they officially began. In some cases, the activities of a number of these organizations began earlier than the stated dates and some sports ministries evolved as suborganizations of others.
95. Especially, in America a significant number of Christian colleges run courses on sport and faith, or courses with some content on this topic.

BIBLIOGRAPHY

Abe, S. (1986) Zen and Sport, *Journal of the Philosophy of Sport*, XIII: 45–48.
Ackerman, D. (1997) *Deep Play*, New York: Vintage.
Aitken, B. W. W. (1989) Sport, Religion, and Well-Being, *Studies in Religion*, 18 (4): 391–405.
Allen, L. D. (2002) *Rise Up, O Men of God: The "Men and Religion Forward Movement" and the "Promise Keepers"*, Mercer, MA, USA: Mercer University Press.
Alter, J. S. (2004) Indian Clubs and Colonialism: Hindi Masculinity and Muscular Christianity, *Comparative Studies in Society and History*, 46 (3): 497–534.
Altrogge, S. (2008) *Game Day for the Glory of God: A Guide for Athletes, Fans and Wannabes*, Nottingham, UK: Crossway Books.
Amarasingam, A. (2008) Transcending Technology: Looking at Futurology as a New Religious Movement, *Journal of Contemporary Religion*, 23 (1): 1–16.
Anderson, W. K. (1925) Athletics as an Undergraduate Religion, *Methodist Review*, 591–602.
Archetti, E. P. (2002) The Spectacle of a Heroic Life: The Case of Diego Maradona, in D. L. Andrews and S. J. Jackson (Eds.), *Sport Stars: The Cultural Politics of Sporting Celebrity*, London: Routledge, 151–63.

Ardley, G. (1967) The Role of Play in the Philosophy of Plato, *Philosophy*, 42: 226–44.

Armato, M. and Marsiglio, W. (2002) Self Structure, Identity and Commitment: Promise Keepers' Godly man Project, *Symbolic Intercation*, 25: 41–65.

Arnold, B. (2012) Re-Envisioning the Olympic Games: Paul's use of Athletic Imagery in Philippians, *Theology*, 115 (4): 243–252.

Arnold, P. (1989) Competitive Sport, Winning and Education, *Journal of Moral Education*, 18 (1): 15–25.

Arnold, P. (1994) Sport and Moral Education, *Journal of Moral Education*, 23 (1): 75–89.

Arnold, P. (1997) *Sport, Ethics and Education*, London: Cassell.

Arnold, P. (1999) The Virtues, Moral Education and Practice in Sport, *Quest*, 51: 39–54.

Arnold, P. (2001) Sport, Moral Development and the Role of Teacher, *Quest*, 53: 135–50.

Aune, K. (2010) Fatherhood in British Evangelical Christianity: Negotiating Mainstream Culture, *Men and Masculinities*, 13 (2): 168–89.

Aveyard, H. (2008) *Doing a Literature Review in Health and Social Care: A Practical Guide*, Maidenhead, Berkshire, UK: Open University Press, McGraw-Hill Education.

Baker, W. J. (1988) *Sports in the Western World*, Chicago: University of Illinois Press.

Baker, W. J. (2000a) *If Christ Came to the Olympics*, Sydney: University of New South Wales Press.

Baker, W. J. (2000b) Questioning Tom Brown: Sport and the Character Game, in J. Squires (Ed.), *A Fair Go for All? Current Issues in Australian Sport Ethics*, Sydney: New College Institute for Values Research, 7–18.

Baker, W. J. (2007a) Athletes for Allah, in *Playing with God: Religion and Modern Sport*, Cambridge, MA: Harvard University Press, 218–39.

Baker, W. J. (2007b) *Playing with God: Religion and Modern Sport*, Cambridge, MA: Harvard University Press.

Baker, W. J. (2010) Religion, in S.W. Pope and J. Nauright (Eds.), *Routledge Companion to Sports History*, London: Routledge, 216–28.

Ballou, R. B. (1973) Analysis of the Writings of Selected Church Fathers to A.D. 394 to Reveal Attitudes Regarding Physical Activity, in E. F. Zeigler (Ed.), *History of Sport and Physical Education to 1900: Selected Topics*, Champaign, IL: Stipes Publishing, 187–99.

Balmer, R. (2000) Keep the Faith and Go the Distance: Promise Keepers, Feminism, and the World of Sports, in D. S. Claussen (Ed.), *The Promise Keepers: Essays on Masculinity and Christianity*, Jefferson, AL: McFarland and Company, 194–203.

Bandy, S. J. (2010) Gender, in S. W. Pope and J. Nauright (Eds.), *Routledge Companion to Sports History*, London: Routledge, 129–47.

Barnes, S. (2011) Athletes, the Naughty Vicars of the 21st Century, *The Times* (London), 23 September, 93.

Barrajón, P. (2012) Overcoming Dualism, in M. Mieth, N. Müller and K. Lixey (Eds.), *Sport and Christianity: Anthropological, Theological and Pastoral Challenges*, Washington, DC: Catholic University of America Press, 45–67.

Barth, K. (1981) *Church Dogmatics: Lecture Fragments*, trans. Geoffrey W. Bromiley, Grand Rapids, MI: Eerdmans.

Bartowski, J. P. (2004) *The Promise Keepers: Servants, Soldiers, and Godly Men*, New Brunswick, NJ, USA: Rutgers University Press.

Battista, G. (2004) *The Runner's High: Illumination and Ecstasy in Motion*, Halcottsville, NY: Breakaway Books.

Batts, C. (2010) 'In Good Conscience': Andy Flower, Henry Olonga and the Death of Democracy in Zimbabwe, *Sport in Society*, 13 (1): 43–58.

Bauer, O. (2011) *Hockey as Religion: The Montreal Canadiens*, Champaign, IL: Common Ground Publishing.

Baum, G. and Coleman, J. (eds.) (1989) *Sport (Religion in the Eighties, Concilium 205)*, Edinburgh: T & T Clark.

Beal, B. (1997) The Promise Keepers' Use of Sport in Defining "Christlike" Masculinity, *Journal of Sport and Social Issues*, 21 (3): 274–84.

Beamish, R. and Ritchie, I. (2006) *Fastest, Highest, Strongest: A Critique of High-Performance Sport*, London: Routledge.

Bederman, G. (1989) "The Women Have Had Charge of the Church Work Long Enough": The Men and Religion Movement of 1911–1912 and the Masculinization of Middle-Class Protestantism, *American Quarterly*, 41 (3): 432–65.

Begbie, J. (ed.) (2000) *Beholding the Glory: Incarnation through the Arts*, Edinburgh, UK: Dartman, Longman and Todd

Begel, D. and Burton, R. W. (eds.) (2000) *Sport Psychiatry: Theory and Practice*, New York: W. W. Norton and Company.

Bekoff, M. and Byers, J. A. (eds.) (1998) *Animal Play: Evolutionary, Comparative, and Ecological Perspectives*, Cambridge: Cambridge University Press.

Bell, T. N., Johnson, S. R. and Peterson, J. C. (2011) Strength of Religious Faith of Athletes and Nonathletes at Two NCAA Division III Institutions, *Sport Journal*, 14. Available online at http://www.thesportjournal.org/article/strength-religious-faith-athletes-and-nonathletes-two-ncaa-division-iii-institutions (accessed 29 June 2011).

Bellah, R. N. (2007) *Habits of the Heart: Individualism and Commitment in American Life*, 3rd ed., Berkeley: University of California Press.

Beller, J. M., Stoll, S. K., Burwell, B. and Cole, J. (1996) The Relationship of Competition and a Christian Liberal Arts Education on Moral Reasoning of College Student Athletes, *Research on Christian Higher Education*, 3: 99–114.

Benn, T., Dagkas, S. and Jawad, H. (2011) Embodied Faith: Islam, Religious Freedom and Educational Practices in Physical Education. *Sport, Education and Society*, 16 (1): 17–34.

Benn, T., Pfister, G. and Jawad, H. (2010) *Muslim Women and Sport*, London: Routledge.

Bennett, G., Sagas, M., Fleming, D., and Von Roennc, S. (2005) On Being a Living Contradiction: The Struggle of an Elite Intercollegiate Christian Coach, *Journal of Beliefs & Values*, 26 (3): 289–300.

Berger, P. L. (1967) *The Social Reality of Religion*, London: Faber and Faber.

Berger, P. L. (1970) *A Rumour of Angels*, Garden City, NY: Doubleday.

Berger, P. L. (1997) *Redeeming Laughter: Comic Dimension of Human Experience*, Boston: Walter de Gruyter.

Binfield, C. (1973) *George Williams and the YMCA: A Study in Victorian Social Attitudes*, London: Heinemann.

Birley, D. (1993) *Sport and the Making of Britain*, Manchester: Manchester University Press.

Blankenhorn, D. (1995) *Fatherless America: Confronting Our Most Urgent Social Problem*, New York: Harper Perennial.

Blazer, A. (2012) Religion and Sports in America, *Religion Compass*, 6/5: 287–297.

Bloomfield, A. (1994) Muscular Christian or Mystic? Charles Kingsley Reappraised, *International Journal of the History of Sport*, 11 (2): 172–90.

Bolt, B. (2012) Bubba, Tiger and the Nature of Sport, *Christian Courier*, June 11, No. 2938: 10–11.

Bonhoeffer, D. (1955) *Ethics*, London: SCM Press.

Borer, M. I. (2008) *Faithful to Fenway: Believing in Boston, Baseball, and America's Most Beloved Ballpark*, New York: NYU Press.

Borer. M. I. and Schafer, T. S. (2011) Culture War Confessionals: Conflicting Accounts of Christianity, Violence, and Mixed Martial Arts, *Journal of Media and Religion*, 10 (4): 165–184.

Borish, L. (1987) The Robust Woman and the Muscular Christian: Catherine Beecher, Thomas Higginson, and the Vision of American Society, Health and Physical Activities, *International Journal of the History of Sport*, 4 (2): 139–54.

Borish, L. (2002) Women, Sport and American Jewish Identity in the Late Nineteenth and Early Twentieth Century, in T. Magdalinski and T. G. L. Chandler (eds.), *With God on Their Side: Sport in the Service of Religion*, London: Routledge, 71–98.

Borish, L. (2009) Place, Identity, Physical Culture, Religion and Sport for Women in Jewish Americanization Organizations, *Stadion: International Journal of the History of Sport*, 35: 87–108.

Boyers, J. (2000) *Beyond the Final Whistle: A Life of Football and Faith*, London: Hodder & Stoughton.

Boyers, J. (2011) Manchester United FC, in M. Threlfall-Holmes and M. Newitt (Eds.), *Being a Chaplain*, London: SPCK, 81–84.

Bradley, I. (2007) Moral Fibre and Muscular Christianity: The Scottish Contribution, in I. Bradley (Ed.), *Believing in Britain: The Spiritual Identity of "Britishness,"* London: I. B. Tauris, 139–66.

Brailsford, D. (1991) *Sport, Time and Society*, London: Routledge.

Branon, D. (2002) *NIV Sports Devotional Bible: Daily Inspirations for Sports Enthusiasts*, Grand Rapids, MI: Zondervan.

Brasch, R. (1970) *How Did Sports Begin?* New York: David McKay.

Bredemeier, B. L. and Shields, D. (1985) Values and Violence in Sport, *Psychology Today*, 19: 22–32.

Bredemeier, B. L. and Shields, D. (1986) Athletic Aggression: An Issue of Contextual Morality, *Sociology of Sport Journal*, 3: 15–28.

Bredemeier, B. L. and Shields, D. (2005) Sport and the Development of Character, In D. Hackfort, J. Duda and R. Lidor (Eds.), *Handbook of Research in Applied Sport and Exercise Psychology*, Morgantown, WV, USA: Fitness Information Technology, 275–90.

Bredemeier, B. L., Weiss, M., Shields, D. and Cooper, B. (1987).The Relationship between Children's Legitimacy Judgments and Their Moral Reasoning, Aggression Tendencies and Sport Involvement, *Sociology of Sport Journal*, 4: 48–60.

Brierley, P. (2006) *Pulling out of the Nosedive: What the 2005 English Church Census Reveals*, London: Christian Research.

Brock, B. (2012) Discipline, Sport, and the Religion of Winners: Paul on Running to Win the Prize, 1 Corinthians 9: 24–27, *Studies in Christian Ethics*, 25 (1): 4–19.

Brock, B. and Swinton, J. (2012) *Disability in the Christian Tradition: A Reader*, Grand Rapids, MI: Wm. B. Eerdmans Publishing.

Brohm, J. M. (1978) *Sport: A Prison of Measured Time*, London: Pluto Press.

Broneer, O. (1962a) The Apostle Paul and the Isthmian Games, *Biblical Archaeologist*, 25 (1): 2–31.

Broneer, O. (1962b) The Isthmian Crown, *American Journal of Archaeology*, 66: 259–63.

Broneer, O. (1971) Paul and the Pagan Cults of Isthmia, *Harvard Theological Review*, 64: 169–87.

Brown, D. (2012) Seeking Spirituality through Physical Education and Sports, presented at the 12th International Conference on Children's Spirituality: Spirituality and Physicality: Crossing Thresholds, University of East Anglia, UK, 1–5 July.

Brown, D. D., Cutcliffe, D., Herrmann, K. and Welsh, T. F. (2006) *Coach Them Well: Fostering Faith and Developing Character in Athletes*, Winona, MN: Saint Mary's Press.

Brueggeman, W. (2010) *Out of Babylon*, Nashville, TN: Abingdon Press.

Buber, M. (1923/1958) *I and Thou* ,trans. W. Kaufmann, New York: Scribner's.

Burghardt, G. M. (2005) *The Genesis of Animal Play: Testing the Limits*, Cambridge, MA: MIT Press.

Burke, E. (1757/1990) *A Philosophical Enquiry into the Origin and the Sublime and Beautiful*, Oxford: Oxford University Press.

Burstyn, V. (2005) Sport as Secular Sacrament, In D.S. Eitzen (ed.), *Sport in Contemporary Society: An Anthology*, Boulder, CO, USA: Paradigm Publishers, 11–20.

Busch, W. (1932) The Liturgy and Athletics, *Orate Fratres*, 6 (8): 345–51.

Butryn, T. M. and Masucci, M. A. (2009) Traversing the Matrix: Cyborg Athletes, Technology, and the Environment, *Journal of Sport and Social Issues*, 33 (3): 285–307.

Byl, J. and Visker, T. (eds.) (1999) *Physical Education, Sports, and Wellness: Looking to God as We Look at Ourselves*, Sioux Center, IA: Dordt College Press.

Callois, R. (1958) *Man, Play and Games*, trans. Meyer Barash, New York: Free Press.

Campolo, T. (1988) Should Preachers Start Preaching against Sports? in T. Campolo (Ed.), *20 Hot Potatoes Christians Are Afraid to Touch*, Nashville, TN: Word Publishing, 122–31.

Capps, D. (1987) *Deadly Sins and Saving Virtues*, Philadelphia, PA: Fortress Press.

Capps, D. (2006) *A Time to Laugh: The Religion of Humor*, New York: Continuum International Publishing.

Carmody, D. L. (1986) Big-Time Spectator Sports: A Feminist Christian Perspective, *New Catholic World*, (July/August): 173–77.

Caroll, D. M. (2000) *An Interdisciplinary Study of Sport as a Symbolic Hunt: A Theory of the Origin and Nature of Sport Based on Paleolithic Hunting*, Lampeter, Wales: Edwin Mellen Press.

Carpenter, P. (2001) The Importance of a Church Youth Clubs' Sport Provision to Continued Church Involvement, *Journal of Sport and Social Issues*, 25 (3): 283–300.

Carter, J. M. (1984a) Muscular Christianity and Its Makers: Sporting Monks and Churchmen in Anglo-Norman Society, 1000–1300, *British Journal of Sports History*, 1 (2): 109–24.

Carter, J. M. (1984b) *Sports and Pastimes of the Middle Ages*, Columbus, GA: Brentwood University.

Carter, J., Kluck, T. and Morin, M. (2012) Is Cage Fighting Ethical for Christians? *Christianity Today*, May 29: 1–2. Available online: http://www.christianitytoday.com/ct/2012/january/cage-fighting.html (accessed 6 June 2012)

Cashmore, E. (2012) The Malignancy of Sport, *Criminal Justice Matters*, 88 (1): 16–17.

Cashmore, E. (2008) *Chariots of Fire*: Bigotry, Manhood and Moral Certitude in an Age of Individualism, *Sport and Society*, 11 (2/3): 159–73.

Cavallo, D. (1981) *Muscles and Morals: Organized Playgrounds and Urban Reform, 1880–1920*, Philadelphia: University of Pennsylvania.

Cavar, M., Sekulic, D. and Culjak, Z. (2010) Complex Interaction of Religiousness with Other Factors in Relation to Substance Use and Misuse among Female Athletes, *Journal of Religion and Health*. Published Online 6 May. Available at: DOI 10.1007/s10943–010–9360–9.

Centre for Sport Ethics, Josephson Institute. (2011) *Pursuing Victory with Honor*. Available online at http://josephsoninstitute.org/sports/ (accessed 28 March 2011).

Chambers, O. (1936/1962) *Biblical Psychology*, London: Oswald Chambers Publications Association and Marshall Morgan Scott.

Chandler, T. J. L. (2002) Manly Catholicism: Making Men in Catholic Public Schools, 1954–80, in T. Magdalinski and T. J. L. Chandler (Eds.), *With God on Their Side: Sport in the Service of Religion*, London: Routledge, 99–119.

Chen, Q. and Zhao, Y. (2001) Sport Activities of Young Women's Christian Association in China and Its Influence, *Journal of the Wuhan Institute of Physical Education*, 35 (1): 70–72.

Claussen, D. S. (ed.) (2000) *The Promise Keepers: Essays on Masculinity and Christianity*, Jefferson, AL: McFarland and Company.

Clemens, J. (2009) Sporting Activity in the Thought of Joseph Ratzinger/Benedict XVI, *Panel Discussion on 'Soccer, Values in Play,'* LUMSA University Auditorium, Rome, December. Received by email from Father Kevin Lixey, 'Church and Sport' Office, Vatican.

Clifford, C. and Feezell, R. M. (2009) *Sport and Character: Reclaiming the Principles of Sportsmanship*, Champaign, IL: Human Kinetics.

Close, P., Askew, D. and Xin, X. (2007) *The Beijing Olympiad: The Political Economy of a Sporting Mega-Event*, London: Routledge.

Coakley, J. J. (2007) Sport and Religion: Is It a Promising Combination?, in J. J. Coakley (Ed.), *Sport in Society: Issues and Controversies*, 9th ed., Maidenhead, UK: McGraw-Hill Education, 528–63.

Coakley, J. J. (2011) Youth Sports: What Counts as "Positive Development," *Journal of Sport and Social Issues*, 35: 306–24.

Coghlan, T., Schlesinger, F. and Savage, M. (2011) Warship Missiles May Protect Games against Terror Strikes, *The Times* (London), 15 November, 5.

Coleman, J. (1989) Sport and Contradictions of Society, in G. Baum and J. Coleman (Eds.), *Sport*, Edinburgh: T & T Clark, 21–31.

Collins, M. (2007) Editorial: Sport and Spirituality: An International Conference, York St. John University, 28–31 August, 2007, *Implicit Religion: Journal of the Centre for the Study of Implicit Religion and Contemporary Spirituality*, 10 (3): 241–43.

Collins, M. and Parker, A. (2009) Faith and Sport Revival in Britain: Muscular Christianity and Beyond, *Stadion: International Journal of the History of Sport*, 35: 193–210.

Combes, I. (1997) Nursing Mother, Ancient Shepherd, Athletic Coach? Some Images of Christ in the Early Church, in M. Hayes., D. Tombs and S. E. Porter (eds.), *Images of Christ: Ancient and Modern*, Sheffield, UK: Sheffield Academic Press, 113–25.

Connor, S. (2003) *Sports Outreach: Principles and Practice for Successful Sports Ministry*, Scotland: Christian Focus Publications.

Cook, D. L. (1985) Sport Psychology and Christianity: A Comparison of Application, in L. K. Bunker, R. J. Rotella and A. S. Reilly (Eds.), *Sport Psychology: Psychological Considerations in Maximising Sport Performance*, Longmeadow, MA: Mouvement Publications, 206–11.

Cooper, A. (1998) *Playing in the Zone: Exploring the Spiritual Dimensions of Sport*, London: Shambhala Publications.

Corlett, J. (1996) Virtues Lost: Courage in Sport, *Journal of the Philosophy of Sport*, 23: 45–57.

Cornick, D. (2012) The Churches and the Olympics, *Theology*, 115 (4): 266–272.

Costantini, E. (2011) New Approaches and Educational Strategies for Sporting Environments, in Liberia Editrice Vaticana (Ed.), *Sport, Education and Faith: Toward a New Season for Catholic Sports Associations (A Series of Studies edited by The Pontifical Council for the Laity)*, Citta del Vaticano, Italy: Liberia Editrice Vaticana, 63–86.

Costantini, E. and Lixey, K. (2011) *Sport and Paul: A Course for Champions*, London: John Paul Sport Foundation.

Cox, H. (1969) *Feast of Fools*, New York: Harper and Row.

Cronin, M. (2000) Catholics and Sport in Northern Ireland: Exclusiveness or Inclusiveness? *International Sport Studies*, 22 (1): 25–41.

Crosson, S. (2012) *Sport and Film*, London: Routledge.

Csikszentmihalyi, M. (1975a) *Beyond Boredom and Anxiety*, San Francisco, CA: Jossey-Bass.

Csikszentmihalyi, M. (1975b) Play and Intrinsic Awards, *Journal of Humanistic Psychology*, 15 (3): 41–63.

Csikszentmihalyi, I. (1988) Flow in a Historical Context: The Case of the Jesuits, in M. Csikszentmihalyi and I. Csikszentmihalyi (Eds.), *Optimal Experience Psychological Studies of Flow in Consciousness*, Cambridge: Cambridge University Press, 232–48.

Cunningham, H. (1980) *Leisure in the Industrial Revolution c.1780–1880*, London: Croom Helm.

Curran, C. E. (2005) *The Moral Theology of Pope John Paul II*, Washington, DC: Georgetown University Press.

Curry, T. J. (1988) Comparing Commitment to Sport and Religion at a Christian College, *Sociology of Sport Journal*, 5 (4): 369–77.

Cusack, C. M. (2010) Sport, in R. D. Hecht and V. F. Biondo (Eds.), *Religion in Everyday Life and Culture*, Westport, CT: Praeger Publishers, 915–43.

Czech, D. and Bullet, E. (2007) An Exploratory Description of Christian Athletes' Perceptions of Prayer in Sport: A Mixed Methodology Pilot Study, *International Journal of Sports Science and Coaching*, 2 (1): 49–56.

Czech, D., Wrisberg, C., Fisher, L., Thompson, C. and Hayes, G. (2004) The Experience of Christian Prayer in Sport—An Existential Phenomenological Investigation, *Journal of Psychology and Christianity*, 2: 1–19.

Daniels, G. and Weir, S. (2008) Church and Sport, in D. Deardorff II and J. White (Eds.), *The Image of God in the Human Body: Essays on Christianity and Sports*, Lampeter, Wales: Edwin Mellen Press, 297–312.

Deardorff II, D. L. (2000) Sport: Philosophy and Religion, in D. L. Deardorff II (Ed.), *Sports: A Reference Guide and Critical Commentary, 1980–1999*, London: Greenwood Press, 163–91.

Deardorff II, D. L. and Deardorff, J. D. (2008) Escaping the Gender Trap: Sport and the Equality of Christ, in D. L. Deardorff II and J. White (Eds.), *The Image of God in the Human Body: Essays on Christianity and Sports*, Lampeter, Wales: Edwin Mellen Press, 195–216.

Deardorff II, D. L. and White, J. (eds.) (2008) *The Image of God in the Human Body: Essays on Christianity and Sports*, Lampeter, Wales: Edwin Mellen Press.

De Bosscher, V., Bingham, J. and Shibli, S. (2008) *The Global Sporting Arms Race: An International Comparative Study of Sports Policy Factors Leading to International Sporting Success*, Oxford: Meyer and Meyer Sport.

Deford, F. (1976a) Endorsing Jesus, *Sports Illustrated*, 26 April, 54–69.

Deford, F. (1976b) Reaching for the Stars, *Sports Illustrated*, 3 May, 60.

Deford, F. (1976c) Religion in Sport, *Sports Illustrated*, 19 April, 88–102.

Deford, F. (1976d) The Word According to Tom, *Sports Illustrated*, 26 April, 64–65.

Deford, F. (1979) Religion in Sport, in D. S. Eitzen (Ed.), *Sport in Contemporary Society*, New York: St. Martin Press, 341–47.

Deford, F. (1986) A Heavenly Game, *Sports Illustrated*, 3 March, 57–70.

Degraaf, D. G. Jordan, D. J. and Degraaf, K. H. (1999) *Programming for Parks, Recreation and Leisure Services: A Servant Leadership Approach*, State College, PA: Venture Publications.

Delaney, T. and Madigan, T. (2009) *The Sociology of Sports: An Introduction*, Jefferson, NC, USA: McFarland.

DeSensi, J. T. and Rosenberg, D. (2003) *Ethics and Morality in Sport Management*, Morgantown, WV: USA: Fitness Information Technology.

DeVries, C. E. (1975) Paul's "Cutting" Remarks about a Race: Galatians 5:1–12, in M. C. Tenney and G. F. Hawthorne (Eds.), *Current Issues in Biblical and Patristic Interpretation,* Grand Rapids, MI: Eerdmans, 115–20.

Dietrich, A. (2003) Functional Neuroanatomy of Altered States of Consciousness: The Transient Hypofrontaility Hypothesis, *Consciousness and Cognition*, 12 (2): 231–56.

Dirksen, J. (1975) The Place of Athletics in the Life of a Christian, *Sport Sociology Bulletin*, 4 (1): 48–55.

Dixon, N. (2007) Boxing, Paternalism, and Legal Moralism, in W. J. Morgan (Ed.), *Ethics in Sport*, 2nd ed., Champaign, IL: Human Kinetics, 389–406.

Dougherty, A. P. (2007) Aesthetic and Ethical Issues Concerning Sport in Wilder Places, in M. McNamee (Ed.), *Philosophy, Risk and Adventure Sports*, London: Routledge, 94–167.

Dowland, S. (2011) War, Sports, and the Construction of Masculinity in American Christianity, *Religion Compass*, 5/7: 355–364.

Dubay, T. (1999) *The Evidential Power of Beauty: Science and Theology Meet*, San Francisco, CA: Ignatius Press.

Duff, P. B. (1991) Metaphor, Motif and Meaning: The Rhetorical Structure behind the Image "Led in Triumph" in 2 Corinthians 2:14, *Catholic Biblical Quarterly*, 53: 79–92.

Dungy, T. (2008) *Quiet Strength: The Principles, Practices and Priorities of a Winning Life*, Carol Stream, IL: Tyndale House Publishers.

Dungy, T. (2010) *The Mentor Leader: Secrets to Building People and Teams that Win Consistently*, Carol Stream, IL: Tyndale House Publishers.

Dunn, R. and Stevenson, C. (1998) The Paradox of the Church Hockey League, *International Review for the Sociology of Sport*, 33 (2): 131–41.

Dunning, E. and Sheard, K. (1979/2005) *Barbarians, Gentlemen and Players: A Sociological Study of the Development of Rugby Football*, London: Routledge.

Dzikus, L., Waller, S. and Hardin, R. (2010) Collegiate Sport Chaplaincy: Exploration of an Emerging Profession, *Journal of Contemporary Athletics*, 5 (1): 21–42.

Edwards, H. (1973) *Sociology of Sport*, Homewood, IL: Dosey Press.

Eichberg, H. (2009a) Sport and Laughter: Phenomenology of the Imperfect Human Being, *Sport, Ethics and Philosophy*, 3 (3): 286–304.

Eichberg, H. (2009b) Sport as Festivity: Towards A Phenomenology of the Event, *Sport, Ethics and Philosophy*, 3 (2): 215–36.

Eisen, G. (1975) Physical Activity, Physical Education and Sport in the Old Testament, *Journal of History of Sport and Physical Education*, 6: 45–65.

Eisen, G. (1991) The Concept of Time, Play and Leisure in Early Protestant Religious Ethic, *Play and Culture*, 4 (3): 223–36.

Eisen, G. (1998) Jewish History and the Ideology of Modern Sport: Approaches and Interpretations, *Journal of Sport History*, 25 (3): 482–531.

Eldredge, J. (2001) *Wild at Heart: Discovering the Secret of a Man's Soul*, Nashville, TN: Thomas Nelson.

Eldredge, J. (2011) *Beautiful Outlaw: Experiencing the Playful, Disruptive, Extravagant Personality of Jesus*, London: Hodder and Stoughton.

Ellis, R. (2012) The Meanings of Sport: An Empirical Study into the Significance Attached to Sporting Participation and Spectating in the UK and US, *Practical Theology*, 5 (2): 169–188.

Ellis, R. (forthcoming) *The Games People Play: Theology, Religion and Sport*, Eugene OR: Wipf & Stock.

Erdozain, D. (2012a) Does Sport Build Character? A Progress Report on a Victorian Idea, *Studies in Christian Ethics*, 25 (1): 35–48.

Erdozain, D. (2012b) In Praise of Folly: Sport as Play, *Anvil: An Evangelical Journal for Theology and Mission*, 28 (1).

Erdozain, D. (2012c) 'I will Not Cease from Mental Fight'?: Sport and the Protestant Work Ethic, *The Bible in Transmission* (Sp. Ed., Sporting Life: Reflections on Sport, Culture and the Church), Spring: 5–7.

Erdozain, D. (2010) *The Problem of Pleasure: Sport, Recreation and the Crisis of Victorian Religion*, Suffolk, UK: Boydell Press.

Esler, P. F. (2005) Paul and the Agon: Understanding a Pauline Motif in Its Cultural and Visual Context, in A. Weissenrieder (ed.), *Picturing the New Testament: Studies in Ancient Visual Images, WUNT II 193*, Tübingen: Mohr Siebeck, 357–84.

Feeney, F. (1995) *A Catholic Perspective: Physical Exercise and Sport*, Arlington, VA: Aquinas Press.

Feeney, F. (2006) *The Catholic Ideal: Exercise and Sport*, Arlington, VA: Aquinas Press.

Fellowship of Christian Athletes. (2008) *Serving: True Champions Know that Success Takes Surrender*, Ventura, CA: Regal, From Gospel Light.

Folley, M. (2001) *A Time to Jump: The Authorized Biography of Jonathan Edwards*, London: HarperCollins Publishers.

Forney, C. A. (2010) *The Holy Trinity of American Sports: Civil Religion in Football, Baseball and Basketball*, Macon, GA: Mercer University Press.

Freeman, M. (2010) Muscular Quakerism? The Society of Friends and Youth Organisations in Britain, c. 1900–1950, *English Historical Review*, 125: 642–69.

Fredriksen, P. (2002) Paul at the Races, *Bible Review*, 18 (3): 12, 42.

Fretheim, K. (2008) Whose Kingdom? Which Context? Ecumenical and Contextual Theology in the World Alliance of YMCAS, *International Review of Mission*, 97 (384–385): 116–128.

Freyne, S. (1989) Early Christianity and the Greek Athletic Ideal, in G. Baum and J. Coleman (Eds.), *Sport Concilium*, 205 (5): 93–100.

Gallagher, D. B. (2008) Football and Aristotle's Philosophy of Friendship, in M. W. Austin (Ed.), *Football and Philosophy: Going Deep*, Lexington: University of Kentucky Press, 31–40.

Galli, M. (2005) *The Grace of Sports: If Christ Can't Be Found in Sports, He Can't Be Found in the Modern World*. Available online at http://www.christianitytoday.com/ct/2005/109/52.0.html (accessed 8 April 2005).

Galli, M. (2010) And God Created Football: Intimations of the Divine in a Well-Executed Screen Pass, *Christianity Today.Com*, 28 January. Available online at http://www.christianitytoday.com/bc/2010/janfeb/godcreatedfootball.html (accessed 30 June 2010).

Garcia, R. S. and Malcolm, D. (2010) Decivilizing, Civilizing or Informalizing? The International Development of Mixed Martial Arts, *International Review for the Sociology of Sport*, 45: 39–58.

Garner, J. (ed.) (2003) *Recreation and Sports Ministry: Impacting Post-Modern Culture*, Nashville, TN: Broadman and Holman Publishers.

Garnham, N. (2001) Both Praying and Playing: 'Muscular Christianity' and the YMCA in North-East, in County Durham, *Journal of Social History*, 35: 397–407.

Garrison, R. (1993) Paul's Use of the Athlete Metaphor, *Studies in Religion*, 22 (2): 209–17.

Garrison, R. (1997) Paul's Use of the Athletic Metaphor in I Corinthians 9, in R. Garrison (Ed.), *The Greco-Roman Context of Early Christian Literature*, Sheffield, UK: Sheffield Academic Press, 95–104.

Gelfer, J. (2010) Evangelical and Catholic Masculinities in Two Fatherhood Ministries, *Feminist Theology*, 19 (1): 36–53.

Gems, G. R. (1993) Sport, Religion, and Americanization: Bishop Sheil and the Catholic Youth Organization, *International Journal of the History of Sport*, 10 (2): 233–41.

Geertz, C. (1973) *The Interpretation of Cultures*, New York: Basic Books.

Giamatti, A. B. (1989/2011) *Take Time for Paradise: Americans and Their Games*, 2nd ed., London: Bloomsbury Publishing.

Gibbons, T., Dixon, K. and Braye, S. (2008) 'The Way It Was': An Account of Soccer Violence in the 1980s, *Soccer and Society*, 9 (1): 28–41.

Gill, R. (2003) *The 'Empty' Church Revisited*, rev. ed., Aldershot, UK: Ashgate.

Gogarty, P. and Williamson, I. (2009) *Winning at All Costs: Sporting Gods and Their Demons*, London: J. R. Books.

Goldstein, J. (ed.) (1998) *Why We Watch: The Attractions of Violent Entertainment*, Oxford: Oxford University Press.

Gore, W. (2011) I Pray for My Opponents before Fights, *Catholic Herald*, 16 September, 7.

Grace, D. J. (2000) Values, Sport and Education, *Journal of Christian Education*, 43 (2): 7–17.

Green, R. (2007) *Babies by Design: The Ethics of Genetic Choice*, New Haven, CT: Yale University Press.

Greenleaf, R. K. (1977/2002) *Servant Leadership: A Journey into the Nature of Legitimate Power and Greatness*, Mahwah, NJ: Paulist Press.

Griffith, R. (2004) *Born Again Bodies: Flesh and Spirit in American Christianity*, Berkley, CA, USA: University of California Press.

Grimshaw, M. (2012) The Oval Opiate? The History and Analysis of an Idea—and Claim, *International Journal of Religion and Sport*, 2 (Spring).

Gruneau, R. S. (1980) Freedom and Constraint: The Paradoxes of Play, Games and Sports, *Journal of Sport History*, 7 (3): 68–86.

Gudorf, M. E. (1998) The Use of PALH in Ephesians 6:12, *Journal of Biblical Literature*, 117 (2): 331–35.

Gumbrecht, H. U. (2006) *In Praise of Athletic Beauty*, Cambridge, MA: Belknap Press of Harvard University Press.

Gurock, J. S. (2005) *Judaism's Encounter with American Sports*, Bloomington: Indiana University Press.

Guttman, A. (1978/2004) *From Ritual to Record: The Nature of Modern Sports*, New York: Columbia University Press.

Haley, B. (1978) *The Healthy Body and Victorian Culture*, Cambridge, MA: Harvard University Press.

Hall, D. E. (1994) *Muscular Christianity: Embodying the Victorian Age*, Cambridge: Cambridge University Press.

Hamilton, M. (2002) Shamelessness and Its Effects on Contemporary Sport, paper presented at the 30th International Association of Philosophy of Sport Conference, Penn State University, 23–27 October.

Hamilton, M. (2004) There's No Lying in Baseball, in E. Bronson (Ed.), *Baseball and Philosophy*, Chicago: Open Court Press, 126–38.

Hamilton, M. (2006) Elective Performance Enhancement Surgery for Athletes: Should It Be Resisted, *Gymnica*, 36 (2): 39–46.

Hamilton, M. (2008a) Is the Gridiron Holy Ground? in W. M. Austin (Ed.), *Football and Philosophy: Going Deep*, Lexington: University of Kentucky Press, 183–95.

Hamilton, M. (2008b) Sport as Spectacle and the Perversion of Play, in D. Deardorff II and J. White (Eds.), *The Image of God in the Human Body: Essays on Christianity and Sports,* Lampeter, Wales: Edwin Mellen Press, 173–93.

Hamilton, M. (2009) Providence, Prayer and Sport, paper presented at the Annual Conference of the International Association of the Philosophy of Sport, Seattle University, Seattle, Washington, 27–30 August.

Hamilton, M. (2011) An Augustinian Critique of our Relationship to Sport, in J. Parry, M. S. Nesti and N. J. Watson (Eds.), *Theology, Ethics and Transcendence in Sports,* London: Routledge, 25–34.

Hamilton, M. and Bassham, G. (2007) Hardwood Dojos: What Basketball Can Teach Us about Character and Success, in J. Walls and G. Bassham (Eds.), *Basketball and Philosophy*, Lexington: University of Kentucky Press, 44–56.

Hargreaves, J. (2001) *Sporting Females: Critical Issues in the History and Sociology of Women's Sports*, London: Routledge.

Hargreaves, J. (2007) Sport, Exercise, and the Female Muslim Body: Negotiating Islam, Politics and Male Power, in J. Hargreaves and P. Vertinsky (Eds.), *Physical Culture, Power, and the Body*, London: Routledge, 74–100.

Harper, R. (2012) New Frontiers: *Wild at Heart* and Post Promise Keepers Manhood, *Journal of Religion and Popular Culture*, 24 (1): 97–112.

Harrison, J. R. (2008) Paul and the Athletic Ideal in Antiquity: A Case Study in Wrestling with Word and Image, in S. E. Porter (Ed.), *Paul's World*, Leiden and Boston: E. J. Brill, 81–109.

Harvey, L. (2012) Celebrating Contingency: Towards a Christian Theology of Sport, *International Journal of Religion and Sport*, 2.

Hastings, E. (2004) Spirituality in Sport, *Spirituality*, (May/June): 160–66.

Hastings, E. and DelleMonache, L. (2007) Promoting the Spiritual Growth and Character Development of Student Athletes, paper presented at the Institute on College Student Values, 9 February. Available online at http://studentvalues.fsu.edu/Hastings%20and%20DelleMonache_SV%20Paper.pdf (accessed 1 July 2011).

Hastings, E., DelleMonache, L. M., Kelley, J. and Nazar, K. (2006) Mission Integration in Athletic Departments of Catholic Colleges and Universities. Available online at http://www.neumann.edu/mission/ISSCD/ACCU_Study_Report_Color.pdf and http://www.neumann.edu/mission/ISSCD/accu_study.asp (accessed 14 June 2012).

Hawkins, B. (2000) A Critical Reading of a Promise Keepers Event: The Interworkings of Race, Religion, and Sport, *Sociology of Sport Online*, 3 (1): 1–11.

Heddendorf, R. (1994/2006) From Faith to Fun: Humor as Invisible Religion, in G. Van Andel, P. Heintzman and T. Visker (Eds.), *Christianity and Leisure: Issues in a Pluralistic Society*, rev. ed., Sioux Center, IA: Dordt College Press, 252–62.

Hefner, P. (2009) The Animal that Aspires to Be an Angel: The Challenge of Transhumanism, *Dialog: A Journal of Theology*, 48 (2): 158–67.

Heintzman, P. (2003a) Leisure and Spirituality: The Re-Emergence of an Historical Relationship, *Parks and Recreation Canada*, 60 (5): 30–31.

Heintzman, P. (2003b) The Wilderness Experience and Spirituality: What Recent Research Tells Us, *Journal of Physical Education Leisure and Dance*, 74 (6): 27–31.

Heintzman, P. (2006) Implications for Leisure from a Review of the Biblical Concepts of Sabbath and Rest, in P. Heintzman, G. Van Andel and T. Visker (Eds.), *Christianity and Leisure: Issues in a Pluralistic Society*, Sioux Center, IA: Dordt College Press, 14–31.

Heintzman, P., Van Andel, G. and Visker, T. (eds.) (1994/2006) *Christianity and Leisure: Issues in a Pluralistic Society*, Sioux Center, IA: Dordt College Press.

Helman, A. (2008) Sport on the Sabbath: Controversy in 1920s and 1930s Jewish Palestine, *International Journal of the History of Sport*, 25 (1): 41–64.

Henderson, W. E. (1997) The Athletic Imagery of Paul, *Theological Educator*, 56: 30–37.

Henkel, S. (2007) Honouring God through Sports Competition, *Journal of Christian Education*, 50 (2): 33–43.

Heskins, J. and Baker, M (eds.) (2006) *Footballing Lives: As Seen by Chaplains in the Beautiful Game*, Norwich, UK: Canterbury Press.

Hess, J. (2012) *Sportuality: Finding Joy in Games*, Bloomington, IN, USA: BalboaPress.

Higgs, R. J. (1981) *Laurel and Thorn: The Athlete in American Literature*, Lexington: University Press of Kentucky.

Higgs, R. J. (1982) *Sports: A Reference Guide*, London: Greenwood Press.

Higgs, R. J. (1983) Muscular Christianity, Holy Play, and Spiritual Exercises: Confusion about Christ in Sports and Religion, *Arete: The Journal of Sports Literature*, 1: 59–85.

Higgs, R. J. (1985) Religion & Sports: Three Muscular Christians in American Literature, in W. L. Umphlett (Ed.), *American Sport Culture: The Humanistic Dimension*, Lewisburg, PA.: Bucknell University Press, 226–34.

Higgs, R. J. (1990) The Edenic and Agonic: Sports Literature and the Theory of Play, in W. L. Umphlett (Ed.), *The Achievement of American Sport Literature: A Critical Appraisal*, Madison, NJ: Fairleigh Dickinson University Press, 143–57.

Higgs, R. J. (1995) *God in the Stadium: Sports and Religion in America*, Lexington: University Press of Kentucky.

Higgs, R. J. and Braswell, M. C. (2004) *An Unholy Alliance: The Sacred and Modern Sports*, Macon: Mercer University Press.

Hill, D. (2005) *Walking with God: Physically and Spiritually*, Abilene, TX: Coach Book Company.

Hoberman, J. (1992) *Mortal Engines: The Science of Performance and the Dehumanization of Sport*, Caldwell, NJ: Blackburn Press.

Hochstetler, D. R. (2009) Striving Towards Maturity: On the Relationship between Prayer and Sport, *Christian Education Journal*, 6 (2): 325–336.

Hochstetler, D. R., Hopsicker, P. and Kretchmar, S. R. (2008) The Ambiguity of Embodiment and Sport: Overcoming Theological Dichotomies, in D. Deardorff and J. White (Eds.), *A Christian Theology of Sport*, Lampeter, Wales: Edwin Mellen Press, 61–77.

Hoffman, S. J. (1976) The Athletae Dei: Missing the Meaning in Sport, *Journal of the Philosophy of Sport*, III: 42–51.

Hoffman, S. J. (1985) Evangelicalism and the Revitalization of Religious Ritual in Sport, *Arete*, 2: 63–87.

Hoffman, S. J. (1986) The Sanctification of Sport: Can the Mind of Christ Coexist with the Killer Instinct, *Christianity Today*, (April): 17–21.

Hoffman, S. J. (1991) Sport and Religion: A Field of Conflict, *American Baptist*, (December): 19–23.

Hoffman, S. J. (ed.) (1992a) Recovering the Sacred in Sport, in S. J. Hoffman (Ed.), *Sport and Religion*, Champaign, IL: Human Kinetics, 153–59.

Hoffman, S. J. (ed.) (1992b) *Sport and Religion*, Champaign, IL: Human Kinetics.

Hoffman, S. J. (ed.) (1992c) Sport as Religious Experience, in S. J. Hoffman (ed.), *Sport and Religion*, Champaign, IL: Human Kinetics, 63–81.

Hoffman, S. J. (1994/2006) Sport, Play, and Leisure in Christian Experience, in G. Van Andel., P. Heintzman and T. Visker (Eds.) *Christianity and Leisure: Issues in a Pluralistic Society*, rev. ed., Sioux Center, IA: Dordt College Press, 139–54.

Hoffman, S. J. (1999) The Decline of Civility and the Rise of Religion in American Sport, *Quest*, 51: 69–84.

Hoffman, S. J. (2003) Toward Narrowing the Gulf between Sport and Religion, *Word and World*, 23 (3): 303–11.

Hoffman, S. J. (2010a) *Good Game: Christians and the Culture of Sport*, Waco, TX: Baylor University Press.

Hoffman, S. J. (2010b) Whatever Happened to Play? How Christians Have Succumbed to the Sports Culture—and What Might Be Done about It, *Christianity Today*, (February): 21–25.

Hoffman, S. J. (2011) Prayer out of Bounds, in J. Parry. M. S. Nesti and N. J. Watson (Eds.), *Theology, Ethics and Transcendence in Sports*, London: Routledge, 35–63.

Hogan, W. R. (1967) Sin in Sports, in R. Slovenko and J. A. Knight (Eds.), *Motivations in Play, Games and Sports*, Springfield, IL: Charles C. Thomas Publisher, 121–47.

Holmes, A. (1981) Towards a Christian Play Ethic, *Christian Scholar's Review*, XI (1): 41–48.

Holowchak, M. A. (2008) "They Don't Pay Nobody to Be Humble!" in M. W. Austin (Ed.), *Football and Philosophy: Going Deep*, Lexington: University of Kentucky Press, 31–40.

Holt, R. (1990) *Sport and the British: A Modern History*, Oxford: Clarendon Press.

Hong, F. (2006) Innocence Lost: Child Athletes in China, in R. Giulianotti and D. McArdle (Eds.), *Sport, Civil Liberties and Human Rights*, London: Routledge, 46–62.

Hopsicker, P. (2009) Miracles in Sport: Finding the 'Ears to Hear' and the 'Eyes to See,' *Sport, Ethics and Philosophy*, 3 (1): 75–93.

Howe, P. D. (2004) *Sport, Professionalism and Pain*, London: Routledge.

Howson, J. S. (1868) *The Metaphors of St. Paul*, London: Strahan and Co.

Hoverd, W. (2005) *Working out My Salvation: The Contemporary Gym and the Promise of "Self" Transformation*, Sydney: Meyer and Meyer Sport.

Hoverd, W. and Sibley, C. G. (2007) Immoral Bodies: The Implicit Association between Moral Discourse and the Body, *Journal for the Scientific Study of Religion*, 46 (3): 391–403.

Hubbard, S. (1998) *Faith in Sports: Athletes and their Religion on and off the Field*, New York: Doubleday.

Hübenthal, C. (2012) Morality and Beauty: Sport at the Service of the Human Being, in M. Mieth, N. Müller and K. Lixey (Eds.), *Sport and Christianity: Anthropological, Theological and Pastoral Challenges*, Washington, DC: Catholic University of America Press, 68–88.

Huggins, M. (2004) *Victorians and Sport*, rev. ed., London: Hambledon, Continuum.

Hughes, A. (1996) Muscular Judaism and the Jewish Rugby League Competition in Sydney, 1924 to 1927, *Sporting Traditions: Journal of the Australian Society for Sport History*, 13 (1): 61–80.

Hughes, T. (1857) *Tom Brown's Schooldays*, London: Macmillan.

Huizinga, J. (1950) *Homo Ludens: A Study of the Play Element in Culture*, Boston: Beacon.

Hullinger, J. M. (2004) The Historical Background of Paul's Athletic Allusions, *Bibliotheca Sacra*, 161 (643): 343–59.

Hunt, K. (1999) Pressure to Win? But I'm a Christian Coach at a Christian College, in J. Byl and T. Visker (Eds.), *Physical Education, Sports and Wellness: Looking to God as We Look at Ourselves*, Sioux Center, IA: Dordt College Press, 235–47.

Hyland, D. (1978) Competition and Friendship, *Journal of the Philosophy of Sport*, 5 (Fall): 27–37.

Hyland, D. (1988) Opponents, Contestants, and Competitors: The Dialectic of Sport, in W. J. Morgan and K. V. Meier (Eds.), *Philosophic Inquiry in Sport*, 2nd ed., Champaign, IL: Human Kinetics, 177–82.

Hyland, D. (1990) *Philosophy of Sport*, New York: Paragon House.

Ilundian-Agurraza, J. (2007) Kant Goes Skydiving: Understanding the Extreme by the Way of the Sublime, in M. McNamee (Ed.), *Philosophy, Risk and Adventure Sports*, London: Routledge, 149–67.

Jackson, S. A. and Csikszentmihalyi, M. (1999) *Flow in Sports: The Keys to Optimal Experiences and Performances*, Champaign, IL: Human Kinetics.

Jarvie, G. (2012) Sport, Religion and Spirituality, in *Sport, Culture and Society: An Introduction*, 2nd ed., London: Routledge, 324–40.

Jesperson, E. and McNamee, M. J. (eds.) (2009) *Ethics, Dis/Ability and Sports*, London: Routledge.

John Paul II. (1997) *The Theology of the Body: Human Love in the Divine Plan*, Boston: Pauline Books and Media.

Johnson, B. (2006) *Dreaming with God: Secrets of Redesigning Your World through God's Creative Flow*), Shippensburg, PA: Destiny Image Publishers.

Johnston, R. K. (1983) *The Christian at Play*, Grand Rapids, MI: William B. Eerdmans Publishing Company.

Johnston, R. K. (2006) *Reel Spirituality: Theology and Film in Dialogue*, Grand Rapids, MI: Baker Books.

Joisten, K. (2012) Man, Morality and the Athletic Idol—Yesterday and Today, in K. Lixey, C. Hübenthal, D. Mieth and N. Müller (Eds.), *Sport and Christianity: A Sign of the Times in the Light of Faith*, Washington, DC: Catholic University of America Press, 16–44.

Jolley, M. (2005) *Safe at Home: A Memoir on God, Baseball and Family*, Macon, GA: Mercer University Press.

Jones, P. N. (2004) Ultrarunners and Chance Encounters with 'Absolute Unitary Being,' *Anthropology of Consciousness*, 15 (2): 39–50.

Joslin, R. D. (2003) *Running the Spiritual Path: A Runner's Guide to Breathing, Meditating, and Exploring the Prayerful Dimension of the Sport*, New York: St. Martin Press.

Jowett, S. and Wylleman, P. (2006) Editorial: Interpersonal Relationships in Sport and Exercise Settings: Crossing the Chasm, *Psychology of Sport and Exercise*, 7: 119–23.

Kajava, M. (2002) When Did the Isthmian Games Return to the Isthmus (Rereading "Corinth" 8.3.153)? *Classical Philology*, 97: 2.

Kammogne, F. (2011) Promoting Inter-Religious Dialogue through Sport, in Liberia Editrice Vaticana (Ed.), *Sport, Education and Faith: Toward a New Season for Catholic Sports Associations (A Series of Studies edited by The Pontifical Council for the Laity)*, Citta del Vaticano, Italy: Liberia Editrice Vaticana, 157–62.

Kant, E. (1790/1952) *The Critique of Judgement*, Oxford: Oxford University Press.

Kaufman, H. and Galily, Y. (2009) Body Culture, Religion and Jewish Identity, *Stadion: International Journal of the History of Sport*, 35: 27–45.

Kay, T. (ed.) (2009) *Fathering through Sport and Leisure*, London: Routledge.

Keddie, J. W. (2007) *Running the Race: Eric Liddell, Olympic Champion and Missionary*, Darlington, UK: Evangelical Press.

Kelly, P. (2011) Flow, Sport and Spiritual Life, in J. Parry, M. S. Nesti and N. J. Watson (Eds.), *Theology, Ethics and Transcendence in Sports*, London: Routledge, 163–80.

Kelly, P. (2012) *Catholic Perspectives on Sports: From Medieval to Modern Times*, Mahwah, NJ: Paulist Press.

Kelly, B. C. Hoffman, S. J. and Gill, D. L. (1990) The Relationship between Competitive Orientation and Religious Orientation, *Journal of Sport Behavior*, 13 (3): 145–156.

Kerrigan, M. (1986) Sports and the Christian Life: Reflections on Pope Paul II's Theology of Sports, *New Catholic World*, July/August: 182–86.

Kessel, A. (2010) *Six Nations: 'Rugby Is Not What Fuels My Happiness,' Says Murray. Scotland Prop Euan Murray on Why He Refuses to Play on Sundays and Will Not Watch Their First Match.* Available online at http://www.guardian.co.uk/sport/2010/feb/04/six-nations-scotland-euan-murray-interview (accessed 17 May 2011).

Kidd, B. (2010) Epilogue: The Struggles Must Continue, *Sport in Society*, 13 (1): 157–65.

Kimball, R. (2008) Muscular Mormonism, *International Journal of the History of Sport*, 25 (5): 549–78.

King, J. R. (1986) The Moment as a Factor in Emotional Well-Being, *Journal of Religion and Health*, 25 (3): 2017–2220.

Kirk, K. E. (1949) *Some Principles of Moral Theology*, New York: Longmans.

Klein, J. Z. and Austen, I. (2011) Hockey Hangover Turns into Riot Embarrassment, *New York Times*, 16 June. Available online at http://www.nytimes.com/2011/06/17/world/americas/17vancouver.html?_r=1&pagewanted=print (accessed 29 June 2011).

Kliever, L. D. (2001) *God and Games in Modern Culture*, in J. L. Price (Ed.), *From Season to Season: Sports as American Religion*, Macon, GA: Mercer University Press, 39–48.

Kluck, T. (2009a) *The Reason for Sports: A Christian Manifesto*, Chicago: Moody Publishers.

Kluck, T. (2009b) Sports and Humility: Why I Love Muhammad Ali (But Why He Also May Have Ruined Sports), in *The Reason for Sports: A Christian Manifesto*, Chicago: Moody Publishers, 129–38.

Koch, A. (1994) *With All Means to Success? Ethical Reflections on Top-Performance Sports* (originally published in German). Available online at http://www.con-spiration.de/koch/english/success-e.html (accessed 3 January 2012).

Koch, A. (1999) *The Apostle Paul and Sports* (originally published in German). Available online at http://www.con-spiration.de/koch/english/paul-e.html (accessed 3 January 2012).

Koch, A. (2003) *Play and Sport at the Jesuit College "Stella Matutina" Feldkirch* (originally published in German). Available online at http://www.con-spiration.de/koch/english/feldkirch-e.html (accessed 3 January 2012).

Koch, A. (2005a) *Against the Unchaining of the Victory Code: Ethical Notes on Sport* (originally published in German). Available online at http://www.con-spiration.de/koch/english/victory-e.html (accessed 3 January 2012).

Koch, A. (2005b) *The Antique Athletic and Agonistic in the Focus of the Criticism of Tertullian of Carthago and of Other Writers of Early Christianity* (originally published in German). Available online at http://www.con-spiration.de/koch/english/tertullian-e.html (accessed 3 January 2012).

Koch, A. (2005c) *Pierre de Coubertin and His Relation to the Catholic Church* (originally published in German). Available online at http://www.con-spiration.de/koch/english/coubertin-e.html (accessed 3 January 2012).

Koch, A. (2012) The Christian View of Sport: Its Foundations in the Holy Scriptures and in the Church Father's Writings, in K. Lixey, C. Hübenthal, D. Mieth and N. Müller (Eds.), *Sport and Christianity: A Sign of the Times in the Light of Faith*, Washington, DC: Catholic University of America Press, 89–112.

Available online at http://www.con-spiration.de/koch/english/menschenbild-e. html. (accessed 14 June 2012).

Koeing, H. (2001) *Handbook of Religion and Health*, Oxford: Oxford University Press.

Koeing, H. (2008) *Medicine, Religion and Health: Where Science and Spirituality Meet*, West Conshohocken, PA: Templeton Foundation Press.

Kohlberg, L. (1984) *Essays in Moral Development: The Psychology of Moral Development*, San Francisco, CA: Harper and Row.

Kohn, A. (1992) *No Contest: The Case against Competition*, rev. ed., New York: Houghton Mifflin.

Krattenmaker, T. (2010) *Onward Christian Athletes: Turning Ballparks into Pulpits and Players into Preachers*, New York: Rowman and Littlefield Publishers.

Kreider, A. J. (2003) Prayers for Assistance as Unsporting Behaviour, *Journal of the Philosophy of Sport*, XXX: 17–25.

Krentz, E. (2003) Paul, Games and the Military, in J. P. Sampley (Ed.), *Paul in the Greco-Roman World: A Handbook*, Harrisburg, PA: Trinity Press International, 344–83.

Kretchmar, S. (1983) Ethics and Sport: An Overview, *Journal of the Philosophy of Sport*, X: 21–32.

Kretchmar, S. R. (1995) From Test to Contest: An Analysis of Two Kinds of Counterpoint in Sport, in J. W. Morgan and K. V. Meier (Eds.), *Philosophic Inquiry in Sport*, 2nd ed., Champaign, IL: Human Kinetics, 36–41.

Kretchmar, S. R. (1998) Soft Metaphysics: A Precursor to Good Sports Ethics, in M. McNamee and J. Parry (Eds.), *Ethics and Sport*, London: Routledge, 19–34.

Kretchmar, S. R. (2011) Why Dichotomies Make It Difficult to See Games as Gifts of God, in J. Parry, M. S. Nesti and N. J. Watson (Eds.), *Theology, Ethics and Transcendence in Sports*, London: Routledge, 185–200.

Kretschmann, R. and Benz, C. (2012) Morality of Christian Athletes in Competitive Sports—A Review, *Sport Science Review*, XXI (1–2): 5–20.

Krüger, A. (1993) The Origins of Pierre de Coubertin's Religio Athletae, *Olympika*, 2: 91–102.

Kugelmass, J. (2007) *Jews, Sports, and the Rites of Citizenship*, Champaign: University of Illinois Press.

Kuschel, K-J. (1994) *Laughter: A Theological Reflection*, London: CSM Press.

Kwauk, C. (2007) Goal! The Dream Begins: Globalizing an Immigrant Muscular Christianity, *Soccer and Society*, 8 (1): 75–90.

Ladd, T. and Mathisen, J. A. (1999) *Muscular Christianity: Evangelical Protestants and the Development of American Sport*, Ada, MI, USA: Baker Books.

Lasch, N. (1980) The Degradation of Sport, in *The Culture of Narcissism: American Life in an Age of Diminished Expectations*, London: Abacus: 100–24.

Lawrence, I. (2011) Living in a Sectarian Maelstrom: A Christian Professional Football Player's Perspective, in J. Parry, M. N. Nesti and N. J. Watson (Eds.), *Theology, Ethics and Transcendence in Sports*, London: Routledge, 82–102.

Lee, J. W. (2003) Prayer in American Scholastic Sport, *Sociology of Sport Online*, 6 (1). Available online at http://physed.otago.ac.nz/sosol/v6il/v6il_2.html (accessed 18 January 2011).

Lee, J. W. (2005) Prayer and Athletics: A Legal Profile, *Smart Online Journal*, 1 (II): 23–27. Available online at http://www.thesmartjournal.com/prayer.pdf (accessed 27 June 2011).

Lelwica, M. M. (1999) *Starving for Salvation: The Spiritual Dimensions of Eating Problems among American Girls and Women*, New York: Oxford University Press.

Lelwica, M. M. (2000) Losing Their Way to Salvation: Women, Weight Loss, and the Salvation Myth of Culture Lite, in B. D. Forbes and J. H. Mahan (Eds.), *Religion and Popular Culture in America*, London: University of California Press, 180–200.

Leone, C. and Leone, D. (1992) Death in the Ring: A Pastoral Dilemma, in S. J. Hoffman (Ed.), *Sport and Religion*, Champaign, IL: Human Kinetics, 265–70.

Levine, J. (1967) Humor in Play and Sports, in R. Slovenko and J. A. Knight (Eds.), *Motivations in Play, Games and Sports*, Springfield, IL: Charles C. Thomas Publisher, 55–62.

Lewis, C. S. (1952/1997) *Mere Christianity*, New York: Harper Collins.

Lewis, C. S. (1955) *Surprised by Joy*, New York: Harcourt, Brace and World, Harvest Books.

Liberia Editrice Vaticana. (2006) *The World of Sport Today: A Field of Christian Mission (A Series of Studies edited by the Pontifical Council for the Laity)*, Citta del Vaticano, Italy: Liberia Editrice Vaticana.

Liberia Editrice Vaticana. (2008) *Sport: An Educational and Pastoral Challenge (A Series of Studies edited by the Pontifical Council for the Laity)*, Citta del Vaticano, Italy: Liberia Editrice Vaticana.

Liberia Editrice Vaticana. (2011) *Sport, Education and Faith: Toward a New Season for Catholic Sports Associations (A Series of Studies edited by the Pontifical Council for the Laity)*, Citta del Vaticano, Italy: Liberia Editrice Vaticana.

Lipe, R. (2005) *Heart of a Champion: A Year Long Daily Devotional for the People of Sport*, Grand Island, NE, USA: Cross Training Publishing.

Lipoński, W. (2009) Sport: From Profound Religious Expressions to Secular Ritual, *Stadion: International Journal of the History of Sport*, 35: 67–86.

Lixey, K. (2012) Sport in the Magisterium of Pius XII, in K. Lixey, C. Hübenthal, D. Mieth and N. Müller (Eds.), *Sport and Christianity: A Sign of the Times in the Light of Faith*, Washington, DC: Catholic University of America Press, 113–37.

Lixey, K., Hübenthal, C., Mieth, D. and Müller, N. (2012) *Sport and Christianity: A Sign of the Times in the Light of Faith*, Washington, DC: Catholic University of America Press.

Lucas, J. A. (1975) Victorian 'Muscular Christianity': Prologue to the Olympic Games Philosophy (Part 1), *Olympic Review*, 97–98: 456–60.

Lucas, J. A. (1976) Victorian 'Muscular Christianity': Prologue to the Olympic Games Philosophy (Part 2), *Olympic Review*, 99–100: 49–52.

Lumpkin, A., Stoll, S. and Beller, J. (2002) *Sport Ethics: Applications for Fair Play*, 4th ed., St. Louis, MO: McGraw Hill.

Lupson, P. (2006) *Thank God for Football?* Elk Grove, CA, USA: Azure Press.

Lynn, Q., Pargament, K. I. and Krane, V. (2010) Sport and Spirituality: A Review of the Literature, in C. H. Chang (Ed.), *Handbook of Sports Psychology*, New York: Nova, 195–216.

Macaloon, J. J. (ed.) (2009) *Muscular Christianity and the Colonial and Post-Colonial World*, London: Routledge.

Macarthur, J. (2003) *Hard to Believe: The High Cost and the Infinite Value of Following Jesus*, Nashville, TN: Thomas Nelson.

Macdonald, D. (1998) Who Are You? Identity and Religion in Physical Education Teacher Education, *Sociology of Sport Online*, 1 (1): 12. Available online at http://physed.otago.ac.nz/sosol/v1i1/v1i1a4.htm (accessed 18 July 2011).

Macdonald, D. and Kirk, D. (1999) Pedagogy, the Body and Christian Identity, *Sport, Education and Society*, 2 (4): 131–42.

MacIntyre, A. (2007) *After Virtue: A Study in Moral Theory*, Notre Dame, IN: Notre Dame University Press.

Magdalinski, T. and Chandler, T. J. L. (eds.) (2002) *With God on Their Side: Sport in the Service of Religion*, London: Routledge.

Mangan, J. A. (1981/2000) *Athleticism in the Victorian and Edwardian Public School*, London: Frank Cass and Co.

Mangan, J. A. (1982) Philathlete Extraordinary: A Portrait of Victorian Moralist Edward Bowen, *Journal of Sport History*, 9 (3): 23–40.

Mangan, J. A. (2011) *'Manufactured' Masculinity: Making Imperial Manliness, Morality and Militarism*, London: Routledge.

Mangan, J. A. and Hickey, C. (2008) An Exceptional Pioneer: Be Strong for Christ, *Soccer & Society*, 9 (5): 671–89.

Mangan, J. A., Majumdar, B. and Dyreson, M. (2009) Series Editor's Foreword, in J. A. Mangan and D. Jinxia (Eds.), *Beijing 2008: Preparing for Glory: Chinese Challenge in the 'Chinese Century*,' London: Routledge, xii–xiii.

Mangan, J. A. and Walvin, C. (1987) *Manliness and Morality: Middle-Class Masculinity in Britain and America, 1800–1940*, Manchester: Manchester University Press.

Manning, B (2002) *Abba's Child: The Cry of the Heart for Intimate Belonging*, Colarado Springs, C, USA: NavPress.

Mara, E. and Barber, H. (2000) Reconciling Aggression, Moral Reasoning, and Christian Beliefs in Sport, *Research Quarterly for Exercise and Sport*, 71 (1): 102.

Maranise, A. M. J. (2009) Practice Makes Perfect: Growing Spiritually through Sports Participation, *The Catholic World: A Journal at the Intersection of Faith and Culture*, 243 (1453): 1–4.

Martens, R. (1979) About Smocks and Jocks, *Journal of Sport Psychology*, 1: 94–99.

Martens, R. (2004) *Successful Coaching*, Champaign, IL: Human Kinetics.

Martin, J. (2011) *Between Heaven and Mirth: Why Joy, Humor, and Laughter Are at the Heart of the Spiritual Life*, New York: HarperOne.

Marty, M. E. (2007) Blood Sport, *Christian Century*, 27 (November): 47.

Marx, J. (2003) *Season of Life: A Football Star, a Boy, a Journey to Manhood*, London: Simon and Schuster.

Maslow, A. (1968) *Toward a Psychology of Being*, New York: Van Nostrand.

Mason, B. (2003) *Into the Stadium: An Active Guide to Sport and Recreation Ministry in the Local Church*, Uckfield, East Sussex, UK: Spring Harvest Publishing.

Mason, B. (2011) *Beyond Gold: What Every Church Needs to Know about Sports Ministry*, Milton Keynes, UK: Authentic Publishing.

Mathisen, J. (1990) Reviving Muscular Christianity: Gil Dodds and the Institutionalization of Sport Evangelism, *Sociological Focus*, 23 (3): 233–49.

Mathisen, J. (1994/2006) Towards an Understanding of Muscular Christianity: Religion, Sport and Culture in the Modern World, in P. Heintzman, G .E. Van Andel and T. L. Visker (Eds.), *Christianity and Leisure: Issues in a Pluralistic Society*, Sioux Center, IA: Dordt College, 192–205.

Mathisen, J. (1998) "I'm Majoring in SPORT Ministry": Religion and Sport in Christian Colleges. Available online at http://www.goodnewssports.com/support/article/art008.html (accessed 18 January 2011).

Mathisen, J. (2001) American Sport as a Folk Religion: Examining a Test of Its Strength, in J. Price (Ed.), *From Season to Reason: Sports as American Religion*, Macon, GA: Mercer University Press, 141–59.

Mathisen, J. (2002) Toward a Biblical Theology of Sport, paper presented at the Annual Meeting of the Association for Christianity, Sport, Leisure and Health (ACSLH), Wheaton College, IL, 7–9 June.

Mathisen, J. (2005) Sport, in Helen R. Abaugh (Ed.), *Handbook of Religion and Social Institutions*, New York: Springer, 279–99.

Mazza, C. (2012) Sport in the Magisterium of John Paul II, in K. Lixey, C. Hübenthal, D. Mieth and N. Müller (Eds.), *Sport and Christianity: A Sign of the Times in the Light of Faith* Washington, DC: Catholic University of America Press, 138–58.

McCown, L. and Gin, V. J. (2003) *Focus on Sport in Ministry*, Marietta, GA: 360° Sports.

McCuaig, L., Öhmans, M. and Wright, J. (2011) Shepherds in the Gym: Employing a Pastoral Power Analytic on Caring Teaching in HPE, *Sport, Education and Society*, 1–19. Available online at http://www.tandfonline.com/doi/full/10.108 0/13573322.2011.611496. (accessed 14 June 2012)

McDevitt, P.F. (1997) Muscular Catholicism: Nationalism, Masculinity and Gaelic Team Sports, 1884–1916, *Gender & History*, 9 (2): 262–84.

McFadyen, A. (1990) *The Call to Personhood: A Christian Theory of the Individual in Social Relationships*, Cambridge: Cambridge University Press.

McFee, G (2004) The Project of a Moral Laboratory; and Particularism, in G. McFee (author) *Sport, Rules and Values: Philosophical Investigations into the Nature of Sport*, London: Routledge, 129–148.

McGrath, A. (2008) *Christianity's Dangerous Idea: The Protestant Revolution—A History from the Sixteenth to the Twenty First*, New York: HarperOne.

McGuire, B., Cooper, W. and Park, M. (2006) Pastoral Care, Spirituality and Physical Education, *Pastoral Care and Education: The Journal of the National Association for Pastoral Care in Education*, 24 (4): 13–19.

McIntosh, P. (1979a) Ethics of Muscular Christianity, in *Fair Play: Ethics in Sport and Education*, London: Heinemann, 20–36.

McIntosh, P. (1979b) Fair Play and Child's Play, in *Fair Play: Ethics in Sport and Education*, London: Heinemann, 164–74.

McIntosh, P. (1979c) *Fair Play: Ethics in Sport and Education*, London: Heinemann.

McLeod, H. (2003) "Thews and Sinews": Nonconformity and Sport, in D. Bebbington and T. Larsen (Eds.), *Modern Christianity and Cultural Aspirations*, Sheffield, UK: Continuum International Publishing Group, 28–46.

McLeod, H. (2007) Sport and the English Sunday School, 1869–1939, in S. Orchard and J. H. Y. Briggs (Eds.), *The Sunday School Movement*, Milton Keynes, UK: Paternoster Press: 109–23.

McLeod, H. (forthcoming) *Religion and the Rise of Sport in Modern England*.

McNamee, M. (2007a) Editorial: Sport, Ethics and Philosophy: Context, History and Prospects, *Sport, Ethics and Philosophy*, 1 (1): 1–6.

McNamee, M. (2007b) *Philosophy, Risk and Adventure Sports*, London: Routledge.

McNamee, M. (2008) *Sports, Virtues and Vices: Morality Plays*, London: Routledge.

McNamee, M. (2010) *The Ethics of Sports: A Reader*, London: Routledge.

McNamee, M. (2011) Sport and Virtue: Integral to Education of the Person, in Liberia Editrice Vaticana (Ed.), *Sport, Education and Faith: Toward a New Season for Catholic Sports Associations (A Series of Studies edited by the Pontifical Council for the Laity)*, Citta del Vaticano, Italy: Liberia Editrice Vaticana, 35–49.

McNamee, M. J. and Parry, S. J. (1998) *Ethics and Sport*, London: Routledge.

McNeill, J. T. (1948) The Christian Athlete in Philippians 3:7–14, Christianity in Crisis, *Journal of Opinion*, 2: 106–7.

Mead, G. H. (1934) *Mind, Self and Society*, Chicago: University of Chicago Press.

Mead, M. (ed.) (1937) *Cooperation and Competition among Primitive Peoples*, New York: McGraw-Hill.

Mendelsohn, E. (ed.) (2009) *Jews and the Sporting Life: Studies in Contemporary Jewry XXIII*, Oxford: Oxford University Press.

Menninger, K. (1973) *Whatever Became of Sin?* New York: Hawthorn Books.

Merton, T. (1948) *Seeds of Contemplation*, Norfolk, CT: New Directions.

Messner, M. A. (1990) When Bodies Are Weapons: Masculinity and Violence in Sports, *International Review for the Sociology of Sport*, 25 (3): 203–18.

Messner, M. A., McKay, J. and Sabo, D. (eds.) (2000) *Masculinities, Gender Relations, and Sport*, London: Sage Publications.

Metzger, P. L. (2003) *The Word of Christ and the World of Culture: Sacred and Secular through the Theology of Karl Barth*, Cambridge: William B. Eedmans Publishing Company.

Meyer, A. (2009) Jewish and Christian Movements and Sport, In B. Houlihan and M. Green (Eds.), *The Routledge Handbook of Sport Development*, London: Routledge, 22–30.

Meyer, A. (2012) Radical Orthodoxy & Lance Armstrong: Shedding Light on Sport as Religious Experience, *Journal of Religion and Popular Culture*, 24 (3):

Meyer, A. and Watson, N. J. (forthcoming) Radical Orthodoxy and the Emergence of Spiritual Hero-Athletes: Examining Lance Armstrong's "Illness" Narrative, *Journal of Religion, Disability and Health*.

Miah, A. (2004) *Genetically Modified Athletes: Biomedical Ethics, Gene Doping and Sport*, London: Routledge.

Miah, A. (2010) The DREAM Gene for the Posthuman Athlete: Reducing Exercise-Induced Pain Sensations Using Gene Transfer, in R. R. Sands and L. Sands. (eds.), *The Anthropology of Sport and Human Movement: A Bicultural Perspective*, Lanham, MD: Lexington Books, 327–41.

Milbank, J and Oliver, S. (eds.) (2009) *The Radical Orthodoxy Reader*, London: Routledge.

Miller, D. L. (1969) *Gods and Games: Towards a Theology of Play*, Cleveland, OH: World Publishing Co.

Miller, D. L. (1971) Theology and Play Studies: An Overview, *Journal of the American Academy of Religion*, 39: 349–54.

Miller, W. R. and Delaney, H. D. (eds.) (2005) *Judeo-Christian Perspectives on Psychology: Human Nature, Motivation, and Change*, Washington, DC: American Psychological Association.

Millikan, M. (2006) The Muscular Christian Ethos in Post–Second World War American Liberalism: Women in Outward Bound 1962–1975, *International Journal of the History of Sport*, xxiii: 838–55.

Miroslaw, P. (2003) The Attitude of the Roman Catholic Church towards Sport and the Other Forms of Physical Culture in Poland in the Period of Structural Transformation (1989–2000), *Studies in Physical Culture and Tourism*, 10 (2): 57–67.

Moltmann, J. (1972) *Theology of Play*, New York: Harper.

Moltmann, J. (1989) Olympia between Politics and Religion, in G. Baum and J. Coleman (Eds.), *Sport (Concilium, 205.5)*, Edinburgh: T & T Clark, 101–9.

Montez de Oca, J. (2012) White Domestic Goddess on a Postmodern Plantation: Charity and Commodity Racism in *The Blind Side*, *Sociology of Sport*, 29: 131–150.

Moore, A. (2012) "Nearer My God to Thee"?—Theological Reflections on Mountaineering, *Anvil: An Evangelical Journal for Theology and Mission*, 28 (1).

Morgan, G. (2005) Rugby and Revivalism: Sport and Religion in Edwardian Wales, *International Journal of the History of Sport*, 22 (3): 434–56.

Morgan, J. W. (ed.) (2007) *Ethics in Sport*, 2nd ed., Champaign, IL: Human Kinetics.

Morgan, J. W. and Meir, K. (eds.) (1995) *Philosophic Inquiry in Sport*, 2nd ed., Champaign, IL: Human Kinetics.

Müller, N. (2011) Promoting Ecumenical Dialogue through Sport, in Liberia Editrice Vaticana (Ed.), *Sport, Education and Faith: Toward a New Season for Catholic Sports Associations (A Series of Studies edited by the Pontifical Council for the Laity)*, Citta del Vaticano, Italy: Liberia Editrice Vaticana, 151–56.

Müller, N. and Schäfer, C. (2010) *The Pastoral Messages (Homilies, Angelus Messages, Speeches, Letters) of Pope John Paul II that Refer to Sport: 1978–2005*. (Introduction by Monsignore Carlo Mazza), Compiled by Norbert Müller and Cornelius Schäfer with the help of the Office of Church and Sport of the Pontifical Council of the Laity (OCSPCL). Unpublished report received electronically from Father Kevin Lixey, head of the OCSPCL.

Munoz, L. (2009) The Birth of an International Catholic Federation: A European Matter, 1905–11, *International Journal of the History of Sport*, 26 (1): 3–20.

Murphy, M. and White, R. A. (1995) *In the Zone: Transcendent Experience in Sports*, London: Penguin.

Murphy-O'Connor, J. (2002) *St. Paul's Corinth: Texts and Archaeology*, Collegeville, MN: Liturgical Press.

Murray, M. A., Joyner, A. B., Burke, K. L., Wilson, M. J. and Zwald, A. D. (2005) The Relationship between Prayer and Team Cohesion in Collegiate Softball Teams, *Journal of Psychology and Christianity*, 24 (3): 233–39.

Neal, W. (1972) *Making an Athlete of God*, Los Angeles: Campus Crusade for Christ Publication.

Neal, W. (1981) *The Handbook of Athletic Perfection*, Milford, UK: Mott Media.

Neale, R. E. (1969) *In Praise of Play*, New York: Harper and Row.

Neddam, F. (2004) Constructing Masculinities under Thomas Arnold (1828–1842): Gender, Educational Policy and School Life in an Early-Victorian Public School, *Gender and Education*, 16 (3): 303–26.

Nesti, M. (2007a), Persons and Players: A Psychological Perspective, in J. Parry, S. Robinson, N. J. Watson and M. S. Nesti (Eds.), *Sport and Spirituality: An Introduction*, London: Routledge, 135–50.

Nesti, M. (2007b) The Spirit of Sport: An Existential Psychology Perspective, in J. Parry, S. Robinson, N. J. Watson and M. S. Nesti (Eds.), *Sport and Spirituality: An Introduction*, London: Routledge, 119–34.

Nesti, M. (2007c) Suffering, Sacrifice, Sport Psychology and the Spirit, in J. Parry, S. Robinson, N. J. Watson and M. S. Nesti (Eds.), *Sport and Spirituality: An Introduction*, London: Routledge, 151–69.

Nesti, M. (2011) Sport Psychology and Spirit in Professional Football, in J. Parry, M. N. Nesti and N. J. Watson (Eds.), *Theology, Ethics and Transcendence in Sports*, London: Routledge, 149–62.

Newman, J. (1989) *Competition in Religious Life*, Waterloo, Ontario, Canada: Wilfrid Laurier University Press.

Niebuhr, H. R. (1951) *Christ and Culture*, New York: Harper and Brothers.

Nixon, H. L. (1992) A Social Network Analysis of Influences of Athletes to Play with Pain and Injuries, *Journal of Sport and Social Issues*, 16 (2): 127–35.

Norman, E. (1987) Victorian Values: Stewart Headlam and the Christian Socialists, *History Today*, (April): 27–32.

Novak, M. (1967/1994) *The Joy of Sports: End Zones, Bases, Baskets, Balls and Consecration of the American Spirit*, New York: Basic Books.

Null, A. (2004) *Real Joy: Freedom to be your Best*, Ulm, Germany: Ebner and Spiegel.

Null, A. (2008a) "Finding the Right Place": Professional Sport as a Christian Vocation, in D. Deardorff II and J. White (Eds.), *The Image of God in the Human Body: Essays on Christianity and Sports*, Lampeter, Wales: Edwin Mellen Press, 315–66.

Null, A. (2008b) Some Preliminary Thoughts on Philosophies of Sports Ministry and Their Literature, in D. Deardorff II and J. White (Eds.), *The Image of God in the Human Body: Essays on Christianity and Sports*, Lampeter, Wales: Edwin Mellen Press, 241–54.

Oakley, D. (2012) Common Ground?: Sport and the Church, *The Bible in Transmission* (Sp. Ed., Sporting Life: Reflections on Sport, Culture and the Church), Spring: 8–10.

Obama, B. (2008) *Barack Obama: Dreams from my Father* (A Story of Race and Inheritance), Edinburgh, UK: Canongate Books Ltd.

O'Gorman, K. (2010a) Saint Paul and Pope John Paul II on Sport, in K. O'Gorman (Ed.), *Saving Sport: Sport, Society and Spirituality*, Dublin, Ireland: Columba Press, 14–28.

O'Gorman, K. (2010b) *Saving Sport: Sport, Society and Spirituality*, Dublin, Ireland: Columba Press.

O' Keefe, C. (1994/2006) Leisure at L'Arche: Communities of Faith of Persons of Developmental Disabilities, in G. Van Andel., P. Heintzman and T. Visker (Eds.), *Christianity and Leisure: Issues in a Pluralistic Society*, rev. ed., Sioux Center, IA: Dordt College Press, 116–24.

Olgilvie, B. and Tutko, T. (1971) If You Want to Build Character, Try Something Else, *Psychology Today*, 5: 60.

Olonga, H. (2010) *Blood, Sweat and Treason: Henry Olonga, My Story* (with Derek Clements), Kingston Upon Thames, Surrey, UK: Vision Sports Publishing.

Oriard, M. (1991) *Sporting with the Gods: The Rhetoric of Play and Game in American Culture*, Cambridge: Cambridge University Press.

O'Toole, T. A. (2001) *Champions of Faith: Catholic Sports Heroes Tell Their Stories*, Lanham, MD: Sheed and Ward.

Overman, S. J. (1997) *The Influence of the Protestant Ethic on Sport and Recreation*, Sydney, Australia: Ashgate.

Overman, S. J. (2011) *The Protestant Work Ethic and the Spirit of Sport: How Calvinism and Capitalism Shaped American Games*, Macon, GA, USA: Mercer University Press.

Park, J. (2000) Coping Strategies by Korean National Athletes, *Sport Psychologist*, 14: 63–80.

Parker, A. and Weir, J. S. (2012) Sport, Spirituality and Protestantism: A Historical Overview, *Theology*, 114 (4): 253–265

Parry, J. (2007a) Peace and the *Religio Athletae*, in J. Parry, S. Robinson, N. J. Watson and M. S. Nesti (Eds.), *Sport and Spirituality: An Introduction,* London: Routledge, 201–14.

Parry, J. (2007b) Sport, Ethos and Education, in J. Parry, S. Robinson, N. J. Watson and M. S. Nesti (Eds.), *Sport and Spirituality: An Introduction,* London: Routledge, 186–200.

Parry, J. (2011) Part 1 Introduction: Theological Ethics in Sport, in J. Parry, M. Nesti and N. J. Watson (Eds.), *Theology, Ethics and Transcendence in Sports*, New York: Routledge, 21–23.

Parry, J., Nesti, M. and Watson, N. J. (eds.) (2011) *Theology, Ethics and Transcendence in Sports*, New York: Routledge.

Parry, J., Robinson, S., Watson, N. J. and Nesti, M. S. (2007) *Sport and Spirituality: An Introduction*, London: Routledge.

Peale, N. V. (ed.) (1957) *Faith Made Them Champions*, Kingswood, Surrey, UK: World's Work.

Peiser, B. J. (1997) "Thou Shalt Not Kill!" The Judaeo-Christian Basis of the Civilizing Process, *Sports Historian*, 17 (1): 93–108.

Peña, D. (2004) *Scripture and Sport Psychology: Mental-Techniques for the Christian Athlete*, New York: iUniverse.

Penrice, J. (2009) *Living the Eucharist through Sports: A Guide for Catholic Athletes, Coaches and Fans*, New York: St. Pauls/Alba House Publishers.

Pfitzner, V.C. (1967) *Paul and the Agon Motif: Traditional Athletic in the Pauline Literature*, Leiden: E. J. Brill.

Pfitzner, V.C. (1981) Martyr and Hero: The Origin and Development of a Tradition in the Early Christian Martyr-Acts, *Lutheran Theological Journal*, 15 (1–2): 9–17.

Pfitzner, V. C. (2009) We Are the Champions! Origins and Developments of the Image of God's Athletes, in G. Preece and R. Hess (Eds.), *Sport and Spirituality: An Exercise in Everyday Theology*, Adelaide, Australia: ATF Press, 49–69.

Piaget, J. (1951) *Play, Dreams and Imitation in Childhood*, New York: Norton.

Pieper, J. (1948/1998) *Leisure: The Basis of Culture*, South Bend, IN: St. Augustine Press.

Pieper, J. (1965) *In Tune with the World: A Theory of Festivity*, New York: Harcourt, Brace and World.

Poliakoff, M. (1984) Jacob, Job, and Other Wrestlers: Reception of Greek Athletics by Jews and Christians in Antiquity, *Journal of Sport History*, 11 (2): 48–65.

Poliakoff, M. (1987) *Combat Sports in the Ancient World: Competition, Violence, and Culture*, New Haven, CT: Yale University Press.

Pope, S. W. (2010) Imperalsim, in S.W. Pope and J. Nauright (Eds.), *Routledge Companion to Sports History*, London: Routledge, 229–47.

Poulton, E. and Roderick, M. (eds.) (2009) *Sport in Films*, London: Routledge.

Prebish, C. S. (1993) *Religion and Sport: The Meeting of Sacred and Profane*, London: Greenwood Press.

Preece, G. (2009)'When I Run I Feel God's Pleasure': Towards a Protestant Play Ethic, in G. Preece and R. Hess (Eds.), *Sport and Spirituality: An Exercise in Everyday Theology*, Adelaide, Australia: ATF Press, 27–40.

Preece, G. and Hess, R. (eds.) (2009) *Sport and Spirituality: An Exercise in Everyday Theology*, Adelaide: ATF Press.

Prentice, A. and Jebb, S. (1995) Obesity in Britain: Gluttony or Sloth? *British Medical Journal*, 3111: 437–39.

President's Council on Bioethics. (2003) Superior Performance, in L. Kass (Ed.), *Beyond Therapy: Biotechnology and the Pursuit of Happiness*, New York: Dana Press, 115–178.

Pressner, T. (2007) *Muscular Judaism: The Jewish Body and the Politics of Regeneration*, London: Routledge.

Price, J. L. (1984) The Super Bowl as Religious Festival, *Christian Century*, (February): 190–191.

Price, J. L. (1991) The Final Four as Final Judgment: The Cultural Significance of the NCAA Basketball Tournament, *Journal of Popular Culture*, 24 (4): 49–58.

Price, J. L. (1994) Fusing the Spirits: Baseball, Religion, and The Brothers K, *Nine: A Journal of Baseball History and Social Policy Perspectives*, 2 (2): 300–13.

Price, J. L. (1996) Naturalistic Recreations, in P. H. Van Ness (Ed.), *Spirituality and the Secular Quest*, London: SCM Press, 414–44.

Price, J. L. (2001a) From Sabbath Proscriptions to Super Sunday Celebrations, in J. Price (Ed.), *From Season to Reason: Sports as American Religion*, Macon, GA: Mercer University Press, 1–13.

Price, J. L. (ed.) (2001b) *From Season to Season: Sports as American Religion*, Macon, GA: Mercer University Press.

Price, J. L. (2002) Dying to Win: America's Grieving for Athletes, *Journal of American and Comparative Cultures*, 25 (3–4): 405–11.

Price, J. L. (2006) *Rounding the Bases: Baseball and American Religion*, Macon, GA: Mercer University Press.

Price, J. L. (2007) Sports and Faith: United States, in E. Fahlbusch (Ed.), *The Encyclopedia of Christianity, Volume 5 Si-Z*, Grand Rapids, MI: William B. Eerdmans Publishers, 178–81.

Price, J. L. (2009) Playing and Praying, Sport and Spirit: The Forms and Functions of Prayer in Sports, *International Journal of Religion and Sport*, 1: 55–80.

Progen, J. L., and DeSensi, J. T. (1984) The Value of Theoretical Frameworks for Exploring the Subjective Dimension of Sport, *Quest*, 36 (1): 80–88.

Putney, C. (2001a) *Muscular Christianity: Manhood and Sports in Protestant America 1880–1920*, Cambridge, MA: Harvard University Press.

Putney, C. (2001b) Muscular Women, in C. Putney (Ed.), *Muscular Christianity: Manhood and Sports in Protestant America 1880–1920*, Cambridge, MA: Harvard University Press, 144–61.

Quinn, D. and Crocker, J. (1999) When Ideology Hurts: The Effects of the Protestant Work Ethic and Feeling Overweight on the Psychological Wellbeing of Women, *Journal of Personality and Social Psychology*, 77 (2): 402–14.

Quoist, M. (1965) *The Christian Response*, Dublin, Ireland: Gill and Macmillan.

Rahner, H. (1972) *Man at Play*, trans. B. Battershaw, New York: Herder and Herder.

Randels, G. D. and Beal, B. (2002) What Makes a Man? Religion, Sport and Negotiating Masculine Identity in the Promise Keepers, in T. Magdalinski and T. G. L. Chandler (Eds.), *With God on Their Side: Sport in the Service of Religion*, London: Routledge, 159–76.

Raschke, W. J. (1986) *The Archaeology of the Olympics: The Olympics and Other Festivals in Antiquity*, Madison: University of Wisconsin Press.

Ratzinger, J. (2005) Cardinal Ratzinger on Europe's Crisis of Culture, *International Catholic Review Communio (USA)*, 2: 345–56.

Ravizza, K. (1984) Qualities of the Peak Experience in Sport, in J. Silva and R. Weinberg (Eds.), *Psychological Foundations of Sport*, Champaign, IL: Human Kinetics, 452–61.

Ravizza, K. (2002) A Philosophical Construct: A Framework for Performance Enhancement, *International Journal of Sport Psychology*, 33: 4–18.

Redmond, G. (1978) The First Tom Brown's Schooldays: Origins and Evolution of "Muscular Christianity" in Children's Literature, *Quest*, 30: 4–18.

Rieke, M., Hammermeister, J. and Chase, M. (2008) Servant Leadership in Sport: A New Paradigm for Effective Coaching Behaviour, *International Journal of Sports Science and Coaching*, 3 (2): 227–39.

Riesen, R. A. (2007) *School and Sports: A Christian Critique*, Formby, Merseyside, UK: Grasshopper Books.

Rigauer, B. (1981) *Sport and Work*, trans. Allen Guttman, New York: Columbia University Press.

Ringwald, A. (1971) Fight, Prize, Triumph, Victory, in C. Brown (Ed.), *The New International Dictionary of New Testament Theology*, Grand Rapids, MI: Paternoster Press, 644–49.

Robinson, D. (1997) Competition and the Bible, *Journal of Christian Education*, 40: 2.

Robinson, S. (2007) Spirituality, Sport and Virtues, in J. Parry, S. Robinson, N. J. Watson and M. S. Nesti (Eds.), *Sport and Spirituality: An Introduction*, London: Routledge, 173–85.

Rodek, J., Sekulic, D. and Pasalic, E. (2009) Can We Consider Religiousness as a Protective Factor against Doping Behaviour in Sport? *Journal of Religion and Health*, 48 (4): 445–53.

Rohr, R. (2004a) *Adam's Return: The Five Promises of Male Initiation*, New York: Crossroad Publishing Co.

Rohr, R. (2004b) *Soul Brothers: Men in the Bible Speak to Men Today*, Maryknoll, NY: Orbis Books.

Rohr, R. (2005) *From Wild Man to Wise Man: Reflections on Male Spirituality* (with Joseph Martos), Cincinnati, OH: St. Anthony Messenger Press.

Rolheiser, R. (2001) *The Shattered Lantern: Rediscovering a Felt Presence of God*, London: Hodder and Stoughton.

Roubach, S. (2007) In the Name of the Father, the Daughter and Eddie Scrap: Trinitarian Theology in *Million Dollar Baby*, *Journal of Religion and Film*, 11 (1): 1–5. Available online at http://www.unomaha.edu/jrf/vol11no1/Roubach-MillionBaby.htm (accessed 21 June 2011).

Rowland, T. (2003) *Culture and the Thomist Tradition: After Vatican II*, London: Routledge.

Ryan, T. (1985) Towards a Spirituality for Sports, *International Journal for Theology*, 5 (205): 110–18.

Ryan, T. (1986) *Wellness, Spirituality and Sports*, New York: Paulist Press.

Ryken, L. (2006) The Puritan Ethic and Christian Leisure Today, in P. Heintzman, G. Van Andel and T. Visker (Eds.), *Christianity and Leisure: Issues in a Pluralistic Society*, Sioux Center, IA: Dordt College Press, 32–49.

Ryken, L. (1986) *Worldly Saints: The Puritans as they Really Were*, Grand Rapids, MI: Zondervan.

Ryken, L. (1987) *Work and Leisure in Christian Perspective*, Portland, OR: Multnomah.

Sager, S. S., Lavallee, D. and Spray, C. M. (2009) Coping with the Effects of Fear of Failure: A Preliminary Investigation of Young Elite Athletes, *Journal of Clinical Sports Psychology*, 3: 73–98.

Sands, R. R. (2010) Homo Cursor: Running into Pleistocene, in R. R. Sands and L. R. Sands (Eds.), *The Anthropology of Sport and Human Movement: A Biocultural Perspective*, New York: Lexington Books, 143–81.

Sands, R. R. and Sands, L. R. (2009) Running Deep: Speculations on the Evolutionary Relationship between Nature, Spirituality in The Genus *Homo*, *Journal for the Scientific Study of Religion, Nature and Culture*, 3 (4): 552–77.

Sands, R. R. and Sands, L. R. (eds.) (2010) *The Anthropology of Sport and Human Movement: A Biocultural Perspective*, New York: Lexington Books.

Savage, T. B. (2004) *Power through Weakness: Paul's Understanding of the Christian Ministry in 2 Corinthians (Society for New Testament Studies Monograph Series 86)*, Cambridge: Cambridge University Press.

Savant, J. (2003) The Saving Grace of Sport: Why We Watch and Play, *Commonweal*, 130 (16): 14.

Sawyer, T. H. (1997) Separation of Church and State: Are Invocation and Team Prayers Illegal? *Journal of Legal Aspects of Sport*, 7 (1): 24–30.

Scarpa, S. and Carraro, A. N. (2011) Does Christianity Demean the Body and Deny the Value of Sport—A Provocative Thesis, *Sport, Ethics and Philosophy*, 5 (2): 110–23.

Schmid, S. E. (2011) Beyond Autotelic Play, *Journal of the Philosophy of Sport*, 38: 149–66.

Schneiderman, R. M. (2010) Flock is Now a Fight Team in Some Ministries: More Churches Promote Martial Arts to Reach Young Men, *New York Times*, P. A1. Available Online: http://www.nytimes.com/2010/02/02/us/02fight.html?_r=1&pagewanted=print (accessed 7 June 2012).

Schroeder, P. J and Scribner, J. P. (2006) To Honor and Glorify God: The Role of Religion in One Intercollegiate Athletics Culture, *Sport, Education and Society*, 11 (1): 39–54.

Schwarze, C. (2010) The Christian and the Cage Fighter, *Sydney Anglican Network*, 27 January. Available online at http://www.sydneyanglicans.net/life/day-today/the_christian_and_the_cage_fighter/ (accessed 24 August 2011).

Schwobel, C. and Gunton, C. E. (eds.) (1991) *Persons, Divine and Human*, Edinburgh: T & T Clark.

Scraton, S. and Flintoff, A. (2002) *Gender and Sport: A Reader*, London: Routledge.

Seesengood, R. P. (2005) Hybridity and the Rhetoric of Endurance: Reading Paul's Athletic Metaphors in a Context of Postcolonial Self-Construction, *The Bible and Critical Theory*, 1 (3): 1–14.

Seesengood, R. P. (2006a) *Competing Identities: The Athlete and the Gladiator in Early Christian Literature*, New York: T & T Clark.

Seesengood, R. P. (2006b) Contending for the Faith in Paul's Absence: Combat Sports and Gladiators in the Disputed Pauline Epistles, *Lexington Theological Quarterly*, 41 (2): 87–118.

Shedloski, D. (2011) Fixing Tiger's Psyche, *Golf World*, (December): 62–63.

Sheehan, G. (1978) *Running and Being*, New York: Warner Books.

Shields, D. (1996) Friendship: Content and Context for Christian Education, *Religious Education*, 91: 104–21.

Shields, D. (2002) Youth Ministry through Sports, *Living Light*, 39 (2): 36–44.

Shields, D. and Bredemeier, B. L. (1995) *Character Development and Physical Activity*, Champaign, IL: Human Kinetics.

Shields, D. and Bredemeier, B. L. (2005) Can Sports Build Character? In D. Lapsley and F. C. Power (Eds.), *Character Psychology and Education*, Notre Dame, IN: University of Notre Dame Press, 121–39.

Shields, D. and Bredemeier, B. L. (2009) *True Competition: A Guide to Pursuing Excellence in Sport and Society*, Champaign, IL: Human Kinetics.

Shields, D. and Bredemeier, B. L. (2010) Competition: Was Kohn Right? *Phi Delta Kappan*, 91 (5): 62–67.

Shields, D. and Bredemeier, B. L. (2011a) Contest, Competition, and Metaphor, *Journal of the Philosophy of Sport*, 38: 27–38.

Shields, D. and Bredemeier, B .L. (2011b) Why Sportsmanship Programs Fail, and What We Can Do About It, *Journal of Physical Education, Recreation & Dance*, 82 (7): 24–29.

Shields, D., Bredemeier, B. L., LaVoi, N. and Power, F. C. (2005) The Sport Behavior of Youth, Parents, and Coaches: The Good, the Bad, and the Ugly, *Journal of Research in Character Education*, 3: 43–59.

Simmons, F. (2011) Christian Love and Athletic Competition, paper presented at the Annual Conference of the Society for the Study of Christian Ethics: 'Christian Ethics and Sport,' Westcott House, University of Cambridge, 2–4 September.

Simon, R. L. (2004) *Fair Play: The Ethics of Sport*, 2nd ed., Boulder, CO: Westview.

Simon, R. L. (2007) Violence in Sport, in W. J. Morgan (Ed.), *Ethics in Sport*, 2nd ed., Champaign, IL: Human Kinetics, 379–88.

Simonson, T. (ed.) (1962) *The Goal and the Glory: America's Athletes Speak their Faith*, Westwood, NJ: Fleming H. Revell Company.

Sinden, L. J. (2012) The Elite Sport and Christianity Debate: Shifting Focus from Normative Values to the Conscious Disregard for Health, *Journal of Religion and Health*, Published Online 24 March: DOI 10.1007/s10943–012–9595–8.

Sing, S. (2004) *Spirituality of Sport: Balancing Body and Soul*, Cincinnati, OH: St. Anthony Messenger Press.

Sing, S. (2011) The Energy of Play, in J. Parry, M. S. Nesti and N. J. Watson (Eds.), *Theology, Ethics and Transcendence in Sports*, London: Routledge, 201–10.

Slusher, H. (1967) *Man, Sport and Existence: A Critical Analysis*, Philadelphia, PA: Lea and Febiger.

Smith, A. L., Lemyre, P. N. and Raedeke, T. D. (eds.) (2007) Athlete Burnout: Special Issue, *International Journal of Sport Psychology*, 38 (4): all pages of special edition.

Smith, G. S. (2010) *Sports Theology: Playing Inside Out*, Indianapolis, IN: Dog Ear Publishing.

Smith, M. (2002) "Muhammad Speaks" and Muhammad Ali: The Intersections of the Nation of Islam and Sport in the 1960s, in T. Magdalinski and T. G. L. Chandler (Eds.) *With God on Their Side: Sport in the Service of Religion*, London: Routledge, 177–96.

Söll, G. (1972) Sport in Catholic Theology in the 20th Century, in O. Grupe, D. Kurrz and J. M. Teipel (Eds.), *The Scientific View of Sport: Perspectives, Aspects, Issues*, New York: Springer-Verlag, 61–80.

Sowers, J. (2010) *Fatherless Generation: Redeeming the Story*, Grand Rapids, IL: Zondervan.

Sparkes, A. C., Partington, E. and Brown, D. H. K. (2007) Bodies as Bearers of Value: The Transmission of Jock Culture via the 'Twelve Commandments, *Sport, Education and Society*, 12 (3): 295–316.

Spencer, A. F. (2000) Ethics, Faith and Sport, *Journal of Interdisciplinary Studies*, 12: 143–58.

Spencer, D. C. (2011) *Ultimate Fighting and Embodiment: Violence, Gender and Mixed Martial Arts*, London: Routledge.

Spencer, D. C. (2009) Habit(us), Body Techniques and Body Callusing: An Ethnography of Mixed Martial Arts, *Body and Society*, 15: 119–143.

Stakweather, T. (2011) *The Rise and Fall of the Muscular Christian: Sport's Influence on Masculinity in British Literature*, Chicago, IL: The University of Illinois at Chicago.

Stebner, E. and Trothen, T. (2002) A Diamond Is Forever? Women, Baseball, and the Pitch for a Radically Inclusive Community, in C. H. Evans and W. R. Herzog (Eds.), *The Faith of 50 Million: Baseball, Religion and American Culture*, London: Westminster John Knox Press, 167–84.Stevenson, C. L. (2008) Sport and Religion, in J. Crossman (ed.), *Canadian Sport Sociology*, Scarborough, ON, Canada: Thompson Publishers:

Stevenson, C. L. (1991) The Christian-Athlete: An Interactionist-Developmental Analysis. *Sociology of Sport*, 8: 362–79.

Stevenson, C. L. (1997) Christian Athletes and the Culture of Elite Sport: Dilemmas and Solutions, *Sociology of Sport Journal*, 14: 241–62.

Stevenson, C. L. (2008) Sport and Religion, in J. Crossman (ed.), *Canadian Sport Sociology*, Scarborough, ON, Canada: Thompson Publishers.

Stibbe, M. (2010) *I Am Your Father: What Every Heart Needs to Know*, London: Monarch Books.

Stoll, S. K. and Beller, J. M. (2008) Moral Reasoning in Athletic Populations: A 20 Year Review, *Centre for Ethics*, University of Idaho. Available online at http://www.educ.uidaho.edu/center_for_ethics/research_fact_sheet.htm (accessed 11 November 2008).

Storch, E. A. and Farber, B. A. (2002) Psychotherapy with the Religious Athlete, *Annals ofthe American Psychotherapy Association*, 3 (6): 15–17.

Storch, E. A., Kolsky, A. R., Silvestri, M. and Storch, J. B. (2001) Religiosity of Elite College Athletes, *Sport Psychologist*, 15: 346–51.

Storch, E. A., Roberti, J. W., Bravata, E. A. and Storch, J. B. (2004) Strength of Religious Faith: A Comparison of Intercollegiate Athletes and Non-Athletes, *Pastoral Psychology*, 52 (6): 485–89.

Storch, E. A., and Storch, J. B. (2002a) Correlations for Organizational, Nonorganizational, and Intrinsic Religiosity with Social Support among Intercollegiate Athletes, *Psychological Reports*, 91: 333–34.

Storch, E. A. and Storch, J. B. (2002b) Intrinsic Religiosity and Aggression in a Sample of Intercollegiate Athletes, *Psychological Reports*, 91: 1041–42.

Storch, E. A., Storch, J. B. and Adams, B. G. (2002) Intrinsic Religiosity and Social Anxiety of Intercollegiate Athletes, *Psychological Reports*, 91: 186.

Storch, E. A., Storch, J. B., Kovacs, A. H., Okun, A. and Welsh, E. (2003) Intrinsic Religiosity and Substance Abuse in Intercollegiate Athletes, *Sport Psychologist*, 25 (2): 248–52.

Storch, E. A., Storch, J. B., Welsh, E. and Okun, A. (2002) Religiosity and Depression in Intercollegiate Athletes, *College Student Journal*, 36: 526–31.

Stranger, M. (1999) The Aesthetics of Risk: A Study of Surfing, *International Review for the Sociology of Sport*, 34 (3): 265–76.

Stringfellow, W. (1973/2004) *An Ethic for Christians and Other Aliens in a Strange Land*, Eugene, OR: Wipf and Stock Publishers.

Sugden, J. P. and Bairner, A. (1993) *Sport, Sectarianism and Society in a Divided Ireland*, London: Leicester University Press.

Swanson, R. A. (1978) Acceptance and Influence of Play in American Protestantism, *Quest*, 11: 58–70.

Swinton, J. (2011) Who Is the God We Worship? Theologies of Disability; Challenges and New Possibilities (Research Report), *International Journal of Practical Theology*, 14 (2): 273–307.

Sydnor, S. (2012) Sport, Women and the Mystical Body of Christ, *The Bible in Transmission* (Sp. Ed., Sporting Life: Reflections on Sport, Culture and the Church), Spring: 11–13.

Sydnor, S. (2003) The Radical Orthodoxy Project and Sport History, in W. Buss and A. Kruger (Ed.), *Transitions in Sport History: Continuity and Change in Sport History*. Hanover: R. Kunz; Schriftenreihe des Niedersächsischen Instituts für Sportgeschichte, 24–39.

Sydnor, S. (2005) Femininity and the Culture of Sport: The Contribution of John Paul II, invited presentation to the Second International Conference: Sport & Religion: An Inquiry Into Cultural Values, St. Olaf College, Northfield, MN, 29 October.

Sydnor, S. (2006a) Contact with God, Body & Soul: Sport History and the Radical Orthodoxy Project, in M. Phillips (Ed.), *Sport History into the New Millennium: A Postmodern Analysis*, Albany: State University of New York Press, 202–26.

Sydnor, S. (2006b) Controversial Themes in the Study of Femininity and Sport: The Contribution of John Paul II's Theology of the Body, in G. T. Papanikos (Ed.), *An Amalgam of Sports & Exercise Research*, Athens: Athens Institute for Education and Research Press, 343–58.

Sydnor, S. (2009) Sport, Femininity and the Promises of the Theology of the Body, in G. Preece and R. Hess (Eds.), *Sport and Spirituality: An Exercise in Everyday Theology*, Adelaide, Australia: ATF Press, 81–115.

Tamburrini, C. and Tannsjo, T. (2005) *Genetic Technology and Sport*, London: Routledge.

Taylor, C. (2007) *A Secular Age*, Boston: Harvard University Press.

Tebow, T. (with N. Whittaker) (2011) *Through My Eyes*, New York: HarperOne.

Thaden, R. H. (2003) Glorify God in Your Body: The Redemptive Role of the Body in Early Christian Ascetic Literature, *Cistercian Studies Quarterly*, 38 (2): 191–209.

Thoennes, E .K. (2008) Created to Play: Thoughts on Play, Sport and Christian Life, in D. Deardorff II and D. J. White (Eds.), *The Image of God in the Human*

Body: Essays on Christianity and Sports, Lampeter, Wales: Edwin Mellen Press, 79–100.

Thomas, G. (2011) *Every Body Matters: Strengthening Your Body to Strengthen Your Soul*, Grand Rapids, MI: Zondervan.

Thomas, J. J. (1976) The English Puritans: Suppressors of Sport and Amusement? *Canadian Journal of History of Sport and Physical Education*, 7 (1): 33–38.

Thompson, K. (2011) Miracles in Sport: A Reply to Hopsicker, *Sport, Ethics and Philosophy*, 5 (2): 175–77.

Trothen, T. J. (2008a) Redefining Human, Redefining Sport: The Imago Dei and Genetic Modification Technologies, in D. Deardorff II and J. White (Eds.), *The Image of God in the Human Body: Essays on Christianity and Sports*, Lampeter, Wales: Edwin Mellen Press, 217–34.

Trothen, T. J. (2008b) The Sporting Spirit? Gene Doping, Bioethics, and Religion, *International Journal of Religion and Sport*, 1: 1–20.

Trothen, T. J. (2009) Holy Acceptable Violence? Violence in Hockey and Christian Atonement Theories, *Journal of Religion and Popular Culture*, 21. Available online at http://www.usask.ca/relst/jrpc/art(se)-HockeyViolence.html (accessed 28 March 2011).

Trothen, T. J. (2011) Better than Normal? Constructing Modified Athletes and a Relational Theological Ethic, in J. Parry, M. S. Nesti and N. J. Watson (Eds.), *Theology, Ethics and Transcendence in Sports*, London: Routledge, 64–81.

Tucker, T. and Woodbridge, N. (2012) Motivational Factors for a Sports Ministry: A Case Study of Churches in Pretoria, *Theological Studies*, 68 (2): 1–25. Full text available online: http://www.hts.org.za/index.php/HTS/article/view/1199 (accessed 6 June 2012)

Turner, P. and Posner, L. (2010) Selves in Play: Scouts, and American Cultural Citizenship, *International Review of the Sociology of Sport*, 45: 390–409.

Twietmeyer, G. (2008) A Theology of Inferiority: Is Christianity the Source of Kinesiology's Second-Class Status in the Academy, *Quest*, 60: 452–66.

Twietmeyer, G. (2009) Law, Gospel, Play: Martin Luther and the Neglected Influence of Theology on Sport History, *Stadion: International Journal of the History of Sport*, 35: 239–55.

Upton, H. (2011) Can There Be a Moral Duty to Cheat in Sport, *Sport, Ethics and Philosophy*, 5 (2): 161–74.

Vance, N. (1985) *The Sinews of the Spirit: The Ideal of Christian Manliness in Victorian Literature and Religious Thought*, Cambridge: Cambridge University Press.

Van Bottenburg, M. and Heilbron, J. (2006) De-Sportization of Fighting Contests: The Origins and Dynamics of No Holds Barred Events and the Theory of Sportization, *International Review for the Sociology of Sport*, 41: 259–282.

Van Nijf, O. (2001) Local Heroes: Athletic Festivals, and Elite Self-Fashioning in the Roman East, in S. Goldhill (Ed.), *Being Greek under Rome: Cultural Identity, the Second Sophistic and the Development of Empire*, Cambridge: Cambridge University Press, 306–34.

Veblen, T. (1899/1970) *Theory of the Leisure Class: An Economic Study of Institutions*, London: Allen and Unwin.

Vertinsky, P. (1987) Exercise, Physical Capability, and the Eternally Wounded Woman in Late Nineteenth Century North America, *Journal of Sport History*, 14 (1): 7–27.

Vitz, P. (1977/1994) *Psychology as Religion: The Cult of Self-Worship*, Grand Rapids, MI: Williams Eerdmans Publishing.

Voss, T. (1997) How Can Physical Activity and Sports Be Used in Youth Ministries? in R. R. Dunn and M. H. Senter (Eds.), *Reaching a Generation for Christ*, Chicago: Moody Press, 599–613.

Vost, K. (2008) *Fit for Eternal Life: A Christian Approach to Working Out, Eating Right, and Building Virtues in Your Soul*, Manchester, NH: Sophia.

Vost, K. (2011) *Tending the Temple: 365 Days of Spiritual and Physical Devotions*, Waterford, MI: Bezalel Books.

Waldron, J., Lynn, Q. and Krane, V. (2011) Duct Tape, Icy Hot and Paddles: Narratives of Initiation onto US Male Sport Teams, *Sport, Education and Society*, 16 (1): 111–25.

Walford, G. A. (2009) *Sport Humor: A Detailed Analysis*, Frederick, MD: PublishAmerica.

Walker, D. (2009) *Sport and Sundays: Christian BBC Presenter Tells His Story*, Leominster, UK: Day One Publications.

Walker, S. H. (1980) *Winning: The Psychology of Competition*, New York: W. W. Norton.

Waller, S. (2010) Leisure in the Life of the 21st Century Black Church: Re-Thinking the Gift, *Journal of the Christian Society for Kinesiology and Leisure Studies*, 1: 33–47.

Waller, S. N. (2009) Favourite Pew or Seat? Sabbath Beliefs as a Barrier to Sporting Event Attendance on Sunday: A Congregational Study, *Journal of Religion and Popular Culture*, 21 (2): 1–15. Available online at http://www.usask.ca/relst/jrpc/art21(2)-PewOrBoxSeat.html (accessed 22 March 2011).

Waller, S., Dzikus, L. and Hardin, R. (2010) The Collegiate Sports Chaplain: Kindred or Alien? *Chaplaincy Today*, 26 (1): 16–26.

Waller, S., Dzikus, L. and Hardin, R. (in press) Credentialing Sport Chaplains: An Idea Whose Time Has Arrived, *International Journal of Sports & Ethics*.

Walsh, A. J. and Giulianotti, R. (2007) *Ethics, Money and Sport: This Sporting Mammon*, London: Routledge.

Walters, P. and Byl, J. (eds.) (2008) *Christian Paths to Health and Wellness*, Champaign, IL: Human Kinetics.

Ward, G. (1999) Theology and Masculinity, *Journal of Men's Studies*, 7 (2): 281–86.

Ward, G. (2012) A Question of Sport and Incarnational Theology, *Studies in Christian Ethics*, 25 (1): 49–64.

Ward, P. (2011) *Gods Behaving Badly: Media, Religion, and Celebrity Culture*, London: SCM Press.

Watson, N. J. (2007a) Muscular Christianity in the Modern Age: "Winning for Christ" or "Playing for Glory"? in J. Parry, S. Robinson, N. J. Watson and M. S. Nesti (Eds.), *Sport and Spirituality: An Introduction*, London: Routledge, 80–94.

Watson, N. J. (2007b) Nature and Transcendence: The Mystical and Sublime in Extreme Sports, in J. Parry, S. Robinson, N. J. Watson and M. S. Nesti (Eds.), *Sport and Spirituality: An Introduction*, London: Routledge, 222–23.

Watson, N. J. (2011a) Identity in Sport: A Psychological and Theological Analysis, in J. Parry, M. N. Nesti and N. J. Watson (Eds.), *Theology, Ethics and Transcendence in Sports*, London: Routledge, 107–48.

Watson, N. J. (2011b) Introduction, in J. Parry, M. N. Nesti and N. J. Watson (eds.), *Theology, Ethics and Transcendence in Sports*, London: Routledge, 1–11.

Watson, N. J. (2012) Sport, Disability and the Olympics: An Exploration of the Status and Prophetic Role of the Special Olympic Movement in Light of the London 2012 Olympic and Paralympic Games, *The Bible in Transmission* (Sp. Ed., Sporting Life: Reflections on Sport, Culture and the Church), Spring: 14–16

Watson, N. J. (forthcoming) Fatherlessness, Fatherhood and Sports: A Christian Theological Reflection, *Journal of Religion and Society*.

Watson, N. J. and Brock, B. (forthcoming) Christianity, Boxing and Mixed Martial Arts, *Practical Theology*.

Watson, N. J. and Czech, D. (2005) The Use of Prayer in Sport: Implications for Sport Psychology Consulting, *Athletic Insight: The Online Journal of Sport Psychology*, 17: 4. Available online at http://www.athleticinsight.com/Vol7Iss4/PrayerinSports.htm (accessed 18 January 2011).

Watson, N. J. and Nesti, M. (2005) The Role of Spirituality in Sport Psychology Consulting: An Analysis and Integrative Review of Literature, *Journal of Applied Sport Psychology*, 17: 228–39.

Watson, N. J. and Parker, A. (2012) Christianity, Disability and Sport: A Case Study of the Role of Long-Distance Running in the Life of a Father and a Son Who Is Congenitally Blind and Who Has Profound Disabilities, *Practical Theology*, 5 (2): 191–210.

Watson, N. J. and Parker, A. (under review) A Theological Analysis of the Institutions and Governance of Sport: A Case Study of the Modern Olympic Games, *International Journal of Religion and Sport*.

Watson, N. J. and Parker, A. (guest eds.) (forthcoming) *Sports, Religion and Disability (Special Edition), Journal of Religion, Disability and Health*.

Weir, S. and Friend, S. (2005) The Development of Muscular Christianity in Victorian Britain and Beyond, *Journal of Religion and Society*, 7. Available online at http://moses.creighton.edu/JRS/2005/2005–2.html (accessed 18 January 2011).

Watson, N. J. and White, J. (2007) "Winning at All Costs" in Modern Sport: Reflections on Pride and Humility in the Writings of C. S. Lewis, in J. Parry, S. Robinson, N. J. Watson and M. S. Nesti (Eds.), *Sport and Spirituality: An Introduction*, London: Routledge, 61–79.

Watson, N. J. and White, J. (2012) C. S. Lewis at the 2012 London Olympics: Reflections on Pride and Humility, *Practical Theology (Special Edition: Sport), Practical Theology*, 5 (2): 153–169.

Watts, G. (2007) Athletes with a Disability—Mixed Messages from the Bible, paper presented at the Inaugural International Conference on Sport and Spirituality, Centre for the Study of Sport and Spirituality (2003–2009), York St. John University, York, UK, 28–31 August.

Weber, M. (1958) *The Protestant Ethic and the Spirit of Capitalism*, trans. Talcott Parsons, New York: Free Press.

Web-Mitchell, B. (1997) And a Football Coach Shall Lead Them: A Theological Critique of *Seven Promise of a Promise Keeper*, *Soundings*, 80 (2/3): 305–26.

Weinberg, R.S. and Gould, D. (2011a) Arousal, Stress and Anxiety, in *Foundations in Sport and Exercise Psychology*, 5th ed., Champaign, IL: Human Kinetics, 77–100.

Weinberg, R. S. and Gould, D. (2011b) Character Development and Good Sporting Behavior, in *Foundations in Sport and Exercise Psychology*, 5th ed., Champaign, IL: Human Kinetics, 103–24.

Weinberg, R .S. and Gould, D. (2011c) Competition and Cooperation, in *Foundations in Sport and Exercise Psychology*, 5th ed., Champaign, IL: Human Kinetics, 103–24.

Weir, S. (2008) Competition as Relationship: Sport as a Mutual Quest for Excellence, in D. Deardorff II and D. J. White (eds.), *The Image of God in the Human Body: Essays on Christianity and Sports*, Lampeter, Wales: Edwin Mellen Press, 101–22.

Weiss, P. (1969) *Sport: A Philosophic Inquiry*, Carbondale: Southern Illinois University Press.

Wellard, I. (2009) *Sport Masculinities and the Body*, London: Routledge.

Wenkert, S. (1963) The Meaning of Sports for Contemporary Man, *Journal of Existential Psychiatry*, 3: 397–404.

Wertz, S. P. (1977) Zen, Yoga, and Sports: Eastern Philosophy for Western Athletes, *Journal of the Philosophy of Sport*, IV: 68–82.

West, E. (2011) A Muscular Christian Takes on Dawkins: Ed West Talks to Kevin Vost, the Memory Expert, Former Olympic-Level Weightlifter and Heavyweight Defender of the Catholic Faith, *Catholic Herald*, 30 September, 7.

Whannel, G. (1986) The Unholy Alliance: Notes on Television and the Remaking of British Sport, 1965–1985, *Leisure Studies*, 5: 129–45.

White, C., Moon, C., Pugh, P., Uszynski, E. and White, J. (2008) *Passing the Baton: Biblical Foundations for Developing a Sport Ministry*, Xenia, OH: Athletes in Action.

White, J. (2008) Idols in the Stadium: Sport as an "Idol Factory," in D. Deardorff II and J. White (Eds.), *The Image of God in the Human Body: Essays on Christianity and Sports*, Lampeter, Wales: Edwin Mellen Press, 127–72.

White, J. (2012a) The Enduring Problem of Dualism: Shirl Hoffman's *Good Game: Christianity and the Culture of Sports*, *Implicit Religion*, 15 (2).

White, J. (2012b) John Paul II's Interpretation of 1 Corinthians 9:24–27: A Paradigm for a Christian Ethic of Sport, *Studies in Christian Ethics*, 25 (1): 73–88.

White, J. and White, C. (2006) *Game Day Glory: Life-Changing Principles for Sport*, Tallmadge, OH: S. D. Meyers Publishing Services.

White, J. and Hill, B.V. (forthcoming, 2014) *God, Nimrod, and the World: Exploring Christian Perspectives on Sport Hunting*, Macon, GA: Mercer University Press.

Williams, D. J. (1999) *Paul's Metaphors: Their Context and Character*, Peabody, MS: Hendrickson Publishers.

Williams, R. (2003) *Silence and Honey Cakes: The Wisdom of the Desert*, London: Continuum.

Wilson, M. V. (1989) *Our Father Abraham: Jewish Roots of the Christian Faith*, Grand Rapids, MI: Wm. B. Eerdmans Publishing Company.

Winn, W .E. (1960) Tom Brown's Schooldays and the Development of "Muscular Christianity," *Church History*, 29: 66.

Wittmer, M. (2008) A Christian Perspective of Sport, in D. Deardorff II and J. White (Eds.), *The Image of God in the Human Body: Essays on Christianity and Sports*, Lampeter, Wales: Edwin Mellen Press, 43–59.

Wood, S. (2011) *Keeping Faith in the Team: The Chaplain's Story*, London: Longman Dartman and Todd.

Woods, R. (2007) Religion and Sport, in R. Wood (Ed.), *Social Issues in Sport*, Champaign, IL: Human Kinetics, 255–70.

Wooden, J. (2005) *Wooden on Leadership* (with Steve Jamison), New York: McGraw-Hill.

Worthington Jr., E. L. and Berry, J. W. (2005) Virtues, Vices, and Character Development, in W. R. Miller and H. D. Delaney (Eds.), *Judeo-Christian Perspectives on Psychology: Human Nature, Motivation, and Change*, Washington, DC: American Psychological Association, 145–64.

Yamane, D., Mellies, C. E. and Blake, T. (2010) Playing for Whom? Sport, Religion, and the Double Movement of Secularization in America, in E. Smith (Ed.), *Sociology of Sport and Social Theory*, Champaign, IL: Human Kinetics, 81–94.

Yerkovich, J. and Kelly, P. (2003) *WE: A Model for Coaching and Christian Living*, Arlington, VA: National Catholic Educational Association.

Yessick, T. (ed.) (1996) *Sports Ministry for Churches*, Nashville, TN: Convention Press.

Yinger, K. L. (2008) Paul and Asceticism in 1 Corinthians 9: 27a, *Journal of Religion and Society*, 10: 101–21. Available online at http://moses.creighton.edu/JRS/2008/2008–41.html (accessed 22 March 2011).

Yong, A. (2007) *Theology and Down Syndrome: Reimaging Disability in Late Modernity*, Waco, TX: Baylor University Press.

Yong A. (forthcoming) Running the (Special) Race: New (Pauline) Perspectives on Disability and Theology of Sport, *Journal of Religion, Disability and Health* (Special Edition: Sports, Disability and Religion).

Young, K. (2011) *Sport, Violence and Society*, London: Routledge.

Zenic, N., Stipic, M. and Sekulic, D. (2011) Religiousness as a Factor of Hesitation against Doping Behaviour in College-Age Athletes, *Journal of Religion and Health*. Published Online First. Available at: DOI. 10.1007/s10943–011–9480-x.

2 Was St. Paul a Sports Enthusiast?

Realism and Rhetoric in Pauline Athletic Metaphors

Victor C. Pfitzner

SURVEYING THE FIELD

Sports-loving moderns readily tune in to St. Paul's images of the athlete who trains with rigorous self-discipline, runs to the finishing line with total concentration, boxes with well-aimed blows, endures pain to win the contest and finally receives the victor's crown. Such imagery is hardly enough to construct a Christian view of sports,[1] let alone provide biblical foundations for a muscular faith or validation of all athletic competition, but it allows us to draw lines of connection between athletic ideals in the ancient world and those echoed in the modern Olympic oath and competition.[2] Athletic metaphors held such imaginative power for the apostle Paul that he could be confident that his message would be enhanced by their use.

Ancient metaphors derived from the games (Greek, *agones*) reflect their popularity. This is also the case with St. Paul's agonistic imagery and terminology that, with the exception of 2 Corinthians and Philemon, is spread throughout the undisputed Pauline epistles. In three cases the metaphor is explicit:

> Do you not know that in a race the *runners* all compete, but only one receives the *prize*? *Run* in such a way that you may win it. *Athletes* exercise self-control in all things; they do it to receive a perishable *wreath*, but we an imperishable one. So I do not run aimlessly, nor do I *box* as though beating the air; but I punish my body and enslave it, so that after proclaiming to others I myself should not be disqualified. (1 Corinthians 9:24–27; NRSV)[3]

> Only, live your life in a manner worthy of the gospel of Christ, so that . . . I will know that you are standing firm in one spirit, *striving* side by side with one mind for the faith of the gospel, and are in no way intimidated by your opponents . . . For he [sc. God] has graciously granted you the privilege not only of believing in Christ, but of suffering for him as well—since you are having the same *struggle* [*agon*] that you saw I had and now hear that I still have. (Philippians 1:27–30)

> Not that I have already obtained this or have already *reached the goal*;
> but I *press on* to make it my own, because Christ Jesus has made me
> his own . . . ; forgetting what lies behind and straining forward to what
> lies ahead, I *press on* toward the *goal* for the *prize* of the heavenly call
> of God in Christ Jesus. (Philippians 3:12–14)

The image of the runner also appears in Galatians 2:2, 5:7, Romans 9:16
and Philippians 2:16. Though English translations do not always make the
connection clear, athletic terminology appears in 1 Thessalonians 2:2, 19
('opposition' and 'crown'); Philippians 4:1, 3 ('crown' and 'struggle'); and
Romans 15:30 ('join in earnest'). There are allusions to athletic running in
Romans 9:30–10:4 with the words 'pursue,' 'attain,' 'stumble' and 'goal/
end.'[4] The so-called Deutero-Pauline letters continue the use of athletic terminology and images (Colossians 1:29–2:1, 4:12),[5] especially the Pastoral
Epistles where young Timothy is encouraged to train himself in godliness
and to 'contest the good contest' (*agon*) of faith in emulation of Paul himself (1 Timothy 4:7–10, 6:11, 12; 2 Timothy 2:5, 4:7–8).

The general sense of most metaphors in oral and written communication
is grasped with relative ease, yet some metaphors can be 'slippery,' their
precise meaning allusive or even elusive. Language can lose its 'color'; individual terms can lose their original connotation. We 'wrestle' with problems without for a second thinking of two grappling, grunting and sweating
contestants. Separated linguistically and culturally by two millennia from
St. Paul, we cannot always be certain of the exact referent or the extent of
an image. In 1 Corinthians 9:24–27 it is not immediately clear whether
'proclaiming' in verse 27 refers to Paul's role as herald or announcer (*keryx*)
in the games or to his role as apostolic preacher—or perhaps to both. Further, has the term 'disqualified' in the same verse a technical sense?

Problems of interpretation are compounded when language used in one
context is appropriated for another, leading to mixed metaphors. Michael
Gudorf (1998) suggests that the ancient reader would have immediately
understood Paul's image of 'wrestling' (Greek, *pale*) in the larger military unit of Ephesians 6:10–17 as depicting the Christian as a fully armed
warrior (*hoplitopales*), ready for hand-to-hand combat with Satan.[6] The
interchangeability of military and athletic images and vocabulary creates
questions in other instances such as Philippians 1:27–30, 2 Timothy 2:4, 5
and 4:7–8. Is the struggle the agon of the soldier or of the athlete? Edgar
Krentz (2003) reads the letter to the Philippians as couched in the form of a
general's harangue to the troops, so that the letter's athletic terminology is
to be given a military sense. Robert Seesengood (2006b: 99, 100) proposes
that Paul and Timothy in their role as agonists in the Pastoral Epistles are
viewed as gladiators fighting to maintain the faith. Similarly, the image of
wrestling in Ephesians 6:12 is to be seen as a gladiatorial reference.

Despite such occasional uncertainties, Paul's metaphors can tell us much
about the cultural identity and location of speaker and listeners. Authorial

intention may not always have encountered intended audience perception, yet we may assume that Paul was canny enough to use imagery that fitted the situation and could expect, as a result of consistent linguistic usage, that his audience would immediately tune in to his meaning.[7] If we today fail to make the right connections, the problem lies with the 'culture gap.'

WAS ST. PAUL REALLY INTERESTED IN SPORTS?

Could St. Paul the ex-Pharisee, educated under the strict Jerusalem rabbi Gamaliel (Acts 22:3), have had any real interest in what went on in gymnasia and sports arenas? Granted that Paul was a Hellenistic Jew,[8] he would surely have been fully aware that the process of Hellenization in Jewish territories under the Seleucid Antiochus IV Epiphanes in the second century BC and over a century later under Herod the Great, including the introduction of public games and buildings that were foreign, if not offensive, to Paul's compatriots and that presented a major threat to the continuance of their identity and fidelity to the Torah.[9] Given also that Hellenistic athletics still had religious connotations and represented the continuance of Greek competitiveness and the quest for fame and glory,[10] Paul's adoption of agonistic metaphors is not as self-explanatory as it might at first appear. Add the obvious fact that Paul was completely focused on carrying out his apostolic commission with total concentration and constant readiness to face opposition (1 Corinthians 9:16, 17; 2 Corinthians 6:1–10, 11:24–28), and it becomes questionable whether Paul had any interest in witnessing local games. Speculation that he did so lacks any literary basis.[11]

Yet there is sufficient evidence for Diaspora Jews attending athletic spectacles, and not only in Alexandria (Harris, 1976: 30–51; Poliakoff, 1984: 58, 59; Fredriksen, 2002; Krentz, 2003: 334; Brändl, 2006: 140–78). Some Jewish youths probably participated in athletics as part of their education. Certainly, no other writer in the ancient world makes greater use of detailed athletic imagery than does the Jewish philosopher, Philo of Alexandria.[12] Nor should we discount some enthusiasm for Greek games in Palestinian territories. Harold Harris (1976: 50) can even assert, 'The old statement "The Jews would have nothing to do with Greek athletics" is exploded by the stadia of Tiberias and Caesarea, the hippodromes of Jericho and Tarichaea, the sports buildings of Jerusalem and the discus throwing priests of *Maccabees.*'

St. Paul writes as a bilingual, acculturated Hellenistic Jew (Saul and Paul!), reflecting the language and social reality of his day. Yet he never uses athletic similes such as 'I am like a runner, like a boxer.' His pictorial language is absolute: 'I run, I box, I contest.' He never explicitly engages in an evaluation of contemporary athletics, either negative or positive; he simply appropriates metaphors for his own purposes, sometimes with surprising results. The simplest way to explain this ready adoption of agonistic imagery and terminology is to see it anchored in *both social reality*, mean-ing knowledge of contemporary athletics, and in *a tradition* of appropriat-ing athletic metaphors. Our brief survey of research shows that the two elements have often been played off against each other. It also summarizes the adoption of new methodologies being employed to indicate a variety of factors at play in the apostle's rhetorical application of these metaphors.

TRACING THE STATE OF PLAY[13]

'Know ye not that those who run in a race, run all, but one receiveth the prize? So run, that ye may obtain.' St. Paul appeals to the experience of the Corinthians. There was nothing with which they were better acquainted than these famous foot-races. Their own games near their own city were among the most celebrated in the world. They 'knew' well that each race was eagerly contested, and that 'one' obtained the prize. (Howson, 1868: 149, 150)

In this assessment of 1 Corinthians 9:24–27, the Dean of Chester long ago voiced the assumption that the apostle to the Gentiles used athletic imagery because he was personally familiar with athletics and could appeal directly to the Corinthians' firsthand experience of contests at the Isthmian games held near Corinth. Even earlier, J. A. Bengel in his famous commentary *Gnomon Novi Testamenti* asserted that Paul was using a similitude taken from 'something well known to the Corinthians.'[14] The connection with the Isthmian games in 1 Corinthians 9:24–27 was drawn already by C. F. Hofmann (De ludis Isthmicis, 1760).[15]

My own study of *Paul and the Agon Motif* (Pfitzner, 1967) did not rule out direct reference to the public games familiar to St. Paul's readers, but sought to show that the apostle's usage reflected a long tradition of ath-letic metaphors in Greek and Hellenistic (especially Jewish) literature. This tradition,[16] which can be reconstructed from the writings of late Cynic and Stoic moralists such as Dio Chrysostom, Epictetus, Seneca and Mar-cus Aurelius (Pfitzner, 1967: 24–72; 2008: 52–56; see also Freyne, 1989: 98), moved attention from the physical athlete who toiled for corruptible trophies to the moral athlete who trained in true virtue for indestructible prizes. Athletic metaphors were picked up also by Jewish Diaspora writers such as the author of Wisdom of Solomon; Ben Sira; Philo; and, to a lesser extent, Josephus. In Hellenistic Judaism this tradition embraced the heroic Maccabean martyrs as God's athletes, suffering in fidelity to the Torah. Christian use of this imagery, I argued, could be traced from its adaptation by Paul and the writer to the Hebrews to the writings of the Apostolic and later Fathers of the church, until the Christian martyrs came to be viewed as athletes of Christ *par excellence* (Pfitzner, 1981, 2008).

Tracing a tradition was not meant to imply literary dependency. St. Paul's dependence on the Cynic and Stoic diatribe for his athletic metaphors was assumed by Rudolf Bultmann (1910) and other German scholars at the beginning of the last century.[17] Positing direct dependency tended to lead to a generalized and moralistic reading of Paul's metaphors instead of noting what is characteristic of Pauline usage: their prime application to his apostolic task and goals, with an eschatological focus.[18] Paul's indebtedness is mainly to oral traditions, especially those passed down in the Hellenistic Jewish synagogue.[19] His readers could understand references to physical athletes, but nuances in his use of agonistic terms and images are best understood on the background of language that was 'in the air.' Significant is not so much Paul's adoption of traditional imagery, but its adaptation by which he strips it of all individualistic heroics. Self-sacrifice and suffering in the cause of advancing the gospel rather than glory is the key note.

Commentators, while picking up major conclusions in my study,[20] rightly rejected some of its exegetical findings. Hans Conzelmann (1975), Gordon D. Fee (1987) and others have correctly shown that the paraenetic context and logical progression of 1 Corinthians 9:24–27 require that verse 24b be read with the verb in the imperative: 'So run,' not 'You are running' as I had suggested—even though the indicative is grammatically possible. Another corrective was soon under way. From the 1970s on, scholars increasingly argued that St. Paul's metaphors are drawn from firsthand knowledge of sporting contests.[21] Citing the archaeological work of Oscar Broneer (1962, 1971) at Isthmia near Corinth, the home of one of the four ancient Pan-Hellenic games, Carl E. De Vries (1975) asserts that Paul understood the hazards of foot racing when he wrote in Galatians 5:7: 'You were running well; who cut in on you that you do not continue to obey the truth?' The context suggests a play on words: those who *cut in* on the Galatian legalists by arguing for the *cutting off* involved in circumcision should themselves be *cut* (Galatians 5:1–12)! Like Broneer, Rainer Metzner (2000: 574) believes that Paul would have felt free to visit athletic events since in his day they had lost some of their religious character; Paul's travels would have brought him into contact with agonistic events and buildings like gymnasia in the cities he visited.[22] It is certainly reasonable to assume that the apostle would have been in Corinth at a time when the biennial Isthmian games were in full swing in April/May AD 49 or 51 (Murphy-O'Connor, 1983: 16: 2002: 15).

O. Schwankl (1997: 184, 190) sees the extended metaphor in 1 Corinthians 9 as an example of Paul's mission policy of being all things to all people (9:22): Paul assumes in his audience a love of sports and a familiarity with traditional imagery. Amphilochios Papathomas (1997) comes to similar conclusions, as does Michael Poliakoff (1984: 48): athletic images used by Jews and Christians 'reflect far more than fashions of speech and literary traditions. They are documents of social history.' While Paul's metaphors could indicate 'little more than acquaintance with the language of Greek rhetoric and popular philosophy,' imagery such as that in 1 Corinthians 9:24–27 'is too precise and vivid to be derived mechanically from a literary tradition.'

Studies on 'public shows and sporting events' in Paul's day are included in David Williams's study of Pauline metaphors (1999: chap. XII). He is mainly interested in locating allusions to Roman *spectacles*: the triumph in 2 Corinthians 2:14 and Colossians 2:15; the death of prisoners in the arena or theatre in 1 Corinthians 4:9; gladiatorial combats in 1 Corinthians 15:32, 2 Timothy 4:17 and even in Philippians 1:27; and—strangely—chariot races in Philippians 3:12–14. Williams also interprets Paul's trials in 2 Corinthians 4:8–11 in terms of the Roman arena, though the verbs used by Paul to describe his sufferings have no clear gladiatorial connotations. The conclusion that Christian 'gladiators,' the apostles and potentially all Christians are continually exposed to the risk of death is very general (266). Less attention is given to the obviously athletic imagery in 1 Corinthians 9 and elsewhere (266–73). As noted earlier, Williams suggests that Philippians 2:15, 16 pictures the apostle and his addressees as involved in a torch relay race: the latter are to shine as lights in the world so that Paul can eventually say that he has not run in vain. Such a connection is improbable.

RESETTING THE STARTING LINE

Since the turn of the century, a number of studies and two monographs—the first for over three and a half decades—have to some extent reset the agenda for further study of the agon in St. Paul's letters. Of special interest is the introduction of visual data, socio-scientific perspectives, the concept of cultural hybridity, new insights into the nature of metaphors and greater interest in Old Testament traditions present in Paul's metaphors via the Septuagint. Sifting through recent research is necessary before we attempt to summarize a modicum of consensus in reading Paul's metaphors and to indicate where paths of investigation might lead in the future.

Visual evidence such as statues, inscriptions and coins fill out the picture of the cultural significance of athletics in Greco-Roman times and help to determine how St. Paul reflects or reacts to those ideals. Philip Esler (2005: 363–70) rightly objects to interpreting New Testament data merely in terms of ideas without reference to social reality. Using socio-scientific methodology, he proposes that Paul's imagery be located within the grid of Mediterranean anthropological models of 'challenge and response' and 'honour and shame.' Given the agonistic nature of Greek culture and the concept of 'limited good,' sporting contests were competitions in which the winner gained honor for himself, his family and his polis; the loser earned nothing but shame. The visual evidence Esler offers is rather meager and does not directly relate chronologically or geographically to Paul's world. Yet, given the conservative nature of Mediterranean culture, it gives us an insight also into the apostle's social world. Esler concludes, 'Paul has adopted the language of sporting contests from the social world in which he lived in a very positive manner,' one that is 'redolent of Mediterranean culture, with its prioritising of honour as the primary good' (378). But a question remains. Paul's use of the image may well reflect contemporary ideals and values, but is he not in some way critiquing them—perhaps even subverting them?[23] Esler concedes that the apostle can be countercultural, rejecting competitiveness (377), and that there is 'an awkward quality' to the image in 1 Corinthians 9 because of its 'highly individual character.'

James Harrison (2008) offers a larger collection of visual and epigraphic materials trawled from a long time span. Aware of the dangers of anachronism and problems of provenance in citing visual evidence for the athletic ideal in antiquity, he believes that the material is representative of artifacts St. Paul might have observed (91). The apostle may have visited the Isthmian games when in Corinth or watched other local games, but would have been familiar with athletic ideals from boyhood days in Tarsus (90). 'Paul may have sourced his athletic imagery from the sermons of the popular philosophers delivered in the agora of Corinth or at the Isthmian games themselves,' but visual artifacts illustrate the athletic ideals to which Paul reacted. Whereas Esler cites visual data to illustrate Paul's text with its positive attitude to sport, Harrison begins with the question how 'Paul's sophisticated response to the Greek athletic ideal would have critiqued the visual icons of excellence as much as its literary representations' (91). Visual images help us to hear what Paul's audience possibly heard: a critique of individualism, a 'dismissive attitude to coronal honours' and the postponement of rewards (107–8).

Robert Dutch (2005: 95–167) also believes that St. Paul's metaphor in 1 Corinthians offers a critique. Examining the role of gymnasia as centers of education in the Greek world, he proposes that the elite youths in Corinth would have received physical training and philosophical instruction as essential ingredients of a good education. Agreeing with current scholarship that sees social stratification within the church at Corinth as a major factor in the community conflict (302), he identifies the 'strong' of Corinth with the educated elite. Paul rejects the reward culture that is exemplified in ancient athletics and tailors his use of the agon metaphor to the educated elite at Corinth who are glorying in their ephebic education. Dutch concludes: 'It is ironic that the weak Paul has to contend with the socially strong, the intellectual and physical athletes, and get them to adopt another perspective from the values they had learnt and cherished in their gymnasium education' (302).

Problematic here is the suggestion that St. Paul's agon image is directed to a section of the church at Corinth: the educated elite. Despite the undoubted existence of factions, of rich and poor, educated and uneducated, libertines and legalists, the apostle's pastoral policy throughout the letter is to address all in the community. Even the lowliest and uneducated are not excused from the duty of self-denial in the service of others, which is the point of Paul's metaphor in 9:24–27.[24]

Robert Seesengood (2005) brings to the discussion the recently developed concept of cultural hybridity. Hybrids are the product of colonization and fashion their identity through mimicry. 'By definition, the language of hybridity is agonistic and competitive.' Viewing St. Paul as the hybrid synthesis of multiple cultural identities may help us to understand his use of athletic metaphors (3). Traditional rhetorical use of agonistic imagery assumed that physical perfection and prowess established one's identity, marking out status. Thus one can ask: 'Might there be a way . . . to see a hybrid Paul at work on construction of a new identity or, perhaps, identities . . . which are unique and communal simultaneously? Further, could this hybrid identity be one that both "transforms" as well as acquiesces to conventional use of a particular motif?' (4).[25]

In the foregoing quotation, the word 'communal' is important. T. Engberg-Pederson (2000: 33) has noted that St. Paul adopts a rhetorical model in Stoic literature that moves the audience from 'I' to 'we,' from the individual who masters his passions to gain *apatheia* (imperturbability) to a group of successfully enlightened people who pursue the same goal. Similarly, Philo, by using the language of athletics helps to establish a hybridized community, that of Alexandrian Judaism (Seesengood, 2005: 7, 8). Engberg-Pedersen, who sees Paul as a man 'who actively participated in the moral philosophical discourse of his day' (2000: 301), finds the same goal of community building in Paul's images, though the Messianic community is quite different to that which the philosophers seek to create.

Ancient writers, who use athletic topoi, notes Seesengood, occupy 'ambiguous social and ethnic locations.' That is true of Philo, the writer of IV Maccabees, and of philosophers like the exiled Seneca and the ex-slave Epictetus. Seesengood (2005: 8) asks:

> Can it be coincidental that those with threatened or ambiguous cultural identities are those who choose metaphors rooted in competition in order to demonstrate or articulate a desire for an integrated community . . . ? The struggle of the hybrid is the agonistic struggle to fashion an identity in the face of colonization and root that identity in a community.

The conclusion is that Paul in 1 Corinthians 9:24–27 utilizes and mimics 'a conventional trope to create a new communal, hybrid identity' (9). Stress on the community in place of the individual embodying the heroic athletic ideal is on the mark, as is Seesengood's highlighting of mimicry as an essential element of hybridization. That the apostle's own social location was ambiguous and threatened also needs no discussion. Yet not all who used athletic imagery were necessarily culturally dislocated or in socially ambiguous territory. Marcus Aurelius wrote his meditations, replete with athletic topoi, on the military front lines, but his social location was certainly not ambiguous. Perhaps St. Paul was far more comfortable using agonistic imagery than Seesengood suggests, even if the apostle gives his own twist to it.

Hybridity is also, for Seesengood (2006b), a cultural model useful for understanding the agonistic imagery of the Deutero-Paulines.[26] The conflation of athletic and military language in the Pastorals and Ephesians 6:12 is intended to call to mind the image of the gladiator. Similar conflation occurs in Stoic writers and in early Christian martyr acts (96–98). Roman citizens of rank could opt out of public life by *voluntarily* choosing to become gladiators. Because they swore a vow (*sacramentum*) to endure extreme pain, loss of property and even loss of life, their role and fate could be viewed as honorable—in contrast to the dishonorable death of those condemned to fight in the arena as criminals, prisoners of war or rebellious slaves (94, 95). Passages calling Timothy to exercise himself in godliness and to fight the good fight of faith, following the example of St. Paul himself (1 Timothy 4:7–10, 6:11, 12, and 2 Timothy 4:6–8), are 'bracketed by confessional and sacrificial language recalling a prior, public oath of allegiance and the subsequent public (and grueling) execution of that oath' (92). Other texts that use military language (1Timothy 1:18–19) or a combination of military and athletic language (2 Timothy, 2:3–9) appear in association with similar motifs (93, 94).

The voluntary gladiator who swears the *sacramentum* can be seen as a model of endurance, apathy and contempt for the opinions of society, and yet as a metaphor of empowerment.[27] He thus becomes a hybrid mimic.

> Much as Paul is Jewgreek/Greekjew . . . the gladiator conflates the athlete and warrior, slave and noble, condemned and conqueror . . . Much like Paul, the threads of the gladiator are not subject to quick disentanglement. More, the gladiator escapes stable cultural categories in ways both productive and demeaning. A gladiator may be a means for the captive to express a sense or aspect of victory, and, inversely, the means to diminish the conqueror even in victory. (Seesengood, 2006b: 96)

This interpretation allows us to see how Paul and Timothy can, paradoxically, count loss as victory, death as life and dishonor as the prelude to honor. 'Far from beings signs of defeat, Paul's struggles become instead verification of his dedication to his oath' (Seesengood, 2006b: 101). Assuming that the Pastorals are a Deutero-Pauline rhetorical performance of the apostle's life and ministry, they invite the audience to become spectators of Paul the gladiator who is 'transformed from beaten prisoner to noble *invictus* to, finally, coercive presence exemplifying stunning *paideia* for all to imitate' (104).

Whether this final, valid assessment of St. Paul in the Pastorals requires the voluntary gladiator as the point of reference is open to question. It may be that some ancients perceived such to be the point of the mixture of athletic and military language, yet the images can be read as quite discrete: the soldier in 1 Timothy 1:18; the athlete in 1 Timothy 4:7–10, 6:11, 12; 2 Timothy 4:6–8—in the last text Paul's finished 'race' (*dromos*) hardly contributes to a gladiatorial image. In the case of 2 Timothy 2:3–6, three distinct images stand side by side: that of the soldier, the athlete and the farmer. Nevertheless, two aspects of Seesengood's argument remain important for the ongoing discussion: the power of an image to transform values and expectations and the concept of Paul as an exemplar requiring imitation. We will return to these points.

AN ALTERED COURSE? POPLUTZ AND BRÄNDL

Uta Poplutz's motif-historical study, *Athlet des Evangeliums* (2004), makes a valuable contribution to understanding how metaphors function. While all language has a metaphorical quality,[28] metaphors themselves, in relating two horizons of meaning to each other, create tension between their origin and their new context. New meaning arises from the 'semantic irritation' that results from the dialectical relationship between the familiar and the strange (21). Thus the clue to understanding 1 Corinthians 9:24–27 is the 'semantic irritation' between only *one* athlete winning the prize in the games and St. Paul's call to *all* at Corinth to run so as to attain it (269, 270). It is precisely this dissonance that draws the audience to new understanding.

Poplutz locates the origin of St. Paul's agonistic imagery in both rhetorical tradition and cultural reality. Writings of popular moral philosophers and the adaptation of athletic imagery in Hellenistic Judaism, as well as the apostle's contact with local contests (Poplutz, 2004: 409) provide points of reference.[29] Thus, for example, Paul's expression of regret that the Galatians have ceased to run well (Galatians 5:7) must refer to the distance race (*dolichos*), which required stamina and in which runners could be tripped by other runners (342). Tracing the agon motif in Greek and Hellenistic literature, Poplutz finds commonalities between Paul and late Stoic writers such as Seneca and Epictetus, but the illustrative parallel material in Hellenistic Jewish sources such as Philo, Josephus and IV Maccabees brings us closer to Paul's context (174). Her conclusion is that the agon metaphor 'became *the* absolute symbol of the sage striving for wisdom and truth' (215).

In analyzing St. Paul's use of the agon motif, Poplutz looks for hints at local contests, illustrative literary material and elements of literary creativity on the part of Paul. She is also interested in 'tracing in Paul a conceivable personal development which manifests itself in each different application of the agon motif corresponding to the concrete situation in the life of the apostle' (2004: 221). Consequently, it is important for her to list the Pauline letters in chronological order, from 1 Thessalonians to Romans. However, she finally concedes that her attempt to see a development in Paul can locate only a minor shift in meaning from the agon for the gospel to the agon for the *Pauline* gospel (401).

Poplutz rightly contrasts St. Paul's concept of the agon for the gospel with the moral agon of the Cynic and Stoic moral philosophers (2004: 407–9). The inner wrestling of the philosopher has nothing in common with Paul's physical sufferings as an apostle, just as the philosopher's goal of noble strength of character (*kalokagathia*) that can be realized in the present stands in stark contrast to Paul's eschatological hope of reward. So it is surprising that Poplutz sees Paul picturing himself in 1 Corinthians 9:24–27 as a wandering philosopher who conforms to the Cynic model in renouncing his rights and thus becomes a truly wise man according to Cynic-Stoic lights (286, 287).

Brändl's *Der Agon bei Paulus* (2006) arrives at significantly different conclusions. While offering an excellent account of the agon imagery in Greek and Hellenistic tradition, he is insistent that form and content are so entirely different in the case of metaphors in this tradition, on the one hand, and in St. Paul' letters, on the other, that there can be no dependence on a traditional agon motif on Paul's part. Intent on showing that Pauline usage reflects firsthand knowledge of athletics by the apostle and his readers, Brändl repeatedly asserts that Paul's imagery is lively and vivid (*lebendig* and *anschaulich*).[30] Whether such a claim for 'local coloring' can be maintained, even in the case of 1 Corinthians 9:24–27 (186–228), is open to debate. That only one contestant gained the prize was the case not only at the Isthmian games, but true of all four Pan-Hellenic crown games (Esler, 2005: 376). That the reference to a 'perishable crown' in 1 Corinthians 9:25 recalls the withered celery of the Isthmian games in contrast to the fresh celery of the Nemean games has been claimed also by others (Broneer, 1971: 186; Murphy-O'Connor, 2002: 15). However, Paul's point is that *all* earthly crowns are perishable in contrast to those that are eternal. Furthermore, to suggest that Paul had contacts with the Isthmian games as a tentmaker and provider of awnings for spectators is drawing a long bow.

None of this detracts from Brändl's major insight, one that must be taken into account in all future research. Determinative for St. Paul's theological application of agon imagery are motifs taken from the Old Testament, via the Septuagint, and early Judaism.[31] Whether descriptive of the Christian life of faith or of Paul's apostolic ministry, 'running' (Greek, *trechein*) involves intense effort, focus on the goal and gospel proclamation. All three aspects, essential for Paul's self-understanding, are located in the figure of the Suffering Servant in Deutero-Isaiah (Isaiah 49:1–6 LXX). The servant's cry, 'I have *labored* in vain,' is echoed by Paul's hope not to have *run* or *labored* in vain (Galatians 2:2; Philippians 2:16 where 'labor' and 'running' become synonymous). Prophetic vocation means 'running' as God's emissaries, eager to deliver his message (Jeremiah 12:5, 23:21, 51:31; Habakkuk 2:2). Paul is a herald of the good news, a runner with beautiful feet (Romans 10:15, citing Isaiah 52:7).

Another important element in St. Paul's linking of Old Testament motifs is that of the suffering incurred by the righteous who *run* in the paths of God's commandments (Psalm 119:32, with 22f, 41f, 51f) or *strive* after wisdom. Paul knew this tradition expressed in agonistic language in Wisdom 4:2, 10:10–12; Ben Sira 4:28; and in IV Maccabees 17:11–16.[32] That is the conceptual background of the agon of suffering and of Paul and his coworkers (1 Thessalonians 2:2, 19; Philippians 4:1–3). Similarly, the eschatological prize or crown of which Paul speaks (1 Corinthians 9:24, 25; 1 Thessalonians 2:19; Philippians 3:14, 4:1) continues the Old Testament and early Jewish motif of the reward that awaits the righteous who suffer for pursuing God's will and wisdom.

ARE WE NOW RUNNING TOGETHER?

There now is something approaching a consensus on the origin of St. Paul's agon metaphors and on their rhetorical application in Paul's letters, but it is too soon to speak of agreement. For example, Alois Koch recently still judges that Paul shows no immediate familiarity with the games, since his metaphors offer no more than general and vague details; the apostle knew and borrowed from the diatribes of the popular moralists (Koch, 2008: 72).[33] On both counts Brändl and others would strongly disagree.

In my view it is time to call a truce on this question in terms of a simple alternative: either cultural realism or rhetorical tradition.[34] The introduction of Septuagintal motifs by Brändl makes such a simple option impossible. In any case, agonistic exercises and philosophical traditions existed side by side in the gymnasium, the fundamental institution of Greek culture. Physical, mental and moral *askesis* went hand in hand. 'Greek philosophy was, in many ways, born in the locker rooms of the Athenian gymnasia' (Seesengood, 2006b: 88). It was the very valorization of physical athletics that fostered the development and continuation of the ideal of the philosopher-athlete and its attendant imagery down to St. Paul's time. Agonistic imagery assumes, at the very least, a basic understanding of what went on at the public games.[35] One can hardly imagine the hybrid Jewgreek Paul not knowing something of the public games, whether from oral reports, coins, statuary or other visual objects.

It is equally difficult to imagine a Hellenistic Jew like St. Paul not hearing in his travels the language and imagery of the popular moral philosophers who were as omnipresent in the Roman East as athletic festivals themselves. The argument that form, content and purpose differ so markedly in philosophical and Pauline use of athletic metaphors as to allow no relationship between the two overlooks the fact that the agon tradition is no smooth and unified development, even within the philosophical tradition from Xenophanes down to the late Stoics (Pfitzner, 1967: 24–35; Brändl, 2006: 32–68). Hellenistic Jews like Philo and the writers of Wisdom and IV

Maccabees saw no problem in adapting popular Stoic diction and imagery for their own purposes.

There is greater consensus on St. Paul's theological application of athletic imagery. His understanding of himself as an athlete of Christ, advancing the gospel, suffering opposition and drawing others into the same agon, was apparently so characteristic of him that he could use agonistic terminology without explanation or elaboration. Indeed, such language was so typical of the apostle that it was recalled by later writers (Acts 20:24), possibly also by some writing pseudonymously (Colossians 1:29–2:1, 4:12; 1 Timothy 4:7–10, 6:11, 12; 2 Timothy 2:5, 4:7–8). Paul's own ministry as an agon involving both *running* forward and *standing* firm became the basis of his appeal to converts to pursue an eschatological goal and to remain steadfast in the faith (1 Corinthians 16:13), in the Lord (Philippians 4:1; 1 Thessalonians 3:8), in one spirit (Philippians. 1:27), in the freedom of the gospel (Galatians 5:1) and to be 'steadfast and immoveable' in hope (1 Corinthians 16:58; see also Ephesians 6:11–14; 2 Thessalonians 2:15). Progress and passion in resisting opposition belong together.

THE ATHLETE AS IDEAL TYPE

A fruitful approach in future inquiry might be to focus on what the *ideal* athlete in antiquity represented in cultural terms, as that ideal is reflected in the conduct of the actual contests, in visual objects, or in popular imagery. This may help us better to understand the rhetorical impact of Paul's metaphors. Clearly, we cannot read back into the past modern ideals such as the honor of participation rather than winning, seeking the glory of the game itself rather than that of the contestants or teamwork ahead of individual achievement (there were no team games in Greek and Hellenistic times). And clearly we cannot assume that every winning athlete incarnated an accepted ideal.

We are not to conclude from the polemics of philosophers, especially Cynics,[36] against 'merely physical' and therefore inferior athletes that participants in the games were no longer held in honor but seen as mindless, muscle-bound 'jocks'! Any claim to be a true athlete makes little sense unless it rides on the back of popular perception of the athlete as embodying popular virtues apart from strength, courage and endurance. Centuries of philosophical claims to be involved in a superior agon obviously meant no diminution of honor for athletes, especially for victors who were the equivalent of modern sporting idols. In the second century AD, well after Paul, the many victories of the pankratiast M. Aurelius Asclepiades, won from Asia Minor to Italy, were on record.[37] Such heroes were memorialized.

Lucian states what was true for Greek culture down to Hellenistic times. The athlete represented and exemplified what the polis had the right to expect from every citizen: the perfection of physical beauty, prime condition, daring, indomitable resolve and the ardent desire for victory (Anacharsis 12). Athletic exercise and competition were thus the perfect preparation for warfare in the service of the state. Naturally, it was the winning athlete who became an ideal to be emulated, especially if the hero combined brawn, beauty and brains as in the case of the deceased boxer Melancomas, lauded by Dio Chrysostom as:

> the most courageous and the biggest of all mankind and the most beautiful. Had he remained a private citizen and not practiced boxing at all, I believe that he would still have become widely known simply for his beauty . . . And yet he dressed in such a way as to escape rather than to attract attention . . . And although beauty customarily leads to softness, even for one who is only moderately beautiful, Melancomas was the most moderate of men despite his beauty. And though he despised his beauty, he preserved it nonetheless and despite his rough sport.[38]

It is only on the presupposition that the idealized athlete represents a heroic figure that we can understand the endurance of the agon motif in its varied literary history. In the case of the philosophers, the hero can be idealized to assume superhuman proportions. His labors interpreted as moral struggles, Hercules becomes the patron and model for the Stoic in his agon against fate and the dominance of passions (Pfitzner, 1967: 29). The Jewish tradition of the agon for virtue and wisdom also develops the heroic theme. With Philo it is the patriarchs and such figures as Enoch, Noah and Moses who are the proto-agonists to be emulated (41, 42). In Wisdom 10:10–12 (see the metaphor also in 4:1) it is Jacob the wrestler who becomes the heroic paradigm for the pursuit of wisdom.[39] Yet the best encomium for heroic athletes of virtue in fidelity to the law of God is that recorded in IV Maccabees 17:11–16:

> For truly it was a holy contest [*agon*] in which they contended. For on that day virtue, proving them through endurance set before them the prize of victory, incorruption in everlasting life. The first to contest was Eleazar; the mother of the seven sons also joined in the contest, and the sons contended. The tyrant was their opponent [i.e. antagonist], and the world and humanity were the spectators. Godliness won the victory, crowning her athletes. Who but wondered at the athletes of the divine law? Who were not amazed at them?

PAUL'S SUBVERSION OF A METAPHOR AND HEROIC IDEAL

A traditional image can be used to gain attention but then be modified to give an unexpected meaning. It may well be that 1 Corinthians 9:24–27 is not the only example of this. In 2 Corinthians 2:14–16 St. Paul probably

tunes into his opponents' picture of himself as a victim in a Roman triumph, being led to execution, only to turn the image in his favor; the procession in which he participates is an epiphany procession in which Christ
is revealed (Duff, 1991). This process of subversion is described by K. A.
Plank (1987: 77) as follows:

> Through the use of symbolic speech a writer taps the potential of lan-
> guage to estrange ordinary images and notions from their expected
> contexts, thereby jolting readers out of familiar continuities. Arrested
> by the novelty of symbolic speech, its readers are diverted from their
> well-defended patterns of thinking and find their perception of new
> insights blocks any retreat into the familiar system of values.

A 'subversion of the *agon* motif' has been located in Romans 9:30–10:15 by
Douglas Campbell (2009: 789–91). Here St. Paul 'is twisting the normally
heroic discourse into a farce,' a 'comic manipulation of the *agon* motif'
(791), and doing so in three ways. He asserts in 9:30 that those not compet-
ing/running have won the prize. Gentiles not even pursuing righteousness
have received it by God's gracious action. Secondly, in 9:31–32a Paul says
that Israel continues to run in a race for righteousness, but it is a race that
is already over. Thirdly, 10:4 asserts that Christ is the end and goal of the
race. Thus, for Paul the Jewish agon in pursuit of righteousness, subsequent to the Christ event, is misdirected if not ludicrous or farcical. Finally,
9:32b-33 pictures Christ as the stumbling block of Isaiah 8:14, which trips
up Israel as it runs after righteousness according to the law. Clearly, Paul
was not worried by the mixed metaphor: Israel is running in the wrong
direction and is also tripped up by Christ as the stumbling block!

Is there a similar process of subversion in 1 Corinthians 9:24–27? The
usual question is 'What did St. Paul *mean* with the extended metaphor?' It
may be equally helpful to ask 'What did his audience possibly *hear*?' The
opening challenge 'Do you not know?' is an arresting litotes formula meaning, 'You surely know.' Included in the assumed knowledge would be some
familiarity with athletics, but the phrase echoes Paul's repeated challenges
earlier in the letter for his hearers to drawn obvious conclusions about what
they *know* for responsible Christian behavior (3:16, 6:2, 3, 9, 15, 16, 19,
9:13). 'Do you not know' was a standard phrase in diatribal diction and
argumentative rhetoric,[40] but there is a special edge to such challenges in
this letter since they appear in the context of Corinthian claims to possess
knowledge (8:1–7) and freedom (6:12, 10:23). Paul's audience may soon
begin to sense that they know less about freedom than they have thought!

Progression from '*all* run' to 'only *one* receives the prize' to 'so [*all*]
run' may produce some slight 'semantic irritation' (Poplutz) for St. Paul's
audience, but the logic is clear enough on reflection. At issue is the application of energy and concentration on the goal in order to achieve victory,
not winning at the expense of others. Even the sequence of competition

('running' in verse 24) and preparation for competition ('self-control' in verse 25) provides no problem. Listeners are aware of the rigorous training and self-discipline required of physical athletes; some may also be aware that self-control is a common theme in the moral discourses of the philosophers, as is the contrast between fading and lasting crowns. In both cases, physical *askesis* is a sine qua non of participation in the agon to receive the prize.[41]

As the metaphor becomes more elaborate 'conceptual irritation' arises for the hearer, to the extent that one may speak with Robert Seesengood (2005) of a mocking mimicry. That a competitor should run in a haphazard manner without having the mind fixed on the goal, or that a boxer or pankratiast should flail the air with his fists without making each blow count, is risible (1 Corinthians 9:26). However, the picture of St. Paul the athlete thrashing his own body rather than that of the opponent turns the primary image of competing for victory and honor upside down. His own body, that is, his own person with its physical desires and appetites, is treated as a boxer or pankratiast would treat an enemy! Rather than the heroic body beautiful of the victor, the listener is invited to see the apostle with self-inflicted bruised face and black eyes (*hypopiazo* in verse 27a literally means to beat under the eyes). His body is subjected as a slave ('I subdue it,' 27b), pressed into a higher service than that of his personal desires.

How listeners heard the end of verse 27 is impossible to ascertain. Coming at the end of an extended metaphor, 'preaching' (Greek, *keryxas*) might have recalled for some the office of the herald of the games even if St. Paul's primary reference was to his apostolic proclamation of the gospel. It is surprising not only that Paul, the athlete of Christ *par excellence*, should call his converts to imitate him in *limiting* his personal freedom in the service of others, but that he even contemplates the possibility of being disqualified from receiving the prize from the eschatological judge. It is this shocking thought that concludes the apostle's discussion on Christian freedom, while at the same time leading back to the concrete issue that initiated the discussion: the question of eating meat offered to idols. The possibility of losing the prize is picked up in the next chapter as Paul addresses the danger of presuming on God's grace (8:1–12).

St. Paul has used the example of the renunciation of his own apostolic rights to a higher good to illustrate that *true freedom is the ability to surrender it to the claims of one's Christian brother or sister* (1 Corinthians 8:13).[42] Self-control is for the apostle not an element of an ascetic lifestyle but an essential part of responsibility for one's fellow believer.[43] To extend the agon imagery to its logical conclusion, Paul the runner will only win the prize if he helps his fellow runners across the line. Ben Witherington (1995: 214) is right: 'Paul cuts a peculiar figure. His life has a cruciform shape; its rejection of status is what he wishes his converts to exemplify.' Service of others, not one's own honor, is what Paul's agon image is meant to illustrate.

St. Paul's approach to the athletic ideal in antiquity is quite radical. He rejects its individualism, its elitism and the lure of immediate rewards (Harrison, 2008: 108). He can boast of his converts and speak of them as his 'crown' and source of honor (1 Thessalonians 2:19; Philippians 4:1), but there is no reward for his 'running' in the same sense that an athlete is rewarded *immediately* after a race or bout. If final judgment is the prerogative of the eschatological judge (1 Corinthians 4:3–5), so is the allocation of rewards. Only the 'day of Christ' will confirm that Paul's running has not been in vain (Philippians 2:16; Galatians 2:2). Thus Paul's life is a constant striving forward towards the prize, not a retrospective assessment of successes and failures along the way. Philippians 3:12–14 may not subvert the athletic ideal, but it certainly does not conform to it with its deferral of rewards. While the apostle is a type (Greek, *typos*) to be imitated, it is not as a heroic ideal (Philippians 3:17). Those who follow his example reject earthly glory as incurring shame; they look to heavenly glory while running the course marked out by the shameful cross (3:18–21).

Yet Paul the apostle is more than a model or paradigm, as is suggested by his use of verbs with athletic connotations beginning with the prefix 'with' (*synathlein* and *synagonizesthai* in Philippians 1:27, 4:3; Romans 15:30). Agonistic language no longer expresses competition and rivalry in the human quest for honor and status. It instead illustrates the vocation Paul shares with his audience; they are in a common contest (*agon* or *athlesis*) for the gospel, and that in a double sense: it is a struggle to promote the gospel (Philippians 1:27, 4:3) and to withstand opposition in the process (Philippians 1:30; 1 Thessalonians 2:2). Solidarity in prayer is part of this 'striving' together (Romans 15:30). Individual achievement here gives way to total teamwork as fellow believers strive together 'in one spirit, with one mind' (Philippians 1:27). The ultimate reason for this is not some general sense of Christian egalitarianism or comradeship, but the common experience of grace. Where the Hellenistic world pictures the idealized runner as the achiever, Paul says that the common experience of divine compassion 'depends not on human will or exertion [Greek, 'running'] but on God who shows mercy' (Romans 9:16).

A POSTSCRIPT: THE PASTORAL LETTERS

The Pastorals continue a strong Pauline emphasis: in the case of both the apostle and Timothy the pupil, the personal agon *of* faith cannot be separated from the agon *for* the faith.[44] Their calling in each case includes both aspects. Yet the call to Timothy to 'fight the *good fight* of faith,' following the example of Paul (1 Timothy 6:11–16; 2 Timothy 4:7, 8) introduces a slightly different tone. The designation of the agon as 'good' (*kalos*) recalls the language of the philosophical agon tradition (Pfitzner, 1967: 166), as does the contrast between training (*askesis*) in godliness and bodily training.

Such diction is in keeping with the introduction of secular Hellenistic terminology in the Pastorals, for example, the references to emperor worship in the case of the first passage (Mounce, 2000: 352). In the second passage Paul becomes the ideal agonist who stands at the end of his race (*dromos*). The 'crown of righteousness' is still a future reward for faithfulness, but there is no hint of the possibility of Paul having 'run in vain.' Timothy, also, can take hold of the prize of eternal life now.

One can tentatively suggest that the heroization of the athlete of Christ that we see in 1 Clement 5 and 6 (where Paul and Peter are noble paradigms) and in the early martyr acts actually begins in the Pastoral Letters rather than in the undisputed letters of Paul.

NOTES

1. Popular and devotional considerations of biblical sporting metaphors understandably tend to be simplistic, sometimes crass. Higgs and Braswell (2004: 95) cite Neal (1975) for a crass example: Paul gives directions on inculcating team spirit in gridiron football when he writes, 'Therefore encourage one another and build up one another, just as you are doing' (1 Thess. 5:11). Practically, this means showing an underperforming team member how to employ stiff-arm tactics when being tackled!
2. Though ritual remains at the Olympic Games, modern athletics differ in that the religious context is removed, competition is open to all, events require specialization and professionalism and there is an emphasis on rules and records. Attempts to sacralize modern sports in the name of Christianity tend to lead to a God-is-on-our-side triumphalism, to a theology of glory.
3. Unless otherwise stated, all scriptural quotations are taken from the NRSV. Only the obvious athletic terms are here highlighted.
4. Stanley Stowers (1994: 313–16) suggests that Israel's fall or failure in Romans 11:11, 12 pictures Israel as being tripped up while running, with the Gentiles racing ahead; yet recovery is possible, so that Jew and Gentile Christians will together eventually reach the goal of redemption (11:26). The problem of an exact identification of the image in 1 Corinthians 4:9 is well known. Nguyen (2007) argues that Paul's picture of the apostles as people sentenced to death refers neither to gladiatorial combats nor to the Roman triumph, but to the public execution of condemned criminals (*noxii*) in the arena.
5. Imagery is less clear in Col. 2:18: 'Do not let anyone disqualify you' obscures the reference to loss of a prize. In 3:15, 'Let the peace of Christ *rule* in your hearts' alludes to the role of a referee.
6. This explanation is preferable to that of C. E. Arnold (1989: 116, 117), who suggests that the writer of Ephesians is referring to the story of an athlete at the Ephesian games who was undefeated in wrestling until a magical amulet was removed; the Ephesians are to put on spiritual armor to wrestle again spiritual powers, including magic.
7. In the New Testament canon, only the author of Hebrews frequently uses athletic terminology though not with the same consistency of meaning as St. Paul (see Heb. 5:14, 10:32, 11:33, 12:1–4). Athletic connotations of vocabulary in Luke 13:24, John 18:36, 2 Peter 2:14 and Jude 3 mostly disappear in translation.

8. W. van Unnik's argument (1962) that Luke in Acts 22:3 used a conventional biographical progression from birth/origin (Greek, *genesis*) to early childhood nurture (*trophe*) and education (*paideia*) to indicate that Paul came to Jerusalem at an early age has not led to scholarly consensus. For our present discussion it is not important whether Paul's familiarity with Hellenistic culture began with childhood spent in Tarsus or came from his post-conversion stay in that city (Gal. 1:21; Acts 9:30, 11:25); the former is more likely.

9. For the introduction of the games on Palestinian soil as a part of the process of Hellenization under Antiochus IV Epiphanes and Herod the Great, see Harris (1976), Poliakoff (1984: 60) and Brändl (2006: 140–77).

10. On the religious nature of the games, also in the first century AD, see, e.g., Pfitzner (1967: 18–20), Fredriksen (2002) and Guttmann (1992). The inseparable connection between the Greek games and the gods is perhaps best paralleled by the deep nexus between Japanese sumo wrestling and Shinto rituals.

11. Harris (1976: 16) speculates whether Paul might have learned about the games 'as a little Jewish boy running about the streets of Tarsus.' Others have followed this view.

12. Philo certainly watched a wrestling match (Quod omnis probus 26) and may have himself participated in sports as a youth.

13. Fuller summaries of research into Paul's athletic metaphors can be found in Pfitzner (1967), Poplutz (2004) and Brändl (2006).

14. Bengel, Gnomon, 1860 (1773) commenting on 1 Cor. 9:24: 'similitudo a re Corinthiis valde nota.'

15. Cited by Brändl (2006: 15).

16. See also the conclusion by Eidem (1913–1914: 4): 'The relative lack of vivid detail [sc. in Paul's agon metaphors] speaks most of all for their origin in the tradition' (my translation).

17. H. Funke (1970) returned to the thesis of literary dependency on the part of Paul in 1 Cor. 9:24–27 by citing the speech of Antisthenes preserved in the eighth discourse of Dio Chrysostom. However, both context and terminology are markedly different with the Cynic and Paul.

18. Jerry M. Hullinger (2004: 359) still reads Paul's agon metaphors in terms of general Christian ethics; they teach that 'the Christian life requires an earnest, consistent striving, fuelled by the grace of God, and that 'the child of God must be careful to strive according to the rules (2 Tim. 2:5) in order to receive rewards from the Lord.'

19. This is the view also of older scholars Schmid (1921) and Stauffer (1964).

20. Freyne (1989: 98) also deems it likely that Paul reflects a philosophical tradition since his allusions are sparse and lacking in detail when compared with the metaphors of Philo. N. Clayton Croy's study of athletic imagery in the Epistle to the Hebrews, especially 12:1–13, includes a section on 'athletes and exemplars' in Hellenistic moral exhortation (1998: 37–76). His conclusion is that the unknown author of Hebrews uses traditional imagery to picture Jesus as the paradigm of endurance in suffering.

21. The work of Harris (1964, 1976) was not available to me when completing my dissertation in 1964. With attention to source material and studies on the actual Greek games (e.g., by Finley and Pleket, 1976; Gardiner, 1978) my conclusions would have been more nuanced.

22. Finley and Pleket (1976) suggest that, by the end of the New Testament era, over three hundred athletic festivals were celebrated in the Greco-Roman world. On the plurality of games, apart from the classical *periodos* or 'round' of the Pan-Hellenic games (Olympic, Isthmian, Nemean and Pythian) see Gardiner (1978: 37–42).

23. The contrast between 'they' and 'we' and between perishable and imperishable prizes suggests that the apostle is not simply endorsing the accepted social status and significance of sports. His readers are called to activity that is superior, holding promise of superior prizes.

24. For the same reason Ben Witherington's suggestion (1995: 214) that Paul, like Philo (Quod deterius 1.42, 42), is making a point against Sophists in saying he does not 'beat the air' is dubious. In any case, the apostle is talking about effective boxing rather than shadowboxing.

25. Robert Seesengood is here reacting to my stress on Paul's transformation of the traditional agon imagery (Pfitzner, 1967: 188, 189, 194, 202–4). His suggestion that I see Paul's theological assertions as transcending culture is not correct. All theological language, including the use of imagery, is cultural.

26. The discussion here follows Seesengood's article (2006b) 'Contending for the Faith' adopted from the larger monograph *Competing Identities* (2006a).

27. Seesengood is here dependent on the work of Barton (1993).

28. Poplutz is reliant on the work of such people as Gadamer, Ricoeur and Jüngel.

29. Her conclusion that Paul gained a knowledge of sporting contests in Jerusalem rather than in his home city of Tarsus can be contested; Jerusalem had a gymnasium in Hellenistic times but no games (Poplutz, 2004: 411). Quotes from Poplutz's work are in my own translation.

30. A look at the vivid and detailed imagery of Philo in Agric. 113–19 confirms the lack of detail in Pauline usage. For an excellent translation of the passage see Harris (1976: 56). For the extensive range of agonistic vocabulary in Philo, some quite technical, see Harris's index of over three hundred words, and Mayer's *Index* (1974).

31. What follows picks up the chief points made by Brändl (2006: 414–8) in his own summary of the argument.

32. Brändl is here dependent on the work of Kleinknecht, *Der leidende Gerechtfertigte* (1988).

33. The reference is to the English translation offered at www.con-spiration.de/koch/english/paul-e.

34. Recent scholarly commentaries on the relevant texts in 1 Corinthians and Philippians reflect this trend. See also, most recently, Arnold's (2012) essay.

35. Epictetus (3.15.2–4 and 3.20.9–10) reflects a good knowledge of gymnastic training and athletics. On the richness of Philonic imagery see note 31.

36. For texts, particularly from the Orations of Dio Chrysostom, see Pfitzner (1967: 28, 29). Dio (Or. 8.9–12) depicts the Cynic Diogenes at the Isthmian games in c. 359 BC, claiming the superiority of the moral athlete: 'The man who is noble is the one who considers hardship as his greatest competitor and struggles with it day and night, and not, like some goat [sc. the physical athlete!], for a bit of celery, olive, or pine, but for the sake of happiness and virtue throughout his life.'

37. See Nichoff (2003: 282, 283) with the map showing victory locations.

38. Cited by Poliakoff (1984: 57) and Harrison (2008: 103), both of whom provide other examples of outstanding athletes honored for combining training of mind and character with exercise of the body. For athletes as exemplars, see also Croy (1998: chap. 2).

39. The figure of Job as wrestler (*agonistes*) for the truth is postbiblical (Poliakoff, 1984).

40. See Bultmann (1910: 13, 65).

41. Mention of the prize (Greek, *brabeion*) before the 'wreath' in verses 24 and 25 allows the listener to think of any local athletic contest, not only of the Isthmian or the other coronal games.

42. The Greek word *exousia* in 9:5, 6 is related to the verb *exestin* that appears in the Corinthian catch cry of freedom in 6:12 and 10:23 ('We are free to do everything'), and is probably for that reason preferred by Paul over the normal Greek word for freedom, *eleutheria*, which would be expected after the adjective *eleutheros* in 9:1.
43. For a discussion of early Christian asceticism and 1 Cor. 9:27a, see Yinger (2008).
44. The example of the athlete is cited in 2 Tim. 2:5 as part of a threefold illustration, not as a metaphor.

BIBLIOGRAPHY

Note: The following list does not attempt to offer even a selection of the ever-growing literature, including online sites, on the history and characteristics of ancient athletic games and Roman spectacles. Nor are the standard commentaries listed.

Arnold, B. (2012) Re-envisioning the Olympic Games: Paul's use of Athletic Imagery in Philippians, *Theology*, 115 (4): 243–252.

Arnold, C. E. (1989) *Ephesians: Power and Magic*, Cambridge: Cambridge University Press.

Barton, Carlin. (1993) *The Sorrows of the Ancient Romans: The Gladiators and the Monster*, Princeton, NJ: Princeton University Press.

Bengel, J. A. (1860) *Gnomon Novi Testamenti . . . secundum editionem tertiam (1773)*, Berlin: Gust. Schlawitz.

Brändl, M. (2006) *Der Agon bei Paulus: Herkunft und Profil paulinischer Agonmetaphorik*, Tübingen: Mohr Siebeck.

Broneer, O. (1962) The Apostle Paul and the Isthmian Games, *Biblical Archaeologist*, 25: 2–31.

Broneer, Oscar. (1971) Paul and the Pagan Cults of Isthmia, *Harvard Theological Review*, 64: 169–87.

Bultmann, R. (1910) *Der Stil der paulinischen Predigt und die kynisch-stoische Diatribe. FRLANT 13*, Göttingen: Vandenhoeck und Ruprecht.

Campbell, D. A. (2009) *The Deliverance of God: An Apocalyptic Reading of Justification in Paul*, Grand Rapids, MI: Eerdmans.

Conzelmann, H. (1975) *1 Corinthians. Hermeneia*, Philadelphia, PA: Fortress Press.

Croy, N. C. (1998) *Endurance in Suffering: Hebrews 12:1–13 in Its Rhetorical, Religious and Philosophical Context*, Cambridge: Cambridge University Press.

De Vries, C. E. (1975) Paul's "Cutting" Remarks about a Race: Galatians 5:1–12, in *Current Issues in Biblical and Patristic Interpretation*, Gerald F. Hawthorne (Ed.), Grand Rapids, MI: Eerdmans, 115–20.

Duff, P. B. (1991) Metaphor, Motif and Meaning: The Rhetorical Structure behind the Image "Led in Triumph" in 2 Corinthians 2:14, *Catholic Biblical Quarterly*, 53: 79–92.

Dutch, R. S. (2005) *The Educated Elite in 1 Corinthians: Education and Community Conflict in Graeco-Roman Context*, London: T & T Clark.

Eidem, E. (1913–1914) *Pauli Bildvärld I, Athletae et Milites Christi*, Lund, 1913. German summary in *Beiträge zur Religionswissenschaft der religionsw. Gesellschaft zu Stockholm*, 1 (1913/14): 212–22.

Engberg-Pedersen, T. (2000) *Paul and the Stoics*, Louisville, KY: Westminster/John Knox Press.

Esler, P. F. (2005) Paul and the Agon: Understanding a Pauline Motif in Its Cultural and Visual Context, in A. Weissenrieder, F. Wendt and Petra von Gemünden.

(Eds.), *Picturing the New Testament: Studies in Ancient Visual Images*, Tübingen: Mohr Siebeck, 357–84.

Fee, G. D. (1987) *The First Epistle to the Corinthians. The New International Comentary on the New Testament*, Grand Rapids, MI: Eerdmans.

Finley, M. I. and Pleket, H. W. (1976) *The Olympic Games. The First Thousand Years*, New York: Viking Press.

Fredriksen, P. (2002) Paul at the Races, *Bible Review*, 18 (3): 12, 42.

Freyne, S. (1989) Early Christianity and the Greek Athletic Ideal, *Sport, Concilium*, 205 (5): 93–100.

Funke, H. (1970) Antisthenes bei Paulus, *Hermes*, 98: 459–71.

Gardiner, E. N. (1978) *Athletics of the Ancient World*, Chicago: Ares.

Garrison, R. (1997) Paul's Use of the Athletic Metaphor in I Corinthians 9, in R. Garrison (Ed,), *The Greco-Roman Context of Early Christian Literature*, Sheffield, UK: Sheffield Academic Press, 95–104.

Gudorf, M. E. (1998) The Use of PALH in Ephesians 6:12, *Journal of Biblical Literature*, 117 (2): 331–35.

Guttmann, Allen. (1992) From Ritual to Record, in Shirl J. Hoffman (Ed.), *Sport and Religion*, Champagne, IL: Human Kinetics Books, 143–151.

Harris, H. H. (1964) *Greek Athletes and Athletics*, London, UK: Thames and Hudson.

Harris, H. H. (1976) *Greek Athletics and the Jews*. Cardiff, UK: University of Wales Press.

Harrison, J. R. (2008) Paul and the Athletic Ideal in Antiquity: A Case Study in Wrestling with Word and Image, in Stanley E. Porter (Ed.), *Paul's World*, Leiden: E. J. Brill: 81–109.

Higgs, R. J. and Braswell, M. C. (2004), *An Unholy Alliance: The Sacred and Modern Sports*, Macon, GA: Mercer University Press.

Howson, J. S. (1868) *The Metaphors of St. Paul*, London: Strahan and Co.

Hullinger, Jerry M. (2004) The Historical Background of Paul's Athletic Allusions, *Bibliotheca Sacra*, 161 (643): 343–59.

Kleinknecht, K. Th. (1988) *Der leidende Gerechtfertigte*, WUNT II.13, Tübingen: Mohr Siebeck.

Koch, A. (2008) 'Paulus und die Wettkampfmetaphorik', *Trierer Theologische Zeitschrift*, 1: 39–55. Available online with English version at www.con.spiration.de/koch/english/paul.e (accessed 3 August 2011).

Krentz, E. (2003) Paul, Games and the Military, in J. P. Sampley (Ed.), *Paul in the Greco-Roman World: A Handbook*, Harrisburg, PA: Trinity Press International, 344–83.

Mayer, Günter (1974) *Index Philoneus*, Berlin: Walter de Gruyter.

Metzner, R. (2000) Paulus und der Wettkampf: Die Rolle des Sportes im Leben und Verkündigung des Apostels (1 Kor 9.24–27; Phil 3.12–16), *New Testament Studies*, 46 (4): 565–83.

Mounce, W. D. (2000) *Pastoral Epistles. Word Biblical Commentary*, Nashville, TN: Nelson.

Murphy-O'Connor, J. (1983) *St. Paul's Corinth. Texts and Archaeology*, Collegeville, PA: Liturgical Press; third edition, 2002.

Neal, W. (1975) *The Handbook of Athletic Perfection*, Prescott, AZ: Institute of Athletic Perfection.

Nguyen, V. T. (2007) The Identification of Paul's Spectacle of Death Metaphor in 1 Cor. 4:9, *New Testament Studies*, 53 (4): 489–501.

Nichoff, J. (2003) Athlete, in H. Cancik and H. Schneider (Eds.), *Brills New Pauly*, English ed., vol. 2, Leiden: Brill, 282–83.

Papathomas, A. (1997) Das agonistische Motiv 1 Kor. 9:24ff im Spiegel zeigenössischer dokumentarischer Quellen, *New Testament Studies*, 43: 223–41.

Pfitzner, V. C. (1967) *Paul and the Agon Motif. Traditional Athletic Imagery in the Pauline Literature, NovTSup 17*, Leiden: E. J. Brill.

Pfitzner, V. C. (1981) Martyr and Hero: The Origin and Development of a Tradition in the Early Christian Martyr-Acts, *Lutheran Theological Journal*, 15 (1–2): 9–17.

Pfitzner, V. C. (2008) We Are the Champions! Origins and Developments of the Image of God's Athletes, *Sport and Spirituality: An Exercise in Everyday Theology, Interface*, 11 (1): 49–64.

Plank, K. A. (1987) *Paul and the Irony of Affliction, SBL Semeia Studies*, Atlanta: Scholars Press.

Poliakoff, M. (1984) Jacob, Job, and Other Wrestlers: Reception of Greek Athletics by Jews and Christians in Antiquity, *Journal of Sport History*, 2 (2): 48–65.

Poplutz, U. (2004) *Athlet des Evangeliums: eine motivgeschichtliche Studie zur Wettkampfmetaphorik bei Paulus, Herders Biblische Studien, 43*, Freiburg, Germany: Herder.

Schmid, L. (1921) *Der Agon bei Paulus*. Unpublished dissertation, Tübingen, Germany.

Schwankl, O. (1997) 'Lauft so, dass ihr gewinnt': Zur Wettkampfmetaphorik in 1 Kor 9, *Biblische Zeitschrift*, 41: 174–91.

Seesengood, R. P. (2005) Hybridity and the Rhetoric of Endurance: Reading Paul's Athletic Metaphors in a Context of Postcolonial Self-Construction, *Bible and Critical Theory*, 1 (3): 1–14.

Seesengood, R. P. (2006a) *Competing Identities: The Athlete and the Gladiator in Early Christian Literature. Journal for the Study of the New Testament, Supplement Series*, New York: Continuum.

Seesengood, R. P. (2006b) Contending for the Faith in Paul's Absence: Combat Sports and Gladiators in the Disputed Pauline Epistles, *Lexington Theological Quarterly*, 41 (2): 87–118.

Stauffer, E. (1964) Agon; athletes; brabeuo, in G. Kittel (Ed.), *Theological Dictionary of the New Testament*, trans. G. Bromiley, Grand Rapids, MI: Eerdmans, I:134–40, 167–68, 637–39 .

Stowers, S. K. (1994) *A Rereading of Roman: Justice, Jews, and Gentiles*, New Haven, CT: Yale University Press.

Straub, W. (1937) *Die Bildersprache des Apostels Paulus*, Tübingen: J. C. B. Mohr [Paul Siebeck].

Van Unnik, W. P. (1962) *Tarsus or Jerusalem*, London: Epworth.

Williams, D. J. (1999) *Paul's Metaphors: Their Context and Character*, Peabody, MA: Hendrickson.

Witherington III, B. (1995) *Conflict and Community in Conflict: A Socio-Rhetorical Commentary on 1 and 2 Corinthians*, Grand Rapids, MI: Eerdmans.

Yinger, Kent L. (2008) Paul and Asceticism in 1 Corinthians 9:27a, *Journal of Religion and Society*, 10: 1–17.

3 Sport and Religion in England, c. 1790–1914

Hugh McLeod

INTRODUCTION

The Church Congress was an annual conference of Anglican clergy and lay-people at which topical issues were debated. In 1892 they returned after an interval of several years to what was by then an old favorite—the Church's relationship to popular recreations. For the first time the contributors to this debate included both a woman (the manager of a Kensington gymnasium) and a missionary bishop. The latter declared that in tropical Africa 'Athletic Exercises seem by the natives to be associated with Christianity.' He welcomed their enthusiasm for football while regretting that they had not yet shown an interest in cricket (*Official Report*, 1892: 319). By this time sport had become part of the package of British practices and values that missionaries brought with them to Africa, Asia and the Pacific (Mangan, 1986). Indeed an eminent African coach claims, 'When Dr. David Livingstone came to Zambia he brought three things with him in his bag. His medical kit, the Bible and a football.' While granting that Dr. Livingstone was not a footballer, Goldblatt notes that the first footballers in Uganda, Nigeria, the French Congo and probably the Gold Coast were missionaries (Goldblatt, 2006: 479, 484–85). Yet fifty years earlier this association between Christianity and athletics would have been unimaginable.

RELIGION VS. SPORT

In England around 1840 relations between the worlds of religion and of sport had been at their nadir. Clergymen had often been among the leaders of the campaigns to suppress the 'calendar sports' associated with particular days of the church year, such as Shrove Tuesday (Hackwood, 1907). Some, such as throwing at cocks or bullbaiting, were condemned for their cruelty, while others such as street football were seen as a source of disorder, destruction of property and sometimes severe injuries to the participants (Malcolmson, 1973). Newer sports such as horse racing and prizefighting were equally objectionable because of the brutality of the latter and the gambling that was an intrinsic part of both (Huggins, 2000; Brailsford, 1988).

The Evangelicals, whose influence was at its peak between about 1790 and 1860, were engaged in a comprehensive program of moral reformation, which left few aspects of contemporary life untouched (Rosman, 1984). Their ideal was the 'serious Christian,' suspicious of anything that appeared to be 'worldly' and responsible to God for the way that he or she used every hour of the day. The more discriminating critique of popular leisure pursuits by the early Evangelicals was hardening from the 1790s into a wholesale condemnation. As the Birmingham Congregationalist R. W. Dale later recalled, by the 1830s and 1840s, 'To play at cards, or to dance, or to go to the theatre, or to get into an omnibus or a cab on a Sunday, was as great a revolt against an unwritten but authoritative opinion as to reject the Calvinistic theory of original sin or the doctrine of eternal suffering' (Erdozain, 2010: 74–76). So, for instance, in the 1820s, John Angell James, a prominent Dissenting preacher from Birmingham, was willing to grant that recreation was a human need, and he approved of walks in the country, visits to botanical gardens and the reading of works of history and biography. But he condemned any kind of frivolous reading, visits to the theatre or listening to oratorios, and any sport that was violent or involved gambling (Reid, 1985: 91–100). With the possible exception of cricket, this appeared to exclude every currently popular sport. Plebeian sects such as the Primitive Methodists were the most extreme in their exclusion of all 'worldly' amusements. Members of these churches had often undergone a sudden conversion, and ostentatious rejection of sports they had once enjoyed marked a symbolic break from their old way of life (Phillips, 1981).

Even a sport like cricket, which few people saw as bad in itself, was seen as incompatible with the dignity and sacred character of the Christian ministry. Thus J. C. Ryle, later bishop of Liverpool, was an outstanding cricketer at Oxford, but never played again after his ordination in 1841 (Scott, 1970). From the 1830s, the Puritanism of the Evangelicals was reinforced by the sacerdotal concerns of the Tractarians. The Oxford Apostles, though less puritanical, were even more insistent on the separation of the priest from the secular world. Meanwhile, church reformers of all parties were demanding higher standards of pastoral zeal on the part of the clergy. The 'hunting parson' became a symbol of all that was wrong with the Church: from the 1820s bishops were trying to stop the participation of their clergy in this favorite sport of the gentry, and one that had been an important means of strengthening the ties between clerical and lay elites in rural areas (Carr, 1976; Itzkowitz, 1977).

If the clergy members of all denominations were becoming increasingly hostile to the world of sport, this hostility was fully reciprocated. The pages of *Bell's Life in London*, the paper of the sporting gentry, often contained sarcastic references to the clergy, not least when clerical magistrates tried to stop illegal prizefights (*Bell's*, 15 May 1836, 17 May 1846). The attitude of many working-class sportsmen was reflected in the response of a bull-baiter at Darlaston in the Black Country to the vicar's attempt to suppress their sport: 'I say it's a nation shame to stop our sport. He has his fun in sorm-singing, so why can't he let us have our fun' (Reid, 1990: 15). The sporting world was a male world, at a time when the churches of all denominations were appealing most successfully to women, and in a period when Evangeli-calism appeared to exercise a pervasive influence in English society, it formed a counterculture. Ways of thinking and behavior flourished in the sporting world that would have been taboo in the religious world (Obelkevich, 1976). The 'sportsman' represented a counter ideal to that of the 'serious Christian,' one that was attractive to many people. He was admired for his physical strength and courage, as well as his skill, and especially for his willingness to take risks. Violence was intrinsic to most of the sports of the time and acceptance, indeed enjoyment, of this violence was seen as one of the marks of a true man. The biography of Hugh Lowther, 5th Earl of Lonsdale (1857–1944), provides an unusually vivid portrait of this mentality and way of life, albeit in a somewhat later generation. As a young man in the 1870s and 1880s he belonged to a 'brash, hard-living set of young men who put hunting above all else.' The quality they most admired was 'bottom,' reflected in feats of drinking and seduction, 'gambling for more than one could afford (always provided one paid one's debts)' and above all by sporting achievements. He 'worshipped physical fitness and virility in men. For him life was a matter of the survival of the fittest' (Sutherland, 1965: 21–22, 29).

The first signs of a more positive relationship between the world of religion and sport were apparent in the 1840s. *Bell's Life in London* was no friend of the clergy, but in August 1843 it told of a Buckinghamshire vil-lage where the youth were accustomed to gather on Sundays to 'pursue the disreputable game of pitch and toss.' The vicar had formed a cricket club and presented them with a stock of bats, balls and stumps, and 'those per-nicious pursuits have now been discontinued.' The paper called on other gentlemen to follow the clergyman's example (*Bell's*, 6 August 1843). Other gentlemen, and indeed other clergymen (*Bell's*, 25 June 1848), were in fact doing so. The context was partly, as in this case, concern at what was seen as the degrading character of existing working-class leisure pursuits and a recognition that 'rational recreations,' such as going to museums, libraries, concerts or parks, or participation in approved 'manly' sports such as cricket, might provide attractive alternatives. More generally, in this time of acute social crisis, many members of the middle and upper classes had been made vividly aware of the deep gulf separating class from class (Bailey, 1978). Lack of opportunities for leisure was coming to be seen as one of the legitimate grievances of the working class, and it was hoped that sport could provide an arena in which friendlier relationships between members of different classes might develop. Cricket in particular came to be endowed with a kind of magic—the power to heal England's wounds (Sandiford, 1994: 42–43).

Most of these patrons of popular sport were spectators rather than players, but reports in *Bell's Life* show that there were many cricketing clergymen who continued to play after their ordination, and at all levels from village to county cricket, in spite of the opposition of some bishops and the reservations of many of their clerical colleagues. In 1851, for instance, there were three parsons playing for Leicestershire and two for Nottinghamshire (*Bell's*, 29 June 1851).

In the circumstances it was not surprising that the author of the first book extolling cricket as the national game and the supreme embodiment of national virtues was a clergyman, the Reverend James Pycroft, whose *The Cricket Field* appeared in 1851. He praised cricket as 'essentially Anglo-Saxon' and as 'a standing panegyric on the English character.' It required 'patience, fortitude and self-denial,' as well as 'good hands and eyes,' 'intelligence' and an 'unruffled temper.' 'Such a national game as cricket will both humanise and harmonise our people. It teaches a love of order, discipline and fair-play for the pure honour and glory of victory' (Pycroft, 1851: 18, 21–22, 28, 32).

MUSCULAR CHRISTIANITY

It was in the 1850s that the growing rapprochement between the worlds of religion and sport became clear for all to see. In 1857 T. C. Sanders, in reviewing a book by the novelist, clergyman and Christian Socialist Charles Kingsley, had invented the term 'muscular Christianity' to describe the increasingly fashionable involvement of the clergy as practitioners and promoters of sport, and in particular the attribution of religious and moral value to physical activity (Vance, 1985; Hall, 1994). In spite of Kingsley's objections, the name stuck, and is still with us today. Indeed, in that same year appeared *Tom Brown's School Days*, the most famous and influential exposition of the creed. 'Muscular Christianity' represented a new ideal of manhood. Hughes was fighting a battle on three fronts. His rhetoric was directed at religious people who thought sport was not Christian, at sportsmen who thought religion was not manly and also at those who saw their sport simply as a source of personal pleasure and who lacked a social conscience. Above all, he was not merely advocating sport as a remedy for social ills or an alternative to more disreputable recreations: it was a part of the full life that God intended us to live, and thus should be enthusiastically enjoyed by Christians, including clergymen.

Hughes fully shared the sportsman's delight in physical contests of many kinds and in closeness to nature. *Tom Brown* is full of blow-by-blow narratives of sporting contests of all kinds as well as of fishing and bird nesting. And while anxious to distance himself from 'the brutal exhibition of men battering one another for money,' Hughes shared the fascination of so many of his contemporaries with fighting: 'it is no good for Quakers or any other body of men to uplift their voices against fighting. Human nature is too strong for them, and they don't follow their own precepts' (Hughes, 1989: 282–83). Hughes would have agreed with those sportsmen who declared that fighting was natural and it was fun. But the characteristic Hughesian note lay in the higher purposes to which this fighting instinct should be put.

In particular, the muscular Christian's fists were in the service of women and children and 'the weak' generally. The most famous scene in *Tom Brown* is that where the hero comes to the aid of the new boy, George Arthur, who is being bullied by some of his dormitory mates because he goes down on his knees to say his prayers before going to bed. Tom's physical bravery and healthy instincts are of course praised, but the equally important point is that the physically weak may be morally stronger, and moral strength is what counts for most—though the perfection of manhood is the combination of moral and physical strength. Physical strength combined with moral weakness might merely produce a bully. Moral strength and physical weakness might mean a person with the best of intentions but incapable of doing what was needed in a crisis. A typical day in the life of a muscular Christian might include saving someone from drowning, running a five-minute mile in order to fetch a doctor or coming to the aid of a women who was struck in the street. Moreover, Hughes, like Kingsley, was a fervent patriot. 'I take it for granted,' he wrote in a religious periodical, 'that every man who reads this Magazine will come forward [in the event of war], and give his goods, his body, his life if necessary, for the old country and her women and children' (Hughes, 1861: 2, 5).

The pioneers of 'muscular Christianity' were drawn mainly from the 'liberal' or 'Broad Church' wing of Anglicanism, and their advocacy of sport was part of their crusade against the asceticism, Puritanism or, to use one of their favorite terms of abuse, the 'Manicheanism' of their Tractarian or Evangelical opponents. They accused Evangelicals of erecting artificial boundaries between the religious and the secular. Instead of the Tractarian priest they wanted a 'parson,' living in the midst of his people, sharing in their struggles and also in all their legitimate pleasures. They believed that God intended us to enjoy to the full the physical pleasures of football and cricket, swimming and athletics, hunting and fishing and, indeed, the sexual relationship between man and wife (Vance, 1985). They also regretted the divide between the Church and a large part of the masculine world; they blamed this on the narrowly spiritual approach of the Evangelicals and Tractarians and their condemnation of many legitimate pleasures. And as Christian Socialists, Hughes and Kingsley were preoccupied with what was called 'The Condition of England,' including the acute deprivation suffered by large sections of the population.

Although the pioneers of 'muscular Christianity' were mainly Broad Churchmen, recreation in general and sport in particular soon became one of the questions of the day for all sections of the Church of England. It was debated at the Church Congress in 1866 and again in 1869. Though there were some doubters, the majority of speakers had a positive view of sport—or at least of 'healthy' sports. Thus the Reverend J. C. Chambers condemned all those sports that were 'barbarous' or involved gambling, but he wanted the parish club to be the social center of each district, providing a program that included concerts, cricket, football, gymnastics and rifle shooting. As often there was a patriotic dimension to these concerns—Chambers believed that a sporting people would be better able to defend their country against foreign invaders. Many of the arguments would soon become very familiar: for instance, one speaker warned that many men had left the Church because the clergy had not recognized their need for recreation, and a Nottinghamshire curate attributed the high level of morality in that county to the large number of cricket clubs (*Official Report*, 1869: 133–34, 142–44).

In the Nonconformist chapels these debates had hardly begun in 1870 and they were still continuing in 1889 when the London Baptist, Reverend Archibald Brown published *The Devil's Mission of Amusement*. Brown was not claiming that amusement was in itself evil, but he denied that it was any part of the Church's mission to provide amusements. Moreover, their efforts in this field were actually counterproductive: churches with large recreational programs had not brought in outsiders, but they had fed the limitless appetite for amusement that was undermining spiritual concerns and making it more difficult for Christian preachers to gain a hearing (Brown, 1889). By now, however, Brown was rowing against a powerful tide (Erdozain, 2010). The trend was reflected in the *Northamptonshire Nonconformist*, which in that same year introduced a sporting column. The columnist declared that 'every healthy recreation' would receive the paper's 'hearty support' (*Northamptonshire Nonconformist*, February 1889). Women's sports added a new dimension to the debate. These had been of little interest to the pioneers of 'muscular Christianity' but by 1889 the situation was very different. In the 1860s and 1870s women of the upper and upper-middle classes were hunting or were playing croquet and tennis in private gardens. In the 1880s sport became part of the syllabus of the girls' public schools, and a growing number of middle-class and lower-middle-class women were practicing gymnastics, swimming, cricket and above all cycling—in spite of male sarcasm (McCrone, 1987; Molyneux, 1957:). The *Northamptonshire Nonconformist* strongly supported these developments—the ideal of balance between body, mind and spirit applied as much to women as to men, and in any case questions of women's rights were coming on to the agenda of the Nonconformist chapels around this time (*Northamptonshire Nonconformist*, April 1889; Lauer, 1997).

RELIGION AND SPORT ALLIED

The alliance between Christianity and sport had its biggest influence in two quite different environments: the public schools attended by the sons of the upper and upper-middle classes and the working-class districts of the cities. One of the pioneers of this work in the cities was the Reverend John Cale Miller of St. Martin's Birmingham. In 1854 he founded a Working Men's Association, which soon had seventeen hundred members, including three hundred women, and a program that included cricket and football, as well as excursions, lectures and Bible studies. As an Evangelical, Miller would have had little sympathy with the theology of Hughes and Kingsley, but he fully shared their social and political concerns. He was all too aware of the extreme social tensions that had reached a high point in the 1830s and 1840s, and he believed that one of the legitimate grievances of the working class was the lack of opportunities for leisure. He believed that the Church should take the lead in addressing these problems (Reid, 1985). More typically Broad Church in inspiration was the Working Men's College founded in London in the same year, with Thomas Hughes among the tutors, providing both lectures and boxing lessons (Harrison, 1954). In the later decades of the century more and more Anglican parishes, and increasingly Nonconformist chapels too, were establishing 'institutes,' with an extensive social, recreational and educational program. In Leicester, Melbourne Hall, established by the prominent Baptist Reverend F. B. Meyer in 1880, had no less than eighty-three attached organizations. Meyer was bitterly opposed to horse racing, but 'healthy' sports, such as football and cricket, were strongly encouraged. At St. Paul's, Leicester, a new High Church parish established in 1871, the first vicar had been a successful athlete at Oxford. In the 1880s he encouraged sport as well as concerts and dancing, and from 1894 the parish magazine gave detailed reports of matches played by the parish cricket team (Crump, 1985). By the early twentieth century many churchgoers might feel that they knew as much about their minister's sporting achievements as his interpretation of the Bible. A typical case was that of the Baptist Reverend J. A. Roxburgh. When he commenced his ministry in Northampton in 1906 a local paper reported:

> He has all along pleaded for the entire development of manhood and womanhood—body, mind and spirit. He is athletic and a lover of all legitimate sport, an all-round cricketer, having captained several clubs, a swimmer and a seasoned cyclist . . . Perhaps the most outstanding features of his character are its manliness and brotherliness. His piety is of the robust order, and will appeal to young men in particular, in whose interests a large part of his active life has been spent. (McLeod, 2003: 38–9)

Meanwhile, the Catholics were a little behind the Nonconformists. On Merseyside, for instance, where Everton (founded 1878) had Methodist origins, the first Catholic football team, St. Francis Xavier, came in 1888. From then, however, there was a considerable development of Catholic sport, especially in Catholic schools, and in 1900 a Liverpool Catholic Schools

Football League was formed, with the aim, according to a Catholic paper, of keeping 'football enthusiasts in a Catholic atmosphere.' Later there were interschool boxing and swimming competitions (Kennedy, 2007: 896–98). Liverpool was ideal ground for establishing a separate Catholic sporting world, but by the 1920s and 1930s other Lancashire towns, such as Bolton and Oldham, also had Catholic football leagues (Williams, 1996). In towns with fewer Catholics, their teams competed with those from other churches or with no religious links. For instance, the first Northamptonshire Cricket Cup in 1886 was won by the Catholic Club, competing against two Non-conformist, one Anglican and a Temperance team, together with seven that had no apparent church link (Sibley, 1986).

But it was the public schools that would become the greatest strongholds of 'muscular Christianity.' In this period the headmasters of the leading public schools were all Anglican clergymen, and the influence of the Broad Church was especially strong. From the 1850s sport became a central part of life in many of these schools (Mangan, 1981). Eton in 1858 was the first to appoint a games master, and Uppingham in 1859 was the first to build a gymnasium. Reverend Edward Thring, headmaster of Uppingham from 1853 to 1887, was among the most enthusiastic and articulate spokesmen for the new order. He himself played for the cricket team; he made football compulsory; and though these two sports held the highest prestige he also encouraged a wide range of other sports. He saw himself as a prophet and he claimed to have received messages from God about the running of his school. His ideas came not only from liberal Anglicanism but also from Plato and from German educational theories. He wanted his school to provide a complete education for 'the body, the mind and the heart.' Like many of his contemporaries he believed that sport was character forming. It would favor such qualities as courage, discipline, team spirit and above all 'manliness'—one of the keywords of the mid-Victorian era. He was also concerned for the boy without scholastic talents. He himself had bad memories of his school days, and he hoped that Uppingham would be 'a happier place.' 'Manliness,' 'bravery' and 'the joy of strength and movement' were frequent themes in his sermons. He also sent some less popular messages, such as the need for a courageous acceptance of defeat and the dangers of an *excessive* concern with sport (Tozer, 1976: 36–39, 46, 123–27).

The growth of public school sport had an impact much wider than the narrow circles of those who attended these schools. For the schoolboys who imbibed a passion for sport in the mid-Victorian era would often become the politicians, landowners and industrialists—as well as the Anglican clergymen and missionaries—of the later Victorian and Edwardian years. In these various roles, 'muscular Christians' would play a major role in the sporting boom of the later nineteenth century.

The clergy had contributed to the decline or marginalization of traditional sports. Now they played a big part in the diffusion of other sports, some of which were new, while others were reformed or recently codified.

In the 1870s and 1880s the sporting boom reached wider sections of the population, including skilled workers and the lower-middle class. A crucial factor in the growing participation in sports or attendance at matches was the practice of closing factories on Saturday afternoons or shops on Wednesday or Thursday afternoons (Molyneux, 1957; Mason, 1980). Sabbatarian laws or personal scruples limited the use of Sunday, but these newly liberated afternoons, and above all Saturday from 2 p.m. onwards, became the great times for sport. The old sport of cricket enjoyed a great revival, while football (codified by the Football Association in 1863) and rugby (codified by the Rugby Football Union in 1871) enjoyed a rapid rise in popularity (Molyneux, 1957). Athletics and rowing were freed from associations with gambling, and the illegal sport of prizefighting was transformed into the respectable sport of boxing (Crump, 1989; Dodd, 1989; Shipley, 1989). The churches contributed to the growth of all these sports, though they did not regard all of them with equal enthusiasm. For example, boxing was encouraged by many Anglican and Catholic clergy, but it was less popular with the Nonconformists, whose pacifist sympathies it offended (McLeod, 2003). The two great survivors among the older sports were horse racing and foxhunting—both benefiting from aristocratic, even royal, patronage, which helped them to survive religiously motivated attacks. Among the newer sports, golf (new in England, though not of course in Scotland) and cycling had an ambivalent relationship with the churches, mainly because they were often practiced on Sundays (Lowerson, 1993). Indeed, they were often the favored Sunday activity of those who were consciously seeking an alternative to church. Nonetheless, golf was popular with many of the clergy, who practiced it on their own day of rest—Monday. And many churches had a cycling club. The bicycle was even named a 'Christian machine' by Evangelists who used it when going to preach in remote villages (McLeod, 2003: 40).

Anglican clergy and Nonconformist ministers were thus propagandists for sport—for sport in general, and for 'healthy' sports over against those regarded as cruel or brutal or were connected with gambling. This happened not only in the cities, where sports new and old were well established, but also in villages or small towns, like Arundel in Sussex, where the vicar, the Reverend G. Arbuthnot, seems to have been the first sports fanatic. In the 1870s he introduced athletics and swimming championships and founded a cricket club, of which he seems to have been the star. He filled the pages of his parish magazine with accounts of matches and ridiculed the lack of manliness of those male parishioners who practiced no sport (*Arundel Parochial Magazine*, 1874–1877). In particular, the clergy surrounded cricket with a mystique. According to Thring, cricket was more than a game, and it was the greatest bond of English-speaking people (Sandiford, 1994: 43). Preachers often drew on cricketing metaphors. When preaching in the chapel of his old school, Uppingham, the writer E. W. Hornung made comparisons between God and the cricket scorer—though

God used a scoring system rather different from that found in conventional cricket, since he was more impressed by singles eked out in failing light than by easy boundaries off loose bowling (Tozer, 1989).

The clergy also contributed to the sporting infrastructure by forming clubs, supporting those founded by church members or providing facilities, such as a club room or gymnasium. The religious origins of many of the leading football and rugby clubs of the present day are well known, though the circumstances of their foundation varied. For example, Northampton rugby club, originally 'St. James,' was founded by the curate of that parish in 1880 as a branch of the Mutual Improvement Class; Southampton football club, originally 'St. Mary's,' arose from a meeting in 1885 held on the initiative of members of the Young Men's Association, but with the curate in the chair; Aston Villa grew out of a cricket club formed in 1872 by members of a Wesleyan Young Men's Bible Class. Here the minister had no direct involvement though he subsequently gave his approval (Northampton Football Club, 1980; Lupson, 2006). The links between elite clubs and these churches soon became rather tenuous: for example, as Aston Villa became the top team in the Midlands it needed to recruit outstanding players, often from Scotland, regardless of their religious affiliation. However, the role of the churches in amateur sport remained important for much longer. Out of thirty-five football clubs in Leicester in 1893, sixteen had a religious base (eleven Anglican, three Nonconformist, two YMCA), as against two works-based, ten neighborhood and seven 'other' (Crump, 1985). Out of twenty in York's football league in 1900, nine were based in a church (seven Anglican, two Wesleyan) (Jones, 1994). Of the seventeen leading cricket clubs in Northampton in 1922, ten were linked with a church (five Anglican and five Nonconformist) (Sibley, 1986), though the situation certainly varied from town to town. In York by 1930 only fourteen out of seventy-one football clubs were linked with a church (Jones 1994), whereas in Bolton, the proportions were 45 percent of the cricket teams and 48 percent of the football teams. The role of the churches in women's sports in Bolton was even greater. In 1920, 88 percent of the women's hockey teams and all of the rounders teams were linked with a church or Sunday school. Until the end of the nineteenth century the majority of church-based sports teams seem to have been Anglican, but by the interwar years the Nonconformists had caught up: in Bolton, by this time, a higher proportion of Methodist and Congregational chapels than of Anglican parishes had a cricket club. On the other hand, there were some sports, for example, rugby league, golf or darts, where the role of religious organizations was much smaller (Williams, 1990, 1996).

Among the 'muscular Christians' of this time were not only clergymen, but also Christian employers who provided sports fields and swimming baths of their employees. For example, the Quaker chocolate manufacturer, George Cadbury, saw himself as responsible for the welfare of his employees, and he also believed that healthy workers would be more productive.

There was already a works cricket team in the 1860s when his factory was still in central Birmingham. After the move to the garden suburb of Bournville in 1879 there was a big expansion of sporting provision. By 1911 there were thirteen football teams, six for cricket, two each for rugby, hockey, bowls and water polo and one for tennis (Bromhead, 2000). While the Bournville Friends' Meeting House was grand by the normally austere Quaker standards, it was less grand (and less ecclesiastical in appearance) than the swimming baths built for the workers in 1902–1904. The Girls' Athletics Club was founded in 1899 and by 1931 included teams for cricket, hockey, netball, tennis and water polo (Williams, 1931). At the Rowntree cocoa works in York, also owned by Quakers, numerous sports clubs, mainly joined by men, but in principle open to women, were established from 1897 onwards, and girls' hockey and cricket teams were established in 1911 and 1912. However, Parratt notes (and deplores) the degree of encouragement given to swimming and gymnastics as the principal physical recreations for women: these were 'orderly and disciplined and directed to consciously utilitarian ends,' such as cleanliness and improved health, rather than simply having fun (Parratt, 2001: 207).

The 1880s and 1890s saw an unprecedented expansion in the number of those playing and watching sport. Many new sporting papers appeared and the daily press began to give much more coverage to sport. But 'muscular Christians' were often uneasy about the directions that sport was taking. By the 1890s four major eras of tension between the worlds of religion and sport were emerging: the impact of professionalism, the persistence of gambling, differing ideas on the use of time (including Sunday) and the fear that sport was becoming 'a new religion.'

NEW TENSIONS BETWEEN RELIGION AND SPORT

Beginning with professionalism: probably the first professionals were boxers, and by the 1790s star pugilists, such as Daniel Mendoza and Richard Humphries, were household names (Brailsford, 1988). But the most important turning point in the development of professional sport was the legalization of professionalism by the Football Association in 1885. Football was rapidly becoming the most widely popular sport, attracting huge crowds, mainly of working-class men, and football teams were becoming an important part of the identities of particular towns or districts. An important symbolic moment was the 1883 FA Cup Final, when Blackburn Olympic, a team made up mainly of factory workers, defeated Old Etonians. The margin of victory was narrow—a goal in extra time. But never again would the 'gentlemen' effectively challenge the dominance of the 'players' (Walvin, 1994). The Football League was founded in 1888 following an initiative by William McGregor, a Birmingham draper and a leading figure in the management of Aston Villa (Taylor, 2005). In parts of Yorkshire and

Lancashire, rugby was developing in similar ways, and in 1895 the Northern Union broke away from the strictly amateur Rugby Football Union over the issue of payments to players. The basis was thus laid for the eventual emergence of rugby league as a separate sport (Collins, 1998).

The impact of professionalism, especially on football, led to a flood of complaints in the years around 1890 both from 'muscular Christians' and from middle- and upper-class sporting enthusiasts more generally, in which questions of sporting ethics mingled with class prejudice. Many of the critics saw professional sport as objectionable in itself, because it abolished the proper distinction between work and play. But there were also more specific complaints. It was alleged that the need of professionals to win at all costs had led to increasingly violent play, to cheating and to intimidation of referees. The violence also spread to the terraces. The intense rivalries that developed, especially between neighboring teams, led to fights between rival groups of fans, to assaults on players and to verbal abuse, sometimes escalating to physical attacks on referees (Mason, 1980; Lewis, 1996). And, while 'muscular Christians' had often welcomed sport as an alternative to the pub, drink came to be linked at several levels with professional sport (Collins and Vamplew, 2002).

Yet the break between 'muscular Christianity' and professional sport was less clean than might appear at first sight. 'Muscular Christian' values long retained an influence in the governing bodies of professional sport—middle class and mainly Nonconformist in the case of the Football League, and more often upper-middle class or upper class and Anglican in the case of the FA and the MCC. The 'father' of the League, William McGregor, was a Congregationalist (Lupson, 2006) (not a Methodist, as claimed by Taylor), and several leading figures in the period from the 1890s to 1939 were Methodists. According to Matthew Taylor, 'bluntness, honesty, respectability and sobriety' were their typical characteristics. They tended to be strongly opposed to gambling, and in the interwar years they waged an unsuccessful war against the football pools. Many of them were teetotalers (Taylor 2005: 55–58).

As for cricket, Jack Williams devotes a chapter in his history of the game in the interwar years to 'Cricket and Christianity.' The connection between cricket and the Church of England was symbolized, at least in the public imagination, by the familiar image of cricket on the village green with the church tower rising behind. Williams notes the high profile of Anglican clergymen at all levels of the game (even including several county players), and the frequency with which journalists, administrators and sometimes players made links between cricket and Christianity. For instance, he quotes the Yorkshire and England fast bowler, Bill Bowes, who, at a 'sportsmen's service' in a Methodist chapel in 1935, claimed that cricket was 'a game every Christian should be interested in' (Williams, 1999: 144–45).

In one respect, the role of religion in elite sport continues to the present day in the 'Chariots of Fire' phenomenon, whereby some top athletes perceive their sporting talents as gifts from God, and their religious faith provides the driving force behind their will to win and their disciplined training.

One of the major differences, however, between 'muscular Christians' and other sections of the sporting world lay in attitudes to gambling. Wagers had been an essential part both of the sports of the gentry and of those of the working man, and a major objective of the Christian sporting movement had been the promotion of sports that were not dependent on betting. But this was only partly successful. Among the old gambling-based sports, horse racing survived and continued to flourish—indeed, betting on horses was growing during the peak years of 'muscular Christianity' and continued to do so in the twentieth century, assisted by technological advances. A key factor was the electric telegraph, which, first in the 1840s and then with improvements in the 1870s, enabled starting prices and results to be conveyed immediately to bookmakers and newspapers all over the country (Chinn, 1991). The 1880s are seen by historians of gambling as a key phase in the growth of offtrack betting, and 1889 has been identified as the year when opponents of gambling began to panic. The National Anti-Gambling League was founded in 1890 (Munting, 1993).

Gambling was also a frequent source of conflict in church-run sporting organizations. For instance, in 1902 the University Club, a leading center for boxing in the East End of London, was closed by its Anglo-Catholic managers because of the prevalence of betting among its members, and it was only reopened after an extensive purge (Shipley, 1986). Opposition to gambling was widespread and often intense both in the Protestant Churches and in the Socialist movement, though Carl Chinn notes the more tolerant attitude of the Catholic Church. He suggests that a disproportionate number of bookmakers were Catholics, including some who were generous supporters of their church (Chinn, 1991).

Perhaps the most fundamental area of tension between 'muscular Christians' and many other sporting enthusiasts lay in different ideas about the proper use of time. The Christian sporting movement was based on the ideal of a balanced life, in which work, leisure, the duties of citizenship and religious activities each had their proper place. But already in the 1870s some of those who had been most prominent in promoting the alliance between Christianity and sport were concerned that this balance was being lost because the obsession with sport was leaving little time for other interests.

In the early 1870s, Edward Thring was agonizing in his diary as to whether the disproportionate place of cricket in Uppingham life was leading to the loss of his original vision (Tozer, 1976). Thomas Hughes claimed in 1874 that 'one day's rest for six days' work has been God's rule from the first.' The first essential was to have a 'calling'—recreation was a necessary counterpart to work, but could not in itself be a 'calling.' He therefore deplored the existence of 'a large leisure class full of physical energy, but without any desire for a "calling," and setting an undue value on physical prowess of all kinds.' He also objected to the employment of many men in servicing the idle rich as huntsmen, gamekeepers, etc., to professional cricket, and to the excessive space given to sport in the press (*Official Report*, 1874: 430–32).

The most sensitive aspect of time use was the use of Sunday. Most Non-conformists and Evangelical Anglicans were still opposed to Sunday sport in the 1930s. On the other hand, many High Church or Broad Church Anglicans, as well as Roman Catholics, while emphasizing the primary obligation to take part in public worship on Sunday, accepted some Sunday sport outside the hours of service. This was already the case at the height of Sabbatarianism around 1850, and this at least partial acceptance of Sunday sport became increasingly widespread as the anti-Sabbatarian reaction got under way from about 1880. However, many of them were ambivalent about Sunday recreation, accepting it in principle, but remaining uncomfortable about most forms of Sabbath activity in practice.

By the 1880s, and especially the 1890s, concerns were being increasingly expressed at the trends in Sunday recreation. Even non-Sabbatarian clergy regretted the tendency for sport to replace rather than supplement religious observance. Many working men had never taken much notice of Sabbatarian restrictions, but in the last quarter of the nineteenth century a more relaxed view of Sunday was also taking hold in the middle and upper classes. In the 1870s and 1880s Sunday tennis and croquet were becoming popular in the gardens of the wealthy. From about 1890 golf clubs were starting to open on Sunday, and by 1914 nearly half the clubs in England did so. While these were the sports of the wealthy, much more widespread was the popularity of cycling, which from the 1890s was becoming a favorite recreation for those seeking alternatives to churchgoing on Sundays (Lowerson, 1993). At the same time, some clergy and Christian laypeople were making cogent criticisms of strict Sabbatarianism and were arguing that the ideal Sunday might be a mixture of churchgoing with healthy recreation. However, by the 1920s, it was increasingly evident that there were many people for whom Sunday was a day to be devoted entirely to recreation, and for whom sport was, apart from work, the main focus of their life. An article in the *Sunday School Chronicle* clearly presented the situation as contemporary religious observers saw it. On Sunday, the writer claimed, railway carriages were 'full of young men and women clad—not in the sombre garments of respectability associated with church worship—but in white flannels and light frocks. They would be armed, not with prayer-books and Bibles, but with tennis racquets and cricket bats.' Most people's work offered them little fulfillment, so they looked for it in sport: 'Our congregations have largely deserted us, and have migrated to the playing-fields, the golf course, and the river' (*Sunday School Chronicle*, 10 July 1924).

The extent of these changes should not be exaggerated. There was no professional sport on Sundays until the introduction of Sunday cricket in the later 1960s, and until that decade the FA would not recognize even amateur teams that played on Sundays (Mason, 1989). Some local authorities still banned Sunday sport in municipal parks in the 1930s (McLeod, 2000), and again resistance only finally collapsed in the 1860s. Sunday in the 1950s may have seemed very unquiet by the standards of the 1850s, but by comparison with today, or indeed by comparison with Sunday in France or Germany, it was still rather quiet. The 'quiet Sunday' remained a part of 'diffusive Christianity,' which included the recognition of Sunday as a day apart, but without the requirement of regular churchgoing.

But the degree to which sport appeared to have become an all-consuming obsession was already apparent in an article of 1892 on 'The New Football Mania' (Edwards, 1892: 628):

> In all our large towns, and most of the small ones, north of Birmingham . . . from September to April, Saturday is consecrated to football. Saturday evenings are devoted to football symposia, and the newspapers issue special editions one after the other.

Football had become 'a passion and not merely a recreation'—comparable to bull-fighting in Spain. When West Bromwich Albion won the Cup in 1892, the MP gave a dinner in honour of the team, and when a Bolton town councillor was dying he asked that a team of Wanderers footballers act as his pall-bearers.

In their respective neighbourhoods [the players] are the objects of the popular adoration. They go to the wars in saloon carriages. . . . They are better known than the local members of Parliament. Their photographs are in several local shops, individually and grouped. The newspaper gives woodcuts of them and brief appreciative biographical sketches. Even in their workaday dress they cannot move in their native streets without receiving standing ovations enoughto turn the head of a Prime Minister.

The author also mentioned the vulnerability of referees in the face of fanatical supporters. Those who gave a decision against the home side in a local derby were in special danger of being chased by a 'yelling and blaspheming mob' and pelted with mud or snowballs.

Many familiar themes are here in the earliest days of professional football. We can already see the role of sports teams as a symbol of the surrounding community, embodying its identity, even its 'honor.' We can see here too the intense emotions aroused by sporting events and the cult of sporting heroes—also the need of public figures to gain reflected glory by association with these heroes. A few years earlier the 'Cambridge Seven'—sportsmen who had decided to join the China Inland Mission—offered the first example of the use of sporting stars for religious propaganda. In fact, the only one who truly ranked as a star was the Test cricketer C. T. Studd. But the Seven undertook a nationwide tour, giving their testimonies to packed halls before taking the boat to China in 1885. According to a religious paper, these meetings were:

A sight to stir the blood, and a striking testimony to the power of the uplifted Christ to draw to himself not the weak, the emotional, the illiterate only, but all that is noblest in strength and finest in culture. (Scott, 1970: 137)

Perhaps the longest-lasting legacy of 'muscular Christianity' had been the idea that sport makes you a better person. Yet the pioneers of Christian sport, such as Hughes and Thring, never claimed that sport was in itself morally beneficial. Indeed, Flashman, the villain of *Tom Brown's School Days*, was described as a 'sportsman.' He was no hero because he was a bully who used his physical strength to oppress those weaker than himself; he was also a gambler, a drunkard and a coward. Those like Hughes and Thring argued that sport was beneficial when practiced in conjunction with an underlying code of moral values—derived, in their case, from Christianity, though in principle it could come from another religion or from a secular creed.

However, by the later nineteenth century, and increasingly in the twentieth, sport was being canvassed as something inherently good, which brought benefits to the soul as much as the body. At the same time, it came to be bound up with national identities, as the embodiment of national virtues, enjoying a quasi-sacred status. Lowerson notes the irony that while clergymen had been among the most enthusiastic proponents of the benefits of sport, by the end of the century sport was often presented as an alternative to religion: enthusiasts for tennis or football were claiming that these sports offered a moral training superior to that obtained by attending church (Lowerson, 1993: 271–72). Sport even offered new ways of being religious: in a newspaper correspondence of 1905 on Sunday observance one writer praised the man who 'takes his bicycle, entailing no Sunday labour on others, and goes forth to worship God in His bright sunshine, amid his wonderful lakes and fells' (McLeod, 1996: 199).

CONCLUSION

England in the years between about 1860 and 1890 saw the beginnings of the modern sporting world. Association and rugby football were codified; modern boxing, based on the Queensberry Rules, took the place of the discredited sport of prizefighting; lawn tennis was invented; golf moved southward from its Scottish home; cricket saw the first county championship and the first Test Matches. The churches had played an important part in the decline of older sports, and 'muscular Christians' now had a major role in promoting new sports or new ways of practicing sport. With memories still vivid of the acute social conflicts of the 1830s and 1840s, their motives were partly political; and at a time when many men were believed to be alienated from a 'feminized' church, these motives were partly evangelistic.

But above all they were moved by the ideal of the whole man (to be joined towards the end of the century by the whole woman) living the full life that God intended, with body, mind and spirit in balance. This ideal, however, was under threat almost as soon as it was enunciated by such pioneers of 'muscular Christianity' as Hughes, Kingsley and Thring. From the 1880s professionalization was pushing sport in new directions that these pioneers deplored, and amateur enthusiasts increasingly practiced sport as an end in itself, potentially absorbing all their free hours, rather than as one limited part of a balanced life. In the twentieth century there would be none of the enmity between the worlds of religion and of sport that had been seen in the early nineteenth century. But they were rivals for people's limited resources of time; energy; and, above all, emotional commitment.

BIBLIOGRAPHY

Arundel Parochial Magazine. (1874–1877) West Sussex County Record Office, Chichester.

Bailey, P. (1978) *Leisure and Class in Victorian England: Rational Recreation and the Contest for Control, 1830–1885*, London: Routledge.

Bell's Life in London. (Published weekly, 1822–1886).

Brailsford, D. (1988) *Bareknuckles: A Social History of Prize-Fighting*, Cambridge: Cambridge University Press.

Bromhead, J. (2000) George Cadbury's Contribution to Sport, *Sports Historian*, 20: 97–117.

Brown, A. (1889) *The Devil's Mission of Amusement*, London: Morgan& Scott.

Carr, R. (1976) *English Fox Hunting: A History*, London: Weidenfeld and Nicolson.

Chinn, C. (1991) *Better Betting with a Decent Feller*, Brighton: Harvester.

Collins, T. (1998) *Rugby's Great Split: Class, Culture and the Origins of Rugby League Football*, London: Frank Cass.

Collins, T. and Vamplew, W. (2002) *Mud, Sweat and Beers: A Cultural History of Sport and Alcohol*, Oxford: Berg.

Crump, J. (1985) *Amusements of the People: Leicester 1850–1914*. PhD Thesis, University of Warwick.

Crump, J. (1989) Athletics, in T. Mason (Ed.), *A Social History of Sport in Britain*, Cambridge: Cambridge University Press, 44–77.

Dodd, C. (1989) Rowing, in T. Mason (Ed.), *A Social History of Sport in Britain*, Cambridge: Cambridge University Press, 276–307.

Edwards, C. (1892) The New Football Mania, *Nineteenth Century*, 32: 622–32.

Erdozain, D. (2010) *The Problem of Pleasure: Sport, Recreation and the Crisis of Victorian Religion*, Woodbridge: Boydell Press.

Goldblatt, D. (2006) *The Ball Is Round: A Global History of Football*, London: Viking.

Hackwood, F. W. (1907) *Old English Sports*, London: T. Fisher Unwin.

Hall, D. E. (ed.) (1994) *Muscular Christianity: Embodying the Victorian Age*, Cambridge: Cambridge University Press.

Harrison, J. F. C. (1954) *A History of the Working Men's College, 1854–1954*, London: Routledge and Kegan Paul.

Huggins, M. (2000) *Flat Racing and British Society, 1790–1914: A Social and Economic History*, London: Frank Cass.

Hughes, T. (1861) How to Be Bodily Strong in a Town, *St Peter's Derby Parish Magazine*, Derby Local History Library.

Hughes, T. (1989) *Tom Brown's School Days*, Oxford: Oxford University Press.

Itzkowitz, D. C. (1977) *Peculiar Privilege: A Social History of English Foxhunting 1753–1885*. Brighton: Harvester.

Jones, I. (1994) *Leisure in York, 1900–1939: Leisure and Citizen-Making in the Minster City*. MA thesis, University of York.

Kennedy, D. (2007) Ambiguity, Complexity and Convergence: The Evolution of Liverpool's Irish Football Clubs, *International Journal of the History of Sport*, 24: 894–920.

Lauer, L. (1997) *Women in British Nonconformity, circa 1880–1920, with Special Reference to the Society of Friends, Baptist Union and Salvation Army*. D.Phil. thesis, University of Oxford.

Lewis, R. W. (1996) Football Hooliganism in England before 1914: A Critique of the Dunning Thesis, *International Journal of the History of Sport*, 13: 310–39.

Lowerson, J. (1993) *Sport and the English Middle Classes, 1870–1914*, Manchester: Manchester University Press.

Lupson, P. (2006) *Thank God for Football*, London: Azure.

Malcolmson, R. W. (1973) *Popular Recreations in English Society, 1700–1850*, Cambridge: Cambridge University Press.

Mangan, J. A. (1981) *Athleticism in the Victorian and Edwardian Public School*, Cambridge: Cambridge University Press.

Mangan, J. A. (1986) *The Games Ethic and Imperialism*, Harmondsworth: Penguin.

Mason, T. (1980) *Association Football and English Society, 1863–1915*, Brighton: Harvester.

Mason, T. (1989) Football, in T. Mason (Ed.), *Sport in Britain: A Social History*, Cambridge: Cambridge University Press, 146–85.

McCrone, K. E. (1987) Play Up! Play Up! And Play the Game! Sport at the late Victorian Girls' Public Schools, in J. A. Mangan and R. J. Park (Eds.), *From 'Fair Sex' to Feminism: Sport and the Socialization of Women in the Industrial and Post-Industrial Eras*, London: Frank Cass, 97–129.

McLeod, H. (1996) *Religion and Society in England, 1850–1914*, Basingstoke: Macmillan.

McLeod, H. (2000) *Secularisation in Western Europe, 1848–1914*, Basingstoke: Macmillan.

McLeod, H. (2003) "Thews and Sinews": Nonconformity and Sport, in D. Bebbington and T. Larsen (Eds.), *Modern Christianity and Cultural Aspirations*, Sheffield: Academic Press, 28–46.

Molyneux, D. (1957) *The Development of Physical Recreation in the Birmingham District from 1871–1892*. MA thesis, University of Birmingham.

Munting, R. (1993) Social Opposition to Gambling in Britain: An Historical Overview, *International Journal of the History of Sport*, 10: 295–312.

Northampton Football Club. (1980) *Northampton Football Club Centenary, 1880–1980*. Northampton: Northampton Football Club.

Northamptonshire Nonconformist. (1889) Northamptonshire Studies Room, Northamptonshire Central Library.

Obelkevich, J. (1976) *Religion and Rural Society: South Lindsey 1825–1875*, Oxford: Clarendon Press.

Official Report of the Church Congress. (Published annually 1861–1930).

Parratt, C. M. (2001) *'More than Mere Amusement': Working-Class Women's Leisure in England, 1750–1914*, Boston: Northeastern University Press.

Phillips, S. K. (1981) Primitive Methodist Confrontation with Popular Sports, in R. Cashman and M. McKirnan (Eds), *Sport, Money, Morality and the Media*, Kensington NSW: University of New South Wales Press, 289–303.

Pycroft, James. (1851) *The Cricket Field*, London: Longman Green.

Reid, D. A. (1985) *Labour, Leisure and Politics in Birmingham ca. 1800–1875*. PhD thesis, University of Birmingham.

Reid, D. A. (1990) Beasts and Brutes: Popular Blood Sports in England, circa 1780–1865, in R. Holt (Ed.), *Sport and the Working Class in Modern Britain*, Manchester: Manchester University Press, 12–28.

Rosman, D. (1984) *Evangelicals and Culture*, London: Croom Helm.

Sandiford, K. (1994) *Cricket and the Victorians*, Aldershot: Scolar Press.

Scott, P. (1970) Cricket and the Religious World in the Victorian Period, *Church Quarterly*, 3: 134–44.

Shipley, S. (1986) *The Boxer as Hero: A Study of Social Class, Community and the Professionalisation of the Sport in London, 1890–1905*. PhD thesis. University of London.

Shipley, S. (1989) Boxing, in T. Mason (Ed.), *A Social History of British Sport*, Cambridge: Cambridge University Press, 78–115.

Sibley, G. (1986) *Northampton Club Cricket*, Northampton: Town Cricket League.

Sutherland, D. (1965) *The Yellow Earl*, London: Cassell.

Taylor, M. (2005) *The Leaguers: The Making of Professional Football in England, 1900–1939*, Liverpool: Liverpool University Press.

Tozer, M. (1976) *Physical Recreation at Thring's Uppingham*, Uppingham: Uppingham School.

Tozer, M. (1989) A Sacred Trinity—Cricket, School, Empire: E. W. Hornung and His Young Guard, *International Journal of the History of Sport*, 6: 156–71.

Vance, N. (1985) *Sinews of the Spirit*, Cambridge: Cambridge University Press.

Walvin, J. (1994) *The People's Game*, Edinburgh: Mainstream.

Williams, I. A. (1931) *The Firm of Cadbury, 1831–1931*, London: Constable.

Williams, J. (1990) Recreational Cricket in the Bolton Area between the Wars, in R. Holt (Ed.), *Sport and the Working Class in Modern Britain*, Manchester: Manchester University Press, 101–20.

Williams, J. (1996) Churches, Identities and Sport in the North, 1900–1939, in J. Hill and J.

Williams (Eds.), *Sport and Identity in the North of England*, Keele: Keele University Press, 113–36.

Williams, J. (1999) *Cricket and England: A Cultural and Social History of the Inter-War Years*, London: Frank Cass.

4   Harvesting Souls in the Stadium
The Rise of Sport Evangelism[1]

Shirl James Hoffman

In the late nineteenth century, the Christian church in North America found itself awash in what some historians refer to as "the golden age of sports." The first gloved boxing match was held during this period; basketball and volleyball were invented; golf was imported from Scotland. Spectator sports were in the ascendancy. The National Baseball League and the Big Ten Athletic Conference were established. Madison Square Garden in New York City opened with seating for eight thousand spectators. Horse racing and human racing were huge draws as was competitive rowing. While only two thousand people watched the first Harvard–Yale football game in 1875, more than twenty-two thousand were in attendance to watch the teams compete fifteen years later. How the church should respond to this swelling passion for sports became a topic of extraordinary importance to clergy and religious scholars, most of whose ancestors had stood shoulder to shoulder against sport, amusement and play (Baker, 1988; Harris, 2000).

From its inception the Christian church had been famously suspicious and, often, outright hostile to public sports, painfully aware of the power of its foe to entice even the most ardent believers into its clutches. First-century Roman citizens who, before their conversion, had been fans of the savagery of the Coliseum and the excitement of the racecourse found it difficult to excise this entertainment from their lifestyles once committed to the faith. From second-century apologist Tertullian's denouncement of the hippodromes as a "spectacle (that) drives out sound morality and invites childish factiousness" (Tertullian, 1931) to Theodore Mopsuestia's fourth-century warnings to baptismal candidates to shun "the circus, the racecourse, the contest of athletes . . . which the Devil introduced into the world under the pretext of amusement, and through which he leads the souls of men to perdition" (Laistner, 1951:42), the church railed against the ignominies of popular sport, yet the urgency of their pronouncements suggests that many Christians continued to flock to the games. Many centuries later, despite the church's lingering uneasiness with sports—whether the crude town games of the villagers or the more formal jousting tournaments of the nobility—the trend continued: passion for sports always seemed to run ahead of passion for the faith.

By the mid-nineteenth century, thanks in no small part to the pleas of secular writers such as Frederic William Sawyer (1847) and an emerging recognition among the pubic of the social benefits of informal sports, it was becoming clear to liberal clergymen that continuing indiscriminately to condemn sports was a lost cause. In 1887 a minister told the Sixth Annual Baptist Congress: "Time was, when we could shut the question [sports and amusement] out of the church with sweeping prohibitions; wave off its perplexities with some snap-rule of arbitrariness. That time has passed" (Watson, 1887:120).

Although there clearly was an "if-you-can't-beat-'em-join-'em'" flavor to such injunctions, in many cases—especially in liberal denominations—they were stimulated by a renewed interest in theological analysis of sport, play and amusements. Prior to the mid-nineteenth century isolated ecclesiastical endorsements of play as a beneficial adjunct to health and work (and therefore a worthy pursuit of Christians) could be found, but always with the caveat that Christians do not "dwell on them, or make them your great employment," nor pursue them for mere pleasure (Taylor, 1831). Conventional thought was that playing represented a misguided effort to quench the souls' thirst for God. The shallow emotions it stirs are but a synthetic substitute for the spiritual nurture ("sober mirth") that comes from hymn singing, Bible reading and meditation. By mid-century, however, a smattering of theologians and pastors began to rethink such notions and to look more deeply at the spiritual significance of play.

At the forefront was Horace Bushnell, an anti-revivalist, anti-conversionist Congregational pastor whose interest in play culminated in an 1861 book titled *Christian Nurture* (Bushnell, 1861). Bushnell rejected the idea that play belongs as a part of the Christian life simply because it is an adjunct to work, noting that work is "an activity for an end" while play is an "activity *as* an end" (389). We weren't created to work, as religious authorities had long had it, but to play. Work was necessary, but only as a means to play.

But the most distinctive part of Bushnell's radical commentary was his belief that the divine appointment of play in animals and youngsters was God's way of reminding Christians what awaited them at this worldly life's end. Animals naturally play; how odd it would be, he said, if God, "having put the same sportive instinct in their [human's] make [to] restrict them to a carefully sober mood." We begin our lives as playful children, significant because God "set the beginning of natural life in a playful mood that foreshadows the last and highest chapter in immortal life." When adults look back on their play experiences in childhood, he said, they "catch a glimpse of paradise before [them]" (339–40).

Five years after Bushnell published his book, a renowned Congregational pastor and early leader of the progressive social gospel movement, Washington Gladden, stood in the pulpit of his North Adams, Massachusetts, church on a Sunday evening and delivered a sermon calling for the church to move to the playgrounds and provide leadership to the developing public interest in sport, play and amusement. This momentous event in the historical relationship between sport and religion was not merely a plea for Christians to play but for them to control the culture in which play so often took place. So controversial were his remarks that a group of local twenty-seven clergymen, fearing that his sermon was "liable to be misconstrued and misrepresented," asked him to publish it, which he did (Gladden, 1866,8).

"All the best amusements have been given up without a struggle to evil men and seducers, and have been used by them as powerful attractions by which to ensnare and ruin our youth" (10) said Gladden. While Gladden (1866) acknowledged that "amusements . . . which tax heavily on the bodily powers" (28) or which "involve the imminent peril of life or limb to those who practice them" (15) or "so engross the mind that it loses its interest in the serious things of life" (28) have no place in the Christian life, his principal aim was to convince the Christian community to rid sport, play and amusement of their abuses and bring them "under the empire of Christian ideas and forces." The goal of the Christian community, he said, should be to "rescue [games] from his [Satan's] clutches, and surround them with proper safeguards, and guard them against abuses" (20).

Thanks to leaders such as Gladden, the ensuing decades—and especially the early years of the twentieth century—saw the social gospel—a far reaching quasi-theological movement—sweep sport and play into the arms of the church. The movement was, in many ways, a response to mass urbanization, industrialization and immigration. Unlike fundamentalists who saw the ills of the world stemming from individual sin, this amorphous, ecumenical network of "evangelical liberals" and "modernistic liberals" believed sin also could be social and corporate. Fundamentalists were determined to save souls; social gospelers were determined to save society by ensuring social justice and purging it of inhumane working conditions, bad hygiene, abuse of liquor, child labor and inadequate schools.

The theological thread running through the movement was postmillennialism: the belief that the second coming of Christ would not occur until the world had been cleansed of its social ills. The notion that Christians could hasten Christ's return by urgently reforming society had its origin in fallout from the revivalist movements that swept the country, first in the eighteenth century and then again between 1800 and 1860. Once infiltrated with liberal clergy, however, the emphasis gradually shifted from saving souls to redeeming decrepit and sinful social structures. Perfectibility of humanity, elimination of inequalities and redemption of society became the focus of a new kind of evangelism.

Among the methods used in this redemptive process, sport was a favorite of many. All in the movement valued sport for its recreational and therapeutic properties, but increasingly, importance was attached to the emotional release experienced by those who gave themselves utterly to games. For the social gospelers, deep emotional involvement, a red flag for earlier generations of Protestants, was absolutely essential if play was to have its intended emotional catharsis. In one hyperbolic passage of his *The Church and the People's Play*, Henry Atkinson, social services secretary for the Congregational Church, ventured that "playing one game of tiddly winks with zest will do a man more good than to push up a five-pound dumbell a thousand times" (Atkinson, 1915, 40).

But even more important than its contribution to physical and mental health was the potential for sports to set misguided people on the correct moral path. Renting facilities for billiards, bowling and ball playing, said one religion writer, "could do more to keep [the church's] young people from the ways of sin than a Sunday school" (Stowe, 1866: 262). Although it was impelled more by "common sense" than hard evidence, the notion became fodder for a string of theological treatises on play. In one of these titled *The Minister and the Boy*, University of Chicago religion professor Allan Hoben doubted if anything, even the Ten Commandments, "could compete with a properly directed game in enforcing the fair play principle" (Hoben, 1912: 68). Hoben's assertion made explicit a point often buried in the flowery testimonials to play by the social gospelers: the moralisms in the Sunday morning sermon may prick a few consciences, but as a laboratory experience guaranteed to instill strength of character, sensitivity to others and a spirit of justice, the playground was miles ahead of the pulpit.

Tracing the rough progression of the relationship between sport and religion from the mid-nineteenth to the early twentieth century one can see a gradual change in the grounds for integrating sport into the Christian life. Initially, sport was viewed as a handmaiden of work and health; a necessary refreshment, like food and drink. From the beginning this hard instrumental view was accompanied by a deep suspicion of sport's emotional appeal and its enticement to excess. Gradually, and only in some theological quarters, the grounds began to shift: the importance of the expressive-emotional side of play and sports came to be acknowledged. As sport proved useful in meeting the material needs of the oppressed of society, it also became viewed as a moral tutor. In some minds at least, its power to redeem the character of participants was equal to the power of the gospel. But by the mid-twentieth century the relationship between sport and faith had taken a new tack: interest in sport's effect on the emotional and moral lives of individuals had waned in favor of the possibilities of sport as a tool for evangelizing the masses. Concern would shift from what sport could do for the bodies, souls and characters of participants to what it could do to help advertise a particular religious viewpoint to spectators.

SPORTS EVANGELISM

The progressive philosophy of the Social Gospel movement would continue to be associated with liberal theology and practice but its force as a revitalizing and unifying agent for Protestantism had greatly diminished by 1920. So too had serious ruminations about sport and play as part of the divine economy. By the end of World War I the stage was set for a ferocious battle between conservatives and "liberal evangelicals," which would find full fruition in the "fundamentalist–modernist controversy" in the twentieth century. The ire of fundamentalists was especially provoked by what they saw as progressives' tendency to emphasize social betterment for the singularly important matter of personal salvation.

It may not be an exaggeration to say that sport came to the defense of fundamentalism. During the first three decades of the twentieth century conservatives steadily lost their grip on mainline Protestant denominations whose colleges, seminaries and outreach organizations had come under the influence of liberal theology. Not only had fundamentalism lost credibility in theological circles; increasingly (and perhaps undeservedly) it also came to be associated with a lower-middle-class, unsophisticated mentality that distrusted intellectuals, rational criticism and popular social trends. In reaction to criticisms from the left, fundamentalists hardened their stance, emphasized their belief in "the fundamentals of faith" and became an embittered minority with a suspect social image. Sport, especially in the images of famous Christian athletes and coaches, promised fundamentalism what it could find in few other avenues of society: social respectability. If liberals could use sport as a means of social reform, fundamentalists could use it to polish a tarnished social image. If liberals could co-opt sport for its political and social agenda, evangelicals could use it to show that a popular, manly athlete could humble himself to walk the "sawdust trail" in a tent meeting and publicly kneel at the altar.

For liberal reformers like Robert Whitaker, author of the prize-winning book *Laughter and Life*, the ills of sport were traceable to its growing commercialization. "The whole field of healthful merriment has been fenced about with staring walls of artifice, which are painted from top to bottom with the dollar sign" (Whitaker, 1915:134). He called for a Christian transformation of sport, a new kind of "sport evangelism" that didn't shun sports but infused them with a spirit of play and changed their tone and methods to conform to Christian thinking. Such ideas had little appeal for fundamentalists for whom "sport evangelism" meant taking sport virtually as secular forces had shaped it and using it as a way of making the gospel more attractive to the sports-loving masses. Liberals had favored informal sports—-sports-behind-the-bleachers so to speak, but evangelicals favored sport played in front of thousands, highly publicized and backed by rabid followers. Fandom, long suspect by Protestants, had found a home in the evangelical community.

Some of the impetus for mixing sport with evangelism came from late Victorian England where the myths of athleticism and muscular Christianity, originally propagated as part of liberal-social Christianity, were co-opted by English evangelicals and exported to America.[1] The ideal was personified in the Cambridge Seven cricket players, many of whom had been converted at American evangelist Dwight L. Moody's revivals in England in 1884. Shortly after their conversions, all seven volunteered as missionaries to China and spent their lives in mission work. In the weeks before they departed for the mission field, they were featured in a series of "farewell meetings," part of a barnstorming tour of Scotland and England.

The vision of young men of decent social class, well-educated, clean-cut, manly and athletic, sitting on stage at the meetings, singing hymns and telling of their own conversions and callings to the mission field was, in the words of one writer, "a sight to stir the blood, and a testimony to the power of the uplifted Christ to draw unto himself, not the weak, the emotional, the intellectual only, but all that is noblest in strength and finest in culture" (Scott, 1970:138). Fifty years later evangelicals were still polishing the athletic image. Norman Grubb titled his biography of C. T. Studd *C. T. Studd: Cricketeer and Pioneer* even though Studd had played cricket seriously for only five years or so and had been a missionary for forty-five.

The year after the Cambridge Seven set off to China a better than average American baseball player by the name of Billy Sunday became a Christian. Five years later he retired from baseball, entered the ministry and, between 1896 and 1920, became the most popular figure in American religion, courted by presidents and men of wealth. Sunday preached an elementary theology he characterized as "the old-time religion," and set it against what he called the "deodorized and disinfected sermons" of evolution-loving liberals who were making "a religion out of social service with Christ left out" (McLoughlin, 1959:399, 429). His oratorical antics—handsprings, standing on stools, threatening the audience and arm waving—captured the imagination of a public starved for entertainment. Less recognized by historians, however, was Sunday's role in consolidating the link between sport and evangelicalism. Public sports would continue to be suspect in many quarters of conservative Christianity, but there is little question that Sunday's biography helped assuage the consciences of closet sports fans.

Hardly a superstar, Sunday nevertheless had earned his reputation as a better than average ballplayer. After entering the ministry it was perhaps natural that his sermons became sprinkled with baseball analogies and tales from his days on the diamond. Backsliders were chided because their "spiritual batting average(s) were not up to God's league standard." He ridiculed those "who step up to the collection plate at church and fan," depicted lost souls as those "who are dying on second and third base" and urged the Lord to "give us some coaches out at this Tabernacle so that people can be brought home to you" (McLoughlin, 1955: 410–412).

In preaching a no-nonsense gospel blended of equal parts militancy and masculinity, Sunday conjured up a tough, chip-on-his-shoulder Christ who was "the greatest scrapper that ever lived." The image had enormous appeal to those attracted to fierce competition, violence and rough sports. Sunday urged his crowds to be ready to stand and fight against an "off-handed, flabby-cheeked, brittle-boned, weak-kneed, thin-skinned, pliable, plastic, spineless, effeminate, ossified three carat Christianity." When audiences, especially college men, resisted his altar calls he appealed to their masculine instincts: "Do you know why you haven't come down here? You're not man enough. I throw it in your teeth. You're not man enough" (McLoughlin, 1955: 175–79).

Sunday certainly wasn't the only Christian ballplayer of his day, nor was he the only advocate of a gospel of evangelical masculinity. His ministry spanned an age when fundamentalist barriers to a wide range of sports were being lowered—first in northern denominations and later in southern churches; it was an age in which the prototype of the clean, All-American, Christian athlete made its first appearance. Young people began to have paraded before them in the religious press famous Christian athletes who, if not always evangelical in their theology, shared evangelicals' contempt for smoking, drinking, dancing and carousing. The social constraints on evangelicalism, not always attractive to adolescents, were recast as practical benefits of the faith and held up for admiration by young athletes. Typical was an article that appeared in 1911 in *The Amethyst*, an organ of the Northern Presbyterian Church, titled "What Baseball Players Think of Cigarettes." Readers were assured that Clark Griffith, Branch Rickey and "Home Run Baker" didn't think it was right to smoke, and Walker John, "the world's greatest pitcher, does not drink, smoke, or chew and goes to bed early" (Hogan, 1967: 134).

In linking the gospel to sports celebrity, evangelicals came to appreciate early on that the currency of the athletic image depended largely on competitive success. For a sports-crazed society, winning, rather than playing fairly, was what garnered attention. Thus the image of a champion became more salient in the evangelical cause than the image of the good sport. And success often required an adulteration, if not complete abrogation, of Christian principles during competition.

Examples abounded in the late decades of the nineteenth century when, as Robert Higgs (1995) notes, there was "a virtual army of Christian coaches" the most famous of who were better models of the athletic than the Christian ethic. John Heisman, the coach at Georgia Tech and for whom the most prestigious award in college football is named, hated fumbling as much as he loathed profanity; he had a well-earned reputation for "gaming the system." He illegally signaled plays from the sideline, perfected the "hidden ball play" in which the quarterback would stuff the ball under his jersey while pretending to tie his shoe and was repudiated by colleagues for running up the score against hapless Cumberland College (222–0), reportedly in retaliation for a trouncing Cumberland had given to Tech's baseball team a year earlier. Fielding "Hurry Up" Yost at University of Michigan regarded his coaching position as "a pulpit" for preaching football as a "sanctified instrument for the good"; he opposed smoking, drinking and swearing. At the same time he thought nothing about humiliating unmatched opponents. He is reported to have gloated about his team's thrashing (130–0) of the University of West Virginia in 1904, and about his teams having outscored opponents 2,271 to 42 in a span of four years. He was a committed Christian yet described by Stanford's president as a practitioner of "the kind of corruptions in athletics that colleges should eschew" (Higgs, 1995: 264–65).

But the coach whose career best exemplified the preeminence given winning by evangelicals was Amos Alonzo Stagg, arguably the most famous American football coach ever to walk the sideline. Stagg, a student of theology, described coaching as a kind of Christian service. He was hired in 1892 by University of Chicago's president, who liked having a man "who could direct athletics and pray" at the same time. Yet Stagg's religion never interfered with his compulsion to win. Guided by his twin philosophies that "the objective of football is to win rather than to play merely for pleasure" and that football is "a game of war within the limitations of the rules and of sportsmanship," he established a remarkable reputation, not only as a winning coach, but as one who helped put college athletics on a disastrous "win at all cost" trajectory (Iverson, 1996). Rebuked by the president for using ineligible players, he had no qualms about the viciousness that was essential for fielding a winning football team, once remarking to a player that he had picked him for his team "because you can do the meanest things in the most gentlemanly manner" (Dawson, 1989: 280, n 31)).

The success of Stagg's teams was owed not only to his managerial genius and flare for strategy, but to on-the-field trickery and deception that barely skirted the line of cheating, something his critics called "most unchristian." Stagg was unchastened, writing that while the British honor both the letter and spirit of the rules, Americans honor only the letter, something he thought fine: "If we are smart enough to detect a joker or loophole first, then we are entitled not only in law but ethics to take advantage of it" (Dawson, 1989: 282). In an exhaustive dissertation analyzing Stagg's career, Peter Iverson reached the disappointing but probably correct conclusion "that football's 'purity man,' willingly stretched and broke the rules to win, while defending the game as a builder of good character." His "opportunistic nature and drive for recognition," says Iverson, "helped fuel his legendary coaching career and myth as a heroic character" (Iverson, 1996: 223). With time many evangelicals came to expect ethically blighted sports as par for the course. Sports, by and large, were granted an exemption from normal ethical standards. Christian athletes may be expected to lead Christ-inspired lives when off the field, but during competition, another ethic was held to be supreme.

THE BONDS TIGHTEN

In America, the evangelical parade to the playground had already begun to assemble when Billy Sunday began his ministry, but the band didn't start playing until Olympic runner Eric Liddell, popularized in the book

Chariots of Fire and in the 1981 Oscar-winning film by the same name, refused to run in the 100 meters in the 1924 Olympics because the heats were held on a Sunday. A last-minute arrangement permitted Liddell to run in the 400 meters, a fact far less embellished than his willingness to follow the dictates of his evangelical conscience. In his conversations with fans and reporters Liddell talked of correlations between faith and running; he described winning as a God-honoring feat and running as a spiritual obligation, all familiar themes in today's evangelical sport talk.

In retrospect, the uniqueness of the Liddell episode wasn't so much that he publicized his religious commitment, something the evangelical community continues to point to, but his willingness to allow his religious conscience to override the demands of the sporting culture. Liddell may have been the first Christian elite athlete to do this. We would have to wait another sixty years for the second incident when Andrea Jaeger, the number two ranked female tennis player in the world, left the game because of conflicts between aspects of the culture of competition and her faith. Not surprisingly, the evangelical community did not rush to Jaeger's defense or hold her up as a paragon of the intersection of faith and sport.

Sports evangelism was moved to the next level when Billy Graham revival meetings began featuring elite athletes who made facile comparisons between athletics and faith. The first was runner Gil Dodds, who spoke at a 1947 revival. Dodds recently had set the world indoor record for the mile. He ran a mock race around the stadium against a local athlete before the service. Later, at the podium, he asked the crowd, "I wonder how many of you here tonight are doing your best in the race for Jesus Christ?" (Ladd and Mathisen, 1999:96). Dodds set the course for the army of sports evangelists that followed, crediting the Lord with helping them win and preaching variations of Billy Sunday's theme of "muscularity." "It takes a man to become a Christian," said Dodds, thereby unwittingly barring over 50 percent of the population from heavenly glory (Farmer, 1948: 96).

In the 1950s and 1960s, when evangelicals began to move out from under the shadow of a declining fundamentalism, they began seeking visibility, not only in the intellectual marketplace, but in popular culture as well. It was a timely transition since sports occupied an increasingly significant role in American society, deepening its bonds with cultural and political life. During this period several athletic ministries were born, Venture for Victory, Fellowship of Christian Athletes (FCA), Athletes in Action (AIA) and several others. Famous athletes were ushered to microphones; the evangelical press published stories about their lives.

One such athlete was Bill Glass, four-time Pro Bowl player for the Cleveland Browns who, after retiring, established a thriving prison ministry. Glass's genial personality, coupled with a physically intimidating physique, targeted teenage boys with a tough-man, locker-room version of the gospel with a competitive-based brand of Christian ethics. Even though I am a Christian," said Glass, "I can play a rough brand of football. In fact, as a Christian, I ought to play an even rougher brand than anyone else" (Glass, 1981: 81). Glass penned a series of books brimming with athletic mythology. In one such book, containing a foreword by Billy Graham, he tells kids: "If you get beat, after the game is over you ought to congratulate the winner . . . Yes, practice good sportsmanship, but when you get in the dressing room and no one is looking, back off about ten yards and run and ram your head into the locker because you hate to lose so badly. Don't ever be a good loser. Be a bad loser, Good losers usually lose" (Glass, 1965:67–68). Asked how Christians could play a game that teaches players to "run down the weak, hammer your enemy, gouge him where it hurts and the referee can't see," Glass rebuked those who play dirty, but said he saw nothing unchristian about rough aggressive play. "The weak shouldn't play in the first place," he told his interviewer" (Glass and Pinson, 1972:27).

If Glass was the reigning athlete of 1960s evangelicalism, Tom Landry was its reigning coach. Landry, the first coach of the Dallas Cowboys who continued in that role for twenty-nine years, was enormously successful, taking his teams to fifteen divisional title games and five Super Bowls. Firm in his faith and stiff in his demeanor, Landry championed a no-nonsense, corporate-managerial approach to football. When it came to football he was cold and calculating, a strategist who took his football very seriously. "Nothing funny," he once said, "ever happens on a football field" (Meroney, 2000: 43). Landry's style was vastly different from Glass's. He willingly talked of his faith to those who made inquiries, but hesitated to push it on others.

Landry followed in the footsteps of Stagg, Yost or Heisman. He once told a writer: "If you can't play within the rules and play a tough, punishing type of game, you can't play as a Christian. We try to eliminate the vicious side of the game, but you have to punish the opposition" (Flake, 1985). Sportswriter Skip Bayless's book *God's Coach: The Hymns, Hype, & Hypocrisy of Tom Landry's Cowboys* is the most exhaustive analysis of Landry's career. Bayless recounts players' accusations of Landry's "lying to them and the media in the name of 'business' and hiding behind the Bible." Landry's highest compliment of a player was that "he's a pro," which, said Bayless, "meant that (the athlete) played when he was hurt . . . that he agreed to take painkilling injections . . . that he risked serious or permanent injury . . . that he ignored the doctor's warning and all the screaming signals with which God so wondrously equipped the body" (Bayless, 1990: 17). Although the book lauded Landry on many counts, Bayless—a born again believer—struggled to understand how Landry could dismiss the increasing level of violence of the game by saying "but it's just part of this bi'ness" (Bayless, 1990: 162).

Both Glass and Landry helped to cement the bond between big-time sport and evangelicalism, and they also helped forge evangelical understanding of sport as an experience in which flirting with and sometimes skirting ethical boundaries is a normal and understandable reality in big-time sports. In doing this they projected dramatically different images. In his glorification of brutality and manliness Glass was reminiscent of nineteenth-century muscular Christians Hughes and Kingsley, although with a sharper edge. Landry, on the other hand, was more nuanced in his approach. If Glass was the violent knight, Landry was the monk; Glass was the take-no-prisoners warrior, Landry was the hard-driving, Stagg-like CEO. Both images, however, appealed to various segments of the evangelical community: Glass to young athletes, Landry to sport fans.

Glass's career overlapped early efforts to organize sports evangelism, a movement funded in large part by sports-loving, evangelical businessmen who regarded it as a unique and worthy missionary effort. No longer would sports evangelism be left to the *ad hoc*, hit-or-miss postgame stammering of individual athletes. Shaped and nurtured by athletically minded staff members, many of whom had theological training, sports evangelism morphed into a national and international movements, designed and operated according to field-tested methods and intensely honed to produce results. Fawning fans that couldn't quite make the connections between a gospel of grace and humility and a tough, relentless competitive spirit would be helped to understand.

MOVING TO THE NEXT LEVEL

A full telling of the story of the tightening bonds between evangelicalism and big-time sports from the 1930s to present day is far beyond the scope of this chapter. Readers interested in an in-depth examination of organized sports evangelism are referred to the fine book *Muscular Christianity: Evangelical Protestants and the Development of American Sport* by Tony Ladd and James Mathisen, which describes in great detail the events, personalities and organizations that were critical facilitators of the movement. Here we will touch only on some highlights.

The seed for organized sports evangelism in America was planted in 1952 when a small group of talented basketball players, playing under the banner "Venture for Victory," spent eight weeks in Formosa (Taiwan) holding 160 revival meetings, playing seventy-nine basketball games and preaching to sixty-five thousand Chinese. In the ensuing years the team would travel throughout the Orient and South America. Two years later the granddaddy of evangelistic sports ministries was born. FCA was the brainchild of basketball coach Don McClanen, who dreamed of a "harnessing of heroes to reach those who idolized them for a life for the Lord" (Dunn, 1980: 20–25). FCA has grown steadily in both numbers and influence. The "Annual Impact Report" for 2009 claimed that it had reached 1,800,000 people, with 3,694 having made faith commitments (*FCA Annual Impact Report*, 2009).

While the organization has excelled at influencing the lives of athletes away from the field, from its founding it has not favored applying religio-ethical standards to competition or the sports culture. In the 1970s, when he was editor of an FCA publication titled *The Christian Athlete*, Gary Warner published an article drawing uncomfortable comparisons between sports and war and earned the scorn of the leadership. He later wrote "the FCA Board of Trustees slapped the hands of the editorial staff, established an editorial watchdog committee, restated that the magazine was to be a 'house organ' (stories of athletes who win trophies, not articles dealing with touchy subjects)." Later, said Warner, "an issue dealing with violence in sports scheduled for January 1978, was drastically altered and watered down to the point of being largely unintelligible" (Warner, 1979: 185).

In the 1960s, AIA, the second most influential sports evangelism organization, was given life through the efforts of Bill Bright, founder of *Campus Crusade Ministries*, who wanted a "more aggressive evangelism and discipleship training" than offered by the sometimes ecumenical FCA. Gary Warner wrote that his organization did "not produce enough pelts on the salvation barn door to satisfy the Crusade zealots" (Warner, 1979:169). Bright, a firm believer that competition was "a gift from God," was the perfect person to launch a sports ministry that glorifies it (Bright, 1984: 18). He would no doubt have been surprised with the growth of the ministry he started: it now supports a staff of 650 working in ninety-four countries and claims to have a presence on 128 college campuses and "ongoing ministry" with sixteen chaplains serving NFL teams, one NBA team, two major league baseball teams and one major league soccer team. The AIA "Vision Statement" is "a Christ follower on every team in every nation" (see http://www.athletesinaction.org/about/).

Around the same time that AIA was getting its walking legs, the unassuming and very talented second baseman of the New York Yankees, Bobby Richardson, began holding chapel services for interested teammates before Sunday games. His efforts eventually blossomed into the formation of *Baseball Chapel, Inc.* Today the organization sponsors five hundred chapel leaders who lead services before almost all games in Major League, Minor Leagues and Independent Leagues beginning with spring training. Approximately three thousand players, coaches, managers, trainers, umpires, team staff, stadium personnel and families of the players and coaches participate each week.[2] A few years later, in the early 1970s, *Pro Athlete Outreach* (PAO) was founded by Christian professional athletes. Since its founding, PAO claims to have "helped thousands of active and retired athletes and their spouses find lasting solutions for the intense pressures of a career in professional sports" (see http://www.pao.org/who-we-are/history.html). By this time professional sports were flooded with players from evangelical protestant backgrounds, a phenomena that led Billy Graham to tell *Newsweek* that "there are probably more really committed Christians in sports, both college and professional . . . than in any other occupation in America" ("Are Sports Good for the Soul," 1971:51–52).

A few months later it came to light that the 1971 San Francisco Giants baseball team, nicknamed "the God squad," was composed largely of Christians. Around the same time humorist Roy Blount wrote that he set out to select an "All Religious Team" to compete against an "All Heathen Team" in an imaginary "Christians vs. Lions Bowl" but had to abort the project when he couldn't find enough genuine heathens to field a squad. It seemed almost every athlete was a Christian (Blount, 1976: 113).

At about the same time evangelical colleges began to venture into the deeper waters of intercollegiate sports for the professed aim of evangelism. By 1968 the *National Christian College Athletic Association* (NCCAA) was formed "to provide a Christian-based organization that functions uniquely as a national and international agency for the promotion and outreach and ministry, and for the maintenance, enhancement, and promotion of inter-collegiate athletic competition with a Christian perspective.[3] The organization's website covers in great detail season records and accomplishments of its member teams, players and coaches. Awards all focus on athletic successes; unlike websites for secular sports organizations, the NCCAA website offers no information on sportsmanship awards.

The public relations benefits and the perils that can accrue to Christian colleges who wade into the murky waters of big-time sports were discovered firsthand by Tulsa-based Oral Roberts University in the 1970s after it made a major financial commitment to intercollegiate basketball. Going big-time, said founder-evangelist Roberts, wasn't merely to bring attention to the school, but was intended to be a major force for evangelism. Within five years ORU made it to the NCAA playoffs and shortly thereafter found itself involved in a national scandal surrounding their basketball coach.

Late evangelist Jerry Falwell came closer to attaining Robert's dream of building a powerhouse athletic program while avoiding scandal. Two years after he founded Liberty University in 1971 he told a writer from the *Washington Post* that he wanted to field a football team that would beat Notre Dame. "Winning is very important to us," said Falwell. "I agree with Vince Lombardi; if it's not important then why keep score? We want to win and we cry when we don't win." A star running back chipped in: "Our goal is to be the hardest-hitting team anyone has ever played. We don't want them looking at us as a pansy team . . . Their idea of being a Christian is a little-bitty guy carrying a big Bible. What we do is out hustle people, knock their heads off and they'll say 'These guys are different.' . . . Of course it's hard sometimes to show them the love of Christ after we've beat them up and down the field. You say, 'Hey Jesus loves you,' and they don't exactly understand" (Jenkins, 1985:B1).

Falwell pursued his dream of fielding a national champion team by hiring big-name coaches and investing substantial funds and, in effect, assuming the title of "general manager" of the athletic program. "We probably place as high a priority on sports if not higher than many of the major universities," Falwell told reporters. "We don't deify it, but we very nearly do."

The school's website says, "Following games Liberty athletes can typically be seen praying with their opponents and telling them what Christ has done in their lives" (Bechtel and Cannella, 2005:31).

Moran Hout, the school's former stellar football coach, could have used some prayer since, on the same year he was named Virginia Division I Coach of the Year, he was fired by Falwell, simply because Sam Ratigliano, former coach of the Cleveland Browns, became available for the position. In 2005 football coach Ken Karcher, the athletic director and two assistants were fired because of Falwell's disappointment in the progress his teams were making toward the goal of moving from Division IAA to Division IA. Falwell told reporters: "We're not even playing par I-AA football here, so obviously we have to start over, and that's what we're doing" (Bechtel and Cannella, 2005:31).

The evangelical–sport alliance has been abetted by a prodigious output of books and magazines intended to be, more or less, tools of evangelism. A seemingly limitless market for biographies of Christian athletes and coaches is fed by some of the most popular Christian publishing houses. The major evangelical publishing firm Tyndale House has published two of Jim Tressel's books. The most recent—*Life Promises for Success: Promises from God for Achieving Your Best*—came off the presses three months before he was defrocked as coach of the Ohio State University football team for his role in the scandal that rocked the school. Tressel presided over a culture rife with National Collegiate Athletic Association rule violations for more than eight years. The coach with a "prayer request box" on his desk was found to have failed to report known violations and for signing off on a statement declaring that no such violations had been committed (Tressel and Faby, 2011). In *Racing to Win*, Washington Redskins coach and NASCAR owner Joe Gibbs claims to call "his plays by the best selling Book of all time." The blurb on the book's jacket assures readers that "his incredible story of triumph and defeat in the high-stakes world of professional sports, *and in life* will make you a believer too" (Gibbs and Abraham, 2003).

In *From Ashes to Glory*, former University of Colorado football coach and founder of Promise Keepers Bill McCartney tells of his spiritual journey and his rise to the top of the coaching ranks (McCartney and Diles, 1995). In *All Things Possible: My Story of Faith, Football and the First Miracle Season* (Warner, 2001) St. Louis Rams quarterback Kurt Warner describes how his faith played a role in his nearly miraculous rise from anonymity to become the MVP of the Super Bowl. Men's stories dominate the genre just as men tend to dominate the sports evangelism movement (partly it should be noted, because so much of U.S. sports evangelism centers on football, a sport that largely excludes women), but books such as *Competitor's Edge* in which women athletes talk about sports and their faith have also found a market (Branon, 1998).

Books written with breathless adoration of successful college athletic teams are a favorite. Those who would like to know how faith is integrated and demonstrated in the Saturday afternoon exploits of their alma mater can read *Faith of the Sooners: Inspiring Oklahoma Sports Stories of Faith* (Schaller, 2002); *Faith in the Crimson Tide: Inspiring Alabama Sports Stories of Faith* (Atcheson, 2000); and *Lessons from Nebraska Football: Inspirational Stories and Lessons from the Gridiron* (Thiessen and Todd, 1999). Those having difficulty sorting out believer athletes from their less devout teammates can consult *A Sports Fans Guide to Christian Athletes and Sports Trivia* (Branon, 2000), which offers a theologically vetted list of nearly three hundred famous athletes. Athletically slanted devotional books are available for those hesitant to step outside the sport mentality, even for daily meditations. The *Sports Devotional Bible*, a book of general sporting interest, with a dust jacket that promises readers they will learnhow "virtues such as character, trust, perspective, discipline, and faith make both great athletes and strong Christians" (Branon, 2002).

In these writings, strong faith is consistently portrayed as an adjunct rather than a modulator or a restraint to competitive zeal, and it isn't always clear where self-help stops and spirituality begins. Weekend golfers who struggle with their slice can consult *Golf God's Way*, which assures readers that "God is just as interested in the way we play golf as the way we earn a living and the way we spend any of our time" (Bernadoni, 1991: 6).

Two magazines crafted around the theme of faith and sports deserve special mention. *Sharing the Victory*, a publication of FCA with a circulation of eight-two thousand, features inspirational stories by athletes, some famous, some not so famous; almost all have an impressive resume of competitive victories, which receive big play in articles. Athletes and coaches tell how their faith has helped them overcome adversity and how it helps them deal with the stresses of competition. ("Adversity" is a term widely applied to losing seasons as well as personal struggles.) There is little to be found here to deepen anyone's understanding of the meaning of sport in the Christian life, very little about the impact of the experience on the writers' character or understanding of Christian virtues. Nor are there any stories describing how an athletes' spiritual calling might put him or her at odds with the dominant ethos of big-time sport. You won't find much in these pages to chasten the sports establishment but you will find much to whitewash its sins.

Sports Spectrum, with a circulation of twenty-five thousand, is in many ways a slicker, more interesting and varied periodical. The magazine was launched in 1990 under the auspices of the Radio Bible Broadcast in Grand Rapids, Michigan. It is a sleek, evangelical knockoff of the worldly *Sports Illustrated*. Lively articles describing the accomplishments of Christian athletes from all levels of competition, upbeat takes on the glories of sports, columns on topics of general as well as special interest, exceptionally good photographs of athletes in action, expertly designed layouts and a limited number of advertisements, all interlaced with punchy devotionals based on athletic analogies, fill its pages. Its editors and writers are obviously fascinated by the world of sports.

Left unmentioned in the pages of the magazine, is anything that might reflect untoward on sports. Unlike *Sports Illustrated*'s conscientious coverage of both the good and the bad in sports, *Sports Spectrum* is all about the good. You won't find much mention here about racism, recruiting scandals, ill treatment of athletes, cheating, over-the-top competitive coaching or tensions between sports and higher education. Sport, one could easily presume, poses no thorny problems for Christians. In an exhaustive review of the publication, sociologist James Mathisen concluded that it holds to "a persisting individualistic moral orientation toward sport—-root out individual selfishness and cheating, perhaps, but do not confront the more structural dimensions of racism, sexism, and corporate irresponsibility in education or politics or big business" (Mathisen, 1992: 15).

CONCLUSIONS: EVANGELIZING SPORT

This brief historical excursus reviews in a most general way the evolution in Christian thinking about sport that has played out over the centuries. The grounds for rejection of popular sports by church leaders in the first three centuries were based largely on three things: the frenzy produced by games and the way this frenzy destabilized spiritual dispositions, the emotionally toxic effects of watching and participating in violent sports and the pagan religious rites that were incorporated into the games. In mounting these challenges to popular sports—many of which had been in vogue for hundreds of years—the early church leaders were attentive, first and foremost, to the human experience of sport and its implication for spiritual health.

This "interior auditing" of the effects of sport on spiritual and moral sensibilities was the standard for the Christian community's assessments for over eighteen hundred years. Once the vision of sport as a tool for evangelism was cast, however, concern for interior auditing was dimmed; the focus turned away from examining the effects of sport on the individual and society to devise new technologies for advertising the faith. Worries about excess, immoderation, the disharmony brought about by hard-core competition and violence and its impact on physical and moral sensibilities gradually were moved from center stage as excitement grew about sport's role in evangelism. In the process promising possibilities of developing a Christian theology of sport, such as those outlined by Horace Bushnell, were ignored in favor of a hybrid locker-room theology, more hospitable to the orthodoxies of the sports culture, which *Sports Illustrated* writer Frank Deford called "Sportianity." Gradually, thinking about the relationship between sport and religion was dominated by a hard-core evangelical instrumentalism. The power of sport to reach the masses became its own theological rationale.

When the church finally flung open its doors to sport in the late nineteenth century it was with the expectation that the Christian community would offer leadership and moral guidance and, where necessary, lead efforts to reform sport. But the reform movement, such as it was, succumbed to popular pressures to worship the commercialized model of sport that was in vogue. Throughout its entire relationship with sport there is no indication that the Christian community ever mounted a serious attempt to influence the form and function of popular sport, something acutely apparent to Deford, whose criticisms were publicized in a series of articles on sport and evangelicalism in 1976: "Sadly, lost in the shuffle, in the competition for dotted-line converts (sign here, raise your hand, send for literature), is sport itself. In the process of dozens of interviews with people in Sportianity, not one even remotely suggested any direct effort was being considered to improve the morality of athletics. An active churchman, who has long been involved in pro sport, says, 'The trouble with these people is that they worship sport as much as they do Jesus.'"

One must be careful not to paint the entire sports evangelism enterprise with a broad brush; clearly some sectors of the movement have had positive impacts on the off-field lives of athletes and young people, but to date, there is little indication that these incidents of spiritual renewal have had any broad-scale impact on competitive philosophies or on the way games are played. Some sport evangelists truly are concerned with the moral crisis in sport, although the path envisioned for renewal continues to be evangelizing individuals rather than evangelization the sport culture itself. The continued downward spiral in the moral climate of big-time sports—in spite of an unprecedented invasion of sport by Christian athletes—suggests the futility of this approach.

NOTES

1. Portions of this chapter have been adapted with permission from Hoffman (2010).
2. Actually, sport evangelism as a technique may have originated in the third century when Hilarion, a charismatic ascetic, blessed the horse and stable of a Christian charioteer whose subsequent wins, said Jerome, "caused very many people to turn to the faith" (Fox, 1986).
3. See at http://www.baseballchapel.org/.
4. See http://www.thenccaa.org/.

BIBLIOGRAPHY

Are Sports Good for the Soul? (1971) *Newsweek*, 77 (2): 51–52.
Atcheson, W. (2000) *Faith in the Crimson Tide: Inspiring Alabama Sports Stories of Faith*, Kearney, NE: Cross Training.
Atkinson, H. A. (1915) *The Church and the People's Play*, New York: Pilgrim.
Baker, W. J. (1988) *Sports in the Western World*, rev. ed., Champaign: University of Illinois Press.
Bayless, S. (1990) *God's Coach: The Hymns, Hype and Hypocrisy of Tom Landry's Cowboys*, New York: Simon and Schuster.

Bechtel, M. and Cannella, S. (2005) For the Record, *Sports Illustrated*, 103 (22): 31.

Bernadoni, G. (1991) *Golf God's Way*, Lake Mary, FL: Creation House.

Blount, R. (1976) Temple of the Playing Fields, *Esquire*, 111–113: 198.

Branon, D. (1998) *Competitor's Edge: Women Athletes Talk about Sports and Their Faith*, Chicago: Moody.

Branon, D. (2000) *A Sports Fan's Guide to Christian Athletes and Sports Trivia*, Chicago: Moody.

Branon, D. (2002) *Sports Devotional Bible*, Grand Rapids, MI: Zondervan.

Bright, B. (1984) That Winning Spirit, *Athletes in Action Magazine*, 6 (Fall): 21.

Bushnell, H. (1861) *Christian Nurture*, New York: Charles Scribner.

Dawson, H. J. (1989) Veblen's Social Satire and Amos Alonzo Stagg: Football and the American Way of Life, in J. Salzman (Ed.), *Prospects: An Annual of American Cultural Studies*, New York: Cambridge University Press278n23, 280n31.

Deford, F. (1976) Religion in Sport, *Sports Illustrated*, 19 April, 26 April, 3 May.

Dunn, J. (1980) *Sharing the Victory*, New York: Quick Fox.

Farmer, G. (1948) Best Indoor Mile, *Life*, 24 (7): 95–96, 98.

FCA Annual Impact Report. (2009) Available online at http://fca.org/AboutFCA/AnnualImpactReport.lsp (accessed 1 December 2011).

Flake, C. (1985) *Redemptorama*, New York: Penguin.

Fox, R. L. (1986) *Pagans and Christians*, New York: Knopf.

Gibbs, J. and Abraham, J. (2003) *Racing to Win*, Sisters, OR: Multnomah.

Gladden, W. (1866) *Amusements: Their Uses and Abuses*, North Adams, MA: James Robinson.

Glass, B. (1965) *Get in The Game*, Waco, TX: Word.

Glass, B. (1981) *Expect to Win*, Waco, TX: Word.

Glass, B. and Pinson, W. M. (1972) *Don't Blame the Game*, Waco, TX: Word.

Grub, N. (1933) *C. T. Studd, Cricketer and Pioneer*, London: Lutterworth Press.

Harris, J. C. (2000) History of Physical Activity, in S. J. Hoffman and J. C. Harris (Eds.), *Introduction to Kinesiology*, Champaign, IL: Human Kinetics, 179–206.

Higgs, R. J. (1995) *God in the Stadium*, Lexington: University of Kentucky Press.

Hoben, A. (1912) *The Minister and the Boy*, Chicago: University of Chicago Press.

Hoffman, Shirl James. (2010) *Good Game: Christianity and the Culture of Sport*, Waco, TX: Baylor University Press.

Hogan, W. R. (1967) Sin and Sports, in C. Slovenko and J. A. Knight (Eds.), *Motivations in Play, Games and Sports*, Springfiled, Il: Charles C. Thomas, 134–37.

Iverson, P. B. (1996) *A Mission on the Midway: Amos Alonzo Stagg and the Gospel of American Football*. PhD dissertation, Michigan State University.

Jenkins, S. (1985) "Liberty U Hits First, Saves Later," *Washington Post*, 5 October, B1.

Ladd, T. and Mathisen, J. A. (1999) *Muscular Christianity: Evangelical Protestants and the Development of American Sport*, Grand Rapids, MI: Baker Books.

Laistner, W. (1951) *Christianity and Pagan Culture in the Later Roman Empire*, Ithaca, NY: Cornell University Press.

Mathisen, J. A. (1992) The Rhetoric of Modern 'Muscular Christianity': Taking a Second Look at Sports Spectrum, paper presented at the annual meeting of the Society for the Scientific Study of Religion, Washington, DC.

McCartney, B. and Diles, D. (1995) *From Ashes to Glory*, Nashville, TN: Nelson.

McLoughlin, W. C. (1955) *Billy Sunday Was His Real Name*, Chicago: University of Chicago Press.

McLoughlin W. C. (1959) *Modern Revivalism*, New York: Ronald Press.

Meroney, J. (2000) *Sports City*, American Enterprise, 11 (7): 44–45.

Sawyer, F. (1847) *A Plea for Amusements*, New York: D. Appleton.

Schaller, B. (2001) *Faith of the Sooners: Inspiring Oklahoma Sports Stories of Faith*, Kearney, NE: Cross Training.

Scott, P. (1970) Cricket and the Religious World of the Victorian Period, *Church Quarterly*, 3: 137–39.

Stowe, H. B. (1866) The Chimney Corner for 1866, *Atlantic Monthly*, 18, 340.

Taylor, J. (1831) The Rules and Exercise of Daily Living, in T. Hughes (Ed.), *The Works of Jeremy Taylor*, London: A. J. Valpy, 301.

Tertullian. (1931) *Apology: De Spectaculis*, trans. T. R. Glover, London: W. Heinemann.

Thiessen, G. and Todd, M. (1999) *Lessons from Nebraska Football: Inspirational Stories and Lessons from the Gridiron*, Kearney, NE: Cross Training.

Tressel, J. and Fabry, J. (2011) *Life Promises for Success: Promises from God on Achieving Your Best*, Carol Stream, IL: Tyndale House.

Warner, G. (1979) *Competition*, Elgin, IL: David C. Cook.

Warner, K. (2001) *All Things Possible: My Story of Faith, Football and the First Miracle Season*, New York: HarperOne.

Watson, C. H. (1887) The Proper Attitude of the Church toward Amusements, *Sixth Annual Baptist Congress Proceedings*, 6: 120.

Whitaker, R. (1915) *Laughter and Life*, Philadelphia: American Sunday School Union.

5   Stereotypes and Archetypes in Religion and American Sport

Robert J. Higgs

Drawing upon the writings of Aristotle and Aquinas, Hugo Rahner (1972: 93–94) builds a case for both play *and* seriousness and the happy mean between them, *eutrapelia*. The *eutrapelos* averts the extremes of those who make fun of everything and those who never laugh at anything. Though he takes a different view of *eutrapelia* from that of Rahner, David Miller (1970: 137–69) argues that 'Religion is Play' and 'Play is Religion.'

When *eutrapelia* is not practiced, *enantiodromia* is the result, a term hinted at by Heraclitus and coined by Carl Jung, meaning that the superabundance of any force inevitably seeks equilibrium or turns into its opposite, empires, for example.

According to Robert Frost (1968: 91), 'Prowess of course comes first, the ability to perform with success in games, in the arts and, come right down to it, in battle. The nearest of kin to the artists in college . . . are their fellow performers in baseball, football, and tennis. That's why I am so particular college athletics should be kept from corruption. They are close to the soul of culture. At any rate the Greeks thought so.'

From American-based searches during 2011, Google lists under 'scandals in religion' about seventy-eight million references and under 'scandals in sport' about 169 million (Kuper, 2009).

INTRODUCTION

In the modern world, religion and sport could not be more relevant. Major religions figure directly in the future of us all, that is, whether peace shall prevail on earth or war. As for sport, it is hands down the most popular topic in the world. In 2008, 'the world carried out many more Google searches for the footballer Cristiano Ronaldo than for the then U.S.

president George Bush' (Kuper, 2009: 1). Like news and weather, sport is ubiquitous. The study of the breadth and depth of sport is vast, as revealed in the impressive bibliography of psychological and religious themes in *Sport and Spirituality: An Introduction* (Parry et al., 2007). On Google there are four million references to archetypes in sport and six million to stereotypes. Why, then, would I write about both? My response is simple: I want to explore one aspect common to both stereotypes and archetypes, how they intersect and react to make our games and religions what they are and what they are not. What follows is exploratory in the sense that little, if anything, has been written specifically on this topic.

SEEKING DEFINITIONS AND UNDERSTANDING OF STEREOTYPES AND ARCHETYPES

According to *Webster's Tenth New Collegiate Dictionary* (1999), stereotypes are 'standardized' mental pictures 'held in common by members of a group' and that represent 'an oversimplified opinion, affective attitude, or uncritical judgment.' Often a stereotype is defined as 'a metal plate cast from a printing surface,' in other words, that which establishes the 'cookie-cutter' form of production. In *Webster's Second*, a stereotype is 'anything conforming to a fixed and general pattern and undistinguished by individual marks.' As a rule, stereotypical images tend to reflect familiar themes and habits of everyday life. What, though, is an archetype?

Volumes have been written on the subject, perhaps more in 'depth-psychology' than elsewhere, and the one most often cited on the topic is Carl Jung (1964), who defined the term and theorized on its meaning. What Freud called 'archaic remnants' of our prehistoric past Jung called 'archetypes' or 'primordial images.' Just as the fetuses of humans resemble those of other animals and thus provide an indication of man's physical evolution, the psyche has also 'evolved' so that, suggested Jung (1964: 66), 'some contents of modern man's unconscious resemble products of the mind of ancient man.' Further, says Jung (1964: 69), 'archetypes represent an instinctive *trend*, as marked by the impulse of birds to build nests, or ants to form organized colonies.' In the case of the athlete the instinctive trend is to run, jump, throw and compete; in the case of the minister/priest and those of faith it is to worship a transcendent being.

While Jung (1964: 69; italics added) pointed to the similarity between instincts and archetypes, he also noted crucial differences and identified a biological element:

> What we properly call instincts are physiological urges, and are perceived by the senses. But at the same time, they also manifest themselves in fantasies and often reveal their presence *only by symbolic images*, and these manifestations are what I call the 'archetypes.' They are

without known origin; and they reproduce themselves in any time and in any part of the world—even where transmission by direct descent or 'cross fertilization' through migration must be ruled out.

Therefore, the Jungian archetypes of the unconscious are principally biological. According to Joseph Campbell (1988: 51), however, 'the Freudian unconscious is a personal unconscious; it is biographical' but 'secondary' to the biological. To J. E. Cirlot (1962: xxxiv) 'the archetype is, in the first place, an epiphany, that is, the revelation of the latent by way of the recondite: vision, dream, fantasy, myth . . . they are fruits of the inner life perpetually flowing out of the unconscious, in a way which can be compared with the gradual unfolding creation.' While these varying conceptualizations of the archetype from pioneering thinkers, such as Jung, Freud and Campbell, have differences, the fact that they are all characterized by 'patterns' is an important similarity that helps analyze their application to the world of sports.

ARCHETYPES AND STEREOTYPES AS 'PATTERNS'

At this point, then, let us further explore this notion of stereotypes and archetypes as 'patterns.' For stereotypes this means general conformity to established ways of thinking and acting of groups. Archetypes too are patterns generated by instincts in the collective unconscious (a Jungian term) but entering the conscious mind as ideas or symbols suggesting, say, 'change,' 'withdraw' or 'conform and serve.' Broadly speaking, stereotypes are visible patterns of manners of cultures; archetypes are those of the collective unconscious of the human race.

In one of her most popular poems, Emily Dickinson (1961: 1) provides a metaphor that gives startling meaning to the phenomenon of archetypes, 'Bulletins all day / From immortality,' and the effects of those 'bulletins' on the here and now:

The only news I know
Is bulletins all day
From immortality:
The only shows I see
Tomorrow and today.
Perchance eternity.
The only one I meet
Is God, the only street
Existence; this traversed.
If other news there be
Or admirabler show,
I'll tell it you.

Archetypes are also evident in the artful arrangements of nature, including floral displays, inspired by the eternal archetype of beauty, both forms of 'patterns,' the name of the following poem by Amy Lowell (2008: 1):

> In Summer and in Winter I shall walk up and down
> The patterned garden-paths
> In my stiff, brocaded gown.
> The squills and daffodils
> Will give place to pillared roses, and to asters, and to snow
> I shall go up and down,
> In my gown
> Gorgeously arrayed,
> Boned and stayed.
> And the softness of my body will be guarded from embrace
> By each button, hook, and lace.
> For the man who should loose me is dead,
> Fighting with the Duke in Flanders,
> In a pattern called a war.
> Christ! What are patterns for?

Much of the reflection on archetypes and stereotypes from psychologists, anthropologists and literary figures of the modern era, such as Emily Dickinson and Amy Lowell, has been informed by what Mortimer Adler calls the 'Great Ideas' that emerged from Ancient Greece.

ARCHETYPES IN THE 'GREAT IDEAS': GREEK IDEALS AND THE QUEST FOR EXCELLENCE

Whatever else they may be, archetypes are ideas, 'ground' or 'elementary,' and I am not reluctant to refer to some of them by another name, the 'Great Ideas.' According to Mortimer Adler (1981), in his work *Six Great Ideas*, the most important of these are 'truth,' 'goodness' and 'beauty' (ideas we seek to live by) and 'liberty,' 'equality' and 'justice' (ideas we seek to act on). In all, Adler identifies sixty-four that 'should be in the possession of human beings at all times' (18). Adler (1981) approaches ideas as a philosopher drawing mainly on the thinking of Plato and Aristotle, while Campbell (1988), a folklorist and anthropologist, finds his 'elementary ideas' in the bountiful symbols of Gods and heroes among primitive societies. Adler's treatment of ideas is what Campbell referred to as 'headwork,' but before ideas were 'headwork' they were 'spirit work' manifested by totemic symbols and other forms of primitive art. Adler speaks of the 'six great ideas' as 'the Chosen Ones.'

Among the 'Chosen Ones,' there are two sets of three, reflective of the importance of the archetype of trinity in Greek culture, as well as Christian, and no doubt other religions as well. In this category falls Plato's famous metaphor of the Charioteer and the two winged horses, one black and one white, pulling in different directions and representative of the contrasting inclinations of the human soul requiring reins of the driver to move in the direction of enlightenment. Similarly, the tripartite ideal identified by Socrates talking with Glaucon, is expressive of the parts latent in every individual. 'And he who mingles music with gymnastic in *the fairest proportions and best attempers them to the soul* may be rightly called the true musician and harmonist in a far higher sense than the tuner of the strings' (Plato, 1942: 298–300; italics added).

'Music' in the academic world of Greece, according to Rachel Robinson (1980: 125), 'included reading, writing, mathematics, harmony, poetry, drawing, (and music in its narrowest sense)' and 'gymnastic, in which . . . youth are to be trained . . . to continue through life.' Accordingly, Plato did not believe that 'the good body by any bodily excellence improved the soul, but on the contrary, that the good soul, by her own excellence, improves the body as far as this may be possible' (Robinson, 1980: 123). The related concept of *Eutrapelia* is also a way of seeking excellence or *arête*, a composite ideal based upon integration of virtues, wisdom and strength, as opposed to success, or displaying status often according to the dapper styles of expensive advertising. Granted that success and excellence share features of prominence, they are not the same either in Greek culture or the Bible where success is scarcely mentioned, a term for distinction as opposed to the continual search after virtue and understanding, a quality even beyond wisdom as in Proverbs 4:7. Also on the Temple at Delphi is the engraving, 'Know Thyself,' which means, 'to know what one lacks' (O'Connor, 1970: 35). This advice comes from Flannery O'Connor's book on writing entitled *Mystery and Manners* (1970), which itself is an expression of the ongoing intersection between Archetypes (mystery) and Stereotypes (manners).

For ordinary Greeks, nothing upset the equilibrium of the soul like losing (e.g., in sport), leading at times to suicide (see Higgs and Braswell, 2004). Losing, though, was not just one kind of shame, for there was another type that was guard against it, 'that shame which holds men back from wrongdoing' (Plato, 1942: 12). Known as the quality of *Aidos*, it was, argues Werner Jaeger (1945: 1:7), 'dedication to an ideal. In Homer, the real mark of the nobleman is his sense of duty. He is judged and proud to be judged by a severe standard. That sense of duty is *Aidos*.' For Norman Gardiner (1930: 70):

> *Aidos* is the exact opposite of insolence . . . It is the feeling of reverence, modesty, honor. It distinguishes the athlete from the bully. Strength may tempt a man to abuse it; success may begat 'braggart insolence.' It is a feeling incompatible with the commercial spirit, for '*Aidos* is stolen away by secret gain.'

There are some parallels between Greek stereotypes and archetypes present in ancient sports, the arts and literature and those found in the modern era, a topic to which I now turn.

GREEK 'PATTERNS' IN MODERN AMERICAN SPORTS

Countering much media rhetoric and confusion, Steven Overman (1999) has clearly demonstrated that the motto 'Winning is not the most important thing but the only thing' was not proclaimed by Hurry-Up Yost, General Douglas MacArthur or Vince Lombardi, but by a successful football coach at Vanderbilt in the 1940s, Red Sanders, who later won a national championship at UCLA. Further, it was Grantland Rice, a Phi Beta Kappa first baseman, a graduate of Vanderbilt and later 'Dean of American Sports Writers' who penned an opposite view of winning in a poem called 'Alumnus Football,' ending with these lines that were later turned into a quatrain: 'For when the one great scorer comes to mark against your name, He writes—not that you won or lost—but how you played the Game' (Rice, 1954: 154).

While Grantland Rice (1954: 306; italics added) may be remembered mostly for the poem, which *Time* magazine called 'classic corn,' he captured realistically what was happening to sport in the middle of the last century in his autobiography:

> Sport today is . . . much more commercial and *stereotyped* than in my heyday. I doubt if we will ever again have the devil-may-care attitude and the spirit of the Golden Twenties, a period of boom, screwballs, and screwball antics. The almighty dollar or what's left of it, hangs high. The magnificent screwballs have been crowded to the wall. The fleet Washington outfielder who, when asked to race Mickey Mantle against time before a recent Yankee-Senators night game, replied, 'I'll do it for five hundred dollars' is testimony to the times.

It is then incumbent upon scholars in the field of sports studies to ask why such fragmentation has occurred in college sport, as recently suggested by a lead headline in the *Chronicle of Higher Education* (2011): 'What the Hell has happened to College Sport? And What Should We Do about It?' One of the main reasons for the question, according to a prefatory excerpt from the article, is that 'Big Time College Athletics pull in about $10.6 billion in revenue annually' (1). There are of course numerous other reasons for the current state of American college sports, not least the deeper psychological and spiritual meanings that are attached to stereotypes and archetypes.

Some evidence of character traits in terms of stereotypes and 'spiritual manifestations' of archetypes can be inferred from the types of athletes that populate American culture, as seen in modern imitations of ancient gods,

'Apollo,' 'Dionysus' and 'Adonis.' The Apollonian worldview, according to Otto Rank (1964: 293), rests on likeness to others and acceptance of a universal ideal. Rank goes on to note that 'it is not knowledge for the sake of the self but knowledge for the sake of adaptation.' Examples of popular fictional athletes are the 'Dumb Athlete,' the 'Busher,' the 'Sporting Gentleman,' the 'Apotheosized WASP,' the 'Booster Alumnus,' the 'Muscular Christian,' the 'Model or the Hollow Apollo' and the 'Brave New Man' (Higgs, 1981: 22–90).

In contrast, the Dionysian principle in the analysis of Rank (1964: 294) 'repudiates likeness and improvement based on it,' leading instead 'to ecstatic–orgiastic destruction . . . The true self, if it is unchained in Dionysian fashion, is not only anti-social but also unethical and therefore the human being goes to pieces on it.' Among Dionysian types of fictional athletes is the 'Naked Beast,' who cannot transcend his perverted nature, and at the other extreme the 'Darling,' also known as 'golden boy,' pretty boy,' 'lover boy' and 'sonny boy,' beloved pet of the witnessing woman (Higgs, 1981: 91–118).

Rank (1964) favors the model he calls 'Kantian,' which incorporates both constructive doing and being and a way to 'determine thyself from thyself.' A much older term for this type of athlete is 'Adonis,' an admirable figure with a dual history ironically unappreciated by his immediate society, Thoreau at Walden, Whitman on the road or Huck Finn striking out for 'the territory,' all celebrants of play. Types of athletes falling into this classification are the 'Natural' or 'Folk Hero,' the 'Country Boy from the City,' the 'Absurd Athlete' and the 'Secret Christian' (Higgs, 1981: 119–82), each very much in the world but not of it.

These Adonic athletes bring to mind another observation by Jung (1964) about archetypes, that we lose our souls through devotion to a god all outside, or to a goal with a single purpose, for example, 'winning is the only thing.' We inhabit two worlds, one outside, the place of our work and games, and, if we are wise enough, one inside, as Emily Dickinson (1961: 36) says in 'A Certain Slant of light,' 'Where the meanings, are.' Historically, the internal and external quest for 'meanings' in the realms of sport and religions has manifested itself in a range of socio-theological 'movements,' for example, 'Acrobatic Christianity' and 'Muscular Christianity,' both of which, I argue, deserve critical reflection.

'ACROBATIC CHRISTIANITY' OF THE CAMPGROUND AND THE 'MUSCULAR CHRISTIANITY' OF THE STADIUM

Whatever the nature of the displays of 'spirit' and 'soul' in the future, it is doubtful that they will be as captivating as those in the past, especially those, unimaginably hyper, emerging on the southern frontier at Cane Ridge, Kentucky, in 1802, judging from the astonishing motions of

'Acrobatic Christianity,' as much a sporting event as religious. These manifestations included 'holy jerks' and other 'holy exercises' such as 'barking,' 'dancing,' 'falling,' 'laughing' and 'rolling.' Of the effect of diverse spirits at the revival often known as the American Pentecost (Conkin, 1990), Peter Cartwright, the famous Methodist Evangelist, seeing five hundred people fall down as if struck by artillery, said that he 'wished he had staid home' (Johnson, 1955: 64–65). Constance Rourke, in her famous book *American Humor* (1986: 132), sums up the phenomenon of frontier revivals in a single sentence: 'The movement was toward the theater.'

To some degree what occurred in 'Acrobatic Christianity' on the frontier is still taking place in exhibits of 'Muscular Christianity' in huge stadia not only with 'dancing' (in the end zone), 'falling' and 'rolling,' but also praying between plays and pointing fingers to the sky in gratitude for success (e.g., Tebow). A Bible verse that obviates the need for such public thanksgiving is Matthew 6:5, but it asks something of athletes that seems impossible in the show-business world of American sports. 'And when you pray, you shall not be as the hypocrites are: for they love to pray standing in the synagogues and in the corners of the streets, that they may be seen of men. Verily I say unto you, They have their reward.' On a similar theme, the explicit use of religion in sports marketing and advertising is also something that has come under critical scrutiny in recent times.

STEREOTYPES FOR ADVERTISING, ARCHETYPES FOR METAPHORS

It is much too complex to delve into in-depth, but I would like to raise the issue of rampant stereotyping by one new religion in the eyes of some, that is, advertising. Two scholars who have been studying the subject for a number of years, Sut Jhally (2006) and James Twitchell (2000), consider advertising to be:

> the central meaning-maker in our culture, the key storyteller; both concern themselves not with what advertising is supposed to do—sell stuff—but what it does while doing it; for them, whether advertising sells goods or not is largely beside the point. Both argue that advertising works as a form of religion, that it has even supplanted religion as the key institution of our time. And yet Jhally and Twitchell come to opposite conclusions about what all this means. Jhally says advertising is destroying society; Twitchell says it's holding it together. (Jhally and Twitchell, 2012: 1)

If advertising has supplanted traditional religion it has created another, the 'Church of Sport,' where marketing has become the modern work in missions and the Super Bowl the national mecca of materialism.

Whatever is true of advertising in sport has in large measure become true of religion, especially the evangelical variety, the booster version of Christianity. 'If you get the Christian community behind your film and supporting it, they're very strong at word-of-mouth and grass-roots (marketing), and bringing friends to the theater,' suggests Melisa Richter, who runs Richter Strategic Communications (cited in Higgs and Braswell, 2004: 88). The film referenced is the *Passion of the Christ*. Producer and director Mel Gibson even 'scored' prime advertising on the hood of a NASCAR race car, just in time for Sunday's Daytona 500, which draws a television audience of about eleven million. Interstate Batteries chairman Norm Miller reported that a friend asked him to paint the advertisement on his company-sponsored race car (Cobb, 2004).

The advert on Bobby Labonte's car read as follows: 'The PASSION of the Christ in Theaters 02.25.04' (Cobb, 2004). Here we had the Labonte Car in the race with Mark Martin's Viagra car; one promising victory over sexual dysfunction and the other over mortality. The winner was Dale Earnhardt, Jr., driving a car sponsored by 'Budweiser,' makers of still another kind of passion and spirit. These adverts may be good for business, but in another context they are signs of the apocalypse in regard to humanities and religion.

What we see here is the triumph of the sign and demise of the metaphor in which imagination and the invisible world co-relate. Metaphors have two parts, a 'vehicle' and 'tenor,' the material object and the emotion, idea or quality symbolized by it. Advertising not only makes us want to buy but to 'buy into' any number of things, but poetry as a traditional form of art 'makes us see' and connect and understand.

In *Education by Poetry*, Robert Frost (1968: 43), a lover of sport who was still playing baseball at seventy, does not look to the trillions of victories in sports over the ages for the glories of humankind but to something else: 'The richest accumulation of the ages is the noble metaphors we have rolled up.' This is a very different from the *Spectacle of Accumulation* intimated at in the title of Sut Jhally's (2006) book. Are we *mind* people or *thing* people? Each can judge. Similarly, the subtitle of Paul Newberry's (2004) article, 'From Gospel Tent to Fast Lane,' is telling, since this is what has happened in America, where lines between religion and sport have become so blurred that distinctions are hard to identify when finger pointing to the sky and genuflecting for gratitude to God for success are possibly more common than ever.

There are, though, other views on the accessibility of Jesus and his assumed presence on the pro football scene, one presented in 1906 by Albert Schweitzer (1964: 312, 403), a German theologian, organist, philosopher, physician, medical missionary and winner of the Nobel Peace Prize: 'Jesus of Nazareth will not suffer himself to be modernized. As an historic figure, he refuses to be detached from his own time. He has no answers for the question. "Tell us thy name in our speech and for our day!"' Instead, 'He

comes to us as One Unknown, without a name, as of old, by the lake-side.'
As brilliant, versatile and kind as Schweitzer was, his view on either the
historical Jesus or the 'One Unknown' does not square with the evangelical
followers of Jesus. Schweitzer's Jesus waits by the lake; the Jesus of camp-
grounds and ball games is on the move, always booked up. Billy Graham
said he never saw a stadium he didn't like and that we should be selling
Jesus like soap. Recently, jerseys with Jesus's name on the back are being
marketed in connection with the Tebow phenomenon (see Dorrien, 2010).

My advice to church folk, considering the hilarity of bloopers in
church bulletins, is to get out of advertising entirely and stick to defense
of their stock and trade: the ageless metaphors of scripture, the sermons
of the age, and wondrous hymns are now being supplanted by simplistic
signs of the modern world, even those on the hoods of racing cars. My
advice also extends to those signs on church marquees such as the one
that reads: WHAT WILL HELL BE LIKE: COME HEAR OUR CHOIR
NEXT SUNDAY.

Notice the vast difference between the advert for the Hollywood movie
The Passion and a poem of 'racin' automobiles. The poem is based on a
true event, the arrival in our college town in Appalachia in the 1970s of a
car with Bible verses painted on it, meant to be seen, yes, a type of advertisement that, like sin, is unavoidable. Flannery O'Connor (1970) would
have rejoiced upon seeing literary possibilities in such a vehicle, but Marita
Garin (1974: 12), a student poet at the time at East Tennessee State University, filled in brilliantly, winning first place in the ballad category in the
campus literary magazine with the following entry:

> *Ballad of the Jesus Car*
> A few years ago, in Spring it was,
> A car appeared in town.
> A strange vehicle painted gold,
> It was driven up and down.
>
> The car was covered from front to back
> With messages from the Bible.
> The words, taken from Revelations,
> Spoke of the fires of hell.
> 'Jesus is coming, beware,' it said.
> 'The day is soon at hand,
> When the judgment of God shall visit us
> And his scourge shall cover the land.'
>
> A sign on top in the shape of a cross
> Stood out clean and clear.
> It said, 'Beware the false prophets of God,
> Repent, Jesus is here.'

The young man who drove the car that day
Had come from parts unknown.
His name was Darrell, and when he spoke,
His voice had a spiritual tone.

He told his story, his eyes intense:
'I was filled with the spirit one day!
I left my wife, my children, and home
To follow in God's way.'

I've printed here on my car,' he said,
'The true message of the Bible.
The church is not the home of God
But the hiding place of the Devil.'

'I am a Jesus man,' he said.
Fervor shook his voice.
'Heathens, hypocrites, those who sin,
Beware the anti-Christ!'

'I'm a hard-driving man for Jesus,' he said.
'Praise God, he will save all men.
I must drive my car til Jesus comes,
Praise God, He is coming again.'

'The Bible says that those who believe
Can overcome all evil.
God has chosen me to drive my car,
I'll even race with the Devil.
Let Satan come and drive with me.
We'll see who has more power.'

Not long after that, a car appeared.
It was black and low to the ground.
With a sloping hood and a high chrome grill,
It drove without a sound.

It pulled up beside the Jesus car.
The driver spoke not a word,
Just nodded his head with a beckoning glance.
But Darrell understood.

They drove out of town at a furious speed
And raced off down the road.
The Jesus car made a thunderous sound,
The other silently rode.

Into the distance they disappeared,
The white cross riding high,
Faster than ever before, and still
There was a low, black shape by its side.

Whoever won the race that day
Was lost from sight forever.
Perhaps somewhere in a distant place
They are still riding together.

In comparing 'The *Passion* Car' and the 'Jesus Car,' the lessons become clear. The poet affirms the mystery of things, not claiming to know who won or who lost in contending cosmic forces. In pronouncing certainty about the winner, the *Passion* advert ironically explains away the mystery and eliminates faith and wonder in the process.

CONCLUSIVE REFLECTIONS: SPORTS AND THE HUMANITIES, HOW STANDS THE UNION?

The aim of this chapter has been to examine the role of stereotypes and archetypes in modern-day American sports. It is clear that further scholarly attention on this subject may provide some invaluable insights with regard to the deeper religious meanings, status and direction of elite-sporting practices. I conclude my analysis with some poetic reflections on sport, which implicitly touch upon notions of stereotypes and archetypes. These, I hope, will stimulate others to explore this avenue of research.

A number of years ago professor and author Neil D. Isaacs wrote to the president of the University of Tennessee the following: 'If we have to have an invocation before every football game, how about an invocation to the Muses in honor of the liberal arts education we are so proud of at U-T?' (personal correspondence). Similarly, Jack Ridl (personal correspondence), poet and Professor Emeritus at Hope College in Michigan, addressed the current philosophy of winning on college campuses. The son of a college basketball coach, Charles Ridl, formerly of Westminster College and the University of Pittsburgh, had this to say:

> My father never thought of the other team as an 'opponent.' The other team was the other team, be it UCLA, Marquette, UNC, Marist, NC State. If we toss this stuff to those less inclined toward sports and more inclined to bridge or chess or any thoughtful game they play, my hunch is that they play to win.
>
> How else does one make it an honest game, and one that the other can fully take part in and enjoy, and shall we say, how else can there be integrity or fun or an embodiment of some ineffable reason why one plays, and it is play?

Dad never used the word 'beat.' He *would* say, 'I play to win. How else does one show respect for the other?' And he always believed in, and wanted his players to believe in, the now rather clichéd and cynically responded to idea that winning is a result not a goal, and that one plays not to, as I said before, not to beat. Thus, his retiring in disappointment when he saw the shift toward 'beatin',' toward the vindictive rather than the competitive.

The result in his son is that a poem is a result not a goal, the result of knowing your stuff and then entering that mysterious place where poetry offers realization.

Also in his son is the gift he gave me of how to love watching a game even when one team is ahead by 40. Most of my pals leave once the game is decided. I'm grateful he gave me that. It's always been a bumpy road for me, being a poem guy and a sports guy. Within each world there is so much that is mean-spirited. I don't get that.

What an epitaph for a poet: 'I kicked Whitman's ass.'

Whitman would appreciate the humor and the wisdom, too, hopeful as he was for poets of the future just as Emerson had been hopeful for him. Appreciating the same understanding of Ridl and his father, 'The Good Grey Poet' would be honored in passing on the torch to a poet and athlete, for, as he says in "Song of Myself" in *Leaves of Grass* (section 47):

I am the teacher of athletes,
He that by me spreads a wider breast than my own proves the width
    of my own,
He most honors my style who learns under it to destroy the teacher.

ACKNOWLEDGMENTS

With immense gratitude I would like to dedicate this chapter to the following pioneers in the study of sports and the humanities: Neil Isaacs, Professor Emeritus, University of Maryland, and prolific author, for generously sharing in class and out his encyclopedic knowledge of sport and literature; the late Andrew J. "Andy" Kozar, All-American Fullback at the University of Tennessee and author of *R. Tait McKenzie: Sculptor of Athletes*; the late Lyle Olsen, professional athlete, college baseball coach and founder of the Sport Literature Association and *Aethlon: The Journal of Literature of Sport*; and Don Johnson, college athlete, poet, critic, professor, and editor of *Aethlon* from 1988 to 2005, later poetry editor (see "Sport Literature Association" on Wikipedia).

BIBLIOGRAPHY

Adler, M. (1981) *Six Great Ideas*, New York: Macmillan.
Campbell, J. (with B. Moyers) (1988) *The Power of Myth*, New York: Doubleday.

Cirlot, J. E. (1962) *A Dictionary of Symbols*, trans. Jack Sage, New York: Philosophical Library.

Cobb, J. (2004) Marketing the Passion of the Christ. Available online at http://www.msnbc.msn.com/id/4374411/ns/business-cnbc_tv/t/marketing-passion-christ/ (accessed 2 April 2012).

Conkin, P. K. (1990) *Cane Ridge: America's Pentecost*, Madison: University of Wisconsin Press.

Dickinson, E. (1961) *Final Harvest: Emily Dickinson's Poems*, ed. Thomas H. Johnson, Boston: Little, Brown, and Company.

Dodd, P. (2011) Tim Tebow: God's Quarterback, *Wall Street Journal*, 10 December.

Dorrien, G. (2010) *Economy, Difference, Empire: Social Ethics and Social Justice*, New York: Columbia University Press.

Frost, R. (1968) 'A Day of Prowess,' in H. Cox and E. C. Lathem (Eds.), *Selected Prose of Robert Frost*, New York: Macmillan Company, 91.

Gardiner, E. N. (1930) *Athletics of the Ancient World*, London: Clarendon Press.

Garin, M. (1974) 'The Ballad of the Jesus Car,' *The Mockingbird*, 1 (May): 12.

Higgs, R. J. (1981) *Laurel and Thorn. The Athlete in American Literature*, Lexington: University Press of Kentucky.

Higgs, R. J. and Braswell, M. C. (2004) *An Unholy Alliance: The Sacred and Modern Sports*, Macon, GA: Mercer University Press.

Jaeger, W. (1945) *Paideia: The Ideals of Greek Culture*, 3 vols., trans. Gilbert Highet, New York: Oxford University Press.

Jhally S. (2006) *The Spectacle of Accumulation: Essays in Culture, Media, and Politics*, New York: Peter Lang Publishing.

Jhally, S. and Twitchell, J. (2012) On Advertising: Sut Jhally and James Twitchell. Available online at http://www.stayfreemagazine.org/archives/16/twitchell.html (accessed 2 April 2012).

Johnson, C. A. (1955) *The Frontier Camp Meeting: Religious Harvest Time*, Dallas, TX: Southern Methodist University Press.

Jung, C. G. (1964) *Man and His Symbols*, Garden City, NY: Double Day and Co.

Kuper, S. (2009) What Google Tells Us about the Global Obsession with Sport, *Financial Times*, 24 July, 1.

Lowell, A. (2008) *Men, Women, and Ghosts*. Salt Lake City, UT: Project Gutenberg. E Book 841. Available online at http://www.gutenberg.org/files/841/841-h/841-h.htm.

Miller, D. A. (1970) *Gods and Games: Toward a Theology of Play*, New York: World Publishing Co.

Newberry, P. (2004) Racin' and Religion . . . Witnessing Has Moved from Revival Tent to Fast Lane, AP *Greeneville* (TN) *Sun*, 10 February, B1.

O'Connor, F. (1970) *Mystery and Manners*, New York: Farrar, Straus and Giroux.

Overman, S. J. (1999) 'Winning Isn't Everything. It's the Only Thing': The Origin, Attributions and Influence of a Famous Football Quote, *Football Studies*, 2 (2): 77–99.

Parry, J., Robinson, S., Watson, N. J. and Nesti, M. (2007) *Sport and Spirituality: An Introduction*, London: Routledge.

Plato. (1942) *Republic, Book III. Five Great Dialogues*, trans. Benjamin Jowett, New York: Walter J. Black.

Rahner, H. (1972) *Man at Play*, trans. Brian Battershaw and Edward Quinn, New York: Herder and Herder.

Rank, O. (1964) *The Myth of the Birth of the Hero and Other Writings*, ed. Philip Freund, New York: Vintage.

Rice, G. (1954) *The Tumult and the Shouting*, New York: Dell.

Robinson, R. S. (1980) *Sources for the History of Greek Athletics*, Chicago: Ares.

Rourke, C. (1986) *American Humor,* Gainesville: University Press of Florida.

Schweitzer, A. (1964) *The Quest of the Historical Jesus: A Critical Study of Its Progress from Reimarus to Wrede,* New York: Macmillan.

The Chronicle of Higher Education. (2011) What the Hell Has Happened to College Sports? And What Should We Do about It? 16 December. Available online at http://chronicle.com/article/What-the-Hell-Has-Happened-to/130071/ (accessed 2 April 2012).

Twitchell, J. B. (2000) *20 Ads that Shook the World: The Century's Most Groundbreaking Advertising and How It Changed Us All,* New York: Three Rivers Press.

Whitman, W. (1959) 'Song of Myself,' *Leaves of Grass,* 1855, in James E. Miller (Ed.), *Completed Poetry and Selected Prose,* Cambridge: The Riverside Press, 65.

Part II

Contemporary Perspectives on Sport and Christianity

6 Special Olympians as a 'Prophetic Sign' to the Modern Sporting Babel

Nick J. Watson

INTRODUCTION

> This is after all a time that cries out for the Special Olympics. The world is hungry for what we have. Look around. Everywhere you look, people are hungry for authenticity. Everywhere you look there is a crisis in trust. Everyone is asking: where are the role models of optimism and peace. How can I make a difference and feel a part of something bigger? . . . the lesson is clear: we're sports rebels [prophets?] and we need to be sports rebels with spirit and fight forever! (Shriver, 2010c: 4–6)

> American commercial sports . . . represent a prominent and aggressive principality—and one might suppose—a more or less innocuous one. Yet the operation of this demonic power has significant *political* importance . . . markedly similar to that of circuses and athletic spectacles in Imperial Rome. (Stringfellow, 1973/2004: 90)

Amid the generic growth of publications on the relationships between sport and all major world religions, there has been a particular groundswell of academic publications on sport and the Christian faith (see Watson and Parker, this volume). However, a comprehensive review of the literature in the disciplines of 'theology of disability' and 'disability sport' indicates that there is virtually no empirical research or scholarship on disability sport from a Christian perspective . Exceptions include recent essays and empirical work (Brock, 2012; Watson, 2012; Watson and Parker, 2012), a short chapter on the uses of leisure and sport in a *L'Arche* community (O'Keefe, 2006), reflections on the *Special Olympics* (SO) in Yong's (2007: 114–15) book on the theology of Down Syndrome, a handful of papal addresses (John Paul II, 2000b, 1985), a conference presentation (Watts, 2007), and empirical research and essays on women's disability sport from an Islamic perspective (Limoochi, 2012; Gaad, 2011, 2006).

The overarching aim of this chapter is to begin a discussion on this topic by synthesizing ideas and literature from both these areas[1]. While no academic literature exists that has addressed the Christian theological dimensions of disability sport, there are some helpful popular books (Hoyt and Yaeger, 2010; Strike, 2010; St. John, 2009; Papievis, 2008; Molsberry,

2004; Nall, 2002; Driscoll, 2001; Stallings and Cook, 1997)[2] and media sources (e.g., Ironman, 2006) that tell inspirational stories of those with a Christian faith who are involved in disability sport. There is also a significant body of empirical research and scholarship on disability sport that should not be neglected when undertaking theological reflection, in order to contextualize analysis (e.g., Smith and Sparkes, 2012; Le Clair, 2012; Winnick, 2011; Brittain, 2010; Fitzgerald, 2009; Jesperson and McNamee, 2009; Horne and Howe, 2009; Thomas and Smith, 2009; Bailey, 2008; Howe, 2009a, 2008a). Issues of embodiment, social exclusion, governance, media and cinematic representations of disability sports and competitive classification of athletes are some of the topics that have been examined.

The ongoing debate concerning the classification and inclusion (Howe and Jones, 2006), or not, of athletes with intellectual disabilities (ID) in the 2012 London Paralympics is also a controversial topic, not least due to violation of eligibility rights by the Spanish disability (ID) male basketball team at the 2000 Sydney Paralympics (Jobling, Jobling and Fitzgerald, 2008), where it was found that ten out of twelve players did not have an ID. Generally speaking, it can be argued that the level of media coverage, funding and empirical research on athletes with ID and the events in which they participate and compete, the SO being the most well known, is far less than for athletes with physical disabilities (PD).There are deeply embedded sociocultural, historical and theological reasons for this situation that I will explore in more detail. Due to the growing profile of the SO and the recent reinclusion of athletes with ID in the 2012 London Paralympics and beyond,[3] there is a growing literature in the sports and leisure disciplines but again, nothing that addresses the religious or spiritual dimension of athletes with ID and the SO.

In addition to literature that provides a summary of the history,[4] governance, nature and issues surrounding the SO movement (Lenox, 2012), including the SO relation to the Olympics and Paralympics (Brittain, 2010),[5] there is a range of systematic empirical research studies (2004–) and information on program monitoring and evaluation (see Siperstein, Kersh and Bardon, 2007) published mainly by staff from the *Special Olympics Global Collaborating Centre* (University of Massachusetts, Boston) that are available on the official SO website.[6] In addition, there is recent peer-review research on ID in sport, which has examined physical activity levels and behaviors of youths (Smith and Sparkes, 2012; Frey, Stanish and Temple, 2008), leisure patterns (Patterson and Pegg, 2009), the motivations of Special Olympians (Farrell et al., 2004), and a national survey exploring the general sporting experience of athletes with ID and their families (Harada and Siperstein, 2009). It is interesting to note at the outset that those studies that explore the motives for participation and long-term adherence show that although external rewards are of some importance (e.g., medals, winning and the perception of others), the intrinsic motives of fun, friendship and relationships are by far the most important reasons.

This, however, does not mean that Special Olympians are not motivated to excel, win and achieve, as historically there has been a gradual shift toward a more achievement-oriented model in the SO movement (Songster et al., 1997; Bale, 1994). This is not dissimilar to the ethos of the Paralympics, that is, 'building on and celebrating ability,' which Howe (2008a: i) suggests, has been the 'politicised raison d'être for [elite] disability sport for more than twenty years,' since the evolution of PD sport from rehabilitative and participatory models pre-1960s. Thus, it is crucial to note, that irrespective of the presence or absence of a disability, a major principle of the SO (and Paralympics) has always been that, 'athletes are athletes' (Harada and Siperstein, 2009). Notwithstanding, some of the commonalities in the motivations and experiences of individual able-bodied and disabled athletes, there are, however, marked differences in the institutional structures and the economic basis of the modern commercialized sport model and the SO.[7] It is, nonetheless, important to acknowledge that the SO movement has not been devoid of criticism in regard to financial issues, claims of segregation, paternalism, the promotion of national corporations and negative disability images that reinforce stereotypes (Storey, 2004; Wolfensberger, 1995; Hourcade, 1989; Brickley, 1984).[8] This does not, however, mean that a legitimate comparison of these institutions cannot be made to highlight the prophetic potential of the SO movement and athletes with IDs, a central aim of this chapter.

While adding a theological caveat, this follows the work of Howe (2008a: 108), a former Paralympic athlete, anthropologist and disability scholar, who suggests that 'paralympians can challenge the prejudices that restrain the impaired in sport and the society it mirrors.' I will illustrate how the dominant motivations of athletes in the SO and the movement itself, as described above, are often diametrically opposed to able-bodied professional sport, in which external motivations, such as financial gain, celebrity status and winning at all costs often hold sway. It is hoped that this brief overview of key research and interest areas from the discipline of disability sport is helpful in providing some initial resources to enable reflection upon the multifaceted nature of disability sport.

To ensure a clear starting point to my discussion, it is pertinent to clarify a number of key terms, issues and concepts, which underpin the remainder of the chapter. I will adopt 'person first' terminology when describing someone with a PD or ID, as is generally the norm in the UK, Australian and North American contexts. The scope of my deliberations in terms of what 'sport' means will focus mainly, yet not exclusively, on competitive sport. Clifford and Feezell's (1997: 11), definition of sport is useful: 'a form of play [or should be], a competitive, rule-governed activity that human beings freely choose to engage in.' Indeed, participation in sport might ideally include a strong emphasis on fun and play (e.g., Thoennes, 2008; Moltmann, 1972; Huizinga, 1950) and, in turn, an accurate understanding and application of the etymology of the word 'competition,' which renders a sport contest as a 'mutually acceptable quest for excellence' (Weir, 2008; Hyland, 1988), in which excitement, courage, physical and mental endurance, dedication, aesthetic beauty and emotional intensity are all possible. This 'intense passion,' however, also presents the risk that 'such intensity will devolve into alienation . . . violence' (Hyland, 1988: 177) and mental and physical harm, for example, through cheating, drug abuse, greed and trash talk on an individual, team or national level. These commonly recognized elements of corruption will form a major part of my critique of the nature of modern professional sport and how persons with disability, in particular those with ID, arguably can be viewed as one prophetic sign of God's kingdom in the current age.[9]

Hence, what follows is highly critical of the values and institutions of modern-day professional and commercialized sport (Hoffman, 2010; Watson and White, 2007; Higgs and Braswell, 2004) and therefore I emphasize from the outset that I am in no way decrying the quest for human excellence and success, determined performances and displays of aesthetic beauty in able-bodied or disabled sport. I have been a lifelong sports participant, spectator and, more recently, sports coach and university lecturer. This raises the 'insider-versus-outsider' question that sports disability scholars (e.g., Macbeth, 2010) and theologians note has been controversial for some time: 'What qualifies one as an expert?' (Creamer, 2009: 21). Is some degree of personal involvement with disability a prerequisite if one wishes to authentically write about this topic? For the record, I have coached disability sport and have experienced life in a *L'Arche* community (Liverpool, UK) to familiarize myself with the research context and those about whom I would be writing (Watson and Parker, 2012). Hopefully, my experiences in the disability community will provide some degree of authenticity and insight beyond my academic analysis.

There are two principal aims to my exploratory discussion. First, to provide a foundation for theological analysis of ID sport, I briefly outline some of the key themes that emerge from the literature on the 'theology of disability' and will identify key readings for those wishing to further explore these topics and apply them to the sports world. Second, I attempt to establish the beginnings of a 'theology of disability sport' by contextualizing my discussion within the sociocultural and historical context of modern sport. This is followed by an examination of how persons with disabilities, especially ID, are one prophetic sign to the multibillion-dollar business of sport, which it has been argued is a major edifice in the modern 'Tower of Babel,'[10] alongside other cultural idols such as scientism, healthism, intellectualism, unhealthy perfectionism, commercialism and materialism (Watson and White, 2007). Finally, in an extended conclusion, I identify areas within disability sport that may benefit from further theological reflection and highlight current church and para-church initiatives that seek to raise awareness and affect change in this area. It is my hope that this will encourage scholars and empirical researchers from sports studies and theology alike to take this discussion forward.

THEOLOGIES OF DISABILITY

> This is how the *Christian community prepares for the Lord's second coming*: by focusing on those persons whom Jesus himself favoured, those who are often excluded and ignored by society . . . By your situation you call into question those conceptions of life that are solely concerned with satisfaction, appearances . . . success or well-being . . . speed and efficiency . . ."Blessed are the poor in spirit, those who mourn, those who are persecuted for righteousness' sake," for great will be their reward in heaven! This is the paradox of Christian hope: *what seems humanly a ruin, is in the divine plan always a plan of salvation . . .* its profound reason in the mystery of the cross (Phil. 2:6–8) . . . bearing witness in the world to human dignity, whose source is not the outward condition of the body but the primordial likeness to the Creator. God bless you! (John Paul II, 2000)[11]

Following the publication of Nancy Eiesland's now classic book *The Disabled God* (1994)[12], there has been a growing literature on the theology of PD and ID (e.g., Brock and Swinton, 2012; Yong, 2011, 2007; Reinders, 2010, 2008; Reynolds, 2008; Swinton and Hauerwas, 2005; McCloughry and Morris, 2002; Hauerwas, 1986). This body of empirical research and scholarship has evolved from all the major Christian denominations and numerous disciplines outside of traditional theologies, such as sociology, ethics, education and psychology (Swinton, 2011). There was, of course, theological reflection on disability, more so from the Catholic Church (Watts, 2009), prior to the mid-1990s borne out of the disability rights and other civil rights movements of the 1970s, but one could argue that this was, and still is, viewed as a 'specialist interest' area. Hauerwas and Vanier (2009: 18), however, argue that the biblical themes of weakness, vulnerability, mutuality, hospitality, humility and love are at 'the heart of the gospel,' and thus all good theological reflection. Of course, all these gospel values flow from the cross of Christ, and as Moltmann (1974: 7) notes by drawing on Martin Luther's 'theology of the cross,' 'the inner criterion of whether or not a theology is *Christian* lies in the crucified Christ . . . the Cross is the test of everything' but 'to many it sounds unattractive and unmodern.'

Perhaps what follows will sound unattractive to those wedded to the win-at-all-costs mentality of modern-day commercialized sport, in which the character traits of humility, weakness and vulnerability (all experienced in the cross) in an athlete's makeup are most often viewed as an 'anathema,' suggests consultant sport psychiatrist Begel (2000). This does not mean that we should not actively seek and experience excellence and joy in sports, the focus of a book by the theologian Null (2004). But as Martin Luther emphasized, there are two ways of thinking about God in Christ (McGrath, 1985). These two ways encompass the whole breadth of human experience and salvation, including sport: a *theologia gloriae* (theology of glory, the 'risen Christ') that points to the joy of sport and a *theologia crucis* (theology of the cross, the 'crucified Christ') that emphasizes suffering, humility, dependence and vulnerability in sport.

The reasons for the relative lack of theological reflection on disability are many but, as Reynolds (2008: 68) states, a major determinant is that theology has been 'taken captive by the cult of normalcy'; that is, it has often adopted a starting point rooted in enlightenment philosophies and ideas, especially utilitarianism, rationalism, free-market capitalism, abelism and intellectualism. In thinking about and interacting with those people in society who have disabilities, we are also confronted with our own fragilities and weaknesses (bodily and mental) and, therefore, disability can 'disturb us' (Yong, 2007). The pervasive influence of Kantian rationality and Platonic–Cartesian dualism in theology (Wilson, 1989) and sport (Twietmeyer, 2008; Watson, 2007) has also been a factor in de-emphasizing and devaluing the role of the body, and able-bodied and disabled sport as a whole, in Western culture. Theological reflection on the 'full diversity of experiences of human embodiment' has in turn been sorely lacking in theology (Creamer, 2009: 117), until the recent 'body craze' in the discipline, as is the case in the sports studies field since the 1990s due to the central importance of the appearance (i.e., athletic beauty and muscularity) and physical condition of the body in modern sport and exercise contexts (Wellard, 2009; Howe, 2008b; Messner and Sabo, 1990).

It is beyond the scope of this chapter to provide a more in-depth analysis of theologies of disability and/or issues of embodiment and I will leave this to others. In short, some of the most well-researched topics include: analyses of biblical passages on disability and their relationship to gospel narratives of healing (see Moss and Schipper, 2011; Avalos, Melcher and Schipper, 2007); examination of theological anthropology—*imago Dei*—and its importance for accurately assessing the worth/identity, value and dignity of all human beings, regardless of disability or difference; spiritual and psychological struggle with disablement and transition to disablement; exploration of fundamental gospel values, such as hospitality, friendship, humility, mutuality, vulnerability and weakness, which are often experienced in disability contexts and communities, such as *L'Arche*; how persons with disabilities (particularly, persons with ID) can be seen as prophets to the modern age; and, finally, the sociocultural, political and ecclesiological structures that marginalize and oppress people with disabilities.

To varying degrees publications on the theology of disability critique the sociocultural structures and institutions that marginalize, alienate, oppress and devalue the disabled, principally because 'we are creatures that fear difference' (Hauerwas, 2004: 40). To be sure, disability sport scholars following the foundational work of the Marxist sociologist Oliver (1996/2009, 1990), mainly advocating the social constructivist model of disability, have analyzed how access, provision of facilities in schools and communities, funding, media and cinematic representations and the overall status and perceived importance of disability sports are hugely different to able-bodied sport, for example, the Olympic Games (Thomas and Smith, 2009; Howe, 2008a). A particularly thorough and nuanced analysis of negative and ungodly sociocultural structures is presented by Reynolds (2008), who by drawing insights from sociology (Goffman), philosophy (Foucault), psychology and theology, discusses the 'Economics of Exchange' that fuel the 'Cult of Normalcy' and ultimately configures the lens through which moderns view the disabled. It is worth quoting him at length to set the scene for my analysis of modern sporting subculture (Reynolds, 2008: 56–70):

> Consciousness of worth is something that transpires according to what I call an '*economy of exchange*,' a system of reciprocity that regulates interactions in a community . . . The attribution of worth never occurs in isolated form as an individual's thought process, but rather within a complex set of social arrangements and reciprocal relationships that distribute, and appraise values . . . Bodily practices form the supportive scaffolding . . . this point is not trivial. Our bodies always negotiate social space by participating in an exchange of goods, whether going to school, playing on a sports team, working . . . Each social context—school, sports, employment, family, and friendship—involves its own performance expectations and criteria of value measurement . . . Physical appearance is probably the most obvious marker . . . A social identity is written on the body . . . Economics of exchange, therefore, revolve around identification markers that display what I call *body capital* . . . All kinds of cultural productions are involved, such as beauty, athleticism and intelligence . . . The body is an icon representing the effects of power . . . cast in the form of the dominant culture's sense of the good.

The dominant culture of our age borne from the Enlightenment modernist principles of individuality, self-sufficiency, materialism, rationalism, free-market capitalism and power, then encourage a 'cult of normalcy' that 'tells people with disabilities who they are, forcing them by various societal rituals to bear a name that is depersonalizing,' and this leads to 'alienation, both socially and personally' (Reynolds, 2008: 62). This dangerous 'Tyranny of Normality,' as Hauerwas (2004) has called it, so grips our culture that we are often in denial to its existence, preferring to suppress our own fears and insecurities and thus maintain the status quo. This unconscious denial is what Kierkegaard (1849/1989:74) called a 'spiritless sense of security,' a 'fictitious health' that maintains itself, in-part, through the legion of princi-palities and powers,[13] that is, evil spiritual forces (Luke 8:29–33; Gal. 4:3; Eph. 1:21, 6:12; Col 1:15–16, 2:15)[14] that govern (are behind) many of the ungodly and idolatrous institutions of our society, including sport and the Olympic Games (see Brueggemann, 2010; Stringfellow, 1973/2004; Stott, 1980; Ellul, 1977; Schlier, 1962).[15] This empirical reality will be explored in the following section as I examine the character of the modern sporting institution and then discuss the role of the disabled, within it, and propheti-cally against it.

SETTING THE SCENE: THE MODERN SPORTING INSTITUTION

> If Christ came to the Olympics, He would be impressed with the quasi-religious aspects of the Olympic rituals and sterling athletic performances on the field, but He would also be uneasy with some less positive features of the Games. He might well be inspired to bring out His whip against the modern scene, for he would most certainly recognise some idolatrous tendencies embedded in today's Olympism. (Baker, 2000: 44)

> Should you then seek great things for yourself? Seek them not. (The Prophet Jeremiah 45:5)

Recent scholarly debate surrounding the relationship between Christianity and modern-day sport has often included a critique of the ungodly values of the 'win-at-all-costs ethic' of global commercialized sport that is driven by unbridled free-market capitalism (e.g., Hamilton, 2011; Overman, 2011; Hoffman, 2010; Higgs and Braswell, 2004; Stevenson, 1997; Watson and White, 2007). It is interesting, however, that Savage's (2004)[16] analysis of Paul's paradoxical ministry of 'power through weakness' (the self-emptying gospel of Christ), described in 2 Corinthians, and the self-exalting cultural setting of first-century Corinth, is, I would argue, a mirror image of the decadent Western culture of today:

> It was a time when everyone yearned for an admiring public . . . The pursuit of upward mobility thus turned into a quest for applause and esteem . . . and self-glorification . . . The first century AD was intensely competitive . . . It was an era of . . . great accomplishment, but also anxiety and uncertainty . . . The practice of setting athletes on ped-estals sheds penetrating light on what people in the first century val-ued most . . . The games [Isthmian] thus reflected in microcosm, and more intensely, the competitive spirit of the first century . . . The actor, runner or rhetorician won adulation in the same way as the merchant banker or tanner—by excelling his rivals . . . Indeed the drive to show

oneself better than one's neighbour was perhaps more pronounced in Corinth than anywhere else . . . Competition for honour had two important side-effects. First, it encouraged outward expressions of pride and arrogance. For many boasting itself became an activity worthy of honour. Humility on the other hand was scorned. The lowly had no self-respect, no public standing . . . individuals grew indifferent to the needs of others.

An accurate description of twenty-first-century sport? As with any human activity or institution such as sport, the underlying belief system 'may be used for other purposes, with the danger of corruption and decadence,' suggests the late Pope John Paul II (1980: 64), a champion of sport when played in the right spirit. I would agree and contend that the multibillion-dollar institute of sport that is often (certainly not always) characterized by prideful attitudes and behaviors—self-promotion, financial greed and corruption, drug doping, cheating; violence, trash talk, and, looming on the horizon, genetic performance-enhancement technologies for athletes (Trothen, 2011)—is so encultured that pride of heart 'is now synonymous with virtue' (Higgs and Braswell, 2004: 372); as is the case in other institutions, such as media, government and religion. We would do well to heed the warning of the medieval monk Thomas Á Kempis (1380–1471), who warns that we must 'carefully observe the impulses of nature and grace, for these are opposed one to another, and work in so subtle manner that even a spiritual, holy and enlightened man can hardly distinguish them . . . many are deceived by . . . appearance of virtue' (1952: 53).

Indeed, to 'get on' in our society and professional sports it seems that one must practice unbridled self-promotion, which is diametrically opposed to the consistent biblical teaching of humbling oneself, as Muhammad Ali (1963) clearly understood in stating that 'at home I am nice guy: but I don't want the world to know. Humble people, I've found, don't get very far.'[17] 'Pride is *essentially* competitive above all other vices,' C. S. Lewis (1952/1997: 101) suggested.[18] Therefore, any human activity such as sport that involves competition presents the temptation to become proud. Kohn (1992: 2–3), in his book-length treatment of competition in the West, notes that this striving to be 'better than' has reached 'exaggerated, often ludicrous proportions.' In the sports domain, the legendary American football coach, Vince Lombardi, supports this in stating that 'the zeal to be first in everything has always been American, to win and win and to win' (cited in Overman, 1997: 226). Importantly, C. S. Lewis points out that not all forms of pride are evil and unhealthy. For example, having pride in a good performance (as long as it does not slip into vanity) and experiencing the pleasure of being praised by parents, coaches and fans, what Lewis calls a 'warmhearted admiration for.' Similarly, in his analysis of spiritual pride, the psychiatrist Karl Menninger (1973: 136) notes that 'self-respect, self-approval and self-confidence are favourable aspects of a normal self-concern,' and I would add are vital for a healthy pursuit of excellence and success in able-bodied or disabled sport.

Nevertheless, it has been strongly argued that pride and its empirical outworking are endemic in modern sports and that 'sport is a major edifice in' the 'modern tower of Babel' (Watson and White, 2007: 76). If pride is endemic and 'those embedded in the . . . world of sport, which is constructed from socio-cultural norms and reinforced and manipulated by the mass media' (78); why on the whole are people blind to this disturbing reality? Spiritual blindness of heart, stemming from idolatry of the institution of sport and the moral decadence it manifests, the bible instructs is the principal reason (Matthew 13:14–15; 1 Corinthians 2:14; Isaiah 6:9–10).

Adopting the metaphor of Babel (Genesis 11:1–9; Revelation 18) and the moral death that characterizes it,[19] William Stringfellow (1972/2004) states that 'the principality, insinuating itself in the place of God, deceives humans into thinking as if the moral worth or justification of human beings is defined and determined by commitment . . . to the survival interest, grandeur and vanity of the principality.'[20] For many, it seems, the idol of sport operates as a surrogate religion (Ward, 2011a; Evans, 2002) in that it provides significance and self-worth and therefore is a major source of their identity (Watson, 2011; Harris and Parker, 2009). From a Christian standpoint, it could therefore be argued that sport has become an idol in the hearts of millions of people in the twenty-first century. In this regard, soccer is undoubtedly the chief deity of the English while in America the 'holy trinity' of baseball, basketball and football are shot through with religious zeal and commitment (Forney, 2010). The biographer of basketballing demigod Michael Jordan, Halberstam (2001), perhaps unknowingly conveys this when he describes him as, 'Jesus in Nikes,' the savior of the sports world.[21]

The founder and chairperson of Nike, the company that essentially made Jordan a demigod, acknowledges that sports 'define the culture of the world' (cited in Smart, 2005: 1), and it could be argued they are the most popular global cultural pastime, surpassing previously dominant cultural expressions, such as music and the arts. The magazine *Sports Illustrated* sells 13.2 million copies a month, Americans in 2005 spent $89 billion on the purchase of sports goods and more than 7.6 billion admission tickets were sold at sport spectator events (Hoffman, 2010: 2–3). The voluminous amount of space given to sports in newspapers, on the web and on our television screens is further evidence of the importance of sports in our culture. Not that I in any way denigrate sport itself but I would strongly support Stringfellow's (1973/2004: 77) contention that principalities and powers drive this fallen idolatrous institution and that 'an ethics which ignores or omits the principalities . . . is, biblically speaking, so deficient as to be either no ethics categorically or to be, as has been suggested, an anti-ethics.' Stringfellow (1973/2004: 76–78) describes our current situation:

> The fall concerns the alienation of the whole of Creation from God . . .
> Human beings are fallen indeed! But all other creatures suffer fallen-
> ness too . . . corporations . . . the nations, the institutions, the princi-
> palities and powers . . . the principalities become recognizable and all
> too familiar: they include institutions . . . ideologies . . . corporations
> . . . bureaucracies . . . the Olympics . . . sports . . . the puritan work ethic
> . . . humanism . . . capitalism . . . the principalities are legion.

The fact that the founder of the modern Olympic Games (1896–), Baron de
Coubertin, writes in his *Olympic Memoirs*, 'the first essential characteristic of ancient and of modern Olympism alike is that of being a religion' is
then pertinent (cited in Parry, 2007: 206). This notion of the *religio athletae* has led Null (2008: 325) to affirm that 'Coubertin's vision of sport is
completely antithetical to Christian doctrine.' De Coubertin's Olympic vision
was built on a mix of the amateur ideals of nineteenth-century sport—*esprit
de corps*—the nineteenth-century Victorian movement of muscular Christianity, the philosophy of the Ancient Greek Olympics, a desire to reconcile
warring nations and promote world peace and to restore French pride and
masculinity in the nation's youth after defeat in the Franco-Prussian War
(Young, 2005; Guttmann, 2002). This said, he was staunchly against today's
commercialized professional sport model that permeates the modern Olympic games, which Baker (2000: 48) contends, perhaps too harshly, was 'from
the outset . . . conceived in the womb of rabid nationalism.'[22] Specific examples of modern Olympia and football World Cups that have been marred by
nationalistic fervor (e.g., 1936 Berlin, the so-called Nazi Olympics), political
and financial corruption, human rights abuses (e.g., Beijing, 2008), exploitation and terrorism (e.g., 1972, Munich Olympics) are described in Tomlinson
and Young's (2006) and Lenskyj's (2008) research.

The 'coming out' of China as an emerging global superpower, in part
through the vehicle of the Beijing 2008 Olympiad (Close, Askew and Xin,
2007) and their so-called 'celebration of the Paralympics' (and thus persons
with disabilities), is perhaps the most pertinent example here. In light of
communist China's bleak history of human rights abuses, which includes
the systematic abuse of child athletes (Hong, 2007), many scholars (Oliver, 1996/2009; Lenskyj, 2008), activists (Human Rights Watch, 2008)
and sports administrators were incredulous that the International Olympic
Committee (IOC) ever awarded China the Olympics. Indeed, Kidd (2010)
has subsequently suggested that the IOC should require host nations to
meet a standard human rights criterion to reduce the risk of the Olympic Movement (and its governing body: IOC) losing it's oft-stated, but
questionable, 'moral authority,' as a force for global peace (Kidd, 2010).
The continued discrimination of the disabled despite new legislation and
some positive changes from the Chinese government in the run-up to the
2008 Olympics (Human Rights Watch, 2008), the practice of sex-selective

abortion (Junhong, 2001) and genetic testing to detect fetal disabilities, usually with the goal of abortion ('the new eugenics') or rejecting children who are then commonly sent to orphanages (Ingstad and Whyte, 2007; Saxton, 2006), and harassment of athletes with IDs,[23] are all suggestive that the celebration of the Paralympics is somewhat of smokescreen. This provides substantive evidence of Chinese nationalism, a lack of respect for individual human dignity, unhealthy pride and idolatry, founded in an atheistic communist ideology (Hong, 2007). Of course, it is important to recognize that some of these ungodly values, such as pride, idolatry and nationalism, also characterize much of the Western sports model (Watson and White, 2012, 2007).

The evidence provided in this section that encompasses professional com-mercialized sport across the globe goes some way to supporting the claim that it is 'immediately obvious that Olympia as a religion is an idolatry . . . the classic example of an artificially constructed modern worship of false gods . . . for in Olympia human beings extol themselves, adore themselves, sacrifice themselves and reward themselves' (Moltmann, 1989: 104). To be sure, this extends to the 'nations,' as the previous century shows, in that 'whether communist, democratic, or fascist, modern governments have one thing in common—a reliance upon sports to define and bolster national pride' (Higgs, 1982: 179; also see Brohm, 1971). So, returning to Stringfel-low's (1973/2004) notion that the idolatrous institution of sport is fueled by the 'principalities and powers' that '*are* legion,' let us consider how group pride (e.g., Hong, 2007)[24]—nationalism, tribalism (consider football hoo-liganism) and racism that is widespread in sport—in addition to individual pride and self-glorification manifests itself:

> Collective pride is . . . man's last, and in some respects most pathetic, effort to deny the determinate and contingent character of his existence: The very essence of human sin is in it. This form of human sin is also most fruitful of human guilt, that is, of objective social and historical evil. Prophetic religion had its very inception in a conflict with national self-deification. Beginning with Amos, all the great Hebrew prophets challenged the simple deification between God and the nation, or the naïve confidence of the nation in its exclusive relation to God . . . Judge-ment would overtake not only Israel but every nation, including the great nations who were used for the moment to execute divine judg-ment upon Israel but were also equally guilty of exalting themselves beyond measure (Is. 47; Jer. 25:15; Ez. 24–39). (Niebuhr, 1949, cited in Menninger, 1973: 135–36)

For readers wishing to understand 'group pride' and related issues, the award-winning movie *Chariots of Fire* (1981), which is based on real–life events at the 1924 Paris Olympics, is instructive (see Cashmore, 2008). During the film, one of the principal characters of the movie, Eric Liddell, prophetically reads from Isaiah (40:15, 17) declaring, 'surely the nations are like a drop in the bucket; they are regarded as dust on the scales . . . Before him all nations are as nothing; they are regarded by him as worthless and less than nothing.' To some degree, this scripture portrays the foundation of Liddell's stand under national pressure not to compete on the Sabbath and thus miss the 100 meters qualifying race.[25] In explaining the dynamics of group pride, Menninger (1973: 136) notes that 'soon individuals have identified themselves with the group (and thus with God) and . . . Anything the group leaders decide to do is right.' Liddell stood against the group and avoided the 'herd mentality' that Kierkegaard often wrote of—'the crowd is untruth' (Moore, 1999: 243).

Having briefly surveyed the values of the modern professional able-bodied sports scene, it is important to consider disability sport and thus avoid romanticizing about disability sport as 'innocent and pure' (Howe, 2008a: 10), as the media is often guilty of. The sin of pride, nationalism and the win-at-all-costs ethic is also present in some activities in the disability sport realm. In their paper on the sport-disability docu-movie *Murderball* (2005), which narrates an enduring rivalry between the U.S. and Canadian men's national wheelchair rugby teams, Gard and Fitzgerald (2008: 135–36) find that:

> Wheelchair rugby is presented as an extremely competitive sport requiring the same aggressive outlook and physical excellence of non-disabled elite sport performers . . . *Murderball* offers viewers a window into a world of almost apocalyptic competitive intensity. Team huddles involve red-faced screaming team chants while coaches 'candidly' claim 'we're going to kick the shit out of them' . . . in the film's climax. The build-up to the Athens Paralympics . . . in a collage of short sections of footage accompanied by the obligatory heavy metal music, fans are shown with national emblems tattooed on their face; the Olympic flame burns; lycra-clad athletes carry a USA flag in victory . . . The message is clear: This is *real sport*. There is no 'feel-good' here. This is about winning.

Gard and Fitzgerald (2008: 139) note that some viewers of the film will be alarmed and worried about the 'corrupting influence of corporatized sport on disability sport,' something that Howe (2008a) has also identified. Indeed, I am one of them, and from watching the film I had further anxieties about the explicit marginalization and devaluing of athletes with ID who compete in the SO. The film's main characters used derogatory language about Special Olympians and clearly viewed their form of disability sport (Paralympics, PD) as superior to the SO. This discriminatory hierarchy is widely documented in the theology of disability literature (Yong, 2007; Young, 1990) and is documented in ethnographic research of the Paralympics by Howe (2008a: 31), who observed that 'athletes with intellectual disability were at the bottom of the hierarchy.' Hierarchies of worth based on PD or ID do not exist in the eyes of God. This truth is based on the biblical concept of *imago Dei*, that is, that we are all in essence (our spiritual nature) made in the image of God (Gen. 1:27). Niebuhr (1943: 32) conveys this in stating that it 'is the assurance that because I am, I am valued, and because you are, you are beloved, and because whatever is has being, therefore is worthy of love.' Developing the notion that those with ID in sport (and other aspects of life) are commonly devalued and marginalized raises the possibility that such people might be considered, at least to some degree, to be prophets to the sporting Babel of our age. As Swinton (Hauerwas and Vanier, 2009: 16) has intimated, central to much theological work on disability is the biblical mandate that the 'weakest, and least presentable people are indispensable to the Church' (1 Corinthians 12:22), and I would add the sports realm.

ATHLETES WITH INTELLECTUAL DISABILITIES: A 'PROPHETIC SIGN'?

> We're not leading a program; We're leading a movement—some say a civil rights movement of the heart—powered by sport. (Shriver, 2010c: 2)

> God chose things the world considers foolish in order to shame those who think they are wise. And he chose things that are powerless to shame those who are powerful. God chose things despised by the world, things counted as nothing at all, and used them to bring to nothing what the world considers important. As a result, no one can ever boast in the presence of God. (1 Corinthians 1:27–29)[26]

Over the years, theologians have to varying degrees suggested that persons with disabilities, in particular ID, are a prophetic sign to the age of modernity and the present era that exalts self, celebrity, wealth, outward beauty, the intellect, success and the need to be perfect in all that we do (Harshaw, 2010). These cultural values reflect what we think about ourselves, who we are—our identity and self-worth—and thus how we think and act towards those who do not exhibit these qualities. The controversial figure of Wolf Wolfensberger, who is perhaps most well known for the concept of 'normalization' that he advocates in mainstream disability studies and the SO (Wolfensberger, 1995, 1972), and which Oliver (1996/2009) has strongly critiqued, has been a major proponent of the idea that those with ID carry a prophetic message. Responses to his work reflect those received by the Old Testament prophets, who attempted to call the nation of Israel to repentance over its idolatry. As the modern system of competitive sport is arguably an 'idol factory' in which athletes, fans, coaches and parents have a 'misplaced trust . . . false worship in something other than God' (White, 2008: 127),

Wolfensberger's ideas are applicable here. Some of Wolfensberger's (2001a, 2001b) reasons for interpreting those with ID as a 'Prophetic Voice and Presence . . . in the World Today' that link to the sports world are discussed in the following (also see Brock, 2011; Albl, 2007).

People with ID (and PD) are much more public and visible, which is reflected in the sports community, with the birth and development of the SO (1968–), which is 'the world's largest organization for people with intellectual disabilities' (Siperstein, Kersh and Bardon, 2007: 1) and is a global movement that 'serves 3.1 million Special Olympic athletes [children from eight years old and adults] and their families in 175 countries'[27]. The SO have evolved from a "nice" sport organization for persons with Down syndrome into a global "movement" that champions the cause and dignity of those with IDs, suggests Timothy Shriver, the CEO since 1996 (Shriver, 2010c). It is worth noting that the SO is understood as a 'movement.' Harshaw (2010: 316) notes that all those who have advocated that those with ID are a prophetic sign to the modern world, Jean Vanier, Wolf Wolfensberger and Amos Yong, do so in plurality, 'advancing the idea that the most important aspect of their prophetic activity centres on the role that they hold in common.' The SO has more than 805,000 volunteers; 244,000 coaches; 500,000 officials; and it organizes 44,136 international and regional competitions around the globe each year (Brittain, 2010; Shriver, 2010c). The SO Summer Games were held in Athens in 2011, and seventy-five hundred SO athletes from 185 nations competed in twenty-two Olympic-type sports. Increasing visibility of athletes with ID is also shown in the organization of the first *SO Global Congress* (Marrakech, Morocco, 2010), at which SO leaders from around the world developed the 2011–2015 strategic plan of what Shriver (2010c: 2) calls a 'civil rights movement of the heart—powered by sport.' Similarly, athletes with PD now have high media visibility. Brittain (2010) projects that there will be forty-two hundred athletes from 150 nations participating in 480 events in the London 2012 Paralympics.

People with ID (and PD) are internationally recognized, following the civil and disability rights movement, subsequent changes in legislation of the 1960s–1970s and the rise of 'normalization' and 'social role valorization' theories (Wolfensberger, 1972). Again, this is mirrored in the birth of the *Paralympic Games* (1960, Rome) and the SO (1968, Chicago), which has led to the exponential growth of disability sports provision, global public awareness through increased media coverage (Thomas and Smith, 2009) and government and corporate funding. Under the leadership of Shriver, the SO have undoubtedly also seen exponential growth and international recognition,[28] not unlike the *L'Arche* movement that has, Wolfensberger (2001b: 18) argues, 'unequivocally gained international visibility.'

Further evidence is provided by the fact that some disabled—note they are only physically disabled—have attained 'celebrity status,' for example, British paralympian Dame Tanni Grey-Thompson (Howe and Parker, 2005),

Mark Zupan, one of the main characters of the documentary *Murderball* (Gard and Fitzgerald, 2008) and Ade Adepitan MBE, a wheelchair basketball paralympian and well-known UK television presenter. Of course, these are not in the same world as current able-bodied demigods, such as Tiger Woods (until recently), Roger Federer and Lionel Messi. Brittain (2010: 19) inadvertently summarizes the first two dimensions of Wolfensberger's thesis I have selected and applied to sport by stating that:

> International disability sport has come an amazingly long way since its early beginnings as a rehabilitative tool at a hospital in England over sixty years ago. It has developed into a huge international mega-event that has done a great deal to raise awareness of what people with disabilities are capable of and is increasingly making disability sport and athletes with disabilities an important visible part of the international sporting calendar.

Nondisabled and disabled persons are sharing their lives, often living together. This is personified in *L'Arche* communities where those with disabilities (especially ID) and 'assistants,' live together in a 'spirit of mutuality,' learning from one another. Jean Vanier, the founder of what many see as a prophetic movement (Harshaw, 2010), agrees in principle with Wolfensberger that 'people with handicaps are prophetic' (Vanier, 1995: 114). Disability sport organizations and events, for example, the SO and Paralympics, which have spawned thousands of regional and local events worldwide, to some degree offer this community spirit through relationships and social support. This is supported by the results of Farrell et al.'s (2004: 160, 164) study of motivations for athletes participation in the SO, in which they found that 'athletes identified friendships in the program as the key reason they enjoyed Special Olympics . . . the importance placed on relatedness by these participants was striking.'

People with ID may be parodying intellectualism. Since the European Enlightenment arid intellectualism has slowly pervaded our culture. Not in any way to decry the intellect itself, the university, education and research but it is a well-known maxim that academics often 'talk to themselves' and operate in a 'publish or perish' ethos that is characterized by 'arid scholasticism, crass careerism' and 'pompous posturing' (Steele, 2000: 90), that is just as destructive as the 'win-at-all-costs' sporting attitude. Wolfensberger (2001b: 27) in line with numerous biblical themes that parody the fallible wisdom and intelligence of humans, in relation to Gods wisdom (e.g., 1 Corinthians 1:17–31, 2:1–16) provides a critique:

> Many of the behaviours emitted by . . . [disabled] . . . people irritate and aggravate bright people, and that some of these behaviours may constitute a parodying of some of the intellectualisms of a culture that elevates the intellect and secular achievement to an extreme. Such parodying

would not be malicious, but an innocent acting out of God's derision, so to speak, at our efforts to build intellectual towers of Babel.

God's derision? Is not the multibillion-dollar business of sport, with its financial corruption, boasting and exaltation of human ability and strength, celebrity status and bodily beauty, a focus of God's derision? There is a 'strange logic of Christian witness,' Reynolds (2008: 19) suggests, in that 'the Christological implications of Paul's paradoxical proclamation 2 Corinthians 12:9–10; namely' that 'the saving power of God is made manifest and perfected in weakness or the lack of ability . . . a strength that comes through weakness, or wholeness that manifests itself in brokenness, a power that reveals itself through vulnerability.' While beyond the scope of this study, it is worth noting the clear links here to conceptions of the 'Holy Fool' (for Christ, 1 Corinthians 4:10) and 'Holy Folly' within the Russian Christian tradition of the fourteenth and sixteenth centuries, desert monasticism and the writings of Dostoevsky (Staley, 2012; Cross, 2011; Phan, 2001),[29] in which persons that were feebleminded, vulnerable, weak and idiotic in the eyes of the world, 'unconventionally . . . might be a mouthpiece of the Holy Spirit' (Trevett, 2009: 137). Perhaps then, athletes with ID do have a powerful embodied prophetic message for the modern sporting realm.

Disabled people are gentling others, through their vulnerability, weakness and presence.[30] This, I would argue, is Wolfensberger's most pertinent point for the sports world. It is suggested that those with ID have a 'gentling' influence on others, making them more compassionate, patient and tender in relationships. Yong (2007: 221) calls this a humanizing influence on others, through which we 'meet' with the vulnerability and brokenness of others (see Watson and Parker, 2012; Young, 2011, 1990). Similarly, Timothy Shriver (2010b: 1), in recounting one of many stories from the SO, in which an athlete with IDs has 'changed the way people think,' suggests that it is "soul power" that gentles others and leads them to consider spiritual and relational issues.[31] Gabriel Marcel's notion of 'presence' and Martin Buber's Hasidic teaching of 'hallowing the everyday' and 'healing through meeting,' in an 'encounter' with the other, is useful for understanding this relational mutuality in sport from a Judea-Christian standpoint (Watson, 2006).

In sport, the story of Gene Stallings, a highly competitive professional American football coach who has a son with Down syndrome, provides a good example. Through his relationship with his son, Stallings quickly realized that he 'was becoming more tolerant, more compassionate, and it was carrying over into work [professional sport coaching]' (Stallings and Cook, 1997: 66). This is supported by research that has explored *The Positive Contributions of the Special Olympics to the Family* (Kersh and Siperstein, 2010: 4), which showed increased patience, benevolence, tolerance, appreciation of health and family, improved relationships/

friendships and a 're-examination of personal values' as the result of consistent interaction with a family member with ID. I also have experienced something of this in my coaching disability sport and spending time in a *L'Arche* community (Watson and Parker, 2012). People with IDs often see beyond our masks and defenses,[32] in that they seem to have what Yong (2007: 189) calls a 'spiritual antennae' that is not determined by intellectual capacity (1 Cor. 1:18–31). In their vulnerability and transparency (e.g., hugging others) they relationally touch recesses of our hearts that we may not normally reveal, for fear of appearing weak or incompetent in front of others, which is often due to defensive pride and/or fear of difference. It is interesting to note that in the tradition of the SO, each athlete is not only given a medal but also 'a hug' after competing (Bale, 1994), something that Storey (2004) has questioned because it may encourage 'inappropriate social behavior' with strangers.

As described in the preceding section, able-bodied competitive sport is generally characterized by 'being the best, 'winning at all costs' through a physical and/or psychological domination of your opponent. Sports media perpetrate these notions claiming, 'You don't win silver, you lose gold' (Nike ad), and 'Nice guys finish last . . . every time you lose you die a little' (Kohn, 1992: 118). This understanding of modern sport is supported by Begel (2000: xiv–xvi), who illustrates how thoughts of humility, weakness and vulnerability are diametrically opposed to the identity of athletes:

> If there is any character trait that is anathema to an athlete it is that of weakness. Being unable to handle one's feelings, and confessing that inability to another human being in intimate conversation, is not usually concordant with an athlete's sense of mastery . . . the role of professional athlete may increase the risk of suffering a specific narcissistic vulnerability, and retirement from sports at any level carries with it an increased risk of clinical depression, especially if the retirement is forced by injury, or waning abilities.

This risk of depression is fundamentally tied to the athlete's sense of identity, an idolatrous trust and hope in the vehicle of sport instead of God to provide meaning in life (Watson, 2011). Thus, when sport is taken away a 'symbolic death' occurs in the heart of the athlete and they experience what Martin Buber called a 'shudder of identity' (Katz, 1975). On retiring from sport, Dean Macey, British Olympic decathlete, clearly articulated this: 'Fourth in the Olympics hurt, but retirement is like a death in the family . . . I'd lost a major part of my life, something was dead. Everything I'd lived for was over' (Slot, 2008: 98). This is a description of what sport psychologists call the 'hero-to-zero' syndrome. More often than not an athlete's sense of identity is based on culturally bound hegemonic definitions of masculinity and femininity (the gendered body) that are linked to demonstrations of power, performance and bodily beauty and muscularity (e.g., Wellard,

2009; Hargreaves, 1994; Messner and Sabo, 1990), as is also the case in some PD sports (Hardin and Hardin, 2005; Gard and Fitzgerald, 2008). Indeed, as Weiss (2007: 107) notes, 'this glorification of the physical body has had implications for the devaluation of the disabled body.'

In their analysis of constructions of masculinity and disability in recent movies that have a Christian subtext, that is, a battle between good and evil, such as the *Superman* films, Koosed and Schumm (2009) discuss the concept of a 'Super Jesus' (i.e., a Superman character, such as the late Christopher Reeve) and how this 'American ideal' rooted in the Protestant work ethic shapes modern understandings of Jesus: a 'Super Jesus.' Similarly, some Christians (especially Protestants) involved in modern sport have pedaled a utilitarian 'winning a championship for Christ' mentality (Hoffman, 2010) that often values and adopts the values of sports culture, in which pride is erroneously oft understood as virtue, due to the process of enculturation. I have argued elsewhere (Watson, 2012, 2007) that those who adopt this approach to sport and view Jesus as a competitive 'superhero' or 'teammate' should consider the message of Isaiah 53 and Philippians 2:1–11 and adopt a less utilitarian and more playful approach to sport, while still pursuing excellence and success (see Null, 2008). Perhaps by adopting St. Francis's maxim, 'preach the gospel . . . and when necessary use words,' so that the witness of their lives would bear fruit, rather than always trying to exalt Jesus through winning for him. He does not need us to be the most 'winningest' athlete or coach to advance His kingdom.

The Christian story teaches that God's kingdom advances through human beings first accepting his extravagant offer of grace and salvation and then following the author of salvation, Jesus Christ, in all aspects of their lives. Winning in any aspect of life, including sport, is not a prerequisite. When Pontius Pilate asked Jesus if He was the King of Jews, Jesus replied, 'You are right in saying I am a King' but 'My Kingdom is not of this world' (John 18:33–39). The values of God's kingdom, unselfishness, humility, sacrificial love, patience, kindness, peace, long-suffering, righteousness and moral purity are seldom observed in modern culture and the microcosm of sport. 'I tell you the truth,' Jesus says, 'many who are first will be last, and the last first' (Mark 10:29, 31). Herein lies the rationale for examining narratives of disability sport from a Christian perspective, to uncover any hidden prophetic message.

In summary, it is predictable that there are many dissenters of Wolfensberger's polemical ideas and his contention that Satan (i.e., demonic forces) is involved in some part in people's disablements and worldly affairs. I would concur with Yong (2007: 221–22), however, that Wolfensberger calls 'into question our taken-for-granted assumptions of "normalcy" in exclusive ways' and that his argument 'has to do with Paul's claim that God confounds the wisdom of the world with what the world considers foolishness.' This is not to suggest that persons with ID are in any way foolish, but as Yong goes on to say that 'their lives embody the wisdom of God in ways that interrogate, critique, and undermine the status quo' (221). Thus, Wolfensberger's thesis is a valuable framework to critique and theologically deconstruct the win-at-all-costs culture of sport. An important point to stress at this juncture, is that while we can learn much about the heart of Jesus from relating to those with disabilities, and we can, with strong biblical justification, view them as prophets to this age, we must never see them as 'objects' of ministry or as a means of developing virtuous character traits in ourselves. As Professor Michael Bérubé (2010: 48) notes in reflecting on his relationship with his son, who has Down syndrome and loves competitive sport, 'I've long since grown immune to clichés about children with Down syndrome. Jamie is not an angel sent to humanise the rest of us; not a sweet dollop of smiles and passivity. He is an ordinary human being, full of passions and desires that are . . . admirable.' Following this, any utilitarian, self-pitying and hierarchical mind-set must be avoided and we must view all persons with disabilities as equals in relationships of mutuality, where both the nondisabled and disabled have something to offer and receive as a gift, for example, time, presence and sacrificial love.

CONCLUSIVE REMARKS AND FURTHER RESEARCH

> We need to get even more serious about sharing the gifts of our athletes with the world. To do so, we need to fight harder to get attention for our story while we are confronting the most persistent and stubborn prejudice against our athletes. (Shriver, 2010c: 6)

> In the last days . . . their land is full of idols; they bow down to the work of their hands . . . So man will be brought low and mankind humbled . . . The arrogance of man will be brought low and the pride of men humbled; the Lord alone will be exalted in that day, and the idols will totally disappear . . . Stop trusting in man, who has but a breath in his nostrils. Of what account is he? (The Prophet Isaiah 2:2, 8, 17–18, 22)

I have argued through the presentation of empirical evidence and the application of biblical ethics two things. (i) The institution of professional competitive sport, especially professional big-business sport, is to some degree underpinned by ungodly ideologies and values and thus is an institution that is in part controlled by principalities and powers, that is, demonic spiritual forces. (ii) Sportspeople with ID and the global organization that represents them, the Special Olympics, are arguably *one* prophetic sign, not a panacea, to the modern sporting institution that is an idol for many athletes, fans and coaches. It is important to reemphasize that of course there are many individuals in amateur and professional competitive sport (able-bodied and disabled) that play free from the sinful bondage of selfishness, and pridefully seeking self-glorification and status. Indeed, due to critical tenor of my study some readers may think that I am demonizing all elite able-bodied sportspeople. On the contrary, I strongly support Barry Smart (2005: 198–99), who states that regardless of celebrity status of our sports stars:

> . . . the achievements of high profile professional sporting figures possess a quality that is increasingly rare in a world made cynical (corruption in sport) . . . the excitement and emotion aroused by the uncertainty of sporting encounters . . . the pleasure derived, and frequently collectively shared . . . as a spectator or viewer.

Sports are good, or perhaps more accurately have the potential to be and I am in agreement with the spiritual writer Brennan Manning (2005: 104), who acknowledges that due to their own insecurities and need to feel good about themselves, some 'hypercritical Christians quickly deny the presence of any value anywhere and overemphasize the dark and ugly aspects of a person, situation, or institution at the expense of their noble and valuable facets.' This said, while acknowledging the many positive aspects of modern sports institutions, such as the Olympic and Paralympic Games (see Watson and White, 2012; Ryken, 2004; Moltmann, 1989), when gazing through a Christian theological lens, I argue that much of the idolatrous institution of sport built on free-market capitalist and enlightenment principles (Guttman, 1994) is shot through with sin and corruption and is in need of spiritual rehabilitation.

Why are some Christians, as well as non-Christians, blind to the state of the sports world? Wolfensberger (2001b: 92) suggests the biggest 'obstacle to reading the signs of the time is idolatry, i.e. having excessive attachments to things created rather than to the Creator,' such as sport, as an idolatrous surrogate religion. A 'hardness of heart' that leads to a lack of moral discernment and individual and corporate conscience. Wolfensberger goes on to note that if you are able to detach yourself (in your heart) from these attachments because of intimacy, dependency and trust in God, 'the more apt one is to read the signs and perceive their meaning.' Spiritual blindness of the heart is of course a common occurrence in the history of humanity and of God's chosen people (Keller, 2009), as the prophet Jonah (2:8) proclaimed to the nation of Israel in the eighth century BC, 'those who cling to worthless idols forfeit the grace that could be theirs.' So, as Swinton and Brock (2007: 243) contend, 'our sinfulness . . . is our true disability; all human beings are disabled for all have sinned [Rom. 3:10–12]' and it is sin (especially the primal sin of pride) and ignorance (often unconscious) that makes us blind to the realities of the modern sporting Babel and the many other forms of idolatry in the modern world.[33] Biblical scholar John Stott (1986: 161) sheds light on this and expounds how the doctrine of 'substitution' is an offense to the modern heart: 'This is the great 'scandal,' the stumbling block, of the cross. For our proud hearts rebel against it. We cannot bear to acknowledge either the seriousness of our sin and guilt or our indebtedness to the cross.'[34]

If spiritual blindness is then the norm, and sin in this age is, 'as it was in the days of Noah' (Matt. 24:37),[35] where the majority of people are unaware of and desensitized to the sin that pervades their culture and reject God, what is the solution? The general vision of the SO is to 'transform communities by inspiring people throughout the world to open their minds, accept and include people with intellectual disabilities and thereby celebrate the similarities common to all people' (Brittain, 2010: 147). This is a noble and worthy vision and yet one I argue could be extended from a spiritual perspective. Encouragingly then, in his opening address of the 2010 SO Global Congress, Timothy Shriver seems to extends this vision to the heart and perhaps the spiritual message of the SO: 'We're not leading a program; We're leading a movement—some say a civil rights movement of the heart—powered by sport' (2010c: 2). It would seem that Shriver as a Catholic Christian is referring to the biblical teaching, that the 'heart . . . is the wellspring of life' and healthy relationships (Pv. 4:23).[36] So, in addition to 'opening our minds,' we must also open our hearts to God and then each other and follow what Jesus said to be the most important commandments:

> Love the Lord your God with all your heart and with all your soul and with all your mind and with all your strength. The second is this: 'Love your neighbour as yourself. (Mk.12:28–31)

Notice that love of God precedes love of others: 'we love because he first loved us' (1 Jn. 4:19). Hence, Christian doctrine teaches that health and vitality of our 'vertical relationship' with a Father God (in a *fatherless generation*),[37] through belief in Jesus Christ, will directly impact upon the depth and effectiveness of our 'horizontal relationships' with others, on an individual, familial and national level. In turn, it will determine, along with sound biblical teaching, how we receive, or not, understand and relate to those with disabilities in all walks of life, including sport.

Authentic loving relationships are at the heart of the gospel and Jesus ministry to all, including the disabled. Most writings on the theology of disability give significant space to relational concepts, such as friendship, mutuality, hospitality, vulnerability, humility and giving and receiving love (e.g., Reimer, 2009; Reinders, 2008; Reynolds, 2008; Hauerwas, 1986; Webb-Mitchell, 19934; Young, 1990; McCloughry and Morris, 2002). However, interpersonal relationships in sport settings remains largely 'unexplored territory' (Jowett and Wylleman, 2006; Watson and Nesti, 2005). The importance of building and managing healthy relationships in secular sport coaching and physical education texts has received some attention (e.g., Martens, 2004). Nonetheless, with a handful of exceptions there has been very limited Christian reflection on relationships on able-bodied sport and certainly not for disabled sport (Rieke, Hammermeister and Chase, 2008; Fellowship of Christian Athletes, 2008; Gallagher, 2008; Dungy, 2008; Wooden, 2005;[38] McCown and Gin, 2003; Boyers, 2000).

In this regard, Jean Vanier (cited in Reimer, 2009: 53), the founder of *L'Arche*, suggests that we need to 'rediscover what is essential: Committed relationships, openness and the acceptance of weakness' in a 'world of competition,' if we are to understand the prophetic message of persons with ID, which includes athletes with ID and the SO. As O'Keefe (2006: 113) found in her study of the use of leisure and sport in *L'Arche*, leisure can be used to foster community and 'the Christian focus of love in L'Arche is to announce the ridiculous—that we NEED them to teach us to trust, laugh easily, live more in the moment, enjoy the presence of others, and accept one another unconditionally.' Indeed, sharing and celebrating life and relationships is a central motif of *L'Arche*, which maps closely to the experience of athletes at the SO (Corman, 2003). It is through Jesus's relationships that he ministered God's love and grace to the world and prophetically spoke into people's hearts, for example, the Samaritan woman at the well (Jn. 4:7–26) and the healing of the disabled man at the pool of Bethesda (Jn. 5:1–15). Why has the sports world largely neglected the importance of relationships and how can a Christian understanding of athletes with ID speak into this situation?

Due to the continued secularization and scientization of sport since the evolution of professional sport in the 1960s and the resultant win-at-all-costs ethic (Beamish and Ritchie 2006; Hoberman 1992), I would argue that relationships and especially the discussion of relational dynamics, such as love, humility and vulnerability, have been neglected. This said, it has been argued that athletes can authentically love one another, even in aggressive physical contact sports, when love is properly understood.[39] In Swinton and Brock's (2007: 18) theological analysis of genetic science and its effect on the disabled, they were 'struck by the lack of a rhetoric of love,' as I am in the scientized sports world. In light of the fact that genetic performance-enhancement technologies were identified as a 'potential threat to the London 2012 Olympics' (House of Commons, 2007: 40) and secular analyses of genetic science in sport have pedaled trans-humanist ideas (e.g., Miah, 2004), I strongly support Trothen's (2011) contention that scholars need to adopt a 'Relational theological Ethic' rooted in Mark 12:28–31 and sound biblical anthropology when theologizing on both able-bodied and disabled sport. Also, of vital importance to all theological writing, research and praxis in the area of disability sport is to reflect on all the key theological themes and doctrines, that is, the biblical narrative as a whole. For example the Creation narrative has been often 'glossed over' in disability research and yet these narratives are 'crucial to understand the creation as the context of human love, this being part of a matrix of other theological themes, such as the nature of God, revelation, covenant, providence, salvation, and so on' (Reynolds, 2008: 138). Ontologically, if we are created then we are also dependent (on God and others), which rejects the modern mantra of individualism, self-actualization and freedom that characterizes modern sports (Swinton, 2011; Watson, 2011). How then is the power of God's love in human relationships in the world of sport practically worked out?

The father of a son with Down syndrome and well-known American professional football coach Gene Stallings suggests that 'sport provides a common bond' for the able-bodied and disabled to meet (Stallings and Cook, 1997: 213). Indeed, it is through the vehicle of sport that *Team Hoyt*, a father-and-son team (the son has disabilities), has received global media coverage, been awarded multiple honors,[40] inspired millions of people from around the world and been heavily involved in changing people's attitudes toward the disabled and government legislation. It is also interesting to note that the parents of both Rick Hoyt and Johnny Stallings were advised by doctors at the birth of their sons to institutionalize them due to their 'use-lessness'—the medicalized and utilitarian ideology of the modern world that marginalizes and rejects the disabled. If we reject the disabled though, we miss out on the possibility of learning to love, and in turn 'we suffer because it is only in relationships with other persons that we are most fully alive, whole, and human' (Reynolds, 2008: 112). Perhaps then, relation-ships with persons with disabilities in sport (ID and PD) can prophetically speak to others and allow them to 'see with their eyes, hear with their ears, understand with their hearts and turn' and enter into a relationship with God the Father (Matt. 13:15). As Moltmann (1998: 121) intimates, 'a per-son with disabilities gives others the precious insight into the woundedness and weakness of human life,' and I would add, the heart of Jesus for the world of sport.

Surprisingly then, with some very encouraging exceptions[41] para-church sports ministry organizations, such as the *Fellowship of Christian Athletes* (U.S.), *Christians in Sport* (UK), *Athletes in Action* (U.S.), *Church Sport Recreation Ministries* (U.S.) and *Verite Sport* (Europe), have not formally engaged with disabled sportspersons in terms of ministry focus (i.e., camps, seminars and athlete support), writings or any acknowledgment on web-sites. This is not a direct criticism of these organizations that do untold good in the sports domain but it is perhaps a wake-up call and it certainly reflects the abelist and utilitarian ideology and mind-set of the modern sport and Christian sport organizations.[42]

Recently, however, there has been promising signs that the acknowledg-ment and inclusion of the disabled in the sports world is on the radar of the world church (see Hawkins, 2010). For example, the Catholic bishops of England and Wales appointed James Parker, the Catholic Executive Coor-dinator for the London 2012 Games, who assisted in organizing a 'inter-national seminar on the theology of disability / paralympic sport' in 2012[43] Additionally, in support of the recent United Nations' *Treaty of Rights for the Disabled* (2006), which highlighted the importance of increased access and provision of sport and leisure activities for those with disabilities (article 30),[44] let us hope that, like the *L'Arche* worldwide network of communities and the Vatican's 'Church and Sport' office, others may consider helping to develop more sport and leisure provision for those with ID. For empirical researchers seeking to explore the role of sport and recreation in *L'Arche* communities, the theological ethnographies of Reimer (2009) and Webb-Mitchell (1993), the disability sport research of Howe (2009b, 2008a) and methodological reflections of Ward (2011b), Macbeth (2010) and Swinton and Mowat (2006) are helpful resources.

In conclusion, there is a need for further research on the theology of intellectual and PD sport and, most importantly, change in practice and legislation of sport (Macbeth, 2010). An important caveat though is that while 'disability rights are important' insofar 'as they relate to the coming of the kingdom . . . rights without love won't work' (Swinton, 2011: 305). What is required is a radical vulnerability of heart from those involved in sport, a heart that will be open to 'hear and see' the beauty and prophetic message of those with IDs, while also acting to bring liberation within the political and institutional structures that they inhabit.

This study has focused on athletes with ID. However, following the recent craze of 'body studies' across the disciplines, including the sociology and philosophy of sport (e.g., Wellard, 2009; Howe, 2008b; Schilling, 2003), research synthesizing this literature with Eiesland's (1995) embodiment theology of the 'disabled God' and subsequent developments and alternatives of this idea (Swinton, 2011; Creamer, 2009; Yong, 2007; Reynolds, 2008; Reinders, 2008; Monteith, 2005; Hull, 2003) will be one important area of inquiry.[45] Perhaps the question that this study has posed is best summed up by Swinton and Brock (2007: 241), who ask, 'What does their coming among us require of us?' Jean Vanier comments:

> There is a beautiful story of a young man with a disability who wanted to win the Special Olympics; he got to the hundred meter race and was running like crazy to get the gold medal. One of the others running with him slipped and fell; he turned round and picked him up and they ran across the finishing line together last. Are we prepared to sacrifice the prize for solidarity? It's a big question. Do we want to be in solidarity with others? . . . We have to look at the poorest and the weakest. They have a message to give us.[46]

ACKNOWLEDGMENTS

Firstly, I would like to thank Bishop David Smith (Emeritus, Bradford, UK) for the initial discussion that got me thinking about this topic. Secondly, I am indebted to Anthony Kramers (regional coordinator) and Phil Montanjees (community director) of *L'Arche*, for affording me the opportunity to stay in the Liverpool (UK) community for a number of days. Thirdly, the practical experience of coaching athletes with IDs at the *York St. John Inclusivity Club* has also contributed to my understanding and the writing of this chapter, and for this opportunity I am grateful to Simon Kumar, Paul Anderson and Rob Tyas. Finally, I would like to thank Professors Stanley Hauerwas, Gary Siperstein, Andrew Parker and Father Kevin Lixey for providing helpful comments on a first draft.

NOTES

1. One recent development with regard to further discussion and research on the religious and spiritual aspects of disability sport is a forthcoming Special Edition of the *Journal of Religion, Disability and Health*, which focusses on sports and leisure (see Watson and Parker, forthcoming).
2. Hoyt and Yaeger (2010), Nall (2002) and Stallings and Cook (1997) are father and son (both sons have disabilities) sports stories that have a religious angle. Anne Wafula Strike's (2010) biography tells the inspirational story of how a Kenyan girl who contracted polio at the age of two and a half, was consequently disabled from the waist down and as a result was ostracized by the African village community in which she lived. Through terrible adversity and barriers, Anne became a paralympian representing Kenya in 2004 and is now training to represent Britain in the London 2012 Paralympics. Robert Molsberry (2004), who is a pastor, father and triathlete, provides an insightful narrative that documents his disablement (paraplegic) following a traffic accident and the journey back to an active athletic life. Bonnie St. John's (2009) book details how her faith in God has been the "outrigger" (foundation) for her life as a paralympian and how to live a life of joy amid the challenges and limitations of disability. The book written by Julie Papievis (2008), an athlete, who suffered a severe brain-stem injury in a car accident and experienced deep depression and helplessness due to her disablement, narrates her miraculous and inspirational journey of recovery, in which she ran a 5K race five years later.
3. The most recent memorandum (15 December 2009)—*Re-Inclusion of Athletes with Intellectual Impairment in Paralympic Sports*—published on the *International Paralympic Committee* (IPC) website, indicates that 'the IPC General Assembly (Working Group) voted in favour of the re-inclusion of athletes [after the exclusion following the scandal at the 2000 Sydney Olympics. Athletes with intellectual disabilities were first included in the Athens 1996 Paralympic games] with intellectual impairment in the London 2012 Paralympic games and beyond.' The memorandum is available at: http://www.icsspe.org/news/pdf/2009_12_15MemoIPC%20Memorandum.pdf (accessed 22 June 2012)
4. For a general history of the SO, see Bu.eno (1994).
5. See Chapter 10, "The Special Olympics, Intellectual Disability and the Paralympic Games," of Britain's (2010) book, which is a good starting point to explore this topic.
6. For SO research studies, see: http://www.specialolympics.org/research_studies.aspx. (accessed 22 June 2012).
7. The SO are a nonprofit organization, have an amateur basis and are most often run and organized on a community level, through after-school and community based programs. Rarely is training and competition at a national

or international level, and the concept of "participation" and community are key principles for the SO.

8. For example, considering the SO is a nonprofit organization, Hong (2007: 114) notes: 'Economically, does SO promote corporations and their public-relations projects who support/finance SO rather than people it is designed to serve (witness the high financial salaries of the top SO executives who make upwards of $200,000 per year plus perks)?'

9. There are many different legitimate manifestations of the prophetic. First and foremost, the expository 'prophetic preaching' of God's word (as a large proportion of scripture is prophetic: foretelling/predictive and forth-telling); prophetic writings, for example, those of Kierkegaard, C. S. Lewis, Chesterton, Pascal and Dostoevsky; prophetic painting, art, sculpture and poetry, for example, the work of mystic, William Blake; songs and hymns with a prophetic edge (e.g., John Newton's *Amazing Grace*); prophetic signs (athletes with ID); and prophecy as a personal prophetic gifting (1 Corinthians 12 and 14) or as the 'office of a prophet,' that is, when an individual is assigned this gift/calling by God (Eph. 4:11). For further detail on this, point, see Harshaw (2010: 313–15), who provides an insightful and illuminating discussion of the prophetic in relation to those with IDs and addresses the question, 'What is a Prophet?'

10. The 'Tower of Babel' metaphor that I adopt here, based on Genesis 11, describes the prideful and idolatrous attempt of humans to 'build a city with a tower that reaches to the heavens, so that' they 'make a name for themselves (v.4). The footnote in the NIV study Bible (2002) explains that 'the people's plans were egotistical and proud . . . rebellious man undertook a united and godless effort to establish for himself, by titanic human enterprise, a world renown by which he would dominate God's creation,' a 'proud attempt to take its destiny into its own hands and, by its man-centered efforts, to seize the reigns of history . . . the kingdom of man would replace the kingdom of God' (27). In the modern era, this manifests itself in supposed metanarratives, 'myths of progress,' for example, the disciplines of anthropology (Feuerbach), psychology (Freud), sociology (Comte, Marx and Durkheim et al.) and biology (Darwin and Dawkins). Following the 'Genome Project' in 2000, genetic determinism has arguably become the latest mythic utopia for some. Undisputedly, all these ideas have in varying ways led to very positive scientific, technological and some social advancements that we should be most thankful for. However, the point is that the proponents and followers of these utopias have often slid into idolatry, seeing them as *all-encompassing* explanations for social and cultural existence and in turn ignoring God's guidance for how humanity should live. The history of the twentieth century *and the state of the modern world* clearly shows the folly in this view, which we are warned about in the Bible (1 Cor. 1:18–31, 2). Some of this footnote is cited in Watson and White (2007: 219).

11. This quotation is taken from John Paul II (2000c and 2000a).

12. In Eiesland's (1994) seminal book that focussed entirely on 'physical disability', she specifically states that her theology is not for those with intellectual disabilities.

13. Some scholars have confused (even supplanted) the meaning and spiritual reality of the 'principalities and powers' in their exegesis of these scriptures, with earthly forces/institutions themselves. But as John Stott (1980: 274) notes, if this is the case 'we become too negative towards society and its structures . . . we find it hard to believe or say anything good about them, so corrupt they do appear. Advocates of the new theory warn us against deifying structures; I want to warn them against demonizing them. Both are extremes to avoid.'

14. Unless otherwise stated, all biblical citations are from NIV (2002).
15. The Old Testament scholar Walter Brueggemann (2010) presents arguably the most nuanced and insightful contemporary analysis of the metaphor of Babylon in modern institutions and nations, especially focusing on America.
16. This quote is constructed from pages 19, 23–24 and 44–45 of Chapter 1, "The Social Setting of First-Century Corinth: An Historical Examination."
17. Quote from the *Sunday Express* (London), 13 January 1963, cited in Kluck (2009: 129).
18. Within his chapter "The Great Sin" Lewis does differentiate between 'diabolical pride' and what I would term 'defensive pride.' Lewis defines 'black diabolical pride' as 'when you look down on others so much that you do not care what they think of you' (Lewis, 1952/1997: 104), which is often the root of power-mad dictators. Defensive pride is in some ways (however, a Christian should be able to forgive all sin however despicable, by the grace of God) more forgivable, as it is normally rooted in unconscious emotional and spiritual wounds of the individual acting out of a proud heart, due to their need to appear 'better' than their opponent, or who they have fantasized as their opponent in some human endeavor. This footnote is also cited in Watson and White (2007: 23).
19. Moral death, according to Stringfellow, relates to the empirical outworking of demonic forces (governing principalities and powers) in individuals and institutions—sin—that leads to moral and ethical decline, idolatry, corruption and suffering.
20. William Stringfellow (1928–1985) was a renowned and highly controversial American lay theologian, activist and practicing attorney, whose writings were highly critical of U.S. social, economic and military policies and liberal churches; consequently he was under government surveillance for a number of years. His biblical ethics were based around the influence of the 'powers and principalities,' the metaphor of Babel and the systemic evil that characterizes Western, in particular American, culture and governance. The importance of his theological ideas should not be underestimated. In a panel discussion at the University of Chicago in 1962 the great Protestant theologian Karl Barth turned to the audience and famously said, 'You should listen to this man!' (cited in Johnston, 2007: 1). Wolf Wolfensberger's theories, which I rely on in this chapter, draw extensively on Stringfellow's work to develop his ideas.
21. The term 'demigod' is used here in the colloquial sense to denote a godlike person in the eyes of others (*The Oxford Compact Dictionary and Thesaurus*, 1997).
22. It is important to note that there are of course many very positive aspects of the Olympic Games, even when they are marred by nationalistic fervor (see Ryken, 2004). For example, Baker (2000: 50) provides the famous example of the friendship between German long jumper Lutz Long (a true Aryan) and Jesse Owens, the black American track and field star, which contradicted all that Hitler was trying to do—use the Olympics as a Nazi propaganda event.
23. 'Meng Weina, founder of China's Huiling Community Services, a nongovernmental organization that assists disabled people in eight major Chinese cities, complained of harassment by Shanghai police in a letter to the International Olympic and Paralympic Committees. A group of Meng's mentally disabled students were harassed en route to the SO in Shanghai on 11 October 2007; Meng described the incident as evidence that Chinese police "believe

that events initiated by civil society must be 'dangerous' and 'destructive'" (Human Rights Watch, 2008, 1–2).

24. In analyzing the Beijing 2008 Olympiad, Hong (2007: 55) provides a good example of how 'group pride' manifests itself in modern sport. 'For the Chinese, shame means "losing face" and loss of pride. For a person to "know no shame" is equivalent to saying that he has no decency. In Chinese sport, results must satisfy the requirements of collective pride. It must make others respect and admire China. Chinese sport is concerned with the "best," because above all it increase renown—the sense of pride—and avoids loss of face which Chinese people feel acutely.' This sense of pride is undoubtedly a significant dimension of China's response to a 'century of humiliation,' experienced mainly from Western imperialistic forces.

25. He was heavily 'leaned upon' to change his mind by the British Olympic Committee and members of the royalty, to guard against loss of national pride.

26. This Bible quotation is taken from the *Holy Bible: New Living Translation* (2004).

27. See: http://www.specialolympics.org/ (accessed 22 June 2012).

28. See Shriver (2010c) for evidence of this.

29. The character of the "holy fool" is personified in *The Idiot,* one of Dostoevsky's religious masterpieces. Prince Myskin is the Christlike figure who is mocked and berated by all for his simplicity and foolishness and yet as the story progresses is shown to be the most virtuous and wise of all of Dostoevsky's characters (see Phan, 2001).

30. It is important to note that while interaction with persons with IDs may have a 'gentling' influence on some individuals, there is also potential for the 'hardening of the heart' due to challenging behaviors (i.e., verbal and physical violence). .

31. This term is borrowed from Dr. Martin Luther King, who urged Americans to rely on "soul power" to fuel his *dream* during the race civil rights movement of the 1960s.

32. Of course this spiritual sensitivity—the 'spiritual antennae'—is not unique to persons with IDs.

33. While I have focused on 'institutional sin' in this study, it is important to remember that this of course stems from the individual sins of men and women within the institution.

34. The doctrine of 'substitution,' as Stott (1986: 161) describes it: 'The doctrine of substitution affirms not only a fact (God in Christ substituted himself for us) but its necessity (there was no other way by which God's holy love could be satisfied and rebellious human beings could be saved). Therefore, as we stand before the cross, we begin to gain a clear view both of God and ourselves, especially in relation to each other. Instead of inflicting upon us the judgment we deserved, God in Christ endured it in our place.'

35. 'The Lord saw how great man's wickedness on the earth had become and that every inclination of the thoughts of his heart was only evil all the time' (Gen. 6:5). This verse describes the status of ancient society before the judgment of God fell on humankind—the flood. Perhaps we live in comparable times (see 2 Timothy 3:1–9).

36. Timothy Shriver was raised as a Catholic and undertook a master's degree in Religion and Religious Studies at the Catholic University of America, Washington (1988) and has a column in the *Washington Post*—"Religion from the Heart"—in which he describes himself as a Catholic Christian (see Shriver, 2010a).

37. I have elsewhere noted how identity issues in sport and life are directly related to the *fatherless generation* in which we live (Watson, 2011). For an accessible and yet scholarly analyses of fatherlessness in our times, written from a Christian perspective, see Stibbe (2010) and Sowers (2010).

38. It is interesting that following England's disastrous performance at the Soccer World Cup 2010, Mike Atherton (2010: 84), ex-England cricket captain and now sports journalist for the London *Times*, suggested that what England 'footballers can learn from Wooden's gospel' was the importance of relationships, humility and self-sacrifice.

39. Etymologically the word love has four root meanings (Greek) that are important to understand in the context of relations in sport competition. These are: *storge* (affection), the love we have for family, especially parents to children, but also children to parents; *philia* (platonic), love expressed towards our friends; *eros* (sexual desire), the state of 'being in love,' a healthy sexual desire toward one's partner; and *agape* (unconditional love or charity), the unconditional love of God for humanity (divine gift-love) and the unconditional (as far as it can be) and *willed* love of humans towards others without expecting anything in return, especially to those who do not deserve our love, our enemies, i.e., those who annoy/offend us. While all four aspects of love are interrelated and balance between them in relationships is vital, I would argue that *philia* and *agape* love are those most needed for virtuous and humble relations with others in sport competition, as often one would need to *willfully choose* to love others even when wronged or incited to verbally or physically retaliate. If sport had become an *idol* in an athlete's life leading to familial relational problems, then it would be *storge* that is being neglected. For an overview, see Lewis (1960). This footnote is also cited in Watson and White (2007: 217–18).

40. For example, they have met President Ronald Regan and have been awarded the George Washington Honor Medal, an Honorary Doctor of Law degree for Dick Hoyt (Western New England College, Springfield, Massachusetts) and the Superlative Performance for Courage in Sports *Arete* award.

41. Further to an email correspondence (29 July 2010) with the executive director of CRSM, Dr. Greg Linville, it is encouraging to know that some staff members of this organization work with those facing physical, emotional and intellectual challenges, which has included collaboration with *Joni and Friends*. Similarly, the director of *Verite Sport*, Stuart Weir, has also informed me through email correspondence (12 August 2010) of his awareness of Chaplaincy work and his engagement with Paralympic athletes. Email correspondence with staff from *Christians in Sport* (CIS), revealed that there was at present no formal work with disabled athletes, although some Christian physiotherapists who work with paralympians and have contact with CIS do engage, when opportunities arise, with others in their sporting subculture on these issues.

42. It is then interesting to note that 'evangelical Protestants in the 1940–50's initially had little interest in sports and athletics per se, until they realised the power of sport to attract an audience of potential converts to the faith' (Mathisen, 2002: 10); which is, in part, a utilitarian approach that has historical reasons (see Watson, 2007: 90–94).

43. To my knowledge this event is the first of its kind: Everybody Has a Place: Catholic International Conference (theology of disability/paralympic sport), The Methodist, Westminster Central Hall, London, UK, 2 July, 2012. Co-organized by the Catholic Paralympic 2012 Committee and The Kairos Forum for Cognitive Disabilities (University of Aberdeen).

44. Cited in Howe (2008a: 1).

45. In brief, Eiesland argues that Jesus on the cross and through the resurrection is a 'disabled God,' in that even after his *bodily* resurrection and before his ascension to the father, when he appeared to his disciples and others, he was in some way disabled due to the wounds in his hands, feet and side (for an explanation and critique of this theory in light of subsequent writings, see Swinton, 2011). This obviously has significant ramifications for how those with disabilities understand God, themselves and others, in this life and the next. On this note, it is interesting that Rick Hoyt of *Team Hoyt* (a father–son sports team, in which the son is physically disabled), a self-confessed Mormon, reported that 'the doctrine that ultimately drew him to the church was the idea that when we are resurrected, our bodies are perfect' (Hoyt and Yaeger, 2010: 157).
46. Jean Vanier, cited in Whitney-Brown (2008: 167–68).

BIBLIOGRAPHY

Á Kempis, T. (1952) *The Imitation of Christ*, trans. Leo Sherley-Price, London: Penguin Books.

Albl, M. (2007) For Whenever I Am Weak, Then I Am Strong: Disability in Paul's Epistles, in H. Avalos, S. J. Melcher and J. Schipper (Eds.), *This Abled Body: Rethinking Disabilities in Biblical Studies*, Atlanta, GA: Society of Biblical Literature, 145–58.

Atherton, M. (2010) Footballers Can Learn from Wooden Gospel, *The Times* (London), 24 July, 84.

Avalos, H., Melcher, S. J. and Schipper, J. (eds.) (2007) *This Abled Body: Rethinking Disabilities in Biblical Studies*, Atlanta, GA: Society of Biblical Literature.

Bailey, S. (2008) *Athlete First: A History of the Paralympic Movement*, Chichester, UK: John Wiley and Sons.

Baker, W. J. (2000) *If Christ Came to the Olympics*, Sydney: University of New South Wales Press.

Bale, J. (1994) *Running Culture: Racing in Time and Space*, London: Routledge.

Beamish, R. and Ritchie, I. (2006) *Fastest, Highest, Strongest: A Critique of High-Performance Sport*, London: Routledge.

Begel, D. (2000) Introduction: The Origins and Aims of Sport Psychiatry, in D. Begel and R. W. Burton (Eds.), *Sport Psychiatry: Theory and Practice*, New York: W. W. Norton and Company, xiii–xx.

Bérubé, M. (2010) Learning Curveballs: Michael Bérubé on the Life Lessons to Be Found in Uncompetitive Sport—and a Fiercely Competitive Son with Down Syndrome, *Times Higher Education*, 1 (949): 36–48.

Boyers, J. (2000) *Beyond the Final Whistle: A Life of Football and Faith*, London: Hodder and Stoughton.

Brickley, M. (1984) Normalizing the Special Olympics, *Journal of Physical Education, Recreation and Dance*, 55 (8): 28–29, 75–76.

Brittain, I. (2010) *The Paralympic Games Explained*, London: Routledge.

Brock, B. (2012) Discipline, Sport and the Religion of Winners: Paul on Running to Win the Prize, *Studies in Christian Ethics*, 25, 1: 4–19.

Brock, B. (2011) Praise: The Prophetic Public Presence of the Mentally Disabled, in S. Hauerwas and S. Wells (Eds.), *Blackwell Companion to Christian Ethics*, 2nd ed., Oxford: Wiley-Blackwell, 139–15.

Brock, B. and Swinton, J. (2012) *Disability in the Christian Tradition: A Reader*, Grand Rapids, MI: Wm. B. Eerdmans Publishing.

Brohm, J. M. (1971) *Sport: A Prison of Measured Time*, London: Pluto Press.

Brueggemann, W. (2010) *Out of Babylon*, Nashville, TN: Abingdon Press.

Bueno, A. (1994) *Special Olympics: The First 25 Years*, San Francisco, CA: Foghorn Press.

Cashmore, E. (2008) *Chariots of Fire*: Bigotry, Manhood and Moral Certitude in an Age of Individualism, *Sport and Society*, 11 (2–3): 159–73.

Chambers, O. (1935) *My Utmost for His Highest*, Uhrichsville, TN: Barbour Books.

Cherney, J. L. and Lindemann, K. (2010) Sporting Images of Disability: Murderball and the Rehabilitation of Masculine Identity, in H. L. Hundley and A. C. Billings (Eds.), *Examining Identity in Sports Media*, Los Angeles: Sage Publications, 195–216.

Clifford, C. and Feezell, R. M. (1997) *Coaching for Character*, Champaign, IL: Human Kinetics.

Close, P., Askew, D. and Xin, X. (2007) *The Beijing Olympiad: The Political Economy of a Sporting Mega-Event*, London: Routledge.

Corman, R. (2003) *I Am Proud: The Athletes of Special Olympics*, New York: Barnes and Noble Books.

Creamer, D. B. (2009) *Disability and Christian Theology: Embodied Limits and Constructive Possibilities*, Oxford: Oxford University Press.

Cross, R. (2011) Disability, Impairment, and Some Medieval Accounts of the Incarnation: Suggestions for a Theology of Personhood, *Modern Theology*, 27, 4: 639–658.

Driscoll, J. (2001) *Determined to Win: The Overcoming Spirit of Jean Driscoll*, Tunbridge Wells, Kent, UK: Shaw Books.

Dungy, T. (2008) *Quiet Strength: The Principles, Practices and Priorities of a Winning Life*, Carol Stream, IL: Tyndale House Publishers.

Eiesland, N. L. (1994) *The Disabled God: Towards a Liberation Theology of Disability*, Nashville, TN: Abingdon Press.

Ellul, J. (1977) *The New Demons*, Woonsocket, RI, USA: Mowbray

Evans, C. H. (2002) Baseball as Civil Religion: The Genesis of an American Creation Story, in C .H. Evans and W. R. Herzog (Eds.), *The Faith of 50 Million: Baseball, Religion and American Culture*, London: Westminster John Knox Press, 13–33.

Farrell, R. J., Crocker, P. R. E., McDonough, M. H. and Sedgwick, W. A. (2004) The Driving Force: Motivation in Special Olympics, *Adapted Physical Activity Quarterly*, 21: 153–66.

Feeney, F. (ed.) (1995) *A Catholic Perspective: Physical Exercise and Sport*, Arlington, VA: Aquinas Press.

Fellowship of Christian Athletes. (2008) *Serving: True Champions Know that Success Takes Surrender*, Ventura, CA: Regal, From Gospel Light.

Fitzgerald, H. (2009) *Disability and Youth Sport*, London: Routledge.

Forney, C. A. (2010) *The Holy Trinity of American Sports: Civil Religion in Football, baseball and Basketball*, Macon, GA: Mercer University Press.

Frey, G. C., Stanish, H. I. and Temple, V. A. (2008) Physical Activity of Youth with Intellectual Disability: Review and Research Agenda, *Adapted Physical Activity Quarterly*, 25: 95–117.

Gaad, E. (2006) The Social and Educational Impacts of the First National Down's Syndrome Support Group in the UAE, *Journal for Research in Special Educational Needs*, 3 (September): 134–42.

Gaad, E. (2011) A Case Study on the United Arab Emirates: Women, Disability and Sport, in T. Benn, G. Pfister and H. Jawad (Eds.), *Muslim Women and Sport*, London: Routledge, 211–21.

Gallagher, D. B. (2008) Football and Aristotle's Philosophy of Friendship, in M. W. Austin (Ed.), *Football and Philosophy: Going Deep*, Lexington: University of Kentucky Press, 31–40.

Gard, M. and Fitzgerald, H. (2008) Tackling *Murderball*: Masculinity, Disability and the Big Screen, *Sport, Ethics and Philosophy*, 2 (2): 126–41.

Guttman, A. (1994) *Games and Empires: Modern Sports and Cultural Imperialism*, New York: Columbia University Press.

Guttmann, A. (2002) *The Olympics: A History of the Modern Games*, Champaign: University of Illinois Press.

Halberstam, D. (2001) *Playing for Keeps: Michael Jordan and the World He Made*, London: Yellow Jersey Press.

Hamilton, M. J. (2011) An Augustinian Critique of our Relationship to Sport, in J. Parry, M. Nesti and N. J. Watson (Eds.), *Theology, Ethics and Transcendence in Sports*, London: Routledge, 25–34.

Harada, C. M. and Siperstein, G. N. (2009) The Sport Experience of Athletes with Intellectual Disabilities: A National Survey of Special Olympics Athletes and Their Families, *Adapted Physical Activity Quarterly*, 26: 68–85.

Hardin, B. and Hardin, M. (2005) Performances of Participation . . . Pluralism or Hegemony? Images of Disability and Gender in *Sports n Spokes* Magazine, *Disabilities Study Quarterly*, 25 (4): 1–16.

Hargreaves, J. (1994) *Sporting Females: Critical Issues in the History and Sociology of Women's Sports*, London: Routledge.

Harris, J. and Parker, A. (eds.) (2009), *Sport and Social Identities*, New York: Palgrave Macmillan.

Harshaw, J. R. (2010) Prophetic Voices, Silent Words: The Prophetic Role of Persons with Profound Intellectual Disabilities in Contemporary Christianity, *Practical Theology*, 3 (3): 311–29.

Hauerwas, S. (1986) *Suffering Presence*, Notre Dame, IN: University of Notre Dame Press.

Hauerwas, S. (2004) Community and Diversity: The Tyranny of Normality, in J. Swinton (Ed.), *Critical Reflections on Stanley Hauerwas' Theology of Disability: Disabling Society, Enabling Theology*, New York: Haworth Press, 37–43.

Hauerwas, S. and Vanier, J. (2009) *Living Gently in a Violent World: The Prophetic Witness of Weakness*, Downers Grove, IL, USA: Intervarsity Press.

Hawkins, D. (2010) *Why Churches Should Engage with the Olympics and Paralympic Games and Cultural Olympiad*. Available online at http://www.cofe. anglican.org/olympics/whyengage.html (accessed 28 September 2010).

Higgs, R. J. (1982) *Sports: A Reference Guide*, Westport, CT: Greenwood Press.

Higgs, R. J. and Braswell, M. C. (2004) *An Unholy Alliance: The Sacred and Modern Sports*, Macon, GA: Mercer University Press.

Hoberman, J. (1992) *Mortal Engines: The Science of Performance and the Dehumanization of Sport*, Caldwell, NJ: Blackburn Press.

Hoffman, S. J. (2010) *Good Game: Christians and the Culture of Sport*, Waco, TX: Baylor University Press.

Holy Bible: New Living Translation, 2nd ed. (2004) Carol Stream, IL: Tyndale Publishers.

Hong, F. (2007) Innocence Lost: Child Athletes in China, in R. Giulianotti and D. McArdle (Eds.), *Sport, Civil Liberties and Human Rights*, London: Routledge, 46–62.

Horne, D. and Howe, D. (guest eds.) (2009) Special Edition: Disability and Leisure, *Leisure Studies*, 28 (4): 371–504.

Hourcade, J. J. (1989) Special Olympics: A Review and Critical Analysis, *Therapeutic Recreation Journal*, 23: 58–65.

House of Commons, Science and Technology Committee. (2007) *Human Enhancement Technologies in Sport—Second Report of Session 2006–07*, London: House of Commons London.

Howe, P. D. (2008a) *The Cultural Politics of the Paralympic Movement: Through an Anthropological Lens*, London: Routledge.

Howe, P. D. (2008b) The Imperfect Body and Sport, in *The Cultural Politics of the Paralympic Movement: Through an Anthropological Lens*, London: Routledge, 101–19.

Howe, P. D. (2009a) The Paralympic Movement: Identity and (Dis)ability, in J. Harris and A. Parker (Eds.), *Sport and Social Identities*, New York: Palgrave Macmillan, 29–48.

Howe, P. D. (2009b) Reflexive Ethnography, Impairment and the Pub, *Leisure Studies*, 28 (4): 489–96.

Howe, D. P. and Jones, C. (2006) Classification of Disabled Athletes: (Dis)empowering the Paralympic Practice Community, *Sociology of Sport Journal*, 23: 29–46.

Howe, P. D. and Parker, A. (2006), Celebrating Imperfection: Sport, Disability and Celebrity Culture, paper presented at Celebrity Culture: An Interdisciplinary Conference, School of Media, Language and Music, University of Paisley, Ayr, Scotland, 12–14 September.

Hoyt, D. and Yaeger, D. (2010) *Devoted: The Story of a Father's Love for His Son*, Cambridge, MA: Da Capo Press.

Hull, J. M. (2003) The Broken Body in a Broken World: A Contribution to a Christian Doctrine of the Person from a Disabled Point of View, *Journal of Religion, Disability and Health*, 7 (4): 5–23.

Huizinga, J. (1950) *Homo Ludens: A Study of the Play Element in Culture*, Boston: Beacon.

Human Rights Watch. (2008) *China: As Paralympics Launch, Disabled Face Discrimination*, 5 September. Available online at http://www.hrw.org/en/news/2008/09/03/china-paralympics-launch-disabled-face-discrimination (accessed 12 April 2011).

Hyland, D. A. (1988) Opponents, Contestants, and Competitors: The Dialectic of Sport, in W. J. Morgan and K. V. Meier (Eds.), *Philosophic Inquiry in Sport*, 2nd ed., Champaign, IL: Human Kinetics, 177–82.

Ingstad, B. and Whyte, S. R. (2007) *Disability in Local and Global Worlds*, Berkeley: University of California Press.

IronMan. (2006) *The Dick and Rick Hoyt Story*, DVD video, World Triathlon Corporation.

Jesperson, E. and McNamee, M. J. (eds.) (2009) *Ethics, Dis/Ability and Sports*, London: Routledge.

Jobling, A., Jobling, I. and Fitzgerald, H. (2008) The Inclusion and Exclusion of Athletes with an Intellectual Disability, in R. Cashman and S. Darcy (Eds.), *Benchmark Games: The Sydney 2000 Paralympic Games*, Petersham, NSW, Australia: Walla Walla Press, 201–15.

John Paul II. (1980) Human and Sporting Qualities Make Men Brothers, in R. Feeney (Ed.), *A Catholic Perspective: Physical Exercise and Sport*, Arlington, VA, USA: Aquinas Press, 62–67.

John Paul II. (1985) Address of Pope John Paul II to the Participants in the European Blind Championship, Castel Gandolfo, September 14, in N. Müller and C. Schäfer (Eds.), *The Pastoral Messages (Homilies, Angelus Messages, Speeches, Letters) of Pope John Paul II that Refer to Sport: 1978–2005*. Compiled by Norbert Müller and Cornelius Schäfer with the help of the Office of Church and Sport, of the Pontifical Council of the Laity (OCSPCL). Received electronically from Father Kevin Lixey, head of the OCSPCL.

John Paul II. (2000a) *Address of the Holy Father John Paul II, Jubilee of the Disabled*, 3 December. Available online at http://www.vatican.va/holy_father/john_paul_ii/homilies/documents/hf_jp-ii_hom_20001203_jubildisabled_en.html (accessed 2 August 2010).

John Paul II. (2000b) Address of the Holy Father to the Italian Silent Sports Federation, May 15, in N. Müller and C. Schäfer (Eds.), *The Pastoral Messages (Homilies, Angelus Messages, Speeches, Letters) of Pope John Paul II that Refer to Sport: 1978–2005.* Compiled by Norbert Müller and Cornelius Schäfer with the help of the Office of Church and Sport, of the Pontifical Council of the Laity (OCSPCL). Received electronically from Father Kevin Lixey, head of the OCSPCL.

John Paul II. (2000c) *Homily of John Paul II, Jubilee of the Disabled*, 3 December. Available online at http://www.vatican.va/holy_father/john_paul_ii/homilies/documents/hf_jp-ii_hom_20001203_jubildisabled_en.html (accessed 2 August 2010).

Johnston, R. (2007) *Bombast, Blasphemy, and the Bastard Gospel: William Stringfellow and American Exceptionalism.* PhD thesis, Baylor University. Available online at https://beardocs.baylor.edu/bitstream/2104/5068/1/marshall_johnston_phd.pdf (accessed 17 May 2011).

Jowett, S. and Wylleman, P. (2006) Editorial: Interpersonal Relationships in Sport and Exercise Settings: Crossing the Chasm, *Psychology of Sport and Exercise*, 7: 119–23.

Junhong, C. (2001) Prenatal Sex Determination and Sex-Selective Abortion in Rural Central China, *Population and Development Review*, 27 (2): 259–81.

Katz, R. L. (1975) Martin Buber and Psychotherapy, *Hebrew Union College Annual*, 46 (1): 413–31.

Keller, T. (2009) *Counterfeit Gods: When the Empty Promises of Love, Money and Power let you Down*, London: Hodder and Stoughton.

Kersh, J. and Siperstein, G. N. (2010) The Positive Contributions of Special Olympics to the Family. Available online at http://www.specialolympics.org/uploadedFiles/LandingPage/WhatWeDo/Research_Studies_Desciption_Pages/Athlete%20in%20the%20familiy%20final%20report_10.14.08.pdf (accessed 27 September 2010).

Kidd, B. (2010) Human Rights and the Olympic Movement after Beijing, *Sport in Society*, 13 (5): 901–10.

Kierkegaard, S. (1849/1989) *The Sickness unto Death: A Christian Exposition of Edification and Awakening*, trans. Alastair Hannay, London: Penguin Books.

Kluck, T. (2009) Sports and Humility: Why I Love Muhammad Ali (But Why He Also May Have Ruined Sports), in *The Reason for Sports: A Christian Manifesto*, Chicago: Moody Publishers, 129–38.

Kohn, A. (1992) *No Contest: The Case against Competition*, rev. ed., New York: Houghton Mifflin.

Koosed, J. L. and Schumm, D. (2009) From Superman to Jesus: Constructions of Masculinity and Disability on the Silver Screen, *Disability Studies Quarterly*, 29 (2). Available online at http://www.dsq-sds.org/article/view/917/1092 (accessed 11 April 2011).

Le Clair, J. M. (2012) *Disability in the Global Sporting Arena: A Sporting Chance*, London: Routledge.

Lenox, D. (2012) The Philosophy and Development of the Special Olympics International, and the Perspectives of Athletes with Intellectual Disabilities, in J. M. Le Clair (Ed.), *Disability in the Global Sport Arena: A Sporting Chance*, London: Routledge.

Lenskyj, H. F. (2008) *Olympic Industry Resistance: Challenging Olympic Power and Propaganda*, Albany: State University of York Press.

Lewis, C. S. (1952/1997) *Mere Christianity*, New York: HarperCollins.

Lewis, C. S. (1960) *The Four Loves*, London: Fontanna Books.

Liberia Editrice Vaticana. (2006) *Sport: An Educational and Pastoral Challenge (A Series of Studies Edited by the Pontifical Council for the Laity)*, Citta del Vaticano, Italy: Liberia Editrice Vaticana.

Liberia Editrice Vaticana. (2008) *The World of Sport Today: A Field of Christian Mission (A Series of Studies Edited by the Pontifical Council for the Laity)*, Citta del Vaticano, Italy: Liberia Editrice Vaticana.

Liberia Editrice Vaticana. (2011) *Sport, Education, Faith: Toward a New Season for Catholic Sports Associations (A Series of Studies Edited by the Pontifical Council for the Laity)*, Citta del Vaticano, Italy: Liberia Editrice Vaticana.

Limoochi, S. (2012) Reflections on the Participation of Muslim Women in Disability Sports: hijab, Burkiniw, modesty and Changing Strategies, in J. M. Le Clair (Ed.), *Disability in the Global Sport Arena: A Sporting Chance*, London: Routledge.

Macbeth, J. L. (2010) Reflecting on Disability Research in Sport and Leisure Settings, *Leisure Studies*, 29 (4): 477–85.

Manning, B. (2005) *The Importance of Being Foolish: How to Think Like Jesus*, New York: HarperCollins.

Martens, R. (2004) *Successful Coaching*, Champaign, IL: Human Kinetics.

Mathisen, J. (2002) Toward a Biblical Theology of Sport, Paper Presented at the *Annual Meeting of the Association for Christianity, Sport, Leisure and Health* (ACSLH), Wheaton College, IL, 7–9 June.

McCloughry, R. and Morris, M. (2002) *Making a World of Difference: Christian Reflections on Disability*, London: SCM Press.

McCown, L. and Gin, V. J. (2003) *Focus on Sport in Ministry*, Marietta, GA: 360⁰ Sports.

McGrath, A. (1985) *Luther's Theology of the Cross: Martin Luther's Theological Breakthrough*, Oxford: Blackwell Publishing.

Menninger, K. (1973) *Whatever Became of Sin?* New York: Hawthorn Books.

Messner, M. A. and Sabo, D (eds.) (1990) *Sport, Men, and the Gender Order: Critical Feminist Perspectives*, Champaign, IL: Human Kinetics.

Miah, A. (2004) *Genetically Modified Athletes: Biomedical Ethics, Gene Doping and Sport*, London: Routledge.

Molsberry, R. F. (2004) *Blinded by Grace: Entering the World of Disability*, Minneapolis, MN: Augsburg Books.

Moltmann, J. (1972) *Theology of Play*, New York: Harper.

Moltmann, J. (1974) *The Crucified God*, London: SCM Press.

Moltmann, J. (1989) Olympia between Politics and Religion, in G. Baum and J. Coleman (Eds.) *Sport*, Edinburgh: T & T Clark, 101–9.

Moltmann, J. (1998) Liberate Yourselves by Accepting One Another, in N. L. Eiesland and D. E. Saliers (Eds.), *Human Disability and the Service of God: Reassessing Religious Practice*, Nashville, TN: Abingdon Press, 105–122.

Monteith, G. (2005) *Deconstructing Miracles: From Thoughtless Indifference to Honouring the Disabled People*, Glasgow, UK: Covenanters.

Moore, C. E. (ed.) (1999) *Provocations: The Spiritual Writings of Kierkegaard*, Farmington, PA: Plough Publishing House.

Moss, C. R. and Schipper, J. (2011) *Disability Studies and Biblical Literature*, New York: Palgrave Macmillan.

Nall, S. (2002) *It's Only a Mountain: Dick and Rick Hoyt, Men of Iron*, St. Petersburg, FL: Charybdis Publishing.

Niebuhr, R. H. (1943) *Radical Monotheism and Western Culture*, Louisville, KY: Westminster John Knox Press.

Niebuhr, R. H. (1949) *The Nature and Destiny of Man: A Christian Interpretation*, New York: Scribner.

NIV. (2002) *NIV Study Bible*, ed. Kenneth L. Barker, London: Hodder and Stoughton.

Novak, M. (1967/1994) *The Joy of Sports: End Zones, Bases, Baskets, Balls and Consecration of the American Spirit*, New York: Basic Books.

Null, A. (2008) "Finding the Right Place": Professional Sport as a Christian Vocation, in D. Deardorff II and J. White (Eds.), *The Image of God in the Human Body: Essays on Christianity and Sports*, Lampeter, Wales: Edwin Mellen Press, 315–66.

Null, A. (2004) *Real Joy: Freedom to Be Your Best*, Ulm, Germany: Ebner and Spiegel.

O'Keefe, C. (2006) Leisure at L'Arche: Communities of Faith of Persons of Developmental Disabilities, in G. Van Andel, P. Heintzman and T. Visker (Eds.), *Christianity and Leisure: Issues in a Pluralistic Society*, rev. ed., Sioux Center, IA: Dordt College Press, 116–24.

Oliver, M. (1990) *The Politics of Disablement*, Basingstoke, UK: Macmillan and St. Martin's Press.

Oliver, M. (1996/2009) *Understanding Disability: From Theory to Practice*, New York: Palgrave Macmillan.

Overman, S. J. (1997) *The Influence of the Protestant Ethic on Sport and Recreation*, Sydney: Ashgate.

Overman, S. J. (2011) *The Protestant Work Ethic and the Spirit of Sport: How Calvinism and Capitalism Shaped American Games*, Macon, GA: Mercer University Press.

Papievis, J. (2008) *Go Back and be Happy* (with Margaret McSweeney), Oxford: Monarch Books, Lion Hudson.

Parry, J. (2007) The *religio athletae*, Olympism and Peace, in J. Parry, S. Robinson, N. J. Watson and M. S. Nesti (Eds.), *Sport and Spirituality: An Introduction*, London: Routledge, 201–14.

Patterson, I. and Pegg, S. (2009) Serious Leisure and People with Intellectual Disabilities: Benefits and Opportunities, *Leisure Studies*, 28 (4): 387–402.

Phan, P. C. (2001) The Wisdom of Holy Fools in Postmodernity, *Theological Studies*, 62: 730–52.

Reimer, K. (2009). *Living L'Arche: Stories of Compassion, Love and Disability*, London; Continuum.

Reinders, H. (2008) *Receiving the Gift of Friendship: Profound Disability, Theological Anthropology and Ethics*, Grand Rapids, MI: William B. Eerdmans Publishing Co.

Reinders, H. (2010) *The Paradox of Disability: Responses to Jean Vanier and L'Arche Communities from Theology and Sciences*, Grand Rapids, MI: William B. Eerdmans Publishing Co.

Reynolds, T. E. (2008) *Vulnerable Communion: A Theology of Disability and Hospitality*, Grand Rapids, MI, USA: Brazos Press.

Rieke, M., Hammermeister, J. and Chase, M. (2008) Servant Leadership in Sport: A New Paradigm for Effective Coaching Behaviour, *International Journal of Sports Science and Coaching*, 3 (2): 227–39.

Rojek, C. (2001) *Celebrity*, London: Reaktion Books.

Ryken, P. G. (2004) The Gospel According to the Olympics, in P. G. Ryken (Ed.), *He Speaks to Me Everywhere: Meditations on Christianity and Culture*, Phillipsburg, NJ: P & R Publishing Company, 43–45.

Savage, T. B. (2004) *Power through Weakness: Paul's Understanding of the Christian Ministry in 2 Corinthians (Society for New Testament Studies Monograph Series 86)*, Cambridge: Cambridge University Press.

Saxton, M. (2006) Disability Rights and Selective Abortion, in L. J. Davis (Ed.), *The Disability Studies Reader*, 2nd ed., London: Routledge, 105–16.

Schlier, H. (1962) *Principalities and Powers in the New Testament*, New York: Herder and Herder.

Shilling, C. (2003) *The Body and Social Theory*, 2nd ed., London: Sage.

Shriver, T. (2010a) About 'Religion from the Heart,' *Washington Post*, 10 February. Available online at http://newsweek.washingtonpost.com/onfaith/

religionfromtheheart/2008/02/about_religion_from_the_heart.html (accessed 22 September 2010).

Shriver, T. (2010b) Disabled Have a Dream, Too, *Washington Post*, 10 February. Available online at http://onfaith.washingtonpost.com/onfaith/religionfromthe-heart/2010/01/chubbs_stillman_a_special_education.html (accessed 22 September 2010).

Shriver, T. (2010c) Opening Address of Timothy Shriver (CEO), *Special Olympics Global Congress*, Marrakech, Morocco, 7 June. Available online at http://www.specialolympics.org/slideshow-global-congress-photos.aspx (accessed 15 September 2010).

Siperstein, G. N., Kersh, J. and Bardon, J. N. (2007) A New Generation of Research in Intellectual Disabilities: Charting the Course (Report), presented at A Special Olympics Working Conference, Miami, FL, 6–7 December. Available online at http://media.specialolympics.org/soi/files/healthy-athletes/2007%20Research%20Agenda%20Miami.pdf (accessed 17 September 2010).

Slot, O. (2008) Fourth in the Olympics Hurt, but Retirement Is Like a Death in the Family, *The Times* (London), 19 December, 98–99.

Smart, B. (2005) *The Sport Star: Modern Sport and the Cultural Economy of Sporting Celebrity*, London: Sage Publications.

Smith, B. and Sparkes, A. (2012) Disability, Sport, and Physical Activity. A Critical Review, in N. Watson, C. Thomas and A. Roulstone (Eds.), *Routledge Companion to Disability Studies*, London: Routledge, 336–47.

Songster, T. B., Smith, G., Evans, M., Munson, D. and Behen, D. (1997) Special Olympics and Athletes with Down Syndrome, in S. M. Pueschel and M. Sustrova (Eds.), *Adolescents with Down Syndrome: Toward a More Fulfilling Life*, Baltimore, MD: Paul H. Brookes, 341–57.

Sowers, J. (2010) *Fatherless Generation: Redeeming the Story*, Grand Rapids, IL: Zondervan.

St. John, B. (2009) *Live your Joy*, Boston: Faithwords.

Staley, E. (2012) Intellectual Disability and Mystical Unknowing: Contemporary Insights from Medieval Sources, *Modern Theology*, 28, 3: 385–401.

Stallings, G. and Cook, S. (1997) *Another Season: A Coach's Story of Raising an Exceptional Son*, New York: Broadway Publishing.

Steele, R. B. (2000) Devotio Post-Moderna: On Using a "Spiritual Classic" as a Diagnostic Tool in a Freshman Christian Formation Course, *Horizons*, 27 (1): 81–97.

Stevenson, C. L. (1997) Christian Athletes and the Culture of Elite Sport: Dilemmas and Solutions, *Sociology of Sport Journal*, 14: 241–62.

Stibbe, M. (2010) *I Am Your Father: What Every Heart Needs to Know*, London: Monarch Books.

Strike, A. W. (2010) *In My Dreams I Dance: How One Women Battled Prejudice to Become a Champion*, London: HarperTrue.

Stringfellow, W. (2004/1973) *An Ethic for Christians and Other Aliens in a Strange Land*, Eugene, OR: Wipf and Stock Publishers.

Storey, K (2004) The Case against the Special Olympics, *Journal of Disability Policy Studies*, 15 (1): 35–42.

Stott, J. (1980) *God's New Society: The Message of Ephesians*, Leicester, UK: Inter-Varsity Press.

Stott, J. (1986) *The Cross of Christ*, Leicester, UK: Inter-Varsity Press.

Swinton, J. (2011) Who Is the God We Worship? Theologies of Disability; Challenges and New Possibilities (Research Report), *International Journal of Practical Theology*, 14 (2): 273–307.

Swinton, J. and Brock, B. (eds.) (2007) *Theology, Disability and the New Genetics: Why Science Needs the Church*, Edinburgh: T & T Clark.

Swinton, J. and Hauerwas, S. (eds.) (2005) *Critical Reflections on Stanley Hauerwas' Theology of Disability: Disabling, Society, Enabling Theology*, New York: Haworth Press.

Swinton, J. and Mowat, H. (2006) *Practical Theology and Qualitative Research*, London: SCM Press.

Thoennes, E. K. (2008) Created to Play: Thoughts on Play, Sport and Christian Life, in D. Deardorff II and J. White (Eds.), *The Image of God in the Human Body: Essays on Christianity and Sports*, Lampeter, Wales: Edwin Mellen Press, 79–100.

Thomas, N. and Smith, A. (2009) *Disability Sport and Society: An Introduction*, London: Routledge.

Tomlinson, A. and Young, C. (2006) *National Identity and Global Sports Events: Culture, Politics and Spectacle in the Olympics and World Cup*, Albany: State University of York Press.

Trevett, C. (2009) Asperger's Syndrome and the Holy Fool: The Case of Brother Juniper, *Journal of Religion, Disability and Health*, 13: 129–50.

Trothen, T. J. (2011) Better than Normal? Constructing Modified Athletes and a Relational Theological Ethic, in J. Parry, M. S. Nesti and N. J. Watson (Eds.), *Theology, Ethics and Transcendence in Sports*, London: Routledge, 64–81.

Twietmeyer, G. (2008) A Theology of Inferiority: Is Christianity the Source of Kinesiology's Second-Class Status in the Academy, *Quest*, 60: 452–66.

Vanier, J. (1995) *An Ark for the Poor: The Story of L'Arche*, Toronto: Novalis.

Ward, P. (2011a) *Gods Behaving Badly: Media, Religion, and Celebrity Culture*, London: SCM Press.

Ward, P. (2011b) *Perspectives on Ecclesiology and Ethnography*, Grand Rapids, MI, USA: William Eerdmans Publishers.

Watson, N. J. (2006) Martin Buber's *I and Thou*: Implications for Christian Psychotherapy, *Journal of Psychology and Christianity*, 25 (1): 35–44.

Watson, N. J. (2007) Muscular Christianity in the Modern Age: "Winning for Christ" or "Playing for Glory"? in J. Parry, S. Robinson, N. J. Watson and M. S. Nesti (Eds.), *Sport and Spirituality: An Introduction*, London: Routledge, 80–94.

Watson, N. J. (2011) Identity in Sport: A Psychological and Theological Analysis, in J. Parry, M. N. Nesti and N. J. Watson (Eds.), *Theology, Ethics and Transcendence in Sports*, London: Routledge, 107–48.

Watson, N. J. (2012) Sport, Disability and the Olympics: An Exploration of the Status and Prophetic Role of the Special Olympic Movement in Light of the London 2012 Olympic and Paralympic Games, *The Bible in Transmission*, Spring: 14–16. Full text available online: http://www.biblesociety.org.uk/resources22/ (accessed 22 June 2012).

Watson, N. J. and Nesti, M. (2005) The Role of Spirituality in Sport Psychology Consulting: An Analysis and Integrative Review of Literature, *Journal of Applied Sport Psychology*, 17: 228–39. Available online at http://pdfserve.informaworld.com/657886_731218473_725758807.pdf (accessed 29 July 2010).

Watson, N. J. and Parker, A. (2012) Christianity, Disability and Sport: A Case Study of the Role of Long-Distance Running in the Life of a Father and a Son Who Is Congenitally Blind and has Profound Intellectual Disabilities, *Practical Theology*, 5, 2: 191–210.

Watson, N. J. and Parker, A. (guest eds.) (forthcoming) Sports, Religion and Disability (Special Edition), *Journal of Religion, Disability and Health*.

Watson, N. J. and White, J. (2007) "Winning at all Costs" in Modern Sport: Reflections on Pride and Humility in the Writings of C. S. Lewis, in J. Parry, S. Robinson, N. J. Watson and M. S. Nesti (Eds.), *Sport and Spirituality: An Introduction*, London: Routledge, 61–79.

Watson, N. J. and White, J. (2012) C. S. Lewis at the 2012 London Olympics: Reflections on Pride and Humility, *Practical Theology*, 5,2: 153–169.

Watts, G. (2007) Athletes with a Disability—Mixed Messages from the Bible, paper presented at the Inaugural International Conference on Sport and Spirituality, Centre for the Study of Sport and Spirituality (2003–2009), York St. John University, York, UK, 28–31 August.

Watts, G. (2009) Disability from a Christian Gospel Perspective, *Australian Religion Studies Review*, 21,2: 109–21.

Webb-Mitchell, B. (1993) *God Plays Piano, Too*: *The Spiritual Lives of Disabled Children*, New York: Crossroads.

Weir, S. (2008) Competition as Relationship: Sport as a Mutual Quest for Excellence, in D. Deardorff II and J. White (Eds.), *The Image of God in the Human Body*: *Essays on Christianity and Sports*, Lampeter, Wales: Edwin Mellen Press, 101–22.

Weiss, M. (2007) The Chosen Body and the Rejection of Disability in Israeli Society, in B. Ingstad and S. R. Whyte (Eds.), *Disability in Local and Global Worlds*, London: University of California Press, 107–27.

Wellard, I. (2009) *Sport Masculinities and the Body*, London: Routledge.

White, J. (2008) Idols in the Stadium: Sport as an "Idol Factory," in D. Deardorff II and J. White (Eds.), *The Image of God in the Human Body*: *Essays on Christianity and Sports*, Lampeter, Wales: Edwin Mellen Press, 127–72.

Whitney-Brown, C. (2008) *Jean Vanier*: *Essential Writings*, Maryknoll, NY: Orbis Books.

Wilson, M. V. (1989) *Our Father Abraham*: *Jewish Roots of the Christian Faith*, Grand Rapids, MI: Wm. B. Eerdmans Publishing Company.

Winnick, J. P. (2011) *Adapted Physical Education and Sport*, 5th ed., Champaign, IL: Human Kinetics.

Wolfensberger, W. (1972) *The Principle of Normalization in Human Services*, Toronto: National Institute on Mental Retardation.

Wolfensberger, W. (1995) Of "Normalization," Lifestyles, the Special Olympics, Deinstitutionalization, Mainstreaming, Integration and Cabbages and Kings, *Mental Retardation*, 33: 128–31.

Wolfensberger, W. (2001a) The Most Urgent Issues Facing Us as Christians Concerned with Handicapped Persons Today, in W. Gaventa and C. Coulter (Eds.), *The Theological Voice of Wolf Wolfensberger*, Binghamton, NY: Haworth Pastoral Press, 91–102.

Wolfensberger, W. (2001b) The Prophetic Voice and the Presence of Mentally Retarded People in the World Today, in W. Gaventa and C. Coulter (Eds.), *The Theological Voice of Wolf Wolfensberger*, Binghamton, NY: Haworth Pastoral Press, 11–48.

Wooden, J. (2005) *Wooden on Leadership* (with Steve Jamison), New York: McGraw-Hill.

Yong, A. (2007) *Theology and Down Syndrome*: *Reimaging Disability in Late Modernity*, Waco, TX: Baylor University Press.

Yong, A. (2011) *The Bible, Disability, and the Church*: *A New Vision of the People of God*, Grand Rapids, MI: Wm. B. Eerdmans Publishing.

Young, D. (2005) From Olympia 776 BC to Athens 2004: The Origin and Authenticity of the Modern Olympic Games, in K. Young and K. B. Wamsley (Eds.), *Global Olympics: Historical and Sociological Studies of the Modern Games (Research in the Sociology of Sport, Volume 3)*, Oxford: Elsevier, 3–18.

Young, F. M. (1990) *Face to Face*, Edinburgh: T & T Clark.

Young, F. M. (2011) Wisdom in Weakness, *Theology*, 114, 3: 181–188.

7 The Technoscience Enhancement Debate in Sports

What's Religion Got to Do with It?[1]

Tracy J. Trothen

The desire to improve, become better, or enhance one's performance has long been part of human history. What it means to enhance, however, has not been static but has fluctuated according to context and corresponding normative values. Technoscience developments in genetic modification technologies, cognitive sciences, cybernetics and robotic technologies are fast emerging (Miah, 2005). The increasing availability of technoscience innovations such as cheetah legs, genetic testing, super swimsuits and Repoxygen (the trade name for a type of gene therapy) are forcing a more intentional identification and examination of the values that undergird the assessment of what constitutes acceptable enhancements in sporting competition (Trothen, 2009, 2011).

I approach this chapter as a theological social ethicist, drawing on postmodernism. As such I am attentive to causal dynamics particularly as viewed through a theologically informed lens. The postmodernist insight that all knowledge is limited and its concomitant rejection of grand narratives, universalisms and normative claims is very helpful to the interrogation of the recent confluence of sport, technoscience and religion. I argue that epistemological categorizations that inform (and are informed by) normative values have shaped approaches to enhancement questions in sport. The exploration of causal dynamics including the identification of operative values and interests that shape these and other norms can make possible the reframing of the sport and enhancement issue and the consideration of alternative values and interests.

It has been argued elsewhere that sport—rightly or wrongly—either is a religion or is perceived to function like a religion for many participants and fans (see, for example, Higgs and Braswell, 2004; Ladd and Mathisen, 1999; Mathisen, 1992; Novak, 1993; Prebish, 1993; Price, 2001; Sinclair-Faulkner, 1977; Trothen, 2006). Certainly there are good arguments for and against this relationship and attendant understandings of sport, religion, and spirituality. A view of sport as a way of being religious or experiencing the sacred requires a reconsideration of religion in part challenging accepted normative epistemological categorizations of what constitutes a religion as well as a framing of the sacred and profane as oppositional binaries (Lynch, 2007). This disruption, I argue, also holds the potential to challenge normative ways of distancing and negating the Other. Important for this chapter is that many athletes and fans subjectively experience something that they perceive as the sacred in sport.

This perception is an important, if underconsidered, dimension of sport that deepens the moral and ethical analysis of the use of technoscience for athletic enhancement. Most ethical analyses of the enhancement debate have turned on a critique or acceptance of distinctions between essentialist understandings of what is normal, natural and artificial. Some have begun to explore the relevance of the debate to ontological questions regarding what it means to be human (Nowotny and Testa, 2010; Trothen, 2008; Miah, 2005; Simon, 2001). In this chapter I argue that when the issue is reframed as a theological one, centered on a postmodern feminist understanding of transcendence, ethical interrogation surfaces additional issues concerning values, difference, visibility, relationship, hope and the sacred. When framed in this way, the ethical implications of enhancements in sport assume greater complexity. As will become clear, of particular significance is the question of visibility. Not only are new and visible technoscience enhancements emerging, but technoscience is increasing the visibility of preexisting enhancements or advantages. Through the use of narrative examples, I will demonstrate that this increased visibility has paradoxical implications: opportunities both to recognize and become hospitably disposed to greater human diversity are presented, but at the same time this heightened visibility can lead to a retrenchment of dominant embodiment categories and to the absorption or greater marginalization of those who are different from the norm. From a Christian perspective, the welcoming of the stranger is a strong biblical motif and value. The greater visibility of difference in sport and wider society disrupts the belief of hegemonic sameness and equal opportunity, including any belief claim that sport is a meritocracy in which one can succeed (win) through hard work (Overman, 1997).

I will argue that an adequate ethical analysis of the use of genetic, machine and other technologies in sport must go beyond the individualistically focused issues of cheating and rights to address underlying systemic questions of meaning and values. My intention here is not to arrive at a blanket ethical assessment of the use of technoscience enhancements as this is too complex an issue to judge all cases as one. Instead, my focus is the interrogation of the moral relevance of the relationship between transcendence and technoscience enhancement in sport.

This chapter will demonstrate that normative embodiment discourse and related assumptive values are operative even if not always visible in sport enhancement issues. Although any normative value claim must be viewed critically (Edwards and Jones, 2009), there is a need for alternative norms to be considered if the systemic marginalization of the "Other" and systemic valorization of those with power are to be rejected. Approached from a postmodern feminist theological perspective, transcendence can provide a much needed illumination of the complexity of the sport enhancement issue largely though a valuing of the diverse Other.

THE ENHANCEMENT DEBATE

The most common approaches to the sport enhancement debate have hinged on distinctions between the natural and the artificial with the natural being framed as morally acceptable or good and the artificial being conversely framed as unacceptable or bad (Trothen, 2009). The essentialist concept of 'natural' has become increasingly problematic with science making more visible the diversity that exists within human biology and embodiment. As Nowotny and Testa argue: a "defining feature of the molecular life sciences . . . is that they make things visible that could not previously be seen" (2010: 1). This sense of diversity challenges epistemologies that rely on static categories to understand humanity; there is no one 'natural' way to be human. Further demonstrating the limitations of these essentialisms, as collective constructs of normal have shifted, so too has what is considered natural. For example, the use of vaccinations and vitamins has become considered normal and therefore natural even though both are externally introduced and may alter one's physiology.

The external–internal distinction has been helpful to a degree in that it has made clear that externally introduced drugs, such as anabolic steroids (that may alter one's physiology), are not permitted in elite sports competitions such as the Olympics (World Anti-Doping Agency [WADA], 2012; Simon, 2004). However, not only has the use of some accepted external substances (vitamins, vaccinations, oxygen levels of controversial hypobaric chambers) complicated this moral distinction, but now technoscience is showing that there are many often unsuspected ways of inducing physiological change through external means. For example, prayer and other religious practices including meditation have not been questioned as performance-enhancing techniques even though they can alter brain activity and physiology (Watson and Nesti, 2005). This is of interest given that iPods were banned in the New York City Marathon in November 2007 since the use of music was determined to be a form of emotional doping that had measurable molecular effects (Nowotny and Testa, 2010). Similarly, cutting-edge training techniques and equipment (e.g., titanium tennis racquets, heated skate blades) that are not equally accessible to all athletes are widely accepted enhancements (Simon, 2004; Trothen, 2009, 2011; WADA, 2012).

Technoscience developments are making more visible genetic anomalies that give some athletes a clear advantage. In the 1960s, Finnish cross-country skiing gold medalist Eero Mantyranla had a significant edge over his opponents due to a genetic anomaly that allowed him to absorb increased amounts of oxygen (Aschwanden, 2000; McCrory, 2003). More recently, runner Caster Semenya's gold medal at the 2009 International Association of Athletics Federations (IAAF) World Championships was contested on the grounds that she was too masculine; indeed genetic testing found Semenya to be intersexed.[2] Gold medalist swimmer Michael Phelps also has several genetic anomalies that arguably give him a competitive edge (Dvorsky, 2008).

If the main objective behind assessing some enhancements as unacceptable or cheating is to ensure fairness in sporting competition, then would it not be fairer to equalize, as far as technoscience allows, these inequalities? Yet, as Nowotny and Testa conclude, "the more that equality turns out to be a fiction, the more it seems necessary to cling to it" (2010: 20). The persistence of the notion of a meritocracy in sport, I propose, has to do more with hope and meaning than any rational conviction of equal starting points. Thus, attempts to explain or justify such resistance that rely on a clear-cut dividing line between acceptable and unacceptable enhancements fail to be persuasive. Further, as I will argue, the seeming refusal to let go of this belief is connected to a need for human diversity and relational transcendence.

The concept of a pure meritocracy seems to presume or desire a starting point of (normal) sameness. However, it may presume instead a wish for equity (but not necessarily a willingness to pay the costs) and not necessarily sameness. The recent super swimsuit case demonstrates that sameness and performance are not necessarily the most prized elements of elite sports competitions; rather skill, merit and continuity with past competitions would seem to be most valued (Partridge, 2011). Sometimes called doping on a hangar, these polyurethane-based swim suits such as Speedo's LZR Racer (as worn by multi-Olympic-gold-medalist Michael Phelps), the Arena X-Glide and the Jaked 01 have been found to significantly reduce competition swim times, creating more than 160 new records before the sport's governing body FINA banned them in early 2010.[3] The suits were judged by FINA to give competitors an unfair advantage, prompting reflection on how much technology is too much. It has been argued that the problem is really one of distributive justice and could be resolved by simply providing the same super swimsuit to all competitors (see Partridge, 2011). Aside from the difficult logistics of implementing this, equal access to a super swimsuit would not solve the problem of a pronounced discontinuity with previous competitors' times. Of course, there is a degree of chronological discontinuity in almost every sport due to developing training techniques, equipment and other enhancements. And there have long been discrepancies between resources and genetics possessed by individual athletes and countries. It seems that it is acceptable to have advantages so long as they are not intentional, unduly visible or disruptive of the status quo. Sufficient difference is valued as sports competition is seen largely as being between persons (thus, neither always predictable nor fully controllable) and not simply technologically driven performances (Simon, 2001). The latter usually fail to give inspiration and hope. Difference is necessary and desired in sport, but only to a certain extent.

Threaded throughout these issues are ontological and theological questions about what it means to be human and the degree, if any, to which technoscience can or should alter this condition. Philosophers Hubert Dreyfuss and Sean Dorrance Kelly (2011: 192) write about the struggle in the Western world to find meaning and hope—the "shining"—in a secular and technological age. With concern, they observe that "sports may be the place in contemporary life where Americans find sacred community most easily. . . . [a] great athlete can shine like a Greek god, and . . . in the presence of such an athlete the sense of greatness is palpable." Psychology professor Mihaly Csikszentmihalyi echoes this view (1975, 1979). Their concern has to do with the challenge of discerning what to do with that 'shining' energy that is sometimes created in sport; there is no one clearly accepted set of moral actions in contemporary society. Technology has ambiguous implications in this context: it has improved lives in many ways but has also made meaning much more difficult to find (Dreyfuss and Kelly, 2011). If sport is indeed filling that void—that sense of the shining—then the increasing intersection of sport and technoscience is creating challenges that go far beyond the mere surface problematic of what should or should not be against the rules. The questions of what makes one human and a virtuous human are unclear, and energy generated in subjectively experienced sacred communities has the potential to be actualized in dramatically different ways.

TECHNOSCIENCE ENHANCEMENT THROUGH THE LENS OF TRANSCENDENCE: REDEFINING THE ISSUE

After studying world religions, religious studies scholar Lawrence W. Fagg (2003) concludes that transcendence as a theological concept related to embodied experiences of the sacred is part of most of these religious traditions. Sport, as a way of being religious is, for some, no different. Yet the actual term *transcendence*, in religious studies scholar A. Whitney Sanford's experience, is not often used by others in his sport: U.S. whitewater kayaking. He surmises that the reason behind the anecdotal preference for Asian or First Nations terms such as mindfulness, Zen or flow instead of transcendence is protest: "their language is a form of opposition to traditional Western norms [specifically Christian or Jewish] of what constitutes religious experience" particularly since these dominant discourses have "emphasized experiencing the divine as transcendent rather than as immanent within the material realm" (2007: 879).

This conflation of transcendence with a hierarchical, distant and exterior God implies and emerges from a disturbing view of difference as "antithetical to close relationships." Accordingly, Latina theologian Mayra Rivera (2007: x) asks:

What would divine transcendence look like if we revised our conceptions of difference? What if we no longer assumed that difference entails separation? What if transcendence were not understood as that which radically distances God from creatures, but rather as a theological concept that makes difference significant, especially our differences from one another?

These are significant questions in the context of sport. Somewhat paradoxically sport relies on human difference (otherwise all competitions arguably would be draws) and yet there is a persistent popular belief in a pure meritocracy that mitigates the use of some enhancements. Difference and Otherness have long posed challenges for humanity. The belief that a meritocracy exists in sporting contexts prevents justice through a concomitant refusal to see significant systemic inequities and differences; the dominant is perceived as normative (see Hargreaves, 2001). There can be little critical examination of the values that undergird epistemological categorizations and embracing of the stranger without first seeing these inequities and differences; the invisible must become visible to a degree that these differences can no longer be ignored. But this increased visibility disrupts normative epistemological and power distribution categories and therefore generates resistance. Difference is acceptable and even desirable in sport, but only to a certain extent.

The theological concept of transcendence reconfigures the intersection of technoscience enhancement and sport. Transcendence is critical to the present discussion in two ways: first, as God's holy Otherness and, second, in terms of what is called 'flow,' 'the zone' or for spectators the wave. The metaphor of a magnifying glass or hand lens will assist in exploring these two dimensions. The transcendence of God's Otherness might be approached, through an understanding of God's Spirit alive in people and creation, as looking through a magnifying glass and seeing surprising detail and vibrant color. The latter dimension of transcendence might be considered as looking back at the one gazing through the magnifying glass: a very large blurred eye that is deeply arrested by what is being beheld.

This metaphor does not correspond well with understandings of God as transcendent and therefore distant, exterior to and apart from humanity and the world. Understood in this way, God may not even be discernable through a magnifying glass let alone as the magnifying agent. Although God has been understood to self-reveal both in general ways and in the particular form of Holy Scripture (Migliore, 2004), access to God has often been seen as restricted. The limitations of these glimpses of God we experience through each other and the world around us are emphasized in this view. God's immanence, although important, is seen as the scruffy underside of God's transcendence. In turn, God's transcendence tends to be elevated over God's immanence as the more divine dimension. Further, as many womanist, feminist, mujerista and other liberation theologians with a concern for women's well-being have identified, women and nature tend to be associated with the immanent as representatives of the mutable and dangerous (see, for example, Townes, 1997; Ruether, 1983; and Aquino, 1993). Embodiment and sexuality have been associated with women as the carnal side of humanity that must be kept under tight control. In short, immanence has often been seen as the opposite of transcendence. Prominent normative theologians such as, and perhaps most notably, Karl Barth have been insistent that God's transcendent nature separates God from sinful creation while God's grace maintains this covenant relationship. This binary approach to God's revelation has troubled many theologians including twentieth-century Jurgen Moltmann.

Refusing to elevate God's transcendence at the expense of God's immanence, Moltmann (1985, 1992) proposed not a dialectical relationship between immanence and transcendence, but an immanent transcendence and a transcendent immanence. Linking the human spirit with God's Spirit, Moltmann (1992: 7) argues that "because God's Spirit is present in human beings, the human spirit is self-transcendently aligned towards God. Anyone who stylizes revelation and experience into alternatives, ends up with revelations that cannot be experienced, and experiences without revelation." Rejecting the sacred–profane bifurcation, Moltmann (1992) understood God to be in, of and more than all of creation. He (1992: 37–38) goes on to contend that there can be no "cleavage" or "disjunction" neither among humans nor between humans and creation. This insistence on the interconnection and interdependence of all life emerges from Moltmann's conviction that God's Spirit is present in all aspects of creation waiting for us to respond as our awareness of this pervasive and intimate connection is realized.

Following Moltmann, liberationist and particularly feminist theologians have constructed important alternative understandings of the nature of God and God's revelatory nature. For example, ethicist Grace D. Cumming Long (1993: 15–17) proposes the communal justice-centered norm of "transcending creativity." Rather than accepting a traditional male-centered Euro-North American conceptualization of transcendence as "world-escaping," she redefines transcendence as an "ascending spirit suggest[ing] the power of life of the heart of the people."[4] Simon Robinson (2007: 56–57) proposes a similar understanding of transcendence as experienced particularly in sport: "Transcendence involves a 'going beyond' or a 'reaching-out,' but this doesn't mean a separation, or an escape—but rather an engagement . . . [It] is potentially transformative, in the finding of new meaning." Sport, as any other activity engaged in by humans, is neither profane nor sacred in and of itself. In this view, sport holds the potential for human realization of the presence of God's Spirit, but this realization is not always met. The question of how to discern a revelatory experience of God in sport is part of what a renewed feminist theology of transcendence can begin to illuminate.

Rivera (2007: 54) has recently suggested a systematic theology based on a starting point of "the irreducibility of other human beings . . . see[ing]" them as 'ineffable likenesses of God.'" Instead of refuting a transcendent/immanent binary, vis-à-vis Moltmann, she goes a step further and through her understanding of transcendence as profoundly relational—"an ethical opening of the self to the Other" (2007: 25)—sees no need to include the concept of immanence as a particular component in a systematic theology; transcendence is located among all diverse life. For Rivera, a "multiple relational model of transcendence-within . . . acknowledges and grapples with the multiplicity within the radical singularity of each person as well as the multiplicity of relations between subjects" (100).[5] Further, "God is thus seen as that multiple singularity that joins together all creatures—creatures that are themselves irreducible in the infinite multiplicity of their own singularity" (137). This interconnection is very different from a desire for sameness in which one way of being is elevated over and above others as normal and therefore best. Rather, a relational transcendence involves a genuine desire and openness to meet the Other, who can never be fully and completely "grasped" but can be "touched." To touch, but not grasp or try to pin down, means trying not to impose preconceived notions or categories on the Other, knowing that we can never fully transcend this temptation but can approach it with God's grace (Rivera, 2007).

Similarly to Cumming Long (1993), Rivera (2007) sees God's transcendence as that which can be brought more fully into life through human responsiveness. Rivera (2007: 81) posits a relational transcendence that flows out of the recognition of God as "irreducibly" but, countering Levinas's tendency to exteriority, not "absolutely" Other. Thus, God's multiplicity is not reduced to exteriority or to a singularity that is built on the shared values of a powerful few (Kurzweil, 2005). Rather, God's transcendence arises out of all creation beckoning our responsive engagement with all others and creation.

This interconnection and interdependence of all life is understood by several theologians as core to theologies of transcendence (see, for example, Moltmann, 1985, 1992; Rivera, 2007; Dickey Young, 2002). Such an understanding demands ongoing transformation as one engages more fully with the rest of creation. This transformation includes the political sphere of policy (including sports policies) and other social justice expressions. For example, building on process theology's panentheistic understanding of God as God in and more than the world, theologian Dickey Young connects transcendence to transformation at a political and epistemological level: "The fact that we can envisage the possible but not yet here allows us not only to build ideas of a different social and political world, but also to transcend the traditional categories of philosophical and theological thought, to re-think old categories and invent new ones" (2002: 45). Indeed, a theology of transcendence that destabilizes the immanent–transcendent and profane–scared binaries recasts the meaning of relationship and the discernment of God's Spirit; as through a magnifying glass, the world can become much more colorful, vibrant and challenging as the Other is seen in more authentic and wondrous detail.

A theology of relational transcendence has ethical implications that go far beyond how we engage with sport, but sport presents an important case particularly insofar as it functions as a religion or as a way of experiencing the sacred for many of its diverse followers. In the following section, the application of this theology is considered through two elite sports cases. Before proceeding to that application, it is important to consider what I call the second dimension of transcendence in sport. This concerns not a deliberate choice regarding relational engagement, but the powerful energy that can be generated both by athletes internally and communal gatherings of impassioned fans.

Turning the magnifying glass around, we see the blurred larger-than-life eye. This distorted eye provides a limited window into the ecstatic experience of the wave or a sense of flow. Dreyfuss and Kelly (2011) have referred to these experiences as life's shining moments; moments in which a sense of (or, in Rivera's words, a wondrous touch of) the transcendent sacred *can* be experienced in a particularly exciting way. Flow in sport has been linked to spirituality (e.g., Watson and Nesti, 2005; Dillon and Tait, 2000).[6] Csikszentmihalyi's (1975) research led him to conclude that for athletes flow occurs most often during those times when skill level is commensurate with the challenge and when the performer is fully engaged and distracted neither by anxiety nor overthinking. In such instances athletes describe making the right moves with their bodies "almost automatically" (Csikszentmihalyi, 1979: 260; see also Dreyfuss and Kelly, 2011), and with a paradoxical sense of ease (Kelly, 2011). These experiences are temporary and dynamic but very powerful (Csikszentmihalyi, 1979). For the spectator, moments of flow or the wave can be described as a wellspring of power connected to a communal experience that some interpret as being of the sacred.

Similar to a theology of relational transcendence, flow is characterized (at least in part) by a deep awareness of oneness or connection to all. During moments of flow, the individual ego is no longer important: "some people describe it as a transcendence, as a merging with the environment, as a union with the activity or with the process" (Csikszentmihalyi, 1979: 261); a sense of being "a part of something larger than oneself" often is experienced (Kelly, 2011: 167; see also Jackson and Csikszentmihalyi, 1999; Watson and Nesti, 2005). Yet, how one interprets this sense of connectedness and what one decides to do or not do in response to it are not assured (Csikszentmihalyi, 1979; Dreyfuss and Kelly, 2011) and depend, in large part, upon one's values and faith perspective. Flow experiences are not all theologically transcendent, and it is important to attempt to distinguish between adrenaline-induced excitement and that inspired by the Holy Spirit (Higgs and Braswell, 2004; Watson, 2007). Csikszentmihalyi (1979) and Dreyfuss and Kelly (2011), respectively, insist that although flow may feel exterior and powerful, one always has the ability to control flow experiences (Csikszentmihalyi, 1979) or "retrain our desires" (Drey-fuss and Kelly, 2011: 119) so that our responses reflect what is meaningful and shining or sacred to us. Assuming responsibility does not denigrate the power of flow, but rather upholds the experience of oneness through the recognition that autonomy is relational; interdependence refutes an extreme individualism and demands a communal responsibility to self and Other.

When flow or shining experiences lead to destruction and harm of the Other, the sacred potential is crushed. The 2011 riots on the streets of Vancouver following the Vancouver Canuck's loss to the Boston Bruins in the seventh game of the 2011 National Hockey League Stanley Cup finals are one example of the destructive potential of this shining energy.[7] On the other hand, this energy can invigorate and draw one to recognize the sacred in the Other. For example, the times when elite athletes have assisted a competitor in the midst of what is usually cutthroat competition, or the widespread regard for figure skater Joannie Rochette's resilient bronze medal performance at the 2010 Winter Olympics, a performance that she dedicated to her mother, who had died at the beginning of the Games.[8] These moments challenge the conflation of success with winning through the valuing and prioritizing of relational triumphs arising out of recognition of the Other's wondrous colors.

As will become clear, technoscience is amplifying the consequences of how we choose to manifest this shining energy associated with sport. Both fans and athletes experience this surge of power periodically and have choices to make regarding its meaning. If normative societal values remain unexamined we choose a wave shaped by the status quo. In the following section, we consider briefly two cases concerning technological enhancement and athletes. Both are approached through an application of a feminist theology of transcendence (similar to that which is proposed by Rivera) and ask how such a theologically informed ethic might reshape the enhancement technology and sport question.

THE INVISIBLE MADE VISIBLE

Sport, as a way of being religious, is transgressive in its reclaiming and celebration of embodiment as wondrous and sometimes the purveyor of transcendent experiences. Christianity historically has devalued the body. Yet elite sports authorities often perpetuate the constraints of dominant discourse and fail to value or allow sporting discourse to be transformed by a wide diversity of bodies. A theology of relational transcendence as proposed by Rivera (2007) refuses to accept this denigration or confinement of Otherness and demands a reimagined ethic. As Dreyfuss and Kelly (2011: 175) advise, "Don't try to see what all the colors look like when they're added up. Instead, try to get into as many (revealing) moods as possible, as many ways of responding to the sacred as you can—and this life of serial resonances with the sacred is ultimately a kind of contentedness, happiness, even joy." Technology in sport heightens this possibility by making invisible difference visible or more visible. The same technology also heightens the possibility of greater marginalization of the Other and the entrenchment of an unjust normativity.

One day before the 800 meter race at the August 2009 IAAF World Championships in Berlin, it was announced that South African middle distance runner Caster Semenya would still compete since she had agreed to gender testing. Although the IOC stopped the mandatory sex testing of female athletes in 1999 (men have not been subject to such testing as it has been assumed that female competitive events are easier than those for males), they retained the right to require testing in individual cases (CBC, 2009). After winning gold in the 800 meter race, there was much speculation that Semenya would be stripped of the honor after it was rumored she had "failed" the gender tests. The tests showed that Semenya was intersexed. The IAAF then had to decide if the athlete had a natural but unfair advantage over the other competitors mainly due to a higher than average amount of "male" hormone (McNamee, 2009). Amid allegations of racism and unfair process, the IAAF eventually decided that Semenya could be legitimately categorized as a woman. This process was long and drawn out, with the subsequent formal announcement of the IAAF's findings being issued on 6 July 2010, almost one year after her win (CBC, 2009).

It is telling that Semenya's "masculine" physical appearance caused more concern than the advantages possessed by many elite athletes other glaring inequities including unequal access to approved enhancements such as cutting-edge equipment, financial support and high-caliber training. Instead of recreating (or at least questioning) the ways in which embodiment categories and Olympic competition are constructed, the issue was framed as one of rights with the conclusion that Semenya fit best into the category of woman and therefore had the *right* to compete. Issues of sex and gender identity particularly regarding human diversity and fluidity that make humans category resistant are clearly pointed to through the visibility of Semenya's particularity; should there even be separate "male" and "female" sporting competitions (Jonsson, 2007)? Semenya's differentness (as defined by normative assumptions) was tolerated and absorbed into existing categories. However, the invisible became more visible with the meaning of biological sex and gender being questioned. The inadequacy of dominant gender and sex-talk was highlighted by this increasing visibility of diversity.

A feminist theology of transcendence refuses to uphold human constructs at the expense of growing into closer relationship with each other and the divine; God breaks open and transforms limited human order. But there is choice involved. Transcendence is a relational covenantal dynamic always offered through God's grace. An inclination to preserve what has become normative at all costs resists God's transcendence. As Rivera (2007:

105) argues, "As we continue to use categories to name ourselves and others, these categories tend to appear as natural, as if they were characteristics innate to persons or to the world we live in—as if they were external to ourselves." The question of what is sacred is morally relevant to the technoscience in sport debate. Interestingly, scientists and philosophers often approach this debate with the assumption that current epistemological constructs and norms are not debatable. For example, Nowotny and Testa (2010: 49) conclude that the "question arising for society is how . . . forms of life . . . are to be integrated into the existing social order." Why not ask the question in the obverse? How can increasing revelations of difference transform or even enhance the existing social order?

What are the implications for sport if we take seriously this critique and Rivera's proposal to frame difference as wondrous with the "gleam of transcendence in the flesh of the Other" (Rivera, 2007: 138)? Categories can be helpful constructs through which we begin to make sense of the world. Categories are also both limited and limiting as all knowledge is incomplete and dynamic. A relational transcendence understands this incompleteness to invite ongoing connection with life's diversity. Semenya's case makes more visible epistemological limitations and the oppressive assumptive values that limit collective flourishing.

The second case in point is that of elite athlete Oscar Pstorius, a triple gold medal winner in the 2008 Paralympics. After a long battle, Pstorius qualified on 23 March 2011 for the 400 meter race in the 2012 "regular" Olympics (Davies, 2011). The "Bladerunner" was born without fibulae in his lower legs resulting in a double amputation when he was eleven months old. "Cheetah legs"—high-tech carbon-fiber prosthetics that, according to some experts including research commissioned by the IAAF, give him an advantage over able-bodied athletes (Jones and Wilson, 2009; UltraFuture, 2008; Sutcliffe, 2008)—have enabled Pstorius to run. In 2007 the IAAF instituted a ban on technical devices that included his prosthetics. In 2008 the Court of Arbitration for Sport subsequently overturned Pstorius's exclusion from the Olympic Games. Several scholars who have written regarding the ethics of Pstorius's case agree that it is not justifiable to exclude Pstorius on the basis of unfair advantage for reason of the subjective problematics in the enhancement debate outlined in the preceding (Edwards, 2008; Jones and Wilson, 2009; Swartz and Watermeyer, 2008; Van Hilvoorde and Landeweerd, 2008). Given this general agreement and the Court of Arbitration for Sport's decision, one may wonder why this issue of unfair advantage arising from Pstorius's use of technology only emerged when he indicated his desire to compete in the Olympics. Previously, in the context of Paralympic competition, his supposed advantage was not contested. As Swartz and Watermeyer (2008) query, is this due to a devaluing of the Paralympics? Potentially reinforcing the social marginalization of those who are disabled or differently abled is both Pstorius's strong desire and preference to participate in the Olympics and the resistance to his inclusion. Both belie a systemic devalorization of those who are defined in dominant discourse as other than 'normal.' His 'acceptance' into 'normal' competition may contribute to the further devalorization of the Paralympics and those with nonnormative bodies (Stuart, 2000).

It has been argued that Pstorius's inclusion in the Olympics violates the internal goods and parameters of elite sports competition on the basis that he is not "playing the same game as his opponents" (Van Hilvoorde and Landeweerd, 2008: 108; Edwards, 2008). Jones and Wilson (2009) have challenged further the contention that Pstorius is not playing the same game as other able-bodied runners by interrogating the specified or measurable criteria for running, concluding that this is, at best, a vague area. Further, they raise the question of who ought to be making such judgments; whose interests are served and who has the preponderance of power. As with Semenya, the Pstorius case has been framed predominantly as one of competing individual rights (Salleh, 2010). More deeply rooted questions including the interrogation of epistemological categories (e.g., what makes someone "able"-bodied or not), and valuing of these categories, have been largely avoided. As Rivera (2007: 118) charges, "We constantly fail to encounter the other as Other. Time and again we ignore or deny the singularity of the Other—we don't see even when the face stands in front of us." An additional issue arising as a consequence of the Pstorius case is the degree to which the less visibly different Other is seen or not seen in all sports competitions. By resisting norms and categories in a highly visible manner, Pstorius destabilizes order. As Nowotny and Testa note:

> Oscar Pstorius is punished for the visibility of his prostheses because he publicly displays his difference from normal competitors. . . . It is thought-provoking that a society proud of its ideal of equality sees a threat to sports precisely when technology enables a handicapped person to overtake his nonhandicapped competitors. (2010: 25)

The strong visibility of his different-ness has disrupted normative categories and with that has emerged a threat to the normative distribution of power. While competing in the Paralympics, Pstorius' differentness was fascinating but not unduly threatening; he was visibly different but located within a marginalized context that is predisposed to being more accepting of difference, at least to a point.

CONCLUDING REMARKS

The functional line used for distinguishing between enhancements that are considered good from those which are considered bad is not so much a divide between natural–artificial or exterior–interior; rather, it seems to be the point at which the status quo is disrupted beyond a degree that can be accommodated within existing normative categories and related values.

Difference is good but only to a certain extent. Technoscience innovations in sport threaten the status quo through making visible existing different-ness and creating more differentness. The religious-like dimension of sport that includes a sense of transcendence holds potential for invigorating this tension. A sense of this transcendence is consistent with Castor Semenya's statement regarding her gender test results to South Africa's popular *You* magazine: "God made me the way I am and I accept myself. I am who I am and I'm proud of myself" (*Telegraph*, 2009). Could it be that it is only through the recognition of the holy in the authentic difference of the Other that we can be enlivened and begin to touch divine right relationship? Indeed, athletic competition would hold little meaning and wonder were it not for the remarkable differences caused by genetic anomalies, chromosomal distinc-tions, yet to be determined differences in perceptions or drive and training conditions, among other factors. As Dreyfuss and Kelly (2011: 174) point out, the "multiple meanings of the universe simply don't add up to a single, universal truth. Our only hope is to engage in each of them fully, live con-tentedly in the truths they reveal, but feel no urge to reconcile them to one another." The differences that ought to be distressing are those of our own making through the imposition of systemic values that reduce the value of the Other. If difference was looked upon not as a problem, but as wondrous and amazing, epistemological categories would likely continue to be used but would be regarded as limited, contextual and responsive to the Other. Normative values that privilege some at the expense of others would become more visible and less desirable. Dreams and hopes would change and change again. Instead of searching for a pure and natural normatively defined athlete the search would be for the next glimpse of the irreducible Other.

The intersection of technoscience, elite sport and religion has ambigu-ous implications. On the one hand, this convergence promises to intensify a need to cling to normative constructions. But, on the other, it has the potential to prompt a greater interrogation of values and norms such that the dominant sociocultural order is queried more collectively and critically (Trothen, 2011). The intersection of sport as a religion (that can generate a potentially relational, life-invigorating sense of transcendence connected to the Spirit) with technoscience enhancements (that foster visible difference) has the liberatory potential to destabilize existing order, creating new and more redemptive relational possibilities. This intersection has the potential to evoke a relational transcendence in which hospitable relationships with the diverse Other become more pervasively desired and valued. As theolo-gian Andrew Davey (2002: 85–86) has stated:

> The imagination of faith refuses to be content with human arrange-ments—social, economic, political, urban, rural—that are not based on the practice of human freedom in the presence of God. That imagi-nation will pertinently challenge those arrangements through prophetic speech and action, through the creation of communities that include, strengthen, and give integrity to those at the margins.

NOTES

1. A grant from the Queen's University Senate Advisory Research Council helped to make the research and writing of this chapter possible.
2. "Intersex," as explained by the Intersex Society of North America (ISNA), "is a general term used for a variety of conditions in which a person is born with a reproductive or sexual anatomy that doesn't seem to fit the typical definitions of female or male" (ISNA, 2008).
3. FINA voted 168–6 to ban "all but textile-based suits" in August 2009.
4. Cumming Long (1993, 17) extends her proposal to the question of what it means to be authentically human: "To be created in the image of a creating and transcending God is to be free to create a life that transcends barriers to our full humanity."
5. It is interesting to note that futurist Ray Kurzweil also writes about singularity but with a dramatically different meaning. Well known for his celebration of technological enhancements, Kurzweil argues that an age he calls the "Singularity" is near; the "Singularity will represent the culmination of our biological thinking and existence with our technology, resulting in a world that is still human but that transcends our biological roots. There will be no distinction, post-Singularity, between human and machine or between physical and virtual reality. . . . Although the Singularity has many faces, its most important implication is this: our technology will match and then vastly exceed the refinement and suppleness of what we regard as the best of human traits" (Kurzweil 2005, 9). Although he claims that respect for diversity is important (424), Kurzweil knows that values are not universal and that values will drive the direction of technology. Further, technological enhancements will affect all of humanity. Therefore, it seems clear that the powerful will make the decisions regarding what are the "best of human traits" and increase or enhance these while "fixing" or removing those traits considered undesirable at that point in time. As a result, once again diversity is respected only insofar as it does not disrupt the status quo. For more discussion on transhumanism and sport, see Trothen (2011).
6. Flow is restricted neither to athletes nor sport but can also be experienced by spectators and through other activities that hold similar features.
7. On the night of Wednesday 15 June 2011, the Vancouver Canucks lost the final game of the National Hockey League's Stanley Cup championships to the Boston Bruins. Vancouver fans and possibly others rioted in the streets of downtown Vancouver. There was much destruction of property and numerous people were injured. Over one hundred people were arrested (CBC, 2011).
8. As reporter Erin Valois (2012) in the *National Post* wrote two years after her bronze medal performance, Joannie Rochette's "performance at the Pacific Coliseum is considered one of the greatest moments from the 2010 Games and she was named Canada's flag-bearer for the Closing Ceremony."

BIBLIOGRAPHY

Aquino, M. P. (1993) *Our Cry for Life—Feminist Theology from Latin America*, Maryknoll, NY: Orbis Books.
Aschwanden, C. (2000) Gene Cheats, *New Scientist*, 165 (2221): 24–29.
CBC. (2009) South African Runner Semenya a Hermaphrodite, CBC Online. Available online at http://www.cbc.ca/sports/amateur/story/2009/09/10/sp-iaaf-athletics-semenya.html (accessed 27 February 2012).

CBC. (2011) Riots erupt in Vancouver after Canuck's Loss, CBC Online. Available online at http://www.cbc.ca/news/canada/british-columbia/story/2011/06/15/bc-stanley-cup-fans-post-game-7.html (accessed 26 February 2012).

Csikszentmihalyi, M. (1975) *Beyond Boredom and Anxiety*, San Francisco, CA: Jossey-Bass.

Csikszentmihalyi, M. (1979) The Concept of Flow, in B. Sutton-Smith (Ed.), *Play and Learning*, New York: Gardner Press, 257–74.

Cumming Long, G. D. (1993) *Passion and Reason—Womenviews of Christian Life*, Kentucky: Westminster/John Knox Press.

Davey, A. (2002) *Urban Christianity and Global Order: Theological Resources for an Urban Future*, Peabody, MA: Hendrickson Pub.

Davies, G. A. (2011) London 2012 Olympics: Double Amputee Oscar Pistorius Makes 400m Qualifying Time, London Telegraph Online. Available online at www.telegraph.co.uk/sport/othersports/olympics/8403343/London-2012–Olympics-double-amputee-Oscar-Pistorius-makes-400m-qualifying-time.html (accessed 30 October 2011).

Dickey Young, P. (2002) The Resurrection of the Body? A Feminist Look at the Question of Transcendence, *Feminist Theology*, 30 (5): 44–51.

Dillon, K. M. and Tait, J. L. (2000) Spirituality and Being in the Zone in Team Sports: A Relationship? *Journal of Sport Behavior*, 23 (2): 91–100.

Dreyfuss, H. and Kelly, S. D. (2011) *All Things Shining—Reading the Western Classics to Find Meaning in a Secular Age*, New York: Free Press.

Dvorsky, G. (2008) Michael Phelps: 'Naturally' Transhuman, The Institute for Ethics and Emerging Technologies Online. Available online at http://ieet.org/index.php/IEET/print/2575/ (accessed 8 September 2011).

Edwards, L. and Jones, C. (2009) Postmodernism, Queer Theory and Moral Judgment in Sport, *International Review for the Sociology of Sport*, 44 (4): 331–44.

Edwards, S. D. (2008) Should Oscar Pistorius Be Excluded from the 2008 Olympic Games? *Sport, Ethics and Philosophy*, 2 (2): 112–25.

Fagg, L. W. (2003) Are There Intimations of Divine Transcendence in the Physical World? *Zygon*, 38 (3): 559–72.

Hargreaves, J. A. (2001) *Heroines of Sport*, London: Routledge.

Higgs, R. J. and Braswell, M. C. (2004) *An Unholy Alliance: The Sacred and Modern Sports*, Macon, GA: Mercer University Press.

Hoppenstand, G. (2003) Inaugural Editorial, *Journal of Popular Culture*, 37 (1): 1–6.

Intersex Society of North America. (2008) What Is Intersex? Available online at http://www.isna.org/faq/what_is_intersex (accessed 26 February 2012).

Jackson, S. and Csikszentmihalyi, M. (1999) *Flow in Sports: The Keys to Optimal Experiences and Performance*, Champaign, IL: Human Kinetics.

Jones, C. and Wilson, C. (2009) Defining Advantage and Athletic Performance: The Case of Oscar Pistorius, *European Journal of Sport Science*, 9 (2): 125–31.

Jonsson, K. (2007) Who's Afraid of Stella Walsh? On Gender, 'Gene Cheaters,' and the Promise of Cyborg Athletes, *Sport, Ethics and Philosophy*, 1 (2): 239–62.

Kelly, P. (2011) Flow, Sport and the Spiritual Life, in J. Parry, M. Nesti and N. Watson (Eds.), *Theology, Ethics and Transcendence in Sports*, London: Routledge, 163–77.

Kurzweil, R. (2005) *The Singularity Is Near—When Humans Transcend Biology*, New York: Penguin Books.

Ladd, T. and Mathisen, J. A. (1999) *Muscular Christianity—Evangelical Protestants and the Development of American Sport*, Grand Rapids, MI: Baker Books.

Lynch, G. (2007) What Is This 'Religion' in the Study of Religion and Popular Culture? in G. Lynch (Ed.), *Between Sacred and Profane—Researching Religion and Popular Culture*, London: I. B. Tauris, 125–42.

Mathisen, J. (1992) From Civil Religion to Folk Religion: The Case of American Sport, in S. J. Hoffman (Ed.), *Sport and Religion*, Champaign, IL: Human Kinetics Books, 17–33.

McCrory, P. (2003) Super Athletes or Gene Cheats? *British Journal of Sports Medicine*, 37 (3): 192–93.

McNamee, M. (2009). On Being 'Probably Slightly on the Wrong Side of the Cheating Thing,' *Sport, Ethics and Philosophy*, 3 (3): 283–85.

Miah, A. (2005) *Genetically Modified Athletes: Biomedical Ethics, Gene Doping, and Sport*, New York: Routledge.

Migliore, D. L. (2004) *Faith Seeking Understanding—An Introduction to Christian Theology*, 2nd ed., Grand Rapids, Michigan, USA:William B. Eerdmans Pub Co.

Moltmann, J. (1985) *God in Creation—A New Theology of Creation and the Spirit of God*, trans. Margaret Kohl, San Francisco, CA: Harper and Row Publishers.

Moltmann, J. (1992) *The Spirit of Life—A Universal Affirmation*, trans. Margaret Kohl, Minneapolis, MN: Fortress Press.

Novak, M. (1993) The Joy of Sports, in C. S. Prebish (Ed.), *Religion and Sport—The Meeting of Sacred and Profane*, Westport, CT: Greenwood Press, 151–72.

Nowotny, H. and Testa, G. (2010) *Naked Genes—Reinventing the Human in the Molecular Age*, trans. Mitch Cohen, Cambridge, MA: MIT Press.

Overman, S. J. (1997) *The Influence of the Protestant Ethic on Sport and Recreation*, Aldershot: Ashgate Publishing Company.

Partridge, B. (2011) Fairness and Performance-Enhancing Swimsuits at the 2009 Swimming World Championships: The 'Asterisk' Championships, *Sport, Ethics and Philosophy*, 5 (1): 63–74.

Prebish, C. S. (ed.) (1993) *Religion and Sport—The Meeting of Sacred and Profane*, Westport, CT: Greenwood Press.

Price, J. (2001) *From Season to Season: Sport as American Religion*, Macon, GA: Mercer University Press.

Rivera, M. (2007) *The Touch of Transcendence*, London: Westminster John Knox Press.

Robinson, S. (2007) The Spiritual Journey, in J. Parry, S. Robinson, N. Watson and M. Nesti (Eds.), *Sport and Spirituality: An Introduction*, London: Routledge, 38–58.

Ruether, R. R. (1983) *Sexism and God-Talk*, Boston: Beacon Press.

Salleh, A. (2010) Cyborg Rights 'Need Debating Now,' ABC Science Online. Available online at www.abc.net.au/science/articles/2010/06/04/2916443.htm (accessed 6 September 2011).

Sanford, A. W. (2007) Pinned on Karma Rock: Whitewater Kayaking as Religious Experience, *Journal of the American Academy of Religion*, 75 (4): 875–95.

Simon, R. L. (2001) Good Competition and Drug-Enhanced Performance in Ethics, in W. J. Morgan, K. V. Meier and A. J. Schneider (Eds.), *Sport*, Champaign, IL: Human Kinetics, 119–29.

Simon, R. L. (2004) *Fair Play—The Ethics of Sport*, 2nd ed., Boulder, CO: Westview Press.

Sinclair-Faulkner, T. (1977) A Puckish Reflection on Religion in Canada, in P. Slater (Ed.), *Religion and Culture in Canada/Religion et Culture au Canada*, Ottawa: Corporation Canadienne des Sciences Religieuses/Canadian Corporation for Studies in Religion, 383–405.

Stuart, E. (2000) Disruptive Bodies: Disability, Embodiment and Sexuality, in L. Isherwood (Ed.), *The Good News of the Body—Sexual Theology and Feminism*, New York: New York University Press, 166–84.

Sutcliffe, M. (2008) Amputee Sprinter Treads Uneven Track, The Ottawa Citizen Online. Available online at http://www2.canada.com (accessed 15 August 2011).

Swartz, L. and Watermeyer, B. (2008) Cyborg Anxiety: Oscar Pistorius and the Boundaries of What It Means to Be Human, *Disability & Society*, 23 (2): 187–90.

Telegraph. (2009) Caster Semenya Says Gender Debate Is 'a Joke' after Having Makeover Back Home. Available online at http://www.telegraph.co.uk/sport/othersports/athletics/6156656/Caster-Semenya-says-gender-debate-is-a-joke-after-having-makeover-back-home.html (accessed 27 February 2012).

Townes, E. (ed.) (1997) *Embracing the Spirit—Womanist Perspectives on Hope, Salvation and Transformation*, Maryknoll, NY: Orbis Books.

Trothen, T. J. (2006) Hockey: A Divine Sport?—Canada's National Sport in Relation to Embodiment, Community, and Hope, *Studies in Religion/Sciences Religieuses*, 35 (2): 291–305.

Trothen, T. J. (2008) Redefining Human, Redefining Sport: The Imago Dei and Genetic Modification Technologies, in D. Deardoff II and J. White (Eds.), *The Image of God in the Human Body: Essays on Christianity and Sports*, New York: Edwin Mellen Press, 217–34.

Trothen, T. J. (2009) Sport, Religion, and Genetic Modification: An Ethical Analysis of Gene Doping, *International Journal of Religion and Sport*, 1: 1–20.

Trothen, T. J. (2011) Better than Normal?—Constructing Genetically Modified Athletes and a Relational Theological Ethic, in J. Parry, M. Nesti and N. Watson (Eds.), *Theology, Ethics and Transcendence in Sports*, New York: Routledge, Taylor and Francis, 64–81.

UltraFuture. (2008) Transhumanism and the Olympics, UltraFuture Online. Available online at http://ultrafuture.com/2008/05/19/transhumanism-and-the-olympics/ (accessed 8 August 2011).

Valois, E. (2012) Unplugged: Figure Skater Joannie Rochette on Life after the Olympics, National Post Sports Online. Available online at http://sports.nationalpost.com/2012/02/24/unplugged-figure-skater-joannie-rochette-on-life-after-the-olympics/ (accessed 26 February 2012).

Van Hilvoorde, I. and Landeweerd, L. (2008) Disability or Extraordinary Talent—Francesco Lentini (Three Legs) versus Oscar Pistorius (No Legs), *Sport, Ethics and Philosophy*, 2 (2): 97–111.

Watson, N. J. and Nesti, M. (2005) The Role of Spirituality in Sport Psychology Consulting: An Analysis and Integrative Review of Literature, *Journal of Applied Sport Psychology*, 17 (3): 228–39.

Watson, N. J. (2007) Nature and Transcendence—The Mystical and Sublime in Extreme Sports, in J. Parry, S. Robinson, N. J. Watson and M. Nesti (Eds.), *Sport and Spirituality—An Introduction*, New York: Routledge, Taylor and France, 95–115.

World Anti-Doping Agency. (2012) WADA Play True. Available online at http://www.wada-ama.org/ (accessed 26 February 2012).

8 The Quest for Perfection in the Sport of Baseball
The Magnanimous Individual or the Magnanimous Team?

Jacob L. Goodson

> *Human friendship, too, is sweet in its precious bond because it makes many souls one.*
>
> St. Augustine (1992)

INTRODUCTION

In this chapter, I offer a virtue-centered approach for making judgments on the use of steroids within Major League Baseball in the U.S.[1] Ancient virtue theorists, such as Aristotle, develop a heroic account of the virtuous life where the goal is to become "a magnanimous man" that does not rely on anyone else for the activities and skills involved in their enjoyment of magnanimity. Reacting against this heroic notion of magnanimity, because it downplays equality within the moral life, modern virtue theorists tend to "level the playing field" in order to make it possible for any and everyone to achieve excellence. When it comes to considering the possibility for excellence and perfection within the sport of baseball, I argue that neither individual magnanimity nor the modern concerns of magnanimity provides us with the best description for what baseball players achieve in regards to the activities and skills involved within the game of baseball. I construct a notion of team magnanimity based on charity and friendship that provides a way forward for thinking about excellence and perfection within Major League Baseball.

Why do we need a way forward, right now, for thinking about excellence and perfection within American professional baseball? Because baseball has become overdetermined by performance-enhancing drugs (PEDs) to the extent that excellence and perfection are measured in relation to the use of steroids, rather than the skills and virtues that the game nurtures and requires. Blame goes all around. By relying on steroids, and the deception that accompanies it, baseball players have failed the game that makes their achievements possible. Major League Baseball, as an institution, has failed the players and fans by not offering moral descriptions and proper narratives of the game they love and promote. The sports media invented the language of the "steroid era" in professional baseball. Such language discourages making careful distinctions concerning the quest for perfection, and it distracts from investigations into the nature and purpose of baseball. Lastly, fans blindly bought into the message of the sports media. Following the inventions of the media, fans have been led either to falling into despair and skepticism concerning the institution and sport of baseball or to the tendency of displaying an "anything goes" mentality where steroid use becomes justified—perhaps even expected—because it makes the game more fun to watch. This reasoning remains unsound and reveals a complete lack of imagination, on the part of fans, concerning an appreciation for how the activity of baseball exhibits certain virtues in more interesting ways than other activities require—such as the prudence involved in knowing when, how and where to make a sacrificial bunt (which will be defined later in the chapter).

I challenge the now common assumption that baseball ought to be narrated by steroids. I show how a virtue-centered account of baseball supplies a different way—different from the institution, the sports media and the expectations of fans—of understanding the nature and purpose of the game.[2] I supply ways to make moral judgments on those baseball players who used steroids on their quest for perfection, and I suggest an alternate account of what the quest for perfection looks like within the sport of baseball.

MORAL AND THEOLOGICAL QUESTIONS

In his book *Babies by Design*, Ronald Green (2007) takes on the reasoning of three ethicists: Leon Kass, Paul Ramsey and Michael Sandel. Green argues that all three of these thinkers maintain a 'status quo' reasoning by painting a strictly 'negative' picture of a future determined by medial advancements and technological enhancements. Green counters the descriptions of Kass, Ramsey and Sandel by offering his own 'positive' picture of a future determined by medical advancements and technological enhancements. His book contains a chapter dedicated to the problem of 'playing God,' addressing Ramsey's specifically religious concerns with a world determined by medical and technological research. Additionally, his book offers a chapter on the question of 'creating the superathlete,' countering Kass's and Sandel's concerns of the effects PEDs have on the nature and purpose of sport.

Green quotes Ramsey's famous line from his 1970 book *Fabricated Man*: 'Men ought not to play God before they learn to be men, and after they have learned to be men they will not play God' (1970: 138).[3] For Ramsey, the quest for perfection is equivalent to what he calls 'questionable aspirations to Godhead' (see 1970: 138–51). Rather than seeking 'to elevate or assimilate any risk-filled, vital decision to playing a divine role,' we should be 'asking the critical questions about the meaning of men's *creaturely* responsibilities as [human beings] or the real role of medicine and technology as a human enterprise *serving* human life' (1970: 138). There are two important aspects to Ramsey's reasoning. First, medicine and technology ought to serve the goods of human life; human life should not be judged, or judge itself, against what medicine and technology make possible or deem normative. Ramsey laments the result of allowing medical and technological research determine and narrate our lives within ethics: 'Human virtue and righteousness are now to be re-defined in terms of biological *summum bonum*. . . . [V]ices now name those human attitudes that hinder chosen biological projects and render individual men worthless in the final biological assize. Anyone who does not love the absolute future of man's self-creation with all his heart and soul and mind and strength cannot be judged virtuous in any respect' (1970: 145). Our lives do not have to be determined and narrated by medicine and technology; rather, medicine and technology ought to be used strictly in service to the goods of human life.

Second, Ramsey's proper theological concern is that there is profound significance to being human—to being creaturely. This significance is lost, at least to some degree, when humans seek to be more than human—that is, when humans attempt to overcome their finitude and limitations. What does learning to be human require for Ramsey? He claims: 'We ought rather to live with charity amid the limits of a biological and historical existence which God created for the good and simple reason that, for all its corruption, it is now—and for the temporal future will be—the good realm in which man and his welfare are to be found and served' (1970: 149). For Ramsey, our finitude and limitations are gifts deserving appreciation; they are not problems to be overcome. Therefore, learning to be human is learning to appreciate the gifts of finitude and limitations. However, within Ramsey's moral reasoning, the question remains: does any attempt for excellence or perfection equal an attempt to overcome our humanity?[4]

Within the particular context of sports, Kass and Sandel claim that the problem with PEDs is not so much the health risks that they may or may not have for athletes—as suggested by others.[5] Rather, the problem is that they change—for the worse—the nature and purpose of sport. Sandel makes his concern quite explicit:

> The real problem with genetically altered athletes is that they corrupt athletic competition as a human activity that honors the cultivation and display of natural talents. From this standpoint, enhancement can be seen as the ultimate expression of the ethic of effort and willfulness, a kind of high-tech striving. The ethic of willingness and the biotechnological powers it now enlists are both arrayed against the claims of giftedness. (2007: 29)

Sandel gestures toward the proper response to the problem of PEDs: 'Arguments about the ethics of enhancement are always, at least in part, arguments about the telos, or point, of the sport in question, and the virtues relevant to the game' (2007: 38). He adds that while 'assessing the rules of athletic competition for their fit with the excellences essential to the sport will strike some as unduly judgmental . . . it is difficult to make sense of what we admire about sports without making some judgment about the point of the game and its relevant virtues' (2007: 42). Sandel observes, for example, that it 'is one thing to hit seventy home runs as a result of disciplined training and effort, and something else, something less, to hit them with the help of steroids or genetically enhanced muscles' (2007: 25). Continuing with this example, Sandel remarks that the 'more the athlete relies on drugs or genetic fixes, the less his performance represents his achievement' (2007: 26). Sandel concludes, therefore, that the argument about PEDs in sports requires serious thinking concerning the point 'of the sport in question' as well as 'the virtues relevant to the game' (2007: 38).

Leon Kass, acting as the head of President George W. Bush's Council on Bioethics, raises the following questions:

> What is a human *performance*, and what is an *excellent* one? And what makes it *excellent as a human performance*? For it seems that some performance-enhancing agents, from stimulants to blood doping to genetic engineering of muscles, call into question the *dignity* of the performance of those who use them. The performance seems less real, less one's own, less worthy of our admiration. Not only do such enhancing agents distort or damage other dimensions of human life . . . they also seem to distort the athletic activity itself. (2003: 160)

For Kass, then, PEDs 'distort the athletic activity' because the athletic performance that results from the use of PEDs cannot be considered 'excellent'—that is, the 'performance seems less real, less one's own, less worthy.' An 'excellent' performance requires one to fully possess the skills required as well as remaining truthful about the source of one's abilities.

While Ramsey's theological reasoning concerning the problems of the quest for perfection raise important questions, I say that not all quests for perfection are theologically problematic. Understanding excellence, as well as a version of magnanimity particular to athletics, within a description of the virtues offers ways to think constructively and nonproblematically about the quest for perfection. Additionally, Kass's and Sandel's reflections point us in the right direction for how to think about the use of PEDs within baseball. I advance the claim that we need a better and thicker description of *what* is meant by the nature and purpose of sport and *why* talk of excellence and the virtues is required for understanding sports. In order to provide such a description, I turn to Alasdair MacIntyre's definition of what constitutes a 'practice,' where I develop MacIntyre's observation that the sport of baseball exemplifies his particular definition of a practice.[6] Before turning to MacIntyre's work, further engagement with Green's book displays the significance of my claims.

RONALD GREEN'S MORAL REASONING APPLIED TO BASEBALL

In *Babies by Design*, Ronald Green offers some helpful distinctions for thinking about the use of PEDs within baseball. First, he distinguishes between somatic enhancements ('somatic cell gene enhancements') and germline enhancements ('germline genetics enhancement'). Somatic enhancements are an 'added benefit to an individual who is otherwise perfectly normal' (2007: 57). Somatic enhancements only have consequences for the individual that uses them. When professional athletes use PEDs, they usually take somatic enhancements. Germline enhancements, however, are not usually used within professional sports. Germline enhancements involve developing, implementing and introducing new genes into individuals who then pass on those genetics to their children. Germline enhancements have consequences for generations, not only for the individual, by introducing new genetic traits. According to Green, a 'special problem for germline genetic enhancement is that those who invite the risks are different from those who suffer them' (2007: 91–92). Germline enhancements, in Green's language, have the potential to create and sustain 'superathletes.' However, in Green's judgment, the generational risk that comes with sustaining superathletes is not worth it. Therefore, in Green's view, the use of somatic enhancements is justifiable within sports while taking germline enhancements remains problematic.

Following the analysis of the first distinction, the second distinction that Green makes is one between 'prevention' and 'pure enhancement.' According to Green, there is a mistaken distinction between enhancement and therapy—which is a distinction that both Kass's and Sandel's cases heavily rely upon. Green finds that 'prevention' works as an intermediate zone between therapy and enhancement (see 2007: 60). Prevention 'belongs to the realm of disease and illness, those subnormal bodily states that either cause or significantly increase our risks of suffering pain, disability, or death' (2007: 61). Prevention thus targets 'dangers' found 'in the future': 'the goal is to surpass normal levels of functioning now to prevent them from ever occurring' (2007: 61). In this way, preventions function as 'a kind of enhancement aimed at *maintaining* normalcy' (2007: 61). Because preventions are 'a kind of enhancement,' but have strictly therapeutic purposes, Green finds that the distinction between enhancement and therapy fails. Alternatively, he proposes his own distinction between prevention and 'pure enhancements.' Pure enhancements 'have nothing to do with forestalling disease or disability'; rather, they 'aim at gratifying the wishes of normal and healthy people for improved performance or superior capabilities' (2007:

61). Within Green's moral reasoning, we might say that PEDs are allowable for those baseball players who need them for therapeutic purposes and for preventive measures but not permissible for those baseball players who are healthy and 'normal.'

Based on their own explanations and self-descriptions, Mark McGwire serves as an example of preventive measures whereas Alex Rodriguez exemplifies Green's understanding of 'pure enhancements.' McGwire started taking steroids for therapeutic purposes, to heal a particular injury. He continued to take them, on his account, in order to prevent further injury because of his age and fragility. In 1998, McGwire broke the record for hitting the most home runs within a single season; the record was sixty-one, set by Roger Maris in 1961, and McGwire broke this record by hitting seventy home runs during the 1998 baseball season. We now know that McGwire was using steroids during his chase for the home run record, but Green's distinction between preventive and pure enhancement provides moral justification for McGwire's use of PEDs. Alex Rodriguez took steroids from 2001 to 2003 while playing for the Texas Rangers. Before the 2001 baseball season, Rodriguez signed the largest contract in the history of Major League Baseball: $252,000,000 for ten years. After signing that contract, Rodriguez turned to PEDs to ensure that his performance lived up to the expectations of his contract. Alex Rodriguez had no injury, and he did not anticipate becoming injured because of age or fragility—which is reflected in the longevity of his contract. He was at the height of his game, and he was the best player within Major League Baseball—which is reflected in the enormous amount of money promised in his contract. His only reason for taking PEDs was his expected level of performance. Hence Rodriguez exemplifies using PEDs for purposes of 'pure enhancement.'

Green makes a third distinction that speaks directly to the question of PEDs within baseball. He suggests that those who obviously excel above others should not use PEDs to excel even further, but those who need to catch up with those who excel should be permitted to use PEDs. This argument serves to level 'the playing field,' and it also maintains equality once it is accomplished: 'we should avoid and discourage interventions that confer only positional advantage' (2007: 223). Green observes that the 'disdain that almost all forms of doping have earned in sports derives largely from the combination of increased risks with the quest for positional advantage' (2007: 223). So, within Major League Baseball, Andy Pettitte might be justified in using PEDs, but not Roger Clemens; Jeremy Giambi might be justified, but not Jason Giambi; José Guillén, but not Manny Ramirez.[7] Why? Because Roger Clemens, Jason Giambi and Manny Ramirez obviously excel above others whereas Andy Pettitte, Jeremy Giambi and José Guillén attempt to catch up to those who excel.

These three distinctions comprise how Green negotiates his own 'positive' view of a future determined by medical advancements and technological enhancements within the world of sports. It is not the case that 'anything goes' within Green's moral reasoning: he makes helpful and nec-essary distinctions that encourage moral judgments and maintain ethical norms. But, in relation to Ramsey, Green does not think that a world deter-mined by medicine and technology is dangerous and idolatrous. In relation to Kass and Sandel, Green does not find that PEDs demean the nature and purpose of sports. According to Green, all three of these thinkers—Sandel, Kass and Ramsey—display a 'status quo bias' within their reasoning con-cerning medical advancements and technological enhancements.

However, Green offers his own 'status quo' reasoning. It is not a status quo reasoning based on prioritizing our current historical realities over that of possible future realities—which is how Green describes Kass's, Ramsey's and Sandel's moral reasoning. Instead, Green's reasoning is committed to a status quo determined solely by the world that medical and technological research make possible. In order to imagine another world, one not solely determined by medical and technological research, we need to turn to Alas-dair MacIntyre's notion of a 'practice.'

BASEBALL AS A PRACTICE WITH INTERNAL GOODS

Medical and technological research makes particular kinds of 'goods' pos-sible within baseball. MacIntyre's definition of what constitutes a 'practice' enables a better understanding of what kinds of 'goods' medical advance-ments and technological enhancements make possible. By doing so, MacIn-tyre's work offers us a better and thicker description of what is meant by the nature and purpose of sport and why talk of excellence and the virtues is required for understanding sports. In this section, I stay close to MacIn-tyre's arguments in *After Virtue* and use them to suggest ways that they apply to the current state of baseball.

By a 'practice,' MacIntyre explains that he means:

> any coherent and complex form of socially established cooperative human activity through which goods internal to that form of activity are realized in the course of trying to achieve those standards of excel-lence which are appropriate to, and partially definitive of, that form of activity, with the result that human powers to achieve excellence, and human conceptions of the ends and goods involved, are systematically extended. (2007: 187)

In this definition, MacIntyre introduces his distinction between internal goods and external goods. To talk about baseball as a 'practice,' with MacIntyre's use of the word, is to consider the kinds of goods that medical and technological research offer as external goods—that is, they remain outside of the nature and purpose of the game of baseball. External goods are not necessarily bad for the individuals involved or even for the particular practice in question, but neither do they contribute to the achievement of excellence within the game itself. Excellence, and even the quest for perfection within baseball, requires a profound understanding of the internal goods of the game. These internal goods comprise the nature and purpose of the game. They also allow, encourage and nurture the possibility for excellence—and perhaps even perfection—within the game itself. According to MacIntyre:

> A practice involves standards of excellence and obedience to rules as well as the achievement of goods. To enter into a practice is to accept the authority of those standards and the inadequacy of my own performance as judged by them. It is to subject my own attitudes, choices, preferences and tastes to the standards which currently and partially define the practice. (2007: 190)

This is part and parcel of most descriptions of the virtues: becoming virtuous requires recognizing that one lacks virtue and then modeling oneself after virtuous people. Knowing what counts as 'excellence' within a practice is recognizing what matters as the best achievements thus far within the particular practice in question. MacIntyre (2007: 189) observes that the verb 'excel' suggests precisely this understanding of excellence: 'excellence . . . has to be understood historically. The sequences of development find their point and purpose in a progress towards and beyond a variety of types and modes of excellence.'

What does MacIntyre mean by 'the achievement of goods'? In his own answer to this question, he further distinguishes between external goods and internal goods:

> It is characteristic of . . . external goods that when achieved they are always some individual's property and possession. Moreover characteristically they are such that the more someone has of them, the less there is for other people. This is sometimes necessarily the case, as with power and fame, and sometimes the case by reason of contingent circumstance as with money. External goods are therefore characteristically objects of competition in which there must be losers as well as winners. Internal goods are indeed the outcome of competition to excel, but it is characteristic of them that their achievement is a good for the whole community who participates in the practice. (2007: 190–91)

External goods are usually 'objects of competition,' like fame or money, which concretely benefit only the individual receiving the particular goods. Internal goods, on the other hand, impact 'the whole community.' Competition is not the difference: internal goods require competition in order to 'excel' within the practice. The difference is the purpose involved in the competition: is it for an individual achievement or for the whole community?

Internal goods are those goods that have positive effects on the community as a whole. Moreover, internal goods also contribute to the particular practice in question because they allow, encourage and nurture excellence across the board with the participants involved in the practice. In this way, internal goods maintain what must be sustained within a practice, in order to recognize it as *that* practice, but also improve what needs to become better. Internal goods define the nature and purpose of a particular practice.

The way to know the difference between external and internal goods is not purely theoretical. Rather, knowing that difference—for the purpose of describing what is best for a particular practice—is the purpose of the virtues. MacIntyre correctly observes that a 'virtue is an acquired human quality the possession and exercise of which tends to enable us to achieve those goods which are internal to practices and the lack of which effectively prevents us from achieving any such goods' (2007: 191).[8] MacIntyre emphasizes the importance of both the 'possession' and 'exercise' of those human qualities that are virtues. Without possession of the virtues, exercising them would never be our doing; it would be some other agent's accomplishment. In this sense, MacIntyre's use of the word 'possession' implies deliberation and intentionality. Exercising the virtues, without possessing them, would never allow the qualities to be 'ours.'

Possessing without exercising the virtues, however, risks a kind of self-righteousness. It places too much emphasis on intentionality at the cost of action. Possessing a virtue without exercising it puts a person on a pedestal, but that person does not model the virtues for others. Rather, *this person stands over the community and not with the community*. Therefore, MacIntyre rightly emphasizes both possession and exercise of the virtues. The result of both possessing and exercising the virtues is that the goods 'internal to practices' are properly achieved. Achieving these goods, on MacIntyre's account, is what is best for the individual as well as for the practice itself. For the participants to not continually achieve the goods of the practice is to let the practice slowly die out, and the internal goods of the practice allow and encourage the participants to excel in that practice— oftentimes beyond what the participants can imagine on their own. Lacking the virtues 'prevents us from achieving any such goods.' Concentrating only on external goods negatively affects both the participants as well as the practice itself. Perhaps surprisingly, concentrating only on external goods does not name the problem itself. It only names a symptom of the deeper problem. The deeper problem, in MacIntyre's view, is lacking the proper virtues for sustaining the nature and purpose of that particular practice.

How, we might ask, does this work? MacIntyre explains his understanding of what constitutes cheating within a practice:

> It belongs to the concept of a practice . . . that its goods can only be achieved by subordinating ourselves within the practice in our relationship to other practitioners. We have to learn to recognize what is due to

whom; we have to be prepared to take whatever self-endangering risks
are demanded along the way; and we have to listen carefully to what we
are told about inadequacies and to reply with the same carefulness for
the facts. In other words we have to accept as necessary components of
any practice with internal goods and standards of excellence the virtues
of justice, courage, and honesty. For not to accept these, to be willing
to cheat . . . so far bars us from achieving the standards of excellence or
the goods internal to the practice that it renders the practice pointless
except as a device for achieving external goods. (2007: 191)

MacIntyre introduces the particular virtues of courage, honesty and justice as necessary for any practice and the possibility for excellence within
that practice. What deserves our full attention is MacIntyre's description
of cheating. MacIntyre argues that goods are achieved only 'by subordinat-
ing ourselves within the practice in our relationship to other practitioners.'
MacIntyre clarifies his position: 'Every practice requires a certain kind of
relationship between those who participate in it' (2007: 191). He continues,
'Now the virtues of are those goods by reference to which, whether we like
it or not, we define our relationships to those other people with whom we
share the kind of purposes and standards which inform practices' (2007:
191). To cheat is to deny these relationships, and it is to deny our dependence on these relationships. Denying these relationships, and our dependence upon them, results in: (a) not being able to achieve 'the standards
of excellence' that the practice makes possible; (b) making the practice,
itself, pointless other than as a means to achieving external goods—such
as becoming wealthy.

If this dependence remains a necessary aspect of the virtuous life, then
how does MacIntyre account for self-sufficiency? This question becomes
important, especially within the context of athletics and the sport of baseball, because it seems that self-sufficiency ought to be the highest goal for
the athlete as well as for the baseball player. After all, hitting a home run
represents the pinnacle of self-sufficiency within baseball: this is the most
efficient way to help other base runners score, and it guarantees the hitter a
run without relying on others to get him back to home plate. However, all
of this might not be quite right. To better understand self-sufficiency, we
need to examine the question of what constitutes magnanimity.

INDIVIDUAL MAGNANIMITY VS. TEAM MAGNANIMITY

For Aristotle, 'the magnanimous man' exemplifies virtue because he
achieves self-sufficiency through constancy and steadfastness to the proper
moral life (see Aristotle, 1962: 1103a–1129a). It remains unclear, however,
if magnanimity requires such robust self-sufficiency within MacIntyre's
recovery of the virtues. For instance, MacIntyre concludes *After Virtue*

by recommending that who we seek as a moral exemplar might be another humble St. Benedict (see 2007: 263). He also recommends St. Francis of Assisi as exemplary of the virtuous life (see 2007: 199), and the virtuous life for St. Francis is not based on self-sufficiency but a radical account of dependency on animal life as well as reliance upon other humans through disciplined forms of poverty. These are not examples of the 'magnanimous man' as envisioned by Aristotle!

Following MacIntyre's argument, as explained in the previous section, we should distinguish between two versions of magnanimity: first, as an individual rising above the game, on their own and being rewarded by money, fame, etc.; second, to understand it as an individual who becomes a skillful team player that betters the game of baseball by making it a more interesting practice—in MacInytre's use of the term *practice*. These possibilities for understanding magnanimity can be distinguished in terms of individual magnanimity and team magnanimity—which might be misleading at first, because individual magnanimity remains a possibility within team magnanimity. The difference between the two is that individual magnanimity displays how the game of baseball becomes a means to achieving external goods for the individual baseball player rather than the game that makes his achievements possible whereas understanding magnanimity in terms of 'team' exhibits the necessity of the skills and virtues of the team to work as one unit. The notion of team magnanimity also maintains and contributes to the nature and purpose—in short, the internal goods—of baseball as a practice worthy of participation through managing, playing and watching.[9]

To play baseball is to enter into a practice, in MacIntyre's use of the term. 'To enter into a practice,' according to MacIntyre, 'is to enter into a relationship not only with its contemporary practitioners, but also with those who have preceded us in the practice, particularly those whose achievements extended the reach of the practice to its present point' (2007: 194).[10] *Cheating* is the term MacIntyre uses to describe the denial of these relationships as well as the denial of dependence on these relationships within a particular practice. This results in not achieving the standards of excellence that baseball makes possible or making the practice itself a means to some other end desired by an individual that remains independent of the practice itself.

Desiring external goods is not bad in and of itself. In fact, as MacIntyre observes, 'external goods genuinely are goods. Not only are they characteristic objects of human desire, whose allocation is what gives point to the virtues of justice and generosity, but no one can despise them altogether without a certain hypocrisy' (2007: 196). The problem arises when the desire for external goods becomes dominant for the participants within the particular practice:

> [While] we may hope that we can not only achieve the standards of excellence and the internal goods of certain practices by possessing the virtues

and become rich, famous and powerful, the virtues are always a potential stumbling block to this comfortable ambition. We should therefore expect that, if in a particular society the pursuit of external goods were to become dominant, the concept of the virtues might suffer first attrition and then perhaps something near total effacement. (2007: 196)

This account of what happens when external goods are prioritized over internal goods offers an apt description for the current state of Major League Baseball within the U.S. Through a discussion on chess, the British political theorist David Miller explains MacIntyre's distinction between external and internal goods—which offers a bridge for understanding the problems currently in Major League Baseball.

The good that consists in playing chess well is an internal good, whereas the money one may earn through being a champion chess player is an external good: it is merely contingent that playing chess should be the means whereby somebody enriches himself, whereas the good of playing well can for obvious reasons only be achieved by the actual playing of chess. Moreover the good in question has to be achieved by attempting to excel, that is by endeavouring to rival or outdo those previous practitioners whose activities make up the history of the practice. (1994: 247–48)

It might be difficult for us to imagine how 'it is merely contingent' that playing baseball is a means to financial bliss and fulfillment, but it remains true that this aspect of the game remains contingent. The nature and purpose of baseball is not equivalent to the money players make for playing baseball. To think that it is, is to confuse external goods with internal goods.

Confusing external goods with internal goods is not the only problem within the current state of Major League Baseball in the U.S. Problems also arise when certain internal goods are prioritized over other internal goods. Working from MacIntyre's notion of a practice as applied to baseball, the American theological ethicist Joel Shuman contends:

Baseball is a kind of activity that the philosopher Alasdair MacIntyre calls a *practice*, a complex, inherently social activity directed first of all toward goods *intrinsic* to that activity. The intrinsic goods achieved by participating in a practice, MacIntyre explains, are never solely the possession of those individuals who achieve them; in some sense they remain the possession of the practice and all of its participants. We participate in practices because our participation is good in itself; our pursuit of such common goods binds us together as members of communities and makes us better than we would otherwise have been. (2004: 301)

For example, this means that Alex Rodriguez's (who is also known as 'A-Rod') 'achievements—like his 57 home runs in 2002—never belong solely to Alex Rodriguez. For as a baseball player, A-Rod is part of a traditioned community formed by the practices of playing, coaching, umpiring, and yes, of watching and appreciating baseball' (2004: 301–2). When any one part of the practice begins to threaten other internal or intrinsic goods within the practice, then that is when that part of the practice becomes a problem. Shuman concludes his discussion on Rodriguez by arguing: 'When it threatens the integrity of the game, whether by alienating fans or creating a competitive imbalance or by pricing small-market teams out of the league, it has become something other than part of the tradition that is baseball' (2004: 302).

Beginning to talk about how the achievements of baseball players 'never belong solely' to them provides a useful starting point for thinking about Major League Baseball in terms of the virtues. Thinking about baseball in terms of the virtues helps us appreciate the possibility for excellence within the sport, and the combination of the possibility for excellence and the emphasis upon the internal goods of baseball offer the tools for us to start thinking about what the quest for perfection looks like within baseball: a game that includes certain skills as well as particular virtues in order for those skills to be nurtured within a team setting.[11]

My contention is that there are at least two reasons for the use of steroids within baseball. The first is for external goods: to make more money and possibly enjoy more fame. These reasons are not bad, in and of themselves; as MacIntyre says, 'external goods genuinely are goods' (2007: 196). But they become problematic when they are prioritized over the internal goods of the game. The second reason that Major League Baseball players have turned toward steroids is for the sake of excellence within the game itself. This reason is slightly more complicated and suspicious: not only does it prioritize some internal goods over others, but in so doing renders excellence and the quest for perfection in terms closer to celebrating—and upholding as a standard—individual magnanimity rather than team magnanimity.

I understand the cases of Mark McGwire and Alex Rodriguez to be examples of this individual magnanimity. Ultimately, even the distinction between prevention and pure enhancement does not provide moral justification for McGwire's reliance on PEDs. By using PEDs in order to excel, both sought the quest for perfection in a way determined solely by what medicine and technology make possible. They failed the game; they failed their teammates; they failed themselves, because they did not achieve excellence within the nature and purpose of baseball as a practice. In other words, they neither maintained the integrity of the game nor contributed to its improvement.

FRIENDSHIP AND TEAMWORK

The quest for perfection within baseball, therefore, does not have to be determined by the world narrated by medical and technological research. Instead, the quest for perfection within baseball can be understood through being disciplined by productive crafts. As MacIntyre says: 'The aim internal' to productive crafts, when in good order, is 'in a manner consonant with the excellences of the craft, so that not only is there a good product, but the craftsperson is perfected through and in her or his activity' (1994: 284). Perfection comes about through how an individual baseball player participates in activities particular to the game and not what is determined and narrated outside of those activities—such as what medical advancements and technological enhancements make possible. So, how should an individual baseball player cultivate their skills within professional baseball? Answering this question requires developing a notion of team magnanimity.

According to the British philosophical ethicist John Casey, 'Magnanimity is a . . . crown of the virtues' (1991: 199–200). The promise of talking about professional baseball players in terms of magnanimity is that we can begin to think about the magnanimous man in the way that Aristotle did—namely, in a way that 'offends the [modern] spirit of equality' (1991: 200)—but does so in the specific context of the sport of baseball where only a handful of elite players truly excel at their craft. Continuing his explanation of Aristotle's understanding of magnanimity, Casey remarks: 'Aristotle says that in so far as the magnanimous man deserves most, he must be good in the highest degree; for the better man always deserves more, and the best man [the] most' (1991: 200). Casey also reminds us that 'moral luck' plays a significant role within Aristotle's account of magnanimity, which requires us to consider magnanimity in terms of friendship: both *the need for others* and *the needs of others*. In the context of the sport of baseball, these 'others' are teammates. What kind of friends are teammates within baseball?

Following Aristotle, the American Christian ethicist Stanley Hauerwas distinguishes between three kinds of friendship: usefulness, pleasure and 'friendship based on virtue' (1997: 34–38). The first kind of friendship is often 'the shortest lived,' because it always changes based on our concrete and practical needs. This form of friendship is not necessarily bad or problematic, so long as it is made explicit and people's expectations are formed properly. The second kind of friendship, based on pleasure, is often seen among 'young people' who have a knack for quickly becoming friends and, as suddenly, ceasing being friends. Basing friendship on pleasure applies to romantic relationships as well as those friends who have no obvious utility but simply feel a void left by the vulnerability of new situations. The third kind of friendship, based on virtue, seeks 'good to the friend for the sake of the friend' (1997: 35). Friendship based on utility seeks benefits for oneself based on the abilities or position of one's friend, and friendship based on pleasure seeks emotional good for oneself based on how the person makes one feel. However, friendship based on virtue primarily seeks the good of the other—the good of one's friend. Aristotle employs the language of 'perfect friendship' to describe this third version of friendship, but Hauerwas interprets 'perfect' not as complete and final, but as constant and enduring.

In this sense, perfection signals the ability of a friendship to endure difficult times. A 'perfect friendship' is a friendship that lasts no matter what. It is not 'perfect' because it is free from complexity or difficulty; rather, it is 'perfect' because it makes it through a host of complexities and difficulties. My claim here is that the teamwork involved within baseball looks like this kind of friendship: 'friendship based on virtue.'

According to Hauerwas, a sign of a 'bad' person is that he or she 'lack[s] the constancy of character that is necessary for friendships of character' (1997: 36)—for friendships based on virtue. In this way, an individual person does not possess constancy; instead, constancy is necessarily communal. Constancy relies on others to maintain their consistent presence when there is no pleasure or utility involved in those friendships. In Hauerwas's words, 'constancy [is] a communal virtue. It is not something one of us possesses alone, but something we share and into which we help each other grow' (1997: 36). What is the implication of Hauerwas's observations concerning constancy? He remarks, 'As such, constancy taken as an integral part of the life of virtue excludes the popular but mistaken idea that the virtuous person is self-sufficient, entirely capable of sustaining his or her happiness alone' (1997: 36).

Significantly, for our purposes, Hauerwas's reflections on Aristotle shift 'the magnanimous man' from being understood in terms of individual magnanimity team magnanimity—which requires friendship, sacrifice and suffering with others. For Aristotle, 'the magnanimous man' achieves excellence and becomes magnificent because he is self-sufficient. Aristotle claims that when the magnanimous man:

> encounters misfortunes that are unavoidable or insignificant, he will not lament and ask for help. That kind of attitude belongs to someone who takes such matters seriously. He is a person who will rather possess beautiful and profitless objects than objects which are profitable and useful, for they mark him more as self-sufficient. (1962: 1125a5012)

Hauerwas interprets this passage in the following way: 'The magnanimous man . . . recognizes and lives the truth that the life of virtue demands a steadfastness of character that steels against so many frivolous distractions' (1997: 22). The self-sufficient magnanimous man allows neither the distractions of the world nor the lack of excellence of those around him to keep him from constancy and virtue. However, reflecting on friendship in Aristotelian terms leads us to conclude that virtuous friendships do not lead to self-sufficiency, but deepen and further our dependence on one another. Aristotle fails to make this connection. Hauerwas muses on Aristotle's oversight:

> But if through some terrible stroke of misfortune . . . we are stripped of our happiness, what then? What becomes of our friendship[s], nurtured in virtue and enjoyed in happiness? Here Aristotle's answer is

clear. It must be surrendered, or at least suspended, to be resumed in better times. For in our misfortune the encroaching world has . . . won the battle. And it is now our turn to bear our suffering and misfortune alone. For we must see [for Aristotle] that friendship and happiness . . . are finally to be understood in distinction from suffering and misfortune. We enjoy the best of friendship and virtue when we are in the best of positions, when our characters are firm and our coffers overflowing. Indeed, being in such a position allows us to claim with confidence the mark of perfect friendship, namely that the friend is chosen for his own sake and not for some other purpose. In contrast [on Aristotle's account], if we are suffering, we are needy, like old people . . . as such our friendship is better understood as one of usefulness rather than as perfect friendship. (1997: 43)

Hauerwas describes suffering differently from Aristotle. Instead of being a mark of losing friends, 'friends will suffer with friends . . . [and] friends will suffer *because* of friends' (1997: 48) within friendships based on virtue. Hauerwas contrasts his argument with Aristotle's:

For Aristotle there are a limited number of human circumstances or narrative sequences about which it makes sense for us to say that good can be found in them, or that the person who passes through them can reasonably be called happy. Virtue, of course, is necessary happiness; moreover, it works effectively to extend the number of circumstances or narratives through which a person can live and still be properly called happy by making her more constant. But there is a limit. Part of virtue is to know when the limit is reached, especially in one's own case. There is, simply, no redemption possible of a life that has been plunged into great suffering; the sufferer does best to recognize this and let go the hand of any yet remaining on the metaphorical island of happiness. Heroically, he cuts himself loose to be carried away from his friends by the raging current. (1997: 48)

Hauerwas summarizes what is at stake: 'To be clear, the settled view that a life of virtue must be a shared life is one of the most compelling features of Aristotle's account' (1997, 48). In this way, Aristotle's 'quest for happiness [should] not . . . be mistaken as that of a solitary hero' (1997: 48–49). However, Hauerwas alleges 'that something like this heroic model reappears at the edge of Aristotle's happy life where the sufferer stoically bears his suffering without friends' (1997: 49).

In relation to Hauerwas's argument with Aristotle, British philosophical theologian John Milbank raises the stakes concerning Aristotle's reflection on the magnanimous man as a solitary hero. According to Milbank, Aristotle's:

ideal of the virtuous person, the 'magnanimous man,' [remains] heroic, and decidedly aristocratic. Although this person must only seek honours as rewards for true exercise of virtue, he is still primarily motivated by this seeking for public acclaim. Hence magnanimity is the crown of the virtues in parallel to the way virtues receive honour as their prize. . . . Aristotle's ideal of virtue is not perfectly separable from a heroic pursuit of honour. (1991: 354–55)

Aristotle's commitment to heroism and honor,[12] on Milbank's account, renders Aristotle's reflections on friendship problematically incomplete. Instead of following his own descriptions on friendship to its logical ends, and including the need for others as well as the needs of others in his account of magnanimity, Aristotle fails to 'place friendship . . . at the apex of civic achievement' (1991: 355). Milbank's criticism of Aristotle comes in the form of a contrast with Thomas Aquinas's success in addressing these questions:

> Aristotle . . . did not, like Aquinas, place friendship quite at the apex of civic achievement. Friends, for Aristotle, share a common love of the good, but this good is ultimately that fine economy of honour which is magnanimity. If friendship becomes the actual summit of virtue, then this suggests that virtue itself is a relational, rather than self-contained, internal matter. And, indeed, Aquinas says that charity and friendship are not just the sharing of a good otherwise available, but rather that mutual benevolence is itself *fundatur super aliqua communicatione* [established beyond communication to some extent]. In other words, a transitive giving of something to someone else is constitutive of friendship, and therefore the thing most ultimately characteristic of virtue. (1991: 363)[13]

Rather than Aristotle's heroic approach to excellence and perfection, Milbank develops a quest for perfection based on the virtue of charity: 'a gradual approach to *perfection*, a perfect suffusion by charity, will mean that we no longer possess . . . impulses that are excessive or deficient' (1991: 364). Basing friendship on charity helps us to consider the kind of friendship necessary for a professional baseball team to pursue excellence and perfection. If we consider the skills and virtues involved in making a sacrificial bunt within baseball, we immediately recognize that the use of steroids for the purposes of achieving external goods actually hinders the skills and virtues required for pulling off a sacrificial bunt. A sacrificial bunt, which is sometimes called a sacrifice hit, takes place when a batter intentionally bunts the ball in order for a base runner to advance to the next base. The batter sacrifices his opportunity to get on base, and he sacrifices his statistics. How are the batter's statistics sacrificed? Because a successful sacrifice does not count toward the player's total at bats, which means that the batter does not get credit for the sacrifice within his statistics concerning his hits. Sacrifice bunts occur when there is a base runner on first base, second base or third base; when a runner is on third base, then a sacrifice bunt will often be called a 'suicide squeeze play,' which depicts how the runner ought to run to home plate as quick as possible no matter the outcome. When a runner is on first or second base, then the runner ought to advance to the next base as soon as the batter bunts the ball. With a runner on first base, the batter ought to bunt the ball down the third base line; with a runner at second base, then the batter ought to put the ball down the first base line. The strategy for both of these concerns keeping the ball as far as possible from the base where the runner is heading. The batter who puts down the sacrifice bunt must avoid putting the ball into the field in a way that invites a 'double play,' where both the batter and runner are called out. A sacrificial bunt requires the batter to get himself out (exceptions to the batter getting out take place when a fielder mishandles the ball, which results in a error, or if the batter is faster than the instincts of the fielders), but the batter ought to do whatever it takes to prevent the runner from the getting out. The religious ethicist Willie Young notes that the sacrifice bunt is 'the most central sacrifice in baseball,' and it displays how a sacrifice 'is an act by which someone renounces something [their base running opportunity and their statistical at bat], so as to achieve an end [advancing the runner on base], thereby also forming a social group [the baseball team]' (2004: 57).

What are the skills and virtues required for a successful sacrificial bunt? First, in terms of the virtue of charity, a batter performs a sacrificial bunt for the sake of the team. The charitable batter bunts the ball down the first base line in order for the runner on third to get to home plate, all the while the batter knows that his bunt most likely will result in him being called out at first base. The circumstances have to be right for a sacrifice bunt to make sense; for instance, it would not be an act of charity—because it would be imprudent—to lay down a sacrificial bunt when one's team is way far ahead of the other team in runs scored. When the circumstances call for it, such as a quick (skills) and prudent (virtues) base runner on third base in a tied ball game in an inning with one out, then it requires charity on the part of the batter not to 'swing for the fences' but to lay down a bunt where the whole team has more control concerning achieving that go-ahead run. While 'swinging for the fence' with a runner on third base might result in hitting a home run, it does not display team magnanimity because the batter fails in exercising the virtue of charity—which shows that the team lacks the ability to control their strategy. Attempting to hit a home run with a runner on third base is better described as self-indulgence—which is one aspect of our lives that continually opposes virtue.

Second, like Aquinas's description of friendship as requiring communication and some aspect beyond communication, a 'sacrifice bunt is . . . a communicative event involving understanding and trust' (Young, 2004: 58). This remark comes from Willie Young's reflections on the ethical significance of the sacrificial bunt (see Young, 2004: 56–68). Young also observes: 'only if it [the sacrificial bunt] enacts these qualities will it be successful' (2004: 58). Who has to communicate, and what are the skills required for the sacrificial bunt to actually work? Young answers this question: 'The manager or base coach must communicate to both the runner and the batter. The runner must trust that the bunt will be laid down, so as to properly advance on contact' (2004: 58). He continues, 'In the case of a suicide squeeze, the base runner must *believe* that the bunt will be laid down, in order to break for home during the [opposing pitcher's] windup' (2004: 58).

Third, the sacrifice bunt only works because the runner assumes that the batter—his teammate—excels at bunting, and the batter assumes that the runner excels at his timing in running. In Young's more descriptive words, 'The bunter promises to lay down a sacrifice, and the runner reciprocally promises to run the bases' (2004: 58). Young continues, saying that keeping 'this promise requires excellence on the part of both players: a popped-up bunt or poor baserunning will kill an inning, with no good achieved for the team' (2004: 58). On the baseball field, excellence is achieved in players fulfilling their roles with deliberation, intentionality and purpose.

While Stanley Hauerwas approvingly cites Milbank's account of the magnanimous man (see Hauerwas, 1997: 61–66), Hauerwas's own descriptions of magnanimity provide a better notion of team magnanimity within the sport of baseball. Hauerwas clarifies what magnanimity looks like when charity is taken as a required virtue for magnanimity. He argues that friendship is best understood as heightening, increasing and intensifying the possibility for magnanimity:

> The magnanimous man is [patient] . . . because he recognizes and lives the truth that the life of virtue demands a steadfastness of character that steels us against so many frivolous distractions. . . . [T]he magnanimous man is on a journey and therefore knows he must be steadfast, since he will often be unsure where he is or where is heading. This demands from him concentration and determination, which in turn demand that he have a center that is not easily destroyed by the good and evil fortune that he is bound to meet along the way. (1997: 22)

The crucial aspect of this quotation concerns what Hauerwas means by 'journey,' and he claims that the:

> point is deepened when we consider that the purpose of journey that the person of virtue undertakes is not merely to get him from here to there, not just to arrive—that would be a trip—but it is the journeying itself that is crucial. In this respect Aristotle's contrast between the arts and the virtues is illuminating. In the arts, excellence lies in the results themselves . . . but in matters of virtues an act is not just or temperate unless the agent has certain characteristics as he performs it. (1997: 22)

First, the moral agent must know what he or she is doing. Second, he or she must choose to act the way he or she does; he or she must choose those particular actions for the sake of the actions themselves. Third, the action ought to come from within character shaped by the constancy of their community. As Aristotle describes it, 'The just and self-controlled man is not he who performs these acts, but he who also performs them in the way just and self-controlled men do' (1962: 1105b7–9).

Baseball is best understood as a 'journey,' played for the sake of virtue itself. The sport of baseball should not be understood as a 'trip,' in which the goals and results are known ahead of time in clear and distinct ways. While winning the World Series is an obvious goal or makes the sport of baseball look more like a 'trip,' stating this so clearly and distinctly degrades and downplays the process through which a World Series is won and makes no reference to the elements of the game that players and fans equally and truly enjoy.

As a fan of the Chicago Cubs team, an organization that has not won the World Series since 1908, the continuous suffering that I have endured mandates the virtue of patience—in some extreme ways. It also requires an appreciation of baseball in Hauerwas's term of 'journey' as opposed to merely a 'trip.' When baseball is understood as a journey, skills and virtues are cultivated for the sake of those virtues and skills and not strictly for the World Series title. While winning the World Series is an admirable goal, the process through which it was won—including Spring Training games in March, scouting reports, draft strategies and building and maintaining a healthy Minor League system—deserves more appreciation, discussion and moral reflection. The journey remains more significant than the end result on its own. This journey displays magnanimity in more important and substantial ways than taking steroids does, which makes possible trip-like achievements.

Baseball fans celebrate individual and team accomplishments as the season goes along—like when a pitcher achieves a 'perfect game' by not allowing the other team to get any hits or runners on base for a whole game and when a team wins its particular division assuring their place in the playoffs—because such accomplishments display the importance of the virtues and the satisfaction of such virtues along the way. These accomplishments are not belittled if a player's team fails to win a championship; they remain appreciated as part of the journey, and we should understand the World Series title as one of these accomplishments. The evidence for this is that ballplayers return to the field after winning a championship and continue their journey through into the following season. Winning a World Series does not allow a team to 'arrive'; if it did, then the sport of baseball would be merely a trip. Instead, the World Series title celebrates and validates the skills and virtues continually cultivated. No matter how many championships a professional ballplayer might win, virtuous baseball players constantly develop their skills by playing the game and relying on their teammates.[14]

CONCLUSION

If baseball is best described as a journey, and not a trip, then might baseball players be morally justified in taking steroids in order to prolong their athletic careers—in order to maintain their journey? While I am sympathetic to injured or older players who use steroids in order to continue on their journeys, morally we have to say that baseball players are not justified in taking steroids in order to continue their careers. There are at least three reasons for this. First, we are not justified in continuing particular activities 'at all costs.' To continue the journey, to continue to play baseball 'at all costs,' is to deny the virtues of charity and prudence within the game. Such behavior denies the virtue of charity, because it does not serve the interests of the other teammates; rather, it serves only the interests of that individual player who takes steroids in order to extend his own career. Similarly, such behavior denies the virtue of prudence, because it does not exercise practical wisdom concerning the limitations of the individual body (see Hauerwas, 1997: 176). I find it fitting and logical, for instance, from the perspective of virtue-centered reasoning, that the San Francisco Giants were able to win the World Series only after deciding not to resign Barry Bonds. Bonds continued to play with the San Francisco Giants, not to contribute to the purposes of the team, but in order to break certain individual hitting records. Bonds displayed an extreme amount of imprudence and selfishness in continuing to play, for the sake of the home run record, way past his the time allotted to him to be an actual team player. After his retirement from Major League Baseball in 2007, the Giants went on to win the World Series championship in 2010.

The second reason that baseball players are not morally justified in taking steroids in order to continue their career is that it misconstrues the kind of friendship shared within the dynamics of team magnanimity. It denies the ways in which players should be present with those players who cannot play and suffer from their inabilities to continue on the journey as a contributing part of the team. This rationale builds from and takes into account Hauerwas's reflections on the role of constancy within friendship, where constancy knows how to suffer along with friends rather than attempting to overcome suffering. When a player suffers from injury, then the goal of the team should become—through the virtue of charity—to find particular function or task for that player. When a player gets too old to contribute to the team in the ways in which both he and they are accustomed, then his task becomes—through the virtue of charity—to actively redefine his role on the team. A good recent example of this is Greg Maddux, a pitcher who played most of his career for the Atlanta Braves. Recognizing that he could not contribute in the same ways that he had for several years as a premier starting pitcher in the league, he slowly took on a different role, resembling a 'pitching coach' in relation to the young pitchers on the team.

The third reason that players should not prolong their careers by taking steroids is that it refuses what Alasdair MacIntyre calls our acknowledged dependence on one another through vulnerability (see MacIntyre, 1999: 119–28). By taking steroids, we take upon ourselves an unreasonable amount of independence and refuse to make ourselves vulnerable to our own bodies as well as vulnerable to others. The sports ethicist Tracy Trothen puts it this way: 'Vulnerability means dependency; mutual vulnerability in community means interdependence' (2008: 231). This vulnerability is necessary for team magnanimity, and taking steroids denounces our vulnerabilities. It makes players rely too heavily on what medical advancements and technological enhancements make possible rather than the skills and virtues acquired and nurtured within the sport of baseball. Steroids deny the team for the sake of the individual player. Baseball exemplifies how excellence and the quest for perfection are team endeavors; a game that, when performed with the particular virtues of charity and prudence, exhibits individual skills that the game of baseball makes possible. Fans, players, sports media and the institution of Major League Baseball all need to recognize the moral bases of the game that they celebrate, enjoy and love.[15]

NOTES

1. In this sense, I develop Tracy Trothen's suggestion that the 'meaning of human virtue must be more critically examined before decisions regarding the use of genetic technologies can be made responsibly' (2008: 231).
2. For other moral ways forward concerning the sport of baseball see Feezell's (2004: 109–25) well-crafted essay; I describe Feezell's essay as 'well-crafted' because he constructs a philosophical dialogue between Abbey the 'absolutist' or Kantian deontologist, Ron the 'realist' and Trev the 'traditionalist' or virtue theorist.
3. Note that Green (2007) plays his subtitle, 'The Ethics of Genetic Choice,' off Ramsey's subtitle, 'The Ethics of Genetic Control,' from thirty-seven years before.
4. See D. Stephen Long (2007: 195): 'Unfortunately he [Ramsey] viewed the use of the . . . doctrine of perfection as another form of that optimistic utopianism symptomatic of Calvinism gone to seed.' The doctrine of perfection Long claims that Ramsey dismisses is not the same version of perfection through an understanding of the virtues that I suggest later in this chapter. It remains an open question whether Ramsey would dismiss an account of perfection grounded in the virtues.
5. Tara Magdalinski (2009: 71–90) makes an important case concerning the health risks that athletes take. She claims that sport itself requires a high degree of health risk. Therefore, to criticize the use of PEDs based on their health risk alone requires one to also question the health risk any professional athlete takes simply to be a professional athlete.
6. See Alasdair MacIntyre (2007: 190): 'If, on starting to play baseball, I do not accept that others know better than I when to throw a fast ball and when not, I will never learn to appreciate good pitching let along to pitch.'
7. I mention José Guillén because he is an outfielder who served a suspension previous to Manny Ramirez's first suspension. Another outfielder, Jay Gibbons,

served a suspension during the same time as José Guillén. These two outfield-ers served their suspensions during the 2008 season, and Ramirez served his during the 2009 season.

8. Interestingly, this is MacIntyre's first definition of virtue within his *After Virtue*.

9. Perhaps the most recent account of this is Michael Lewis (2004). My only hesitation in citing this book is that the premise of Lewis's account of Billy Beane, who is the general manager of the Oakland Athletics, is that Beane's concerns are economic and not with the internal goods of the game itself. The way that Lewis tells the story, which may or may not accurately portray Beane's intentions, is that Beane and the A's gave more attention to particu-lar skills in order to save money (an external good) yet still win. But, at the least, Beane makes concrete attempts to discipline his players and managers in ways that display team magnanimity rather than individual magnanimity alone.

10. There is a bit of arbitrariness in the list of practices MacIntyre provides as examples for his argument. MacIntyre lists some activities that he claims do not count as a 'practice' (like bricklaying), in his use of the term, but does not offer convincing reasons why. For more on this problem within MacIntyre's *After Virtue*, see Stanley Hauerwas and Paul Wadell (1982). For a better rationale than MacIntyre provides for some activities being considered 'prac-tices,' see David Miller (1994: 247–48).

11. At this point, my other disagreement with Green's book arises—the first dif-ference being that he falls into a status quo reasoning concerning medical and technological research—in that he offers no moral framework to make sense of his own claims such as: 'When anyone pursues personal advantage in the hope that others will not do so, a process sets in that ends by damaging everyone' (2007: 223); and 'because the temptation in these circumstances to seek personal gain is great, competitors usually cannot rely on good faith and trust. They must agree to set up an authority with the power to prohibit and punish cheating' (2007: 224). While I agree with the content of these claims made by Green, he offers no substantial moral framework to make sense of how to actually ground such claims. MacIntyre's work provides such grounds for a more substantial understanding of the significance of these claims.

12. For a fascinating development of the notion of heroism and honor, from a particularly Christian perspective, see Brian Hook and R. R. Reno (2000).

13. I am grateful to Allison Hicks for the helpful translation of the phrase *fun-datur super aliqua communicatione* as 'established beyond communication to some extent'—which, I think, gets to the heart of Thomas Aquinas's argu-ments concerning charity and friendship.

14. Through personal correspondence, the collegiate basketball player Quinn McDowell wrote a reflective response in relation to the argument that I have presented here. McDowell connects my reasoning on baseball to Michael Jordan's basketball career: 'Michael Jordan, for example, had to learn early in his career that unless he competed in a way that made his teammates bet-ter, he would never aspire to the career he wanted.' McDowell continues, 'He had to make a choice: to play for himself or to play for his community.' According to McDowell, we all know what he chose: 'he chose to play for his community and was often praised for his knack to bring out the best in the players around him (even if they were of a lower quality).' By doing this, McDowell observes, Jordan 'became the single best player of all time. He accented the abilities of the teammates around him, and he slowly grew to trust them during critical points in the game.' McDowell's concluding

reflections are thus: 'As M.J. became more virtuous in his interactions with his teammates, he became less dependent on himself and more dependent on the community. The results of such a talented player submitting to the community were incredible.' I completely concur with McDowell's assessment of Michael Jordan as a player who prioritized the internal goods of the game of basketball, as well as aspired to team magnanimity rather than individual magnanimity. However, I also think that emphasis also needs to be placed upon the character of the player 'outside the lines.' While a virtuous basketball player, Jordan is well known for his lack of prudence and temperance when it comes to gambling. I do not address this question anywhere else in this chapter, but McDowell's reflective response to the present chapter provides an opportunity for such a consideration.

15. The following students, at the College of William and Mary, read drafts of this chapter and improved its overall quality: Daniel Falloon, Zachary Kmetz and Sean Sweeney.

BIBLIOGRAPHY

Aristotle. (1962) *Nichomachean Ethics*, trans. Martin Ostwald, Indianapolis, IN: Bobbs-Merrill.

Augustine. (1992) *Confessions*, trans. Thomas Williams, ed. James J. O'Donnell, Oxford: Oxford University Press.

Casey, J. (1991) *Pagan Virtue: An Essay in Ethics*, New York: Oxford University Press.

Feezell, R. (2004) Baseball, Cheating, and Tradition: Would Kant Cork His Bat? in E. Bronson (Ed.), *Baseball and Philosophy: Thinking outside the Batter's Box*, Chicago: Open Court, 109–25.

Green, R. (2007) *Babies by Design: The Ethics of Genetic Choice*. New Haven, CT: Yale University Press.

Hauerwas, S. (1981) *A Community of Character: Toward a Constructive Christian Social Ethic*, Notre Dame, IN: University of Notre Dame Press.

Hauerwas, S. (1997) *Christians among the Virtues: Theological Conversations with Ancient and Modern Ethics*, Notre Dame, IN: University of Notre Dame Press.

Hauerwas, S. and Wadell, P. (1982) Review of MacIntyre's *After Virtue*, *The Thomist*, 46 (2), 313–322.

Hook, B. and Reno, R. R. (2000) *Heroism and the Christian Life*, Louisville: Westminster John Knox Press.

Lewis, M. (2004) *Moneyball: The Art of Winning an Unfair Game*, New York: W. W. Norton and Company.

Long, D. S. (2007) *Tragedy, Tradition, Transformism: The Ethics of Paul Ramsey*, Eugene, OR: Wipf and Stock Publishers.

MacIntyre, A. (1994) A Partial Response to My Critics, in J. Horton and S. Mendus (Eds.), *After MacIntyre: Critical Perspectives on the Work of Alasdair MacIntyre*, Notre Dame, IN: University of Notre Dame Press, 283–304.

MacIntyre, A. (1999) *Dependent Rational Animals: Why Human Beings Need the Virtues*, Chicago: Open Court.

MacIntyre, A. (2007) *After Virtue: A Study in Moral Theory*, 3rd ed., Notre Dame, IN: University of Notre Dame Press.

Magdalinski, T. (2008) *Sport, Technology, and the Body: The Nature of Performance*, New York: Routledge.

Milbank, J. (1991) *Theology and Social Theory: Beyond Secular Reason*, Malden, MA: Blackwell Publishing.

Miller, D. (1994) Virtues, Practices, and Justice, in J. Horton and S. Mendus (Eds.), *After MacIntyre: Critical Perspectives on the Work of Alasdair MacIntyre*, Notre Dame, IN: University of Notre Dame Press, 245–264.

President's Council on Bioethics. (2003) *Beyond Therapy: Biotechnology and the Pursuit of Happiness*, with a Special Foreword by Leon Kass. New York: Dana Press.

Ramsey, P. (1970) *Fabricated Man: The Ethics of Genetic Control*, New Haven, CT: Yale University Press.

Sandel, M. (2007) *The Case against Perfection: Ethics in an Age of Genetic Engineering*, Cambridge, MA: Belknap Press.

Shuman, J. (2004) Does A-Rod Deserve So Much Money? In E. Bronson (Ed.), *Baseball and Philosophy: Thinking outside the Batter's Box*, Chicago: Open Court, 300–302.

Trothen, T. J. (2008) Redefining Human, Redefining Sport: The Imago Dei and Genetic Modification Technologies, in D. Deardorff and J. White (Eds.), *The Image of God in the Human Body: Essays on Christianity and Sports*, Lewiston, NY: Edwin Mellen Press, 217–34.

Young, W. (2004) Taking One for the Team: Baseball and Sacrifice, in E. Bronson (Ed.), *Baseball and Philosophy: Thinking outside the Batter's Box*, Chicago: Open Court, 56–68.

9 The Vatican's Game Plan for Maximizing Sport's Educational Potential

Kevin Lixey

> *The educational and spiritual potential of sport must make believers and people of good will united and determined in challenging every distorted aspect that can intrude . . . so that sport, without losing its true nature, can answer the needs of our time: a sport that protects the weak and excludes no one, that frees young people from the snares of apathy and indifference, and arouses a healthy sense of competition in them . . . a sport which contributes to the love of life, teaches sacrifice, respect and responsibility, leading to the full development of every human person.*
>
> John Paul II[1]

INTRODUCTION

Having been accused in the past of banning the Ancient Olympics, and scorning the body, who would ever imagine that now the Catholic Church is insisting on putting play back into sport? That is right; we are talking about play—as in fun and enjoyment . . . pure leisure. One would readily expect the Church to condemn doping or admonish its faithful against neglecting the Sabbath rest due to sports, but who would think that a Pope would adamantly defend the spirit of play and the joy of sport? Yet, is not this the point that John Paul II was making in his remarks to FIFA, which can be applied to all sports? For all its importance and popularity, John Paul II (2000a: 1099) observed that:

> football remains a game. It is a form of play, both simple and complex, in which people take joy in the wonderful possibilities of human life—physical, social and spiritual. It would be a sad day if the spirit of play and the sense of joy in fair competition were to be lost.

In fact, perhaps contrary to popular belief, the Church considers sport in a most positive light: as a gift from God! John Paul II (2000b: 1) considered the Jubilee for Sport in 2000 "a fitting occasion to give thanks to God for the gift of sport" and offered us a positive valuation of this phenomenon. He highlighted how sport possesses a universal language, educational potential and a facility for overcoming indifference and contributing to a love of life. Yet, following the logic of this pontiff, sport is not only a gift, but also a responsibility. Thus the sporting Pope called on all people of goodwill "to allow sport, without losing its true nature, to answer the needs of our time." What are these needs? In particular, John Paul II (2000b: 1) noted "a sport that protects the weak and excludes no one, a sport that frees young people from the snares of apathy and indifference, and arouses a healthy sense of competition in them; a sport which contributes to the love of life."

Some of these points raised by John Paul II—such as a sport that protects the weak and excludes no one—will be addressed elsewhere in this book. In this chapter, I wish to especially focus on a sport that can contribute to the love of life by freeing young people from the snares of apathy and indifference and a sport that can teach sacrifice, respect and responsibility. These are some of the distinguishing characteristics of the type of sport that the "Church and Sport" Section of the Pontifical Council for the Laity seeks to promote.[2] In a nutshell, we can say that the Vatican's game plan for sport consists in recuperating and strengthening sport's recreational, educational and pastoral dimensions.

I will begin this chapter with a brief consideration of three constitutive elements of sport: play, competition and asceticism. Organized sports should be fun as well as serious and formative, but this depends in great part how they are staged. Consequently, the second section of this chapter will explore the importance of the educator's role in sporting activities. Coaches, parents, teachers and volunteers must all have a clear understanding of sports' recreational and educational dimensions and their specific role therein. I believe we are beginning to witness a type of paradigm shift in some parts of the world where some Catholic youth sports directors and coaches are starting to be considered more and more as agents in "pastoral ministry" instead of mere "neutral" volunteers or staff. Consequently, the Vatican's "Church and Sport" office is placing greater importance and emphasis on the mentoring aspects of coaching as an important means to assist the youth of today in reaching their full spiritual and human development.

Thus the following pages will consider the need for recuperating and strengthening: sport's playful dimension; its healthy sense of competition; its ascetical dimension; and, lastly, the teaching moments afforded by a mentoring approach to coaching.

THE FASCINATION OF PLAY AS AN ANTIDOTE TO APATHY

What is the attraction of sport and game playing? How is it possible that sports are played by billions of children around the world and watched by millions on television? Before the World Cup of football in 1978, the then Archbishop of Munich Cardinal Joseph Ratzinger (1978/1992: 262) posed a similar question in a radio interview:

What is the fascination of play that it can have equal importance as food? One can answer that by looking back at ancient Rome, in which the cry for bread and circuses was really the expression of a desire for a paradisiacal life, for a life of satiety without effort, and of fulfilled leisure. Because that is what play means: action, that is truly free—without a goal and without a need to do it—while harnessing and fulfilling all of one's personal forces. In this sense, sport becomes a sort of foretaste of Paradise: a stepping out of the slavish earnestness of our daily life and its concerns into the free seriousness of something that should not be serious and is therefore beautiful.

Sports and recreation, by their very nature, must be first and foremost this break from the frenzy of work and studies, a "stepping out of the slavish earnestness of daily life." As we often have a built-in utilitarian mentality, we like to see everything in terms of what purpose or what benefit is in it for me, and this can eclipse sport's primary characteristic: that of being a spontaneous and free activity, serving no other immediate purpose than that of play. Within this perspective, we can see that youth sports themselves have developed considerably since the time of ancient Greece. Consequently, sport today—as an end or practice pursued in and of itself—lies somewhere between the concept of recreational play in Aristotle (2000: 195) and that concept he calls pure leisure.[3] Although sport is often considered in contrast to work, it is itself no mere rest. It is action, and it harnesses and actualizes one's personal energy in an immediate and earnest pursuit of something which is a non *necessarium*.

Nor is sport devoid of tension and seriousness. Contrary to what some sociologists say, Elias and Dunning (1986: 80) see sporting activities not as a means for a release from tension, but, on the contrary, as a source for experiencing a specific type of tension, a form of excitement that would often be avoided in ordinary life. In fact, these same authors (1986: 81) cite the passage in *The Confessions* where St. Augustine, while reproaching himself for having frequented the theaters, asks himself why it should be that we regard as "entertainment" those very events that arouse in us fear, anxiety, rage, anger and a good many other feelings that if we could we would avoid in real life.

Although these sociologists do not give us a reason why this is so, they do conclude that this arousal of tensions is an essential ingredient of all types of leisure enjoyment, sport included. Elias and Dunning (1986: 80), in fact, consider as a common characteristic of all leisure events this capacity to arouse emotions that are related to those experienced by us in real-life situations, while transposing them into a different "controlled" key and blended with a certain delight. Perhaps in the playing or watching of sports, this drama of emotion might be found in a lesser degree than that of watching a heart-wrenching drama, but the uncertainty of the outcome of a game always weaves a certain element of suspense and excitement into the playing of sports. Although we cannot thoroughly analyze the concept of play in this chapter, allow me to accentuate that emotional tension is central to sport. Whether we play them or watch them, sports excite our passions and captivate our interest; "excitement is, as it were, the spice of all play-enjoyment" (Elias and Dunning, 1986: 74, 80).

Holocaust survivor and Noble Laureate Elie Wiesel once said: "The greatest source of infinite danger in the world, to the world, is indifference. I've always believed that the opposite of love is not hate, but indifference . . . Indifference is the enemy."[4] In Western culture especially, indifference plagues our youth today in epidemic proportions. What can be done? John Paul II (2000b: 1) suggested that we take another look at how sport can offer us a means of freeing young people from the snares of apathy and indifference. Sport is not a panacea. But, with regard to apathy, sporting activities can be a spark that ignites enthusiasm for life; it can offer young people an opportunity to awake from a state of passive slumber, from the passivity of going through life as a mere bystander to becoming an active player: a true protagonist in actively shaping their own lives and the future.

It is interesting to contrast the vision of the human person as a player as offered by Huizinga (1950) and summarized in his book's title, *Homo Ludens*, with that of *Homo Consumens*, the title of a book by Zygmunt Bauman (2007). Instead of being characterized by play and creativity, Bauman offers a diagnosis of contemporary society in which the human person is distinguished by passivity: for his or her capacity of consuming the latest and greatest illusion offered by the market. Yet, one remnant that still stands in opposition to consumerism is manifested in the playing of a sport. (Here we are not so bold as to suggest that sports have nothing to do with consumerism!) There is something within the very dynamism of sports play that impels the person to move outside of himself and in the direction of the other, which is fundamental to the very social dimension of humanity.

If we take a closer look at the nature of the human person, we discover two essential movements that seem apparently in contrast to each other. On one hand, the person is incomplete, a work in progress, who strives to perfect or "complete" his- or herself. Yet, on the other hand, we possess a type of overabundance or richness of being that overflows as we seek to give ourselves, to pour ourselves out.

These two dimensions are akin to the two movements of love, offered by Pope Benedict XVI in *Deus Caritas Est* (2005: 18–19), where he explains how *eros* is that outward movement that seeks to fulfill our incompleteness, and *agape* that dimension of self-giving:

> By their own inner logic, these initial, somewhat philosophical reflections on the essence of love have . . . led us to consider two fundamental words: *eros*, as a term to indicate "worldly" love and *agape*, referring to love grounded in and shaped by faith. The two notions are often contrasted as "ascending" love and "descending" love. [. . .] Yet *eros* and

agape—ascending love and descending love—can never be completely separated. The more the two, in their different aspects, find a proper unity in the one reality of love, the more the true nature of love in general is realized. Even if *eros* is at first mainly covetous and ascending, a fascination for the great promise of happiness, in drawing near to the other, it is less and less concerned with itself, increasingly seeks the happiness of the other, is concerned more and more with the beloved, bestows itself and wants to "be there for" the other. The element of *agape* thus enters into this love, for otherwise *eros* is impoverished and even loses its own nature. On the other hand, man cannot live by oblative, descending love alone. He cannot always give, he must also receive. Anyone who wishes to give love must also receive love as a gift.

Along very similar lines, sports philosopher Drew Hyland (1990: 141) considers sports play as a type of "responsive openness" that is an expression of our unique nature that is both incomplete and overflowing. Hyland notes how we are open-ended beings in need of perfection; yet we also possess a rich inner depth, a source of creativity and strength that we tap into in order to 'respond' to various situations. The point to be made here is that both this desire to complete ourselves and this creative force and capacity for us to "pour ourselves out" and to give our best is at the heart of play. Furthermore, the argument can be made that sports themselves, as a manifestation of this richness of being and zest for life, reveal something about the very nature of the human person. This was already pointed out by John Paul II (1984: 4) at the first Jubilee of Sport when he noted how sport is "joy of life, a game, a celebration . . . an expression of the richness of being, much more valid and to be prized more than having."

On another occasion, John Paul II (1990: 4) publicly recognized athletes for the capacity of expressing in their actions a "zest for life and for everything that makes life great" and stressed how young people of today are in need of such a witness.[5]

To inspire and convey to the youth a zest for life is a great challenge as well as a responsibility for athletes, coaches and directors of youth sports programs today. Nonetheless, it is a possibility within reach of sporting activity and connatural to it. It is no wonder then that in his address during a Vatican Sport Seminar in 2009, Philip Craven (2011: 116) highlighted that one of the key goals of the *International Paralympic Movement* is "to inspire and excite the world." Especially today when considering how the youth are left disenfranchised by the empty promise of materialism, we should not belittle the powerful testimony of athletes and Paralympians especially who can eloquently convey a zest for live and the primacy of being over having.

Obviously, this does not happen automatically, but depends on the goodwill and example of those involved. Because of this, John Paul II (1984: 4) urged that sport:

be properly used and "freed from excess technical perfection and professionalism through a recovery of its free nature, its ability to strengthen bonds of friendship, to foster dialogue and openness to others, as an expression of the richness of being, much more valid and to be prized than having, and hence far above the harsh laws of production and consumption and all other purely utilitarian and hedonistic considerations in life.

In summary, in order for sport to continue to excite and fascinate people and arouse this *homo consumens* from his apathy, the spontaneous dimension of play needs to return front and center to sporting activities.

A HEALTHY SENSE OF COMPETITION

As we noted at the outset, John Paul II suggested a link between freeing young people from the snares of apathy and indifference and arousing in them a healthy sense of competition. In fact, we can see how the excitement of play in sport is also rooted in competition. Although we cannot analyze competition in depth in this chapter we can make a few key observations. First of all, we play or compete with someone and for something. Competition presupposes an opponent as winning implies showing oneself superior in the outcome of a game. As Huizinga (1950: 51) points out, "The primary thing is the desire to excel over others, to be the first and to be honored for that." The object for which we play and compete is first and foremost victory; every game has its prize even if the fruits of victory may be simply honor, esteem and prestige. The Popes have certainly acknowledged this, as John Paul II (1984: 4) among others recognizes that sport is "competitiveness, a contest for winning a crown, a cup, a title, a first place."

A second point to consider—and this stands in contrast to indifference—is that competition creates excitement. We can observe how the more difficult the game, that is to say, the greater its requirements for excellence in skill, knowledge, courage and strength, the greater the tension and excitement. Norbert Elias and Eric Dunning (1986: 86) concur that what makes for an exciting football game for both spectators and players are those games that are always closely matched, point for point, and never those that are one-sided. Even children themselves know this. Consequently, when they are selecting players for the spontaneous play of some sporting game, they generally seek equality among the teams so as to be matched up competitively.

Nonetheless, whether at the professional or the amateur level, competition today gets mixed reviews. Certainly a "win-at-all-costs" mentality that fuels doping and other forms of cheating and malicious behavior is to be shunned across the board. Yet, on the other extreme, I do not think that all children need, or want, to cross the finish line in unison holding hands or to see that every game end in a tie. A few rotten apples—and this unfortunately applies to parents as much as players and coaches—should not provide the grounds for eliminating the competitive spirit altogether from sports.

In the past century, the Church has certainly been attentive to the threat of this "win-at-all-costs" mentality. John Paul II (2000b: 2) pointed out in his final remarks at the Jubilee for Sport in 2000 that even "the 'nicest triviality in the world' is often marred by harsh competitive pressure." He went on to point out that "even competition is just a game" and thus the overriding need that "sport should be fun and enjoyable." Even more to the point were the words of John Paul II (2004: 3) to an Italian Catholic youth sports association:

> In our time, organized sport sometimes seems conditioned by the logic of profit, of the spectacular, of doping, exasperated rivalry and epi-sodes of violence. It is also your task to proclaim and to witness to the humanizing power of the Gospel with regard to the practice of sport, which if lived in accordance with the Christian outlook, becomes a 'generative principle' of profound human relations and encourages the building of a more serene and supportive world. I hope that you, especially, dear young athletes, will practice sport with loyalty and a healthy spirit of competition. In this way it will help you to face the demanding competition of life with courage and honesty, with joy and with calm confidence in the future.

Thus, it becomes clear how the Catholic Church recognizes and values the good of a healthy sense of competition as a stimulus for improvement and for bringing out the best in a person. At the same time the Church is atten-tive to warn against sport being conditioned by the logic of victory at all costs. Yet, rather than seeing the drive to win only in a negative light, we should make these deeper inquiries: "Why is it that the human person pos-sesses an innate desire for self improvement?" "What is it about the human person that makes him or her seek to excel?"

Many pontiffs have seen the physical exertions in sport as a part of a quest for even higher values that build character and give dignity and a sense of achievement that goes beyond sport. John Paul II (2000b: 2) noted how "life itself is a contest and a striving for goodness and holiness."

During his visit to the Czech Republic, Pope Benedict XVI (2009a: 5) touched on this desire in the human heart to excel, and especially on the need for educators to help the youth of today to nurture their God-given capacity to transcend their very limits. It is interesting to note that the Holy Father considered sport as one of these ways or spheres of life where young people are welcomed to excel:

> Of particular importance is the urgent task to encourage young Euro-peans with a formation that respects and nurtures their God-given

capacity to transcend the very limits which are sometimes presumed to entrap them. In sports . . . young people welcome the opportunity to excel. Is it not equally true that when presented with high ideals they will also aspire to moral virtue and a life of compassion and goodness? I warmly encourage parents and community leaders . . . to promote the values which integrate the intellectual, human and spiritual dimensions of a sound education worthy of the aspirations of our young.

Healthy competition, in this sense, promotes excellence and contributes to a zest for life and for overcoming challenges. It can provide the youth especially with a stimulus for self-betterment and personal growth. Following the argument set forth by Pope Benedict XVI, the promotion of the pursuit of excellence in sport can be a step in the direction of inspiring the youth to seek "moral virtue and a life lived with compassion, interest and goodness," which is just the opposite of a life lived in indifference, apathy and selfishness.

A NEW APPRECIATION OF SPORT'S ASCETICAL POTENTIAL

When the inherent fascination of play is combined with a healthy spirit of competition and self-improvement, sport becomes charged with great educational potential. This is because a key component to education is motivation, and sport, as we have seen, motivates and can be a stimulus for the pursuit of excellence. In light of this, it should be no wonder then that sport entered onto the Church's concern through the doorway of education. The case is often made that the Catholic Church was totally opposed to sport since Chrysostom, Augustine and Tertullian forbade Christians to view public spectacles that included games of sport. Yet, this is not the total picture. Clement of Alexandria approved of physical exercise and games among children. Centuries before Thomas Arnold and Pierre de Coubertin recognized the contribution sport could play in the education of youth, Sylvius Piccolomini, a key figure in the humanistic movement in the 1400s and the future Pope Pius II, approved of children playing ball games and encouraged teachers to include recreational activities within school curriculum in his letter *De liberorum educatione*.[6]

Pontiffs in the last century have also pointed out sport's educational potential. In his *Encyclical on Christian Education*, Pius XI (1929: 26) expressed an appreciation for physical exercise and the body in general as he makes the case for a well-rounded, integral education. His successor, Pope Pius XII (1945: 129), also noted to a group of military sport instructors at universities from around the U.S. that:

Sport, properly directed, develops character, makes a person courageous, a generous loser, and a gracious victor; it refines the senses, gives intellectual penetration, and steels the will to endurance. . . . Sport is an occupation of the whole person, and while perfecting the body as an instrument of the mind, it also makes the mind itself a more refined instrument for the search and communication of truth.

Even the Second Vatican Council addressed sport: its conciliar document on education, "Gravissimum Educationis" (Vatican Council II, 1965/1975a: 730) includes sporting activity among the educational resources that belong to the common patrimony of humanity and facilitate moral development and human formation. Also, the Second Vatican Council (Vatican Council II, 1965/1975b: 966), in the "Pastoral Constitution Gaudium et Spes," mentions sport when speaking about the proper use of leisure as a time "to refresh the spirit and strengthen the health of mind and body." It also notes that physical exercise and sport "help to create harmony of feeling on the level of the community as well as fostering friendly relations between men of all classes, countries and races." Thus, in looking back over the last century, we can sum up the teachings of the pontiffs in this way: they manifest an acceptance of sport in principle as a component of youth education while warning against its deviations and offer an occasional description of how sporting activity is a metaphor for the spiritual life.

The pontificate of Benedict XVI has also sought, in the context of youth, to highlight sports educational potential. Nevertheless he also places a *caveat* on these activities so that the necessary conditions must be met in order for sport to be educational such as being practiced with respect for the rules and an acute ethical sense.[7]

Is the Vatican overly optimistic in positively valuing sport as an opportunity for personal growth and maturity? When one considers the commercialization of sports and even the unbalanced interest of some parents to make their child a champion at the detriment of the child's own good, it is no wonder many are less optimistic regarding sport's educational potential and even consider that sports might even lead to the degradation of the human person. In light of this, how is it that sports educate? What is this ascetic dimension that is implicit in the practice of a sport?

Although it is beyond the scope of this chapter to make a complete defense of sport's positive educational potential, it may be helpful to cite two statements from Peter Arnold (1997: 50) in *Sport, Ethics and Education*, which are quite similar to that of recent pontiffs in this regards, although his *caveat* is still more precise and demanding. In the chapter on "Sport, Fairness, and the Development of Character" Arnold states:

Moral character is developed in sport, as in other spheres of life, in so far as such admired human qualities as loyalty, courage and resolution are cultivated and directed to uphold what is fair and just in the interest of all. To this extent it is being argued that the practice of sport is commensurate with moral education and the development of moral character.

Yet, he goes on to raise a key question to which a positive answer might soundly justify the Church's specific solicitude for youth sporting activities. Arnold (1997: 51) asks: "Does the practice of sport provide exceptional opportunities for the nurture and cultivation of admired human qualities?" Arnold (1997: 51) concludes his findings in this chapter in this way:

> Whereas it is empirically unfounded to contend that sports or the sports field is the best training ground for the development of admired qualities of character, it does not seem at all unreasonable to suggest that sports provide an unusually good forum for the encouraged display of such qualities which are not only admired in sport but in other aspects of life. . . . As in all forms of learning, much depends on the attitudes and judgments that are brought to bear upon what is done, and whether what is taught and encouraged is regarded as worthwhile in the context of life.

Ultimately, we can see more clearly from all this that sports do not educate; people do!

One might raise the objection here that sport shouldn't be "tapped" or "used" for anything at all, but should remain true to its purpose as an end in itself and not a means to some other end. Was not this, in fact, the point that was being made in reclaiming sport's playful nature in the face of being "instrumentalized" by other commercial or pragmatic aims? Yes, it was. Yet, at the same time, just as gardening can be enjoyed per se, and not for any instrumental ends, so too the case can be made for sport. One might pursue gardening in itself and still enjoy the beauty of the flowers or the taste of one's own homegrown tomatoes. So too, one can enjoy playing a sport and still benefit from the "seriousness" of competition and the pursuit of excellence and all that this entails. Like gardening or music or the pursuit of other arts, engaging in sports is not pure spontaneous entertainment; it is also a practice that implies the apprenticeship of certain basic skills in order to enjoy the freedom of its play. It is in this sense that, without losing its true nature, we need to recognize and affirm the "educational and spiritual potential of sport." In other words, while upholding the fun and play of sport, we also need to simultaneously recognize that sport is a practice as well as a game. Furthermore, if we pretend that we can consider the practice of sport to be completely "neutral" of any educational purpose and thus void of any values or skills, then we will only be paving the way for sport to be "used" for other aims and purposes that are even further removed from its original end and, unfortunately, even detrimental to a child's development.

In his homily in Olympic Stadium during the Jubilee for Sport, John Paul II (2000b: 1) made an appeal to not only Catholics, but all people of goodwill to promote a "sport which teaches sacrifice, respect and responsibility, leading to the full development of every human person." Thus, in following this appeal made by John Paul II, here are some of the admired human qualities, virtues and skills—in no way a comprehensive list—that can be pursued when sport is considered as a practice.

A Sense of Responsibility

It was mentioned earlier how play has been considered as a stance of "open responsiveness" (Hyland 1990: 141) to others and to particular situations. But this responsiveness implies a minimal amount of self-control. Self-mastery is, in fact, a key factor in sport, where a child learns how to control physical movements and cope with emotions and passions. An old adage states: "At table and at play, a man gives himself a way." Just as self-control is essential to practice good manners at the table, the heat of the game is also a unique place where a person manifests his or her degree of self-dominion over intense emotions and primary inclinations.

Cardinal Ratzinger (1978/1992: 263) observed how sport "compels a man to take himself in hand so that through training, he may gain control over himself; through control, mastery; and through mastery, freedom." As we know, the practice of a sport certainly provides children as well as adults repetitive situations in which they can exercise their self-composure and channel their emotions in a positive way. This self-dominion is sustained especially when children are instructed and encouraged to keep in check their compulsory urges and not to react violently when antagonized or when they disagree with the referee's call.

Sports provide this apprenticeship in responsibility inasmuch as a child is made more aware of the consequences of his or her personal actions in sport. This happens, for instance, when the referee calls a foul or signals an infraction of the rules that results in a penalty; the one responsible for this feels the consequences of his actions in an acute way. The same can be said in a positive way by those individual actions that contribute directly to the benefit of the team.

Discipline and Sacrifice

How crucial and yet how difficult it is for young people who are immersed in a world that offers them all kinds of easy yet fleeting pleasures to learn discipline and sacrifice. Two millennium ago, St. Paul, while addressing the Christian community living amid the licentiousness of Corinth, recalled how: "every athlete exercises discipline in every way" (1 Cor. 9:25). Paul considered the self-discipline in the life of an athlete as something worthy of imitation in his own life and in the life of all Christians who are set on obtaining even more lofty goals than a "perishable crown." Thus, he went on to say: "I do not run aimlessly; I do not fight as if I were shadowboxing. No, I drive my body and train it, for fear that, after having preached to others, I myself should be disqualified" (1 Cor. 9:26–27).

Although the word *sacrifice* is somewhat obsolete today, it is still used in baseball as a "sacrifice" indicates that the batter sacrifices himself by intentionally getting out at first base in order to advance another runner of his team onto another base and thus closer to scoring position. Likewise, a playmaker is he who will "sacrifice" the personal glory of making a basket or a goal by passing to an open teammate. We can also think of the many sacrifices on and off the court an athlete makes—all of the other "nos" that are made in order to follow a strict diet and practice regimen. As John Paul II (2000b: 1) pointed out during the Jubilee of Sport:

> Anyone who plays sports knows this very well: it is only at the cost of strenuous training that significant results are achieved. At the recent Olympic Games in Sydney we admired the feats of the great athletes, who sacrificed themselves for years, day after day, to achieve those results. This is the logic of sport, especially Olympic sports; it is also the logic of life: without sacrifices, important results are not obtained, or even genuine satisfaction.

Respect

The Church takes for granted that every sport, at both the amateur and the competitive levels, requires basic human qualities such as the acceptance of precise rules and respect for one's opponent. Without these basic human qualities, sport would be reduced to a questionable, soulless demonstration of physical strength. Yet let us look at how sporting activities can assist in fostering a respect for the rules, for oneself and for others.

The governance of rules is an essential characteristic of game playing and sports. Athletes accept adhering by rules that limit them in ways far more explicit and arbitrary than everyday life. The rules constitute the parameters of the game and give it its shape; the rules both limit one's action and also grant possibility. Thus we can say that the very nature of game playing requires the honest acceptance of the rules for it to function. Furthermore, we can distinguish between constitutive rules that define the game and regulative (penalty-invoking) rules that govern the behavior of players. Peter Arnold (1997: 13) notes that this distinction "is a formal way of attempting to preserve the social and ethical basis upon which sport was founded." Although the acceptance of rules is taken for granted, its importance today should not be as this can be helpful for the youth who live in a world where personal liberty is often mistaken for pure licentiousness.

Sport can also provide a training in the respect for oneself, which includes both gratitude for one's personal talents as well as the acceptance of one's physical limitations. Within a Christian perspective, the body merits real respect and care as it is invested with natural dignity and a mysterious sacrality. John Paul II (1984: 3), who is well noted for his "theology of the body," offers this perspective:

In the first place, sport is making good use of the body, an effort to reaching optimum physical condition, which brings marked consequences of psychological well-being. From our Christian faith we know that, through baptism, the human person, in his or her totality and integrity of soul and body, becomes a temple of the Holy Spirit: "Do you not know that your body is a temple of the Holy Spirit within you, which you have from God? You are not your own, you were bought with a price (that is, with the blood of Christ the Redeemer). So glorify God in your body" (1 Cor. 6:19–20).

Here coaches, sports directors and parents especially must be the first to respect the limits and health of the children and assist them in giving the body its proper care.

Lastly, sport's activities should also contribute to fostering respect for others. Indeed, sports are a uniquely effective means of building mutual esteem and respect, human solidarity, friendship and goodwill among peoples. Although speaking specifically about football while blessing Rome's Olympic Stadium, these observations of John Paul II (1990: 3) can be applied to sports in general:

> The value of a football competition like this consists basically in the fact that it enables so many people, differing m background and nationality, to come together, get to know one another, to learn to respect one another, and to enjoy competing with one another honestly and in a spirit of healthy rivalry, without giving in to the temptation to selfishness and violence.

We live in a society more and more individualistic. Especially in Europe, where many children have no siblings, these situations can make it more difficult for a child to learn how to operate as a member of a team. Because of this, sports can provide an opportunity to learn how to be a team player. In most team sports, players learn that little acts of self-giving and renunciation are indispensable. Team players know that they cannot go it alone. They must look for the open player, assist their teammates and respect their position. Coaches can also foster team play by praising players for maintaining their position, for making an assist or for helping out on defense as well as offense.

THE IMPORTANCE OF THE SPORTS EDUCATOR

As mentioned previously, sports do not educate youth; people do. It was once assumed and expected that every teacher be considered a moral educator, but many today want to abdicate this responsibility or simply never recognize it at all. In fact, Pope Benedict XVI (2007:3) notes that today "education tends to be broadly reduced to the transmission of specific abilities or capacities for doing." However, the Holy Father (2007:3) sees that this situation cannot satisfy because "it ignores the essential aim of education which is the formation of a person to enable him or her to live to the full and to make his or her own contribution to the common good." The Holy Father goes on to make a point that is also so valid for the sports educator:

> Consequentially, both parents and teachers are easily tempted to abdicate their educational duties and even no longer to understand what their role is in this regards. Yet, in this way, we are not offering to young people, to the young generations, what it is our duty to pass on to them. Moreover, we owe them the true values which give life a foundation . . . Today, in fact, every educational task seems more and more arduous and precarious. Consequently, there is talk of a great "educational emergency," of the increasing difficulty encountered in transmitting the basic values of life and correct behavior to the new generations, a difficulty that involves both schools and families and, one might say, any other body with educational aims.

Here, we cannot debate whether every teacher exercises this role as a moral educator. Yet, we need to stress here in agreement with Arnold (1997: 73) that "the teacher can and should, directly and indirectly, have a moral influence upon the pupils who he or she comes into contact." The sports educator is an initiator and guardian of the intrinsic goods of sport as a practice. This needs to be recognized to a greater degree by the educators themselves and by those responsible for directing youth sports.

In the Catholic Church—at least in the findings of the Vatican's past three international sport seminars[8]—there is a growing consensus regarding the important role that the sport's educator (coach, volunteer, teacher) can play in the lives of the children and youth entrusted to their care. Pope Benedict XVI (2007: 3) also notes that "the demand for authentic education and the rediscovery of the need for true educators" is on the rise. Consequently, with this greater awareness and concern for placing more emphasis on the transcendent role of coaching, there also arises the urgent need of assisting coaches in developing their skills as a mentor for the youth.

Within this perspective of recuperating the educational-formative dimension of sport via coaching, the Church must not remain indifferent to the unique opportunity that is offered to us by those sport activities carried out in Catholic schools or in conjunction with a parish or Catholic association as a point of contact with the youth of today. As hours in catechism class are ever more scarce and church attendance down, the coach, parent or volunteer who is in contact with these children via sports has a precious opportunity to set a good example and to influence them in a positive way. In fact, Pope Benedict XVI (2007: 4) observed how the coach and other educators exercise a role that is complementary to that of parents:

> As children gradually grow up, their inner desire for personal auton-
> omy naturally increases. Especially in adolescence, this can easily lead
> to them taking a critical distance from their family. Here, the closeness
> which can be guaranteed by . . . other educators capable of making the
> friendly face of the Church and love of Christ concrete for the young
> person, becomes particularly important.

On another occasion Pope Benedict XVI (2009b: 5) touched upon the transcendent role that coaches and others can play as experts in guiding the
youth entrusted to their care:

> As part of a coordinated, formative effort, Catholic directors, staff and
> workers must consider themselves expert guides for youth, helping each
> of them to develop their athletic potential without obscuring those human
> qualities and Christian virtues that make for a fully mature person.

From all that has been stated in the preceding, we should be able to recognize
and appreciate all the more the unique and important educational role of a
youth coach. Unfortunately, recent coaching scandals remind us that there
is always a risk that a coach could also be a negative influence on the youth.
Thus, all the more important is the pastoral attention that should be given to
these youth leaders. In fact, the coaching activity that is realized within the
Catholic Church should be considered and appreciated as a type of "youth
ministry" that requires more than mere technical skills. Consequently, there
arises the urgent need to help equip these people for their mission so that they
can be authentic witnesses and expert guides to theses children as well as the
parents with whom they deal with on a weekly basis.

SPORT AND THE SPIRITUAL LIFE

Regarding the interest in establishing a possible link between sports and
the spiritual life, it should be noted that the Church has for centuries
looked favorably upon amateur sports for their contribution to the overall
development of the human person. As sport entered the Church's concern through the door of education, it often has placed emphasis on the
human virtues. As for sport and the development of spiritual virtues, the
relationship has been more indirect: the human virtues acquired through
sport are seen as a pedestal for supporting other virtues as "grace per-
fects nature." Nevertheless, long before sport appeared upon the Church's
radar as an educational activity, it caught the interest of St. Paul as a
metaphor for the spiritual life as he personally considered the athlete and
the Christian to have much in common when it comes to such qualities as
determination, effort and perseverance.

Today, the image of the athlete continues to serve as an analogy for Christians who seek excellence in their spiritual life. Along these lines, several of

the pontiffs, but especially Pius XII and John Paul II, have observed how we can come into contact with the beauty of creation, which leads to praise of the Creator via outdoors sports and leisure time in general.[9] Pope Benedict XVI (2009c: 12) also touches upon this sense of gratitude and wonder that can arise from the contemplation of sporting excellence. In speaking to world champion swimmers, he states:

> Watching these swimming championships and admiring the results achieved make it easy to understand the great potential with which God has endowed the human body and the interesting objectives of perfection it is able to achieve. One then thinks of the Psalmist's wonder who in contemplating the universe, praises the glory of God and the greatness of man: "when I behold your heavens," we read in Psalm 8, "the work of your fingers, the moon and the stars that you have set in place what is man that you are mindful of him, or the son of man that you care for him?" (vv. 3–4). Then, how can one fail to thank the Lord for having endowed the human body with such perfection; for having enriched it with a beauty and harmony that can be expressed in so many ways? The sports disciplines, each in a different way, help us to appreciate this gift which God has made to us.

So gratitude for gifts received, and for life itself, might be one path by which a spirituality of sport or for athletes might be developed. There is also another path: that of considering life itself as a great effort and struggle towards an eternal goal. Pope Paul VI (1964: 894) briefly alluded to this in an audience with cyclists of the *Giro d'Italia*:

> The intuition that you carry in your soul is something that perhaps you do not know how to express; it is that intuition that sport, more than being a reality that is sensible and experiential, is also a symbol of a spiritual reality, that constitutes the hidden goal, but essential to our lives: life is an effort, a struggle, life is a risk, life is a race, life is a hope set upon the finish line, which transcends the scene of common experience where the soul intervenes and religion presents itself.

One other way might be that of developing a spirituality of sport akin to that of work. In the last chapter of the *Encyclical Laborem Exercens*, John Paul II (1981: 85) offers some elements by which there could be constructed a "spirituality of work":

> The Church considers it her duty to speak out on work from the viewpoint of its human value and of the moral order to which it belongs . . . At the same time she sees it as her particular duty to form a spirituality of work which will help all people to come closer, through work, to God, the Creator and Redeemer, to participate in his salvific plan for man and the world and to deepen their friendship with Christ.

Although sport is not a *necessarium* like that of work, some similar elements could be formulated for a spirituality of sport that might enable the athlete to come closer to God through this activity that also is of "human value" and "belongs to the moral order." Needless to say, the elements that could constitute a spirituality of sport require further development. For the present moment, these are simply a few of the many possible ways that a connection might be drawn between the practice of sport and the spiritual life.

CONCLUSION

This chapter attempted to sketch some of the distinguishing characteristics of the type of sport that the "Church and Sport" Section of the Pontifical Council for the Laity seeks to promote, that is to say: "a sport that can contribute to the love of life, that can free young people from the snares of apathy and indifference and a sport that can teach sacrifice, respect and responsibility." (John Paul II 2000b: 1) As we have seen, this Vatican's game plan boils down to recuperating and strengthening sport's recreational, educational and pastoral dimensions and the awareness that this is dependent upon how sports are carried out. The question of how Catholic sports should be best staged is well summarized by Pope Benedict XVI in his message for our last Vatican sports seminar. Thus I wish to conclude this chapter with these words of Benedict XVI (2009b: 5):

> Through sports, the ecclesial community contributes to the formation of youth, providing a suitable environment for their human and spiritual growth. In fact, when sports initiatives aim at the integral development of the person and are managed by qualified and competent personnel, they provide a useful opportunity for priests, religious and lay people to become true and proper educators and teachers of life for the young. In our time when an urgent need to educate the new generations is evident it is therefore necessary for the Church to continue to support sports for youth, making the most of their positive aspects also at competitive levels such as their capacity for stimulating competitiveness, courage and tenacity in pursuing goals.

NOTES

1. John Paul II (2000b).
2. John Paul II established a section for sport within the Pontifical Council for the Laity in 2004, entrusting to it the following goals: 1) To insure a more direct and systematic attention to the vast world of sport on the part of the Church, serving as a point of reference and dialogue with the various national and international sports associations and groups. 2) To solicit a renewed sensitivity on the part of the local Church in this field, favoring synergy among those ecclesiastical

associations involved in sports. 3) To promote a culture of sport in harmony with the true dignity of the human person through youth education, parish centers and other associations. 4) To conduct studies and investigation concerning particular problems and challenges regarding sport, especially those of ethical nature, which are most urgent. 5) To promote any other initiatives that can serve to evangelize the world of sport, especially those that foster the witness of an authentic Christian life among professional athletes.

3. Aristotle makes a distinction between the play of children, which for him was considered in a strict sense a mere recreational break that was subordinate to work of study, and leisure, which was the ultimate goal of man. Cf. Josef Pieper's acute analysis (1952/1999: 1–5).

4. Cited in Staub (2007: 131).

5. Here are both parts of the full citation of John Paul II (1990: 3–4): "Dear young people, you are the very best that your respective nations have to offer for this sporting competition. Be proud of this honor, but also take to heart the responsibility you have to represent your country with dignity, offering in fair exchange the gift or your zest for life and for everything that makes life noble and great." Regarding zest for life and for challenge: "Be conscious of your responsibility! It is not only the champion in the stadium but also the whole person who should become a model for millions of young people, who need 'leaders,' not 'idols.' They need men who can convey to them the zest for challenge, a sense of discipline, the courage to be honest and the joy or unselfishness. Your steady and generous example can inspire them to face life's problems with equal commitment and enthusiasm."

6. See Aiello (2004: 115).

7. See Benedict XVI (2009c: 12)

8. See Pontificium Consilium pro Laicis (2006, 2008, 2011).

9. See Pius XII: 'Lessons of the Mountain' of 26 September 1948, as cited in Feeney (1995: 37–40). Discourse on the mountain and John Paul II, 'Virtue and Contemplation Should Be Your Daily Fare,' 26 April 1986, as cited in Feeney (1995: 81–83).

BIBLIOGRAPHY

Aiello, M. (2004) *Viaggio nello sport attraverso i secoli*, Florence: Le Monnier.

Aristotle. (2000) *Nicomachean Ethics*, trans. R. Crisp, Cambridge: Cambridge University Press.

Arnold, P. (1997) *Sport, Ethics, and Education*, London: Cassell.

Bauman, Z. (2007) *Homo Consumens: Lo sciame inquieto dei consumatori e la miseria degli esclusi*, Trento: Centro Studi Erickson.

Benedict XVI. (2005) *Deus Caritas Est*, Vatican City: LEV.

Benedict XVI. (2007) Address to the Participants of the Convention of the Diocese of Rome, 11 June, in *L'Osservatore Romano*, 3–5n25.

Benedict XVI. (2009a) Address to Civil and Political Authorities in Prague, 26 September, in *L'Osservatore Romano*, 5n224.

Benedict XVI (2009b) Message to the President of the Pontifical Council for the Laity on Sports, in *L'Osservatore Romano*, 5n46.

Benedict XVI. (2009c) Speech to the Participants of the World Swimming Championship, 1 August, in *L'Osservatore Romano*, 12n31.

Craven, P. (2009) Champions against All Obstacles, in Pontificium Consilium pro Laicis (Ed.), *Sport, Education, Faith: Towards a New Season for Catholic Sport Associations*, Vatican City: LEV, 115–21.

Elias, N. and Dunning, E. (1986) *Quest for Excitement*, Oxford: Blackwell.

Feeney, R. (1995) *A Catholic Perspective: Physical Exercise and Sports*, Alexandria, VA: Aquinas Press.

Huizinga, J. (1950) *Homo Ludens: A Study of the Play Element in Culture*, Boston: Beacon.

Hyland, D. (1990) *Philosophy of Sport*, St. Paul, MN: Paragon House.

John Paul II. (1981) *Encyclical Laborem Exercens*, Vatican City: Vatican Polyglot Press.

John Paul II. (1984) International Jubilee of Sport: Homily at Olympic Stadium, 12 April, in *L'Osservatore Romano*, 3–4n17.

John Paul II. (1990) Blessing of Rome's Olympic Stadium: Pope Inaugurates 'Italia 90' Cup, 31 May, in *L'Osservatore Romano*, 3–4n24.

John Paul II (2000a), Address to Members of FIFA, 11 December, in *Insegnamenti di Giovanni Paolo II*, vol. 23, Vatican City: LEV, 1098–99.

John Paul II. (2000b) Even the Greatest Champions Need Christ: Homily and Angelus at the Jubilee for the Word of Sport, 29 October, in *L'Osservatore Romano*, 1–2n44.

John Paul II. (2004) Address to Members of the Italian Sports Centre, 26 June, in *L'Osservatore Romano*, 3n28.

Paul VI. (1964) Address to Cyclists of *Giro d'Italia*, 30 May, in *Insegnamenti di Paolo VI*, vol. 2, Vatican City: LEV, 893–94.

Pieper, J. (1952/1999) *Leisure: The Basis of Culture*, Indianapolis, IN: Liberty Fund.

Pius XI. (1929) *Encyclical on Christian Education*, Vatican City: Vatican Polyglot Press.

Pius XII. (1945) Message to the Central Sports School of the Armed Forces, 29 July, in *Discorsi e Radiomessaggi del Pio XII*, vol. 7, Vatican City: Tipografia Poliglotta Vaticana, 128–30.

Pontificium Consilium pro Laicis. (2006) *The World of Sport Today: A Field of Christian Mission*, Vatican City: LEV.

Pontificium Consilium pro Laicis (2008) *Sport: An Educational and Pastoral Challenge*, Vatican City: LEV.

Pontificium Consilium pro Laicis. (2011) *Sport, Education, Faith: Towards a New Season for Catholic Sport Associations*, Vatican City: LEV.

Ratzinger, J. (1978/1992) *Co-Workers of the Truth: Meditations for Every Day of the Year*, San Francisco, CA: Ignatius Press.

Staub, D. (2007) *The Culturally Savvy: A Manifesto for Deepening Faith and Enriching Popular Culture in an Age of Christianity-Lite*, San Francisco, CA: Wiley.

Vatican Council II. (1965/1975a) Gravissimum Educationis, in A. Flannery (Ed.), *Vatican Council II: The Conciliar and Post Conciliar Documents*, Northport, NY: Costello, 725–37.

Vatican Council II. (1965/1975b) Pastoral Constitution Gaudium et Spes, in A. Flannery (Ed.), *Vatican Council II: The Conciliar and Post Conciliar Documents*, Northport, NY: Costello, 903–1000.

10 Hard-Won Sporting Achievements and Spiritual Humility

Are They Compatible?

Scott Kretchmar

Elite sporting environments that feature chest bumps, end zone dances, superhuman feats of skill or strength and adoring worldwide audiences would seem to be poor sites for the cultivation of humility. In fact, high-level sport is the place where humans rival the gods, reach for supposedly unreachable goals and thereby appear to contradict any claims that they follow the One who was "meek and lowly." In competitive sport settings the claim that "whoever is last shall be first" (Matt. 20:16) would appear to have very little validity. Rather sports are meritocracies where those who work the hardest and become the best shall be first. And currently many of those who are "first" are not at all shy about drawing attention to that fact . . . on the field and elsewhere.

While such hubris and public self-promotion are less visible in recreational and children's sport, and while no godlike deeds are seen at this level of participation, even here we might intuit a kind of incompatibility between sport and humility. When one finally hits a ball over a net, learns how to swim across the deep end of a swimming pool or wins a sandlot game, the natural response is likely to be "I did it!" or in a slightly less self-congratulatory way, "My teammates and I did it!" Even if a player, in Pauline fashion, acknowledged that God had a hand in his success, this young athlete would still seem to deserve a solid pat on the back. After all, it was this individual, not God, who practiced long hours to get the skill right, and it was this person who would likely feel that he or she earned the status that goes with hard-won sporting competence.

These comments portray sporting environments as arid deserts for the cultivation of humility. But the opposite argument may work too. Sport is the kind of activity in which we push the envelope of performance and, because of that, put our human vulnerabilities on display. Novak (1976) captured this fate-tempting, high-risk side of sport when he remarked, "I love the tests of the human spirit. I love to see defeated teams refuse to die. I love to see impossible odds confronted. I love to see impossible dares accepted" (150). Novak went on to say that sometimes these "impassioned efforts are crowned with success." But often, as he readily admitted, they are not. Often—perhaps more often than not—athletes fall short.

From this alternate vantage point, it is clear that sport is just as much about failing as succeeding. Even victories are never perfect. One can always play better. Every achievement always has elements of imperfection in it. High standards, in particular, invite unfavorable outcomes. Paul Weiss (1969) understood this when he wrote many years ago, "Excellence excites and awes. It pleases and it challenges . . . We desire to achieve it. We want to share in it . . . *even though it may point up the fact that we are defective, less than we might have been, [less than] we ought to be*" (3; emphasis added).

If Weiss is right, sport is at once a venue for achievement and a place where we fall short of what we ought to be. Chance events, unexpected encounters, reserves of energy that mysteriously disappear, defective equipment, finding that we are "off" our game, injuries, additional human frailties—there is so much that we cannot fully control. Because of these limitations, patience, grace, gratitude and humility would seem to be natural companions on any serious athlete's successful sojourn through the dangerous and uncertain minefields of athletic performance.

So, which account of sport and athletic attitudes is more compelling? Does sport provide a pedagogy for pride or humility . . . or some of both? If devout individuals wanted to cultivate their spiritual humility, would sport be a good place to do so? Conversely, if serious athletes wanted to become better competitors, would spiritual humility fortify and enhance that project or have precisely the opposite effect?

In this chapter I will attempt to answer these questions. I will first describe the nature of humility philosophically and then briefly discuss its central role in three of the world's great religions: Christianity, Islam and Buddhism. On this foundation, I will then argue for a paradoxical, nondualistic vision of sport as a domain of nervous~confident and secular~spiritual humility.

THE NATURE OF HUMILITY

Something about humility can be learned by looking at its derivation. The term comes from the Latin word humus meaning "of the earth." Thus, humility would seem to connote things that are low, basic or common. To be humble is to be without much dignity, self-worth or merit. The term suggests submissiveness to any and all higher authorities. The humble individual admits to limitations, to being at risk of harm from external agents, to being incapable. When we say that a person comes from humble origins, we suggest that he or she began life with significant handicaps and without the benefit of such privileges as family wealth, advanced education or public stature.

It is precisely this lowliness that makes humility a virtue, one that becomes its possessor. The humble person never pushes to the front of the line. He or she typically gives credit to others. This individual is not a self-promoter, does not want to be a magnet for attention and is typically uncomfortable when others want to celebrate his or her achievements. The humble individual does not reach beyond personal capacities. Aquinas (1929) put it this way: "The virtue of humility consists in this, that a man keeps to his own place, and does not reach out to things above him, but is subject to his superior" (214).

The humble person is particularly unconcerned about rank, comparison or relative standing. Pride, considered by some to be the opposite of humility, comes most directly from relative assessments, from judgments about being better than others or from being seen positively in another's eyes. This is why humility is such a difficult virtue to pursue. Taking pride in one's achievement of humility is, of course, a contradiction. This led C. S. Lewis (1943/1960) to conclude: "If we find that our religious life is making us feel that we are good—above all that we are better than someone else—I believe we may be sure that we are being acted on, not by God, but by the Devil" (96).

Humility needs to be distinguished from several varieties of false humility. One of these comes from various public displays of low self-regard—by demeaning oneself, never taking credit, falsely understating one's contribution to a project or cultivating a public posture of downcast eyes and meek comportment. This kind of humility is too concerned with how one looks in the eyes of others. In other words it is a self-conscious, calculated kind of self-deprecation. It is humility for show, a competitive, prideful humility that announces, in effect, "I can be more humble than you." Again, C. S. Lewis indicated why this is not genuine humility. Humility is not thinking less of yourself. It is thinking of yourself less. Lewis called this a blessed forgetting of the self (1943/1960: 99).

A second form of false humility is similarly extreme in nature. It is the attitude that refuses to take pride in anything. It is a kind of agnostic humility, one that will not identify something that is, in fact, truly wonderful as genuinely good and then celebrate it. It ignores accomplishments. It fails to allow a pride that is justly deserved. It fails, in religious terms, to distinguish between boastful or sinful pride, on the one hand, and what might be called grateful pride, on the other.

Another form of false humility is seen among those who revile themselves to such an extent that they withdraw from all duties and projects. Seeing themselves as utterly unworthy and incapable, they do not act. They are even incapable of being the Good Samaritan or responding to a friend in need. In effect, they mistake a realistic fallibility for worthlessness, dependency for helplessness, relational or derived power for no power at all.

HUMILITY IN CHRISTIANITY

The stories, traditions and theology of Christianity are thoroughly homogenized with the virtue of humility. Jesus came to the earth in humble circumstances—as a baby, the child of an unwed mother, born in the basement of a house amid animals in an obscure town and in an equally obscure part of the world. After he grew up, began his ministry and gained a degree of notoriety, he still seemed to prefer the company of common folk, even prostitutes and tax collectors, over the religious elite.

He promoted a spiritual life that had far more to do with relationships, commitment, love, forgiveness and trust than knowledge, achievement, purity and one's standing in the church. It is not surprising, then, that humility was promoted as a prime virtue. To reinforce this fact, Jesus told those seeking entry to the Kingdom that they must come as little children, in wonder, meekness and humility (Matt. 5:3, 5). On the other hand, those who are rich, powerful and prideful would find that it is easier for a large animal to pass through the eye of a needle than their entering the Kingdom of God (Matt. 19:24). Jesus turned egoistic logic on its head when he concluded that those who would humble themselves will be exalted, while those who exalt themselves will be humbled (Luke 14:11, 18:14; Phil. 2:8–9). To top things off, Jesus made a striking and seemingly scandalous promise to his followers. "Blessed are the meek," he said, "for they shall inherit the earth" (Matt: 5:5).

In the sixth century St. Benedict identified three capital virtues; humility was among them. Humility of heart, not just exterior behavior, was so important to Benedict's goal of "mystical union with God through prayer" that it was identified as a specific objective of the monastic disciplines (Fry, 1981). In discussing the role of humility and pride in one's spiritual growth, Benedict noted the only two directions one can move on Jacob's ladder and the virtues associated with each one. "Without a doubt, this descent and ascent can signify only that we descend by exaltation and ascend by humility. Now the ladder erected is our life on earth and if we humble our hearts the Lord will raise it to heaven" (Benedict in Fry, 1981: 193). In order to promote such an ascent, Benedict identified twelve steps of humility that began with the fear of God and ended with the thorough integration of humility into all that the monk thinks and does "so that [humility] is evident . . . in the oratory, the monastery or the garden, on a journey or in the field, or anywhere else" (201).

Centuries later, those who followed the Pauline, Augustinian, Neoplatonic and Lutheran lineage would emphasize the virtue of humility in relationship to human depravity and incapability. Very little room existed in this theology for human achievement and self-congratulations, let alone self-perfection and pride. Luther captured the gist of human dependency when he interpreted the third article of the Apostle's Creed as follows.

> I believe that I cannot, by my own reason or strength, believe in Jesus Christ my Lord or come to him; but the Holy Spirit has called me by the Gospel, enlightened me with His gifts, sanctified and kept me in the true faith. (Luther in Wagener, 1991: 60)

For Augustine and Luther, humility was not a sometimes, partial or occasionally useful virtue. It was the only appropriate posture or attitude for a fallen human being in relationship to the Divine. Even for those who were compelled more by Aristotelian, Thomistic and Roman Catholic traditions that honored experience, the careful observation of particulars, inductive logic and the power of the human intellect, humility was still given a lofty position. While philosophy and science, for Thomas, could provide important insights into the infinite mystery and majesty of God's creation, while reason and faith were complementary, not contradictory, and while human reason was a force that could "magnify the profundity of the Christian faith" (Tarnas, 1991: 189), the virtue of humility was important for restraining the individual "to his own place" (Aquinas, 1929: 214). Human knowledge would always be imperfect. Reason would always need to be complemented with faith. The conduct of science and philosophy, in short, required a posture of humility—for both secular and theological reasons.

HUMILITY IN ISLAM

The stories, history and theology of Islam are also inseparable from the virtue of humility. In fact, the word *Islam* itself is usually translated to mean "surrender" or "submission." The so-called five pillars of Islamic practice are all designed to reinforce day-to-day experiences of humility through ritual profession of faith, prayer, acts of charity, fasting and pilgrimages to holy sites like Mecca, Medina and Jerusalem. As is well known, most Muslims pray five times a day to Allah. During these sessions, they move through a variety of postures that symbolize their inferior status when addressing the One God. They begin in a standing position and end up kneeling, with head to ground, in a position that connotes complete submission and dependency.

The Prophet Mohammed is said to have founded Islam in 622 CE. At age forty, his life was changed when he was visited by the angel Gabriel. He then took on the task converting his countrymen and, much like prophets in the Hebrew-Christian tradition, opposed moral laxness, materialism, idolatry (particularly in the form of polytheism) and hedonism. Mohammed, seen by adherents as the last of the prophets, attempted to clarify and purify an antecedent religion that had been contaminated by foreign ideas and other errors (Religious Tolerance, 2011: 2). Humility was at the heart of his teachings found in the holy text for Islam, the *Quran*, a volume that was said to have been dictated to Mohammed by the archangel Jibril.

Interestingly, in the *Quran*, the term most often used to refer to worship is *Ibadah*. This is the term from which "ubudiyyah" is derived, meaning to show one's humbleness or humility. This humility is not based merely on an intellectual assent to a proposition about the relative status of humans and

Allah, but rather a complete "sense of humbleness that overcomes one who is totally submitted to the will of God." Worship in Islam is an act of submission, and the foundation of submission is humility (Stacey, 2008: 2).

In Islam, humility is more a way of life than a theological principle. The *Quran* is clear that those who follow Allah must submit to him. "So glorify the praises of your Lord and be of those who prostrate themselves (to Him) (*Quran* 15:98). Arrogance, which is considered in Islam to be the opposite of humility, is unequivocally condemned and is associated with Satan.

> Except Satan, he refused to be among the prostrators. God said, 'O Satan! What is your reason for not being among the prostrators? 'Satan said: 'I am not the one to prostrate myself to a human being, whom You created from sounding clay.' (*Quran* 15:30–35)

If there were any doubt about the commitment human beings should experience in relationship to Allah, this is quelled by Islamic statements like the following: "All men are children of Adam, and Adam was created from soil" (Hadith of Tirmidhi). Humility is supposed to affect everything one does.

> Successful indeed are the believers
> who are humble in their prayers,
> and who shun vain conversation,
> and who are payers of the poor-due
> and who guard their modesty. (*Quran* 23:1–5)

HUMILITY IN ZEN BUDDHISM

The humility required by Zen Buddhism is every bit as demanding as that found in Christianity and Islam even though it is not generated by a relationship to the Divine or "wholly Other." It is demanding because Buddhists think that the ego is an illusion, albeit a deep-seated and difficult-to-transcend kind of self-deception. The source of human suffering and thus the foundation of nonspiritual living is ego desire—the incessant activity of the mind that wants, needs, distinguishes, judges, fixates on and otherwise attempts to control the world and one's life in it. The aggressiveness of the ego creates the "illusion of individuality," and the continuous busyness of consciousness is a product of arrogance and disobedience (Linssen, 1960: 137).

Buddhism requires the humility of one who admits to a chronic, deep-seated dis-ease. The individual who enters a Zen monastery has to admit, in effect, to a grand mistake that has dominated his or her life—namely, reliance on the so-called "I process." The individual has to admit to living a life of ignorance. As D. T. Suzuki (1961) put it, "In ignorance the world is asserted as distinct from the self . . . as soon as cognition takes place there is Ignorance clinging to its very act. When we think we know something, there is something we do not know" (128).

The Buddha figure, then, is not God, nor is he a conduit for the word of God. Rather he is a model. He is one who has had the experience of enlightenment, of transcending the "illusion of individuality." He gave up control, abandoned cherished dichotomies, jettisoned comforting distinctions and submitted to the natural unity of self~other, high~low, yin~yang. In his moment-to-moment experience, he found Life (usually called satori or enlightenment) in the absence of ego-desire. The quieting of the discursive mind did not lead to nihilism or withdrawal from the world, but rather to tranquility, harmony, intuitive productivity, a profound kind of peace in and with the world.

This accomplishment, this ridding oneself of a deep-seated illusion, is a formidable task. Many who begin on this spiritual journey sit and meditate for years and experience only occasional and partial progress. But full enlightenment, according to this tradition, is cataclysmic and unmistakable. According to Mahayana traditions of Buddhism, it floods across one's entire life—every activity, every waking moment. When this happens, one can only bow in humble gratitude. "It" has taken over.

To be sure, this is a kind of achievement. Without a doubt, the Zen practitioner would be tempted to celebrate and congratulate him- or herself. But as was the case with Christianity and Islam, spiritual progress should provide no occasion for the reemergence of pride. It is best just to bow and move on.

> Subhuti, what do you think? Does a holy one say within himself, "I have obtained Perfective Enlightenment"? Subhuti replied, "No, World honored One . . . If a holy one of Perfective Enlightenment said to himself, Such am I, he would necessarily partake of the idea of an ego-identity, a personality, a being, a separated individuality." (Diamond Sutra 9)

From this brief review of three major spiritual traditions—traditions that have attracted roughly four billion adherents worldwide—it is clear that humility plays a central role in each one.[1] For all three, humility is an attitude, a way of comporting oneself, a stance, an approach to life far more than a proposition or a tenet of faith.[2] And in all three spiritual traditions, humility presents something of a paradox.

This is so because humility is both chicken and egg—both a precondition for spiritual experience but also a product of that experience. It is a key that would unlock the front door to the mansion. But it is also something that is at least partly hidden until one moves into the heart of the building. It allows one to start the journey and continue taking steps forward, but it also marks progress of walking in new places. This suggests that there may be a kind of reciprocal relationship at work between two facets of humility—facets that, for sake of simplicity, I will call Humility 1 and Humility 2.

In the Christian tradition, it could be argued that Jesus began his ministry from a posture of Humility 1. This is the kind deference that a Son shows to his Father or an Apprentice to the Master. Niebuhr (1951) remarks that this kind of humility was not a "thing in itself" but a "habit of behavior in the presence of others" (25). This humility coupled with faith and obedience carried Jesus forth on his journey.

But at each step, the "fruits of the spirit," the gifts that are bestowed as a result of humble obedience, evoked a higher order of humility—in my terminology, Humility 2—one that is based more on awe, gratitude and security and less on nervous submission and hope. Humility 2 is generated with various interventions of grace—transformations, miraculous provisions, healings, redemptions, resurrections.

On this line of thought, we could picture Humility 1 and 2 as partners in a kind of reciprocal dance. The reciprocity is so intimate it is hard to say, at times, who is in the lead. Logically, Humility of Apprenticeship would seem to be the initiator, the one in control. The Humility of Gratitude, after all, would not even exist but for the prior work of its partner. But as the dance proceeds, the two elements blend into a kind of unity—seeking promotes new experiences, new experiences promote more seeking, the Humility of Apprenticeship enabling the Humility of Gratitude and the Humility of Gratitude stimulating yet more seeking, on and on in a positive spiral. In circular patterns like this one, it really does not matter who is taking the lead and who is following.

Christianity, Islam and Buddhism agree that Humility 1 has something to do with ego management. In theistic traditions, it is an initial admission of dependency, a promise to let Someone Else dethrone the "I." In non-theistic traditions, it is a willingness to confront an illusion, to change one's ego-driven habits, to exchange the prideful "I want and make" for the harmonious "it happens." But at bottom, the spiritual journeys under all three traditions get under way with the humble two-part admission of the apprentice: 1. I believe there is a better place. 2. I cannot get there on my own. This is the humility of supplication and is symbolized by the posture of kneeling often with head bowed or head to ground.

Humility 2, again in all three traditions, is based on receiving, having better eyes with which to see and better ears with which to hear. It has to do with recognizing the gifted nature of an accomplishment, an unusual experience, a special relationship. Thus, the Humility of Gratitude is grounded in an ontological surprise, an acknowledgment of mystery. It is the humility of those who are thankful. It is often symbolized by a posture of bowing or bowing with one's hands clasped by one's chest.

If this analysis is at all on target, we can conclude that humility plays an enduring and central role in spiritual progress across religious traditions. It might even be called a *sine qua non* or linchpin for spiritual transformations.

Can the same be said for sport? Are there any such things as secular trans-formations? It is to these questions that we need to turn our attention.

HUMILITY IN SPORT

Alasdair MacIntyre (1984) can be helpful in understanding what it means to become an athlete. In his terminology it involves entering something he calls a practice. In rough terms, a practice is a skillful art, a socially established, cooperative, coherent activity that is accompanied by a set of excellences or high standards that are related to that particular art. MacIntyre cites sport, architecture, farming, inquiries in physics, the work of a historian, parenting and the artistic activities of painting and music as examples of practices. Each practice has its own set of excellences. Sport does too, and different sports have different sets of excellences—different blends of skillful movements related to accuracy, power, coordination, grace, timing, balance and so on.

So, we might ask how one enters a practice and how the factor of what I have been calling Humility 1 facilitates these initiation experiences. MacIn-tyre's analysis lends itself to the identification of three brands of humility that allow one to open the front door of sport, as it were, and then open each suc-cessive door as one matures in the practice. These resources for apprentice-ship might be called the humility of place, submission and patience.

Humility of Place

To be humble is to know one's place. In relationship to practices, this means that the new athlete has to acknowledge that the sport, its traditions and its standards of excellence predate and transcend the involvement of this individual. Soccer, baseball, distance running, whatever the sport might be, is bigger than this person. A preexisting community of practitioners in each of these sports supports and partly defines their nature and evolution. The practice, in short, came earlier and will undoubtedly remain well after any single athlete takes up temporary residence in its domain.

Thus, MacIntyre (1984) argues that any who want to enter a practice must acknowledge "the authority of a tradition which [he or she] then must confront and from which [he or she has] to learn" (194). While the new athlete may eventually become someone who helps to redefine the practice and extend its excellences, the starting point is one of encountering a tradi-tion, acknowledging an authoritative community and assuming only a bit part in a much larger play.

Humility of Submission

To be humble is to submit to higher authorities. The beginning athlete not only encounters the authority of an ongoing tradition and community of practitioners. He or she also encounters standards—standards that, to use MacIntyre's terms, define the many excellences of each sporting practice. These excellences, according to MacIntyre, deserve respect, even if they are not fixed for all time. In other words, the new practitioner must submit to them. In order to do so, the athlete needs to confront sporting problems honestly, courageously and with a keen sense of justice. No cheating, no shortcuts, no tricks, no hollow victories will do. In other words, because one submits to the authority of the excellences, one has to pursue them with integrity. It is the authority of the excellences, in short, that begets the virtues of honesty, courage and justice. So, the athlete who would enter any sport's kingdom submits to the authority of excellences that partly define that sporting practice.

Humility of Patience

To be humble is to wait for the right time. Practices, on MacIntyre's analysis, are defined by their unique problems, challenges, dilemmas. Whether one aspires to be a competent architect, physicist, farmer or football player, difficult hurdles will have to be negotiated. Requisite skills, habits, attitudes and virtues will have to be developed, honed and then developed some more. The complexity of these problems is such that rote or repetitive behaviors will not suffice. Pat answers will not do. Practice excellence requires that one be creative, adaptive and able to think on one's feet.

Such achievements are not easily won. Plateaus are encountered. New techniques are attempted, but to no avail. Athletes lift weights, run, change diets, get the latest equipment, work with a new coach. Sometimes the growth is quick and visible. Other times it is not. Breakthroughs are far and few between. The developing athlete cannot simply order them up or will them to appear. The athlete must practice and wait.

MacIntyre (1984) argues that the patient pursuit of practice excellence constitutes a narrative journey that has two essential elements—uncertainty and a telos or goal. MacIntyre tells us that real-life stories, like those that provide an account of our initiation into sport, "are lived before they are told" (212). But eventually they are told, for as MacIntyre claims, a person "is essentially a story-telling animal."

> Deprive children of stories and you leave them unscripted, anxious stutterers in their action as in their words. Hence there is no way to give us an understanding of any society, including our own, except through the stock of stories which constitute its initial dramatic resources. Mythology, in its original sense, is at the heart of things. Vico was right and so was Joyce. And so too of course is that moral tradition from heroic society to its medieval heirs according to which the telling of stories has a key part in educating us into the virtues. (Macintyre, 1984: 216)

The unity of life, for MacIntyre (1984), is won through a patient narrative quest, one that is characterized by integrity and constancy (219). There is no way around it. The cultivation of such a story requires the humility of patience.

Place, submission and patience, then, describe three facets of Humility 1, the Humility of Apprenticeship. These three elements would seem to be inherent in all serious attempts to get past the front door (and all succeeding doors) of any sporting mansion. Those who do not know their place will not acknowledge the larger sporting tradition and community into which they seek admission. Those who will not submit to the authority of the practice excellences will not develop and possess the virtues necessary to genuinely earn and achieve these excellences. Those who lack the humility of patience will regress, stop short of richer goals or substitute an inferior achievement for one that still lays hidden in the practice. Their narrative story will lack coherence as they switch from one pursuit to another. Or their story will lack heroic qualities as they impatiently look for shortcuts to their sporting objectives.

The absence of humility in sport, as in spiritual traditions, is unbecoming. The athlete lacking a sense of place is likely to be seen as brash, disrespectful, naïve, mercenary. The athlete without the humility of submission may be a cheat, an opportunist, one who cares more about fame and fortune than fine play, a person who would be more likely to mine sport than preserve and extend its good traditions. The athletic initiate without the humility of patience will appear to be unrealistic, frustrated, a dabbler, a quitter, ungrounded or aimless.

The lack of Humility 2 is equally unbecoming, but this pushes us ahead of our story. We need to look at this "second partner" in the dance of humility to see how it can also play a central role in sport. This will require that we take a look at what I am calling the humility of identity, grace and harmony. Once again, MacIntyre can help with some of this analysis.

Humility of Identity

When an athlete takes up a sport, the relationship between the person and the activity is distant. This distance and its attendant awkwardness can be experienced in all of our new roles—roles as parents, teachers, researchers and soccer players. We are awkward because it takes time to grow into these roles. We put on the requisite clothing to see how it fits; we begin to absorb the traditions, the ethics, the standards of excellence that go with these roles. Eventually we become more comfortable, more natural.

This development is typically uneven. We take two steps forward and one back. Just as we think we are getting the hang of the practice, a setback seems to present itself. Just as we are getting comfortable and feeling that we belong, a jarring reminder of our ongoing apprenticeship unexpectedly comes down the road. Thus, our quest for intimacy between self and role is chaotic, not linear. One desperately wants to *be* a father (beyond the biological fact), *be* a teacher (beyond having a job as an instructor), *be* a soccer player (beyond spending time on a soccer pitch or on a soccer team).

Eventually, it happens. The desired intimacy is experienced. It is as much granted as it is earned. It is as much a surprise as it was planned for and expected, as much a gift as a payment. It happens when the time is right, and it is always hard to say when that will be. Just as one struggles with one's faith, devotions, meditations and commitment and then realizes gradually or quickly that one *is* a Christian, Muslim or Buddhist, so too the journey in sport, if successful, culminates in an ever-stronger sense of identity. When this intended~surprise happens, the humility of gratitude is an appropriate response.

Sport and Grace

The experience of grace in sport is another fruit of patience and persistence. Grace, of course, is found on the flip side of the effort-achievement coin. Two things are notable about experiences of grace in sport. First, they are neither entirely merited nor predictable. Second, they are not forgettable.

Craig Lambert (1998), a veteran rower, sounded more like a theologian than an athlete when he boldly asserted that "grace has no upper limit" (93). While wall conditions are always presented by physiology, biomechanics and the realities of friction between boat and water, grace will occasionally intervene and seemingly nullify these constraints. Here is how Lambert described one such experience.

> The boat is perfectly level. Set up beautifully, we skim the surface on an invisible laser beam running from horizon to horizon. There is no friction; we ride the natural cadence of our strokes, a continuous cycle. The crew breathes as one. Inhale on the recovery, exhale as we drive our blades through the water: Inspiration and expression. *In. Out.* Row with one body and so with one mind. Nothing exists but: *Here. Now. This.* (1998: 124–25; emphases original)

Lambert (1998) called this particular outbreak of grace in rowing "swing." He proceeded to say that swing is the "coveted, effortless condition where everything falls into place. The experience of swing hooks people on rowing. The appetite for swing is endless." And even though moving a boat through water is factually a difficult, muscular activity, Lambert reported that he and his crewmates were "not so much swinging as being swung." "The boat," he concluded, "swings you" (125).

Swing, just like any other product of grace, cannot be produced on schedule. It appears. It transforms the sporting experience. Amazement and gratitude are far more appropriate responses than any chest-thumping, "I did it" kind of pride. Rather than eliminating humility, this unexpected, unforgettable glimpse of a better world reinforces it and gives it an expanded foundation.

Sport and Harmony

Experiences of harmony might be conceptualized as a species of grace. Undoubtedly, harmony was an element in Lambert's experience of swing. But harmony is so difficult to achieve, it deserves separate mention.

Harmony places a spotlight on the athletic issue of willfulness. Where the athlete makes a willful decision to hit a ball, shoot an arrow, fake out an opponent with a specific tactic—in fact, write a script for success of any sort—harmony between self and world becomes problematic. In short, willfulness generates experiences of self over world or mind over body rather than self with world or mind with body. Eastern cultures point to the possibility of such harmony by using coined terms like "selfworld" and "mindbody."

One kind of sporting harmony is described by Ackerman (1999), who claims that the world of play provides a kind of harmonious, sensible world inside the more chaotic, disparate world of everyday existence.

> Sacred places are playgrounds for deep players. Or to put it another way, whenever one is enraptured by deep play the playground itself becomes sacred. In both cases, special rules must be followed; these may be cricket's rules of play at Lord's famous ground in London, or they may be spiritual or religious rituals. As with all games, a certain air of secrecy reigns. Time shrinks as one gets caught up in the game. The whole universe perfectly contained in that one place, feels harmonious and makes sense. Society's laws give way to higher and more urgent ones. (Ackerman, 1999: 65–66)

Another account of harmony is provided by Herrigel (1953) in the classic book *Zen in the Art of Archery*. This is a mystical harmony between self, act and object. After years of practice with a Zen master, Herrigel still struggled to release the arrow "purposelessly." Each shot, his master told him, must "fall like snow from a bamboo leaf" (73). When Herrigel finally experienced purposeless shooting, he was able to report the following:

> "I'm afraid I don't understand anything more at all," I answered, "even the simplest things have got in a muddle. Is it 'I' who draw the bow, or is it the bow that draws me into the state of highest tension? Do 'I' hit the goal, or does the goal hit me? Is 'It' spiritual when seen by the eyes of the body, and corporeal when seen by the eyes of the spirit—or both or neither? Bow, arrow, goal and ego, all melt into one another, so that I can no longer separate them. And even the need to separate has gone. For as soon as I take the bow and shoot, everything becomes so clear and straightforward and so ridiculously simple."

"Now at last," the Master broke in, "the bowstring has cut right through you." (Herrigel, 1953: 88)

Harmonious, egoless participation causes one to take note. It is not the normal way we experience sport. As Herrigel's Zen master reminded him, it forces a new sense of humility on the participant. "It happened" replaces the more dichotomous and egoistic "I made it happen." All one can do when "it happens" is bow in awe, bow in gratitude, bow to "It."

SUMMARY COMMENTS

Humility can be conceptualized both spiritually and athletically as involving reciprocal experiences of kneeling and bowing. To our logical Western minds, the kneeling comes first. Humility 1 has to precede Humility 2. This brand of humility is the ontological precondition for a renewed sense of being and an epistemological prerequisite for a new way of knowing. Three of the world's great religious traditions appear to be in total agreement on this point. I would like to believe that those who have a deeper appreciation of sport and its demands are unanimous on this point too. We all have to yield to the requirements of the practice whether it be religious or athletic.

In both cases, we desire admission. We are looking for something better. So we kneel in humility. This is a kind of nervous, uncertain, yet hopeful humility. We become apprentices. We risk. We give something up. Of course, such actions assume a degree of self-confidence. On some of the accounts we reviewed, this could be called a kind of pride. But it appears to be a healthy pride, one that is enabling not narcissistic.

This facet of humility is connected to its partner by an unbreakable umbilical cord. Again, three great world religions are unanimous in acknowledging a responsive kind of humility that produces the bow. This is the humility that comes from encountering, even if imperfectly, the Kingdom, grace, harmony, It. It is a grateful and confident humility. Once again, confidence is cited by some as a trait of pride. But here it is a natural response to something beyond the self. And once again, it is not narcissistic. Thus, it is not a contradiction to say that those reach some of the inner chambers of our sporting and spiritual edifices experience a kind of prideful~humility.

Throughout this analysis, the language of reciprocity, paradox, chaos, interpenetration and gradation has replaced terms like dichotomy, dualism, mechanism, logical entailment, linear relationship and the like. This shift seemed necessary to do justice to the lived experiences of our spiritual and athletic journeys. Nevertheless, even without the incisive terminology offered by the language of dualism, we can still say some things with confidence. We can conclude that sporting and spiritual progress is dependent on humility, but in a messy, complicated kind of way, one that does not exclude elements of pride.

To be sure, the phrase "confident humility" sounds like an oxymoron. Confidence and security speak to capability, achievement and status. Humility speaks to incapability, dependency and lack of status. Logically, this does not seem to work.

But that is perhaps one of the strengths of our great religious traditions and our worthy sporting practices alike. They force us to confront and then eventually embrace and reconcile opposites. They give us an experiential vantage point from which to see that opposites are, well, not really opposites . . . or at least they are not disconnected from one another. More and less replaces this or that. Paradox, reciprocity and difference by degree replace black and white, yes and no and other neat and tidy distinctions.

G. K. Chesterton was a fan of paradox. He too felt that the truth of spirituality (in his case Christian spirituality) lay in the experiential reconciliation of apparent opposites. Here is what he said about pride and humility.

> Christianity got over the difficulty of combining furious opposites, by keeping them both, and keeping them both furious. The Church was positive on both points. One can hardly think too little of one's self. One can hardly think too much of one's soul. (1908/1995: 101)

If Chesterton is right, we need not conceptualize pride and humility as existing on some kind of zero-sum scale—the more the pride, the less the humility, and vice versa. Rather, full-blush pride (in the form of confidence) and full-blush humility (in the form of awe and dependency) are compatible. Perhaps it is this kind of undergirding security that moved Lewis to conclude that humility does not so much require that we think less of ourselves but that we think of ourselves less. Security or self-love, as Fromm (1947/1967) argued many years ago, is a precondition for other-directed love and thus, too, self-forgetfulness.

FINAL OBSERVATIONS

We need to return to my original questions and try to nail down some answers. I asked whether sport is more a pedagogy for pride or humility. We are now in a position to see that this was not a good question. I should have asked if sport today is a pedagogy for a healthy version of pride~humility or not. This is partly an empirical question and thus one that moves beyond the scope of this philosophic chapter. But I think the answer would have to be mostly negative.

Since the Enlightenment, we have aimed in one way or another at knowledge, control and perfection. We expected to get it all right and to get it all under control. The fact that this has not happened and, according to many, will never happen, has not dissuaded some scientific materialists, other reductionists and philosophic rationalists of various stripes from still trying. The quest for perfection, the need to win all the time, embarrassment over finishing second, risking health and well-being to chase the gold ring—all of these behaviors suggest that many current athletes, coaches, sport administrators and fans have not abandoned what is, at bottom, a bankrupt ideology.[3]

In *The Case against Perfection*, Michael Sandel (2007) speaks against this ideology by opposing runaway eugenics and genetic engineering and by supporting humility, responsibility and solidarity. The problem with modern versions of the Enlightenment project, he says, is that they represent "a one-sided triumph of willfulness over giftedness, of dominion over reverence, of molding over beholding" (85). Sandel frequently uses sport to show how this rationalistic quest for perfection will end up decreasing the quality of life rather than improving it. Because sport has become spectacle more than a respected practice, according to Sandel, all attempts will be made to produce higher, faster and stronger. With the availability of bioengineering, parents will be able to "dial up" children who have the wherewithal for basketball, music, poetic writing or any other special talent. Arguably, this would be a world dominated by hubris of the wrong kind, one in which we will be able to blame parents not only for raising a child who is ill-manned, but also for having one that is too short. In this kind of world, sport would not offer a good venue for teaching humility.

The second set of questions I asked at the start of this chapter turned out to be very interesting. Is sport a good venue for the cultivation of spiritual humility and vice versa? This is a sacred–secular kind of question, a City of God versus City of Man dilemma. Do lessons on humility transfer from one arena to the other?

In the body of the chapter, I discussed spiritual and athletic humility in terms of similarities, not identities. Spiritual growth, I argued, is analogous to secular growth in sport, but they are not the same thing. Because they are distinct from one another, sport might well be used as a window of sorts for appreciating the plausibility of spiritual truths, and, in turn, religious experiences of humility could help particularly stubborn or willful athletes break through to new and better performances.

However, this conclusion would cut off our previous analysis at the knees. I say this because our discussion of pride and humility led to unsettling conclusions about the nature of differences themselves. We questioned the validity of dichotomous thinking, of separating this from that. If we were to follow this line of thought, we would have to raise questions about traditional lines of demarcation between the sacred and profane or the sacred and the secular.

If the sacred and secular are not separate worlds, if sport and spirituality overlap one another in complicated, messy ways, then it would be misleading to speak simply about the transferability of lessons from one domain to the other. It would be more accurate to claim that the confident humility one feels in different places and on different projects may be sacred~secular. This holistic answer to the pedagogical question, suggests that mystery~explanation abounds and prideful~humility is efficacious across all creation. In other words, if one looks carefully enough, the spiritual can be found in cells, and cells can be found in the spiritual . . . as odd as that sounds.

This is not to say that there are no useful distinctions to be drawn between sporting projects and spiritual practices or the experiences of humility in them. There are! And at times it is important and useful to do so. But it is a warning not to make too much of the differences. These same warnings would be echoed by holistic traditions in Christianity, Islam and Buddhism.

NOTES

1. Humility and a sense of gratitude are also virtues in many secular interpretations of the good life. See Schweitzer (1965) for an early example of a humility-based ethic, and Sandel (2007) for a more recent one.
2. It is always dangerous to make such sweeping statements. All three religions discussed here have sects, leaders or traditions that support different values. For instance, the so-called Gnostic heresy in Christianity put a very different reading on the virtue of humility than more orthodox traditions.
3. See, for example, Wallace (2000) and Midgley (1995), for stinging critiques of scientific materialism and its ambitions.

BIBLIOGRAPHY

Ackerman, D. (1999) *Deep Play*, New York: Vintage Books/Random House.
Aquinas, T. (1929) *The Summa Contra Gentiles*, The Fourth Book, trans. The English Dominican Fathers, London: Burns Oates and Washbourne.
Chesterton, G. K. (1908/1995) *Orthodoxy*. San Francisco: Ignatius Press.
Diamond Sutra 9. (2011) *World Scripture: Humility*. Available online at http://www.unification.net/ws/theme 128.htm (accessed 5 December 2011).
Fromm, E. (1947/1967) *Man for Himself: An Inquiry into the Psychology of Ethics*, New York: Fawcett World Library.
Fry, T. (ed.) (1981) *The Rule of St. Benedict (In Latin and English with Notes)*, Collegeville, MN: Liturgical Press.
Hadith of Termidi. (2011) *World Scripture: Humility*. Available online at http://www.unification.net/ws/theme128.htm (accessed 4 December 2011).
Herrigel, E. (1953) *Zen in the Art of Archery*, New York: Pantheon Books.
Lambert, C. (1998) *Mind Over Water: Lessons from Life on the Art of Rowing*, Boston: Houghton Mifflin.
Lewis, C. S. (1943/1960) *Mere Christianity*, New York: MacMillan Publishing Company.
Linssen, R. (1960) *Living Zen*, New York: Grove Press.
MacIntyre, A. (1984) *After Virtue: A Study in Moral Theory*, 2nd ed., Notre Dame, IN: University of Notre Dame Press.
Midgley, M. (1995) *The Ethical Primate: Humans, Freedom and Morality*, London: Routledge.

Niebuhr, H. R. (1951) *Christ and Culture*, New York: Harper and Row.

Novak, M. (1976) *The Joy of Sports: End Zones, Bases, Baskets, Ball, and the Consecration of the American Spirit*, New York: Basic Books.

Religious Tolerance. (2011) Islam, Introduction, Part I. Available online at http://www.religioustolerance.org/is1_intr.htm (accessed 4 December 2011).

Sandel, M. (2007) *The Case against Perfection: Ethics in an Age of Genetic Engineering*, Cambridge, MA: Belknap/Harvard.

Schweitzer, A. (1965) *Reverence for Life: An Anthology of Selected Writings*, ed. Thomas Kiernan, New York: Philosophical Library.

Stacey, A. (2008) The Role of Humility in Islam. Available online at http://www.islamreligion.com/articles/1693/ (accessed 4 December 2011).

Suzuki, D. (1961) *Essays in Zen Buddhism*, 1st Evergreen ed., New York: Grove Press.

Tarnas, R. (1991) *The Passion of the Western Mind: Understanding the Ideas that Have Shaped Our World View*, New York: Ballantine Books.

Wagener, K. (ed.) (1991) *The Lutheran Confessions Series: Luther's Catechisms*, St. Louis: Concordia Publishing House.

Wallace, B. A. (2000) *The Taboo of Subjectivity: Toward a New Science of Consciousness*, Oxford: Oxford University Press.

Weiss, P. (1969) *Sport: A Philosophic Inquiry*, Carbondale, IL: Southern Illinois University Press.

Contributors

Jacob L. Goodson holds the Hans Tiefel Junior Chair in Religious Ethics at the College of William and Mary in Williamsburg, Virginia. In 2010, he completed his PhD in philosophical theology at the University of Virginia. He is coeditor of *Richard Rorty and Philosophical Theology: Christian Engagements with a Secular Philosopher* (Wipf and Stock, 2011). He serves as the general editor for the *Journal of Scriptural Reasoning*, an academic interfaith peer-reviewed online journal. His research interests include American philosophy, Christian and Jewish ethics and philosophical and theological hermeneutics. Currently, he is completing a manuscript on a virtue-centered approach to biblical hermeneutics and narrative theology.

Robert J. Higgs is Professor Emeritus at East Tennessee State University where for twenty-seven years he taught courses in Appalachian, Southern and American literature and the literature of sport. He is the author, coauthor, editor or coeditor of eight books on sports, including: *An Unholy Alliance: The Sacred and Modern Sports* (2005, with Mickey Braswell); *God in the Stadium: Sports and Religion in America* (1995), which was nominated for a Pulitzer Prize; *Laurel and Thorne: The Athlete in American Literature* (1981), translated into Japanese in 1995; *The Sporting Spirit: Athletes in Literature and Life*, coedited with Neil Isaacs (1977, reprinted 1985); *Sports a Reference Guide* (1982), revised and updated by Donald L. Deardorff; and *Sports: A Reference Guide and Critical Commentary, 1980–1999*. He is the author of over a hundred articles and reviews on Appalachian and American literature and culture, including a solicited feature article for the *London Guardian* for the opening day of Wimbledon, 1985, entitled "A Whiff of Sulfur from the Center Court." In 2008 he was honored by the Sports Literature Association with a Lifetime Achievement Award.

Shirl J. Hoffman is Professor Emeritus of Exercise and Sports Science at the University of North Carolina, Greensboro. He is editor of *Sport and Religion* (1992); *Introduction to Kinesiology* (2009) (both published with Human Kinetics); and author of *Good Game: Christianity and the Culture of Sports* (2010, Baylor University Press). For the past thirty years he has been one of the world's leading thinkers on sport and religion and is presently the executive director of the American Kinesiology Association.

Kevin Lixey is a Catholic priest from the U.S. with degrees in philosophy and theological anthropology from Rome's *Regina Apostolorum*. In 2004, he was called to the Vatican to establish an international observatory for sport on behalf of the Holy See within the Pontifical Council for the Laity at the specific request of John Paul II. Reverend Lixey conducts annual international meetings with experts from various fields of sport that include sociologists, theologians, philosophers and pastors as well as athletes. He is editor of two Vatican Press publications: *The World of Sport Today: Field of Christian Mission* (2006) and *Sport: An Educational and Pastoral Challenge* (2008).

Scott Kretchmar is Professor of Exercise and Sport Science at Penn State University. He is a founding member of the International Association for the Philosophy of Sport and served as its president. He has been editor of the *Journal of the Philosophy of Sport*, is a Fellow in the American Academy of Kinesiology and Physical Education and has authored a popular text in the philosophy of sport. He has written numerous articles on ethics, the nature of sport and the operation of human intelligence in physical activity. He was named Alliance Scholar for AAHPERD in 1996, received the Distinguished Scholar Award from NAPEHE in 1997 and was honored as Distinguished Scholar for the International Association for the Philosophy of Sport in 1998 and again in 2006. Professor Kretchmar has served as chair of the Department of Kinesiology at Penn State on two occasions, has been president of the University Faculty Senate and has served for ten years as the Faculty Athletics Representative to the NCAA. He is the founding editor of the *Journal of Intercollegiate Sport*.

Hugh McLeod is Professor of Church History at the University of Birmingham, UK. His research focuses on the social history of religion in Western Europe and the U.S. in the nineteenth and twentieth centuries. His books include *Piety and Poverty: Working Class Religion in Berlin, London and New York, 1870–1914* (1996) and *The Religious Crisis of the 1960s* (2007). He has published several articles on the relationship between religion, politics and sport.

Michael Novak, holds the George Frederick Jewett Chair in Religion, Philosophy, and Public Policy at the American Enterprise Institute, U.S., and is a theologian, author and former U.S. ambassador. Michael Novak has written numerous books on the philosophy and theology of culture, especially the essential elements of free society. His work includes one of the major texts on sport and religion, *The Joy of Sports: Endzones, Bases, Basket, Balls and the Consecration of the American Spirit* (1967, Basic Books). His writings have appeared in every major Western language, and in Bengali, Korean and Japanese. His seminal work, *The Spirit of Democratic Capitalism*, was published underground in Poland in 1984 and after 1989 in Czechoslovakia, Germany, China, Hungary, Bangladesh, Korea and Latin America. His latest book is entitled *No One Sees God: The Dark Night of Atheists and Believers*. Michael has received many international awards including the million-dollar Templeton Prize for Progress in Religion in 1994.

Andrew Parker is Professor of Sport and Christian Outreach and Director of the Centre for Sport, Spirituality and Religion (CSSR) in the Faculty of Applied Sciences at the University of Gloucestershire, UK. Andrew's research interests include sport and social identity, sport and spirituality and physical activity and schooling. Published outputs reflect these interests and have appeared in periodicals such as the *Sociology of Sport Journal*; the *International Review for the Sociology of Sport, Gender and Education*; and *Qualitative Research in Sport, Exercise and Health*. He has served on the editorial boards of the *Sociology of Sport Journal* (2005–2008) (Human Kinetics) and *Qualitative Research* (2001–present) (Sage), and was coeditor of the *International Journal of Religion and Sport* between 2010 and 2012.

Victor Pfitzner, an Australian Lutheran pastor, lectured in New Testament for nearly four decades in Adelaide, South Australia, and completed guest lectureships in the U.S. and various southeast Asian countries before retirement in 2004. His doctoral dissertation, completed at the University of Münster, Germany, and published in 1967, focused on the use of traditional athletic imagery in early Christian writings, especially in the Pauline literature. A number of later published articles have continued the exploration of the Christian—specifically the apostle and martyr—as Christ's athlete.

Tracy J. Trothen is Head of Theological Studies at Queen's University in Kingston, Ontario. She is Associate Professor of Ethics and a Clinical Pastoral Education Supervisor. Her research interests include sport, spiritual care, theological ethics, sexuality and violence. She is currently completing a manuscript on child sexual abuse and religious institutions.

Nick Watson is Senior Lecturer in Sport, Culture and Religion at York St. John University (YSJU), UK. He was the founding director of the Centre for the Study of Sport and Spirituality (YSJU, 2003–2009) and is now an associate and advisory board member of the Centre for Sport, Spirituality and Religion (CSSR) at the University of Gloucestershire, UK (2009–). In addition to editorial work for a range of theological and sporting journals, Nick is the coauthor and coeditor, respectively, of the books *Sport and Spirituality: An Introduction* (2007) and *Theology, Ethics and Transcendence in Sports* (2011), both published by Routledge. Bridging the 'theory–practice' gap in the world of sport and faith is a major focus of Nick's work, resulting in presentations for, and collaboration with, universities, churches, disability groups and mission organizations. In addition to having coached athletes with disabilities, during the past ten years he has coached soccer in England, Spain and America and enjoys playing golf and hiking with his wife and daughter.

Index